Situated Listening

Situated Listening

THE SOUND OF ABSORPTION IN CLASSICAL CINEMA

GIORGIO BIANCOROSSO

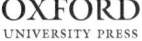
OXFORD
UNIVERSITY PRESS

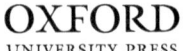
UNIVERSITY PRESS

Oxford University Press is a department of the University of Oxford. It furthers the University's objective of excellence in research, scholarship, and education by publishing worldwide. Oxford is a registered trade mark of Oxford University Press in the UK and certain other countries.

Published in the United States of America by Oxford University Press
198 Madison Avenue, New York, NY 10016, United States of America.

© Oxford University Press 2016

Library of Congress Cataloging-in-Publication Data
Names: Biancorosso, Giorgio, 1968– author.
Title: Situated listening : the sound of absorption in classical cinema / Giorgio Biancorosso.
Description: New York : Oxford University Press, 2016. |
Includes bibliographical references and index.
Identifiers: LCCN 2016001428 | ISBN 9780195374711 (bound book : alk. paper) | ISBN 9780190493196 (epub)
Subjects: LCSH: Motion picture music—History and criticism.
Classification: LCC ML2075 .B53 2016 | DDC 781.5/42—dc23
LC record available at http://lccn.loc.gov/2016001428

This book published with the support of the AMS 75 PAYS Endowment of the American Musicological Society, funded in part by the National Endowment for the Humanities and the Andrew W. Mellon Foundation.

This book is for Yoko Hosoda.

Contents

Acknowledgments

Completion of this book would not have been possible without the support of the following institutions and individuals. Big thanks go to the Music Department at the University of Hong Kong. My colleagues Joshua Chan, Daniel Chua, Kim Youn, Jose Neglia, Deborah Waugh, and Yang Yuanzheng have created the ideal environment to carry out my research. Chan Hing-yan, chair of the department, has been unwavering in his support of my research endeavors. In their capacity as Head of the School of Humanities, Daniel Chua first and then Timothy O'Leary offered a rare example of creative leadership and effective administration. Also at the University of Hong Kong, David Clarke, Gina Marchetti, and Stephen J. Matthews were unfailingly generous with time and ideas, while my former students Chen Chih-ting, Grace Cheng, and Kal Ng offered intellectual companionship when it was most needed.

Michael Ingham and Paisley Livingston, both at Lingnan University, discussed with me many of the central tenets of this book. I am grateful for their feedback. In Singapore, Yung Sai-shing lent a sympathetic ear to my explorations of sound and music in Chinese-language cinemas. In Taiwan, finally, Wang Yin-feng and Chen Jen-yen have been great colleagues and a source of inspiration ever since I visited the Graduate Institute of Musicology (GIM), National Taiwan University, in 2010. During my short tenure there, Professor Shen Tung, also of GIM, made possible a meeting with Director Hou Hsiao-hsien. The ensuing conversation with Mr. Hou and a meeting with Professor Lin Wenchi, director of the Chinese Taipei Film Archive, have helped to shape my understanding of Hou's cinema.

Many ideas in this book originated in discussions or casual conversations with colleagues from around the globe. Exchanges with Paul Anderer, Gil Anderson, Arved Ashby, Gianmario Borio, Roberto Calabretto, Alessandro Cecchi, Joys Cheung, Annette Davison, Vincent Delphine, Joanna Demers, Lawrence Dreyfus, Walter Frisch, Claudia Gorbman, Berthold Hoeckner,

Shuhei Hosokawa, Jean Ma, Su-yin Mak, Ron Sadoff, Emilio Sala, Elaine Sisman, Kate van Orden, Victor Vicente, Joshua Walden, Elisabeth Weis have all found their way into the body of the text. In extending my thanks for their inspiration, I also apologize if I have incorporated their leads and suggestions without the benefit of a fully fledged acknowledgment. Librarians of the Special Collection Research Center, Syracuse University Libraries, were exceedingly kind and efficient in granting access to materials from the *Franz Waxman Papers*.

Parts of this book were presented as colloquia at the Donald Keene Center, Department of East Asian Studies, Columbia University; the English Department, National Taipei University of Technology; and the music departments at Stanford University, Chiaotong University (Taiwan), and Chinese University (Hong Kong), respectively. My thanks to Paul Anderer, Louis Lo, Karol Berger, Kam Lap-kwan, and Lee Tong Soon for their invitations. A portion of chapter 1 was also read as a paper at the Second Biennial Meeting of the East Asian Regional Association of the International Musicological Society, held in Taipei and chaired by Yang Chien-chang and Kam Lap-kwan. An earlier version of my reading of Renoir's *The Rules of the Game* appears in *Music and the Moving Image* 2, no. 3 (2009): 11–33. In chapter 2, I borrow a brief passage from my extended analysis of Spielberg's *Jaws* first published in *Music Analysis* 29, nos. 1–3 (2010): 306–333. Chapter 5, finally, features a revised version of a passage originally published in "Memory and the 'Leitmotif' in Cinema," *Representation in Western Music*, ed. Joshua Walden (Cambridge: Cambridge University Press, 2013), 203–223. I thank University of Illinois Press, Wiley-Blackwell, and Cambridge University Press, respectively, for granting me permission to revise this material for this book.

I am delighted to acknowledge the support of the AMS 75 PAYS Endowment of the American Musicological Society. I also owe a sincere debt of gratitude to my editor, Norm Hirschy, for his guidance, encouragement, and patience. Thanks also to an anonymous reader for the press who read a rough draft of the manuscript and made some invaluable suggestions. Elisabeth Weis, Dawn-joy Leong, Dr. Liu Yen-ling, and Estela Ibáñez-García read all or parts of the manuscript and suggested many improvements. I cannot begin to express my appreciation for their help.

A final round of thanks for their support and inspiration over the years goes to Mrs. Rose Hoffmann, Professor Lee Ou-fan, Margaret Fan, Grace Mak, Yukong Chow, Katrien Jacobs, Andrew Guthrie, and Juan Morales in Hong Kong; Emi Morita, Robert Iolini in Kyoto; Jakub Novak, Nadia Benabid, Ted Friedman, Eve Preminger, Silvia Formenti, Melli Pini, Joe Biancorosso, Siu-yin Mak, and Joshua Cody in New York; Luigi Coiro, Licia Pucella, Gigi Tarallo, and Agnese Gisonni in Naples; Dinko Fabris, Pippo Trezza, Dario Bimbo, Jacopo Pellegrini, and the Rocchetta family in Rome; and Emilio

Sala, Chiara Gelmetti, and Gianni Fodella in Milan. Joshua tipped me on the "Cheese Shop Sketch" and Mia Liu reasoned with me over the notion of "heterological silence." Kal Ng's work on architectural animation and Amanzio Farris's writings on the role of photography in architectural planning, finally, provided an inspiring blueprint for my own understanding of "situated listening." My parents, siblings, and relatives in Seregno, Desio, Milano, Cassino, Paris, and New York deserve my gratitude not only for their unconditional love but also for their patience toward this most elusive member of our extended family.

Situated Listening

Introduction

Behind this way of thinking and evaluating, which is bound to
be hostile to art if it is at all genuine, I had always felt its hostility to life,
a furious, vengeful enmity towards life itself; for all life rests on semblance,
art, deception, prismatic effects, the necessity of perspective and error.
—Friedrich Nietzsche, *"An Attempt at Self Criticism," The Birth of Tragedy (1886)*

The new beauty will be that of THE SITUATION, that is to say, *provisional* and lived.
—Letterist International (January 1954)

In one of its aspects, art is a technique for focusing attention, for teaching skills of attention
—Susan Sontag, *"The Aesthetics of Silence," Styles of Radical Will (1969)*

Remember the notorious Monty Python "Cheese Shop Sketch"? A traveler
(John Cleese), caught by spasms of hunger, stops by a cheese shop in a characteristically gray town in the South East of England (Figure 0.1). As he walks in,
he is welcomed by the incongruous sound of bouzouki music and even more
incongruous presence of two dancers in traditional Greek attire. Walking past
them, he asks the man at the counter for some cheese. Despite his best efforts
and catholic taste in things dairy, he ends up getting none. This is a cheese
shop, apparently, that sells no cheese at all. His inordinately long litany of re-
quests, ranging from the most mundane (cheddar) to the recherché (Perle de
Champagne) or even fictional (Venezuelan beaver cheese), are countered by just
as outrageously long a litany of "nos." The music, meanwhile, has been chiming
in all along, albeit seemingly ignored till, unexpectedly and halfway through yet
another request—for a Limburger, as it turns out—the increasingly frustrated
customer turns toward the bouzouki player and famously screams: "WILL YOU
SHUT THAT BLOODY DANCING OFF?"

Moving one's head in the direction opposite to the source of the sound or
even covering one's ears does not shut down our auditory sense the way closing
the eyes does for our sight. It is a state of affairs we are most keenly aware of, and
often frustrated by, when in the presence of unwanted sounds. Not even during

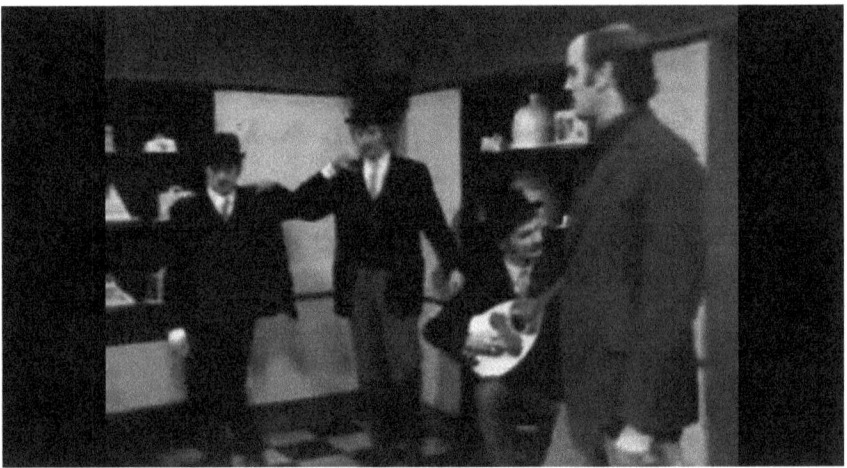

Figure 0.1 "Cheese Sketch Shop."

sleep does the auditory system truly stop working. Constant alertness has its advantages, to be sure. Detecting an unknown, impending, or invisible presence, or
keeping track of a known one, not only complements the information provided
to us by our eyes but also is a highly adaptive function in its own right, an "alert"
system we share with the so-called higher animals.[1] The more invisible, unfath-
omable, or otherwise unknowable the source of a sound is, the more acute our
sensitivity to it—hence our ability to locate, anchor, and eventually respond to
it in the most advantageous manner possible. In the modern world, registering
the constant din of city life or the specific sound quality of a building's interior
tells us where we are and when, and reminds us of the social space we inhabit.[2]
Just because we can hear a sound coming from behind our heads or around corners, however, does not mean that the ear does not discriminate. Many sounds
well within earshot barely register in our day-to-day engagement with the world.
Unannounced, without a proper beginning or a recognizable end, their features
indistinguishable, they blend into a formless background. They disappear just as
discreetly, and without leaving a trace. They are, in one word, *unattended*.[3] The

---

[1] Roland Barthes, "Listening," in *The Responsibility of Forms* (New York: Hill and Wang), 245–
60; Stephen Handel, *Listening: An Introduction to the Perception of Auditory Events* (Cambridge,
MA: MIT Press, 1989), 461–62.

[2] Barry Blesser and Linda-Ruth Salter, *Spaces Speak, Are You Listening? Experiencing Aural
Architecture* (Cambridge, MA: MIT Press, 2007), 317–59.

[3] "The possibility of guarding against the entrance of certain sensations into consciousness—
to annul them, as it were—is of special importance for the sense of hearing since we are not in a
position to close the ear at will, as we can the eye, and to stave off the effects of the outside world.
Thence, perhaps, the almost greater importance that attention claims in the domain of auditory

reason Cleese's sudden and unexpected charge at the bouzouki player is so funny is that, engrossed by the absurd gag playing out at the counter, we are no longer paying any attention to the music—and believe he is not either. The way the gag is prepared neatly deflates the oft-repeated platitude that the ear cannot choose what to hear the way the eye chooses what to see.[4]

Inattentiveness to a sound does not mean that one is not listening (though, as we shall see, the movies often represent it as such). Following Stephen Handel's classic account of auditory perception, in what follows I grant the term "listening" to all kinds of sonic information pickup that involve the perception of an event, and consequently the activation of recognitional, integrative, and predictive capacities.[5] Listening is a skill, and it is nurtured by habits and the environment; hearing is a physiological capacity. On this account, which leaves little scope to the notion of "hearing" except as a theoretical notion, even the casual apprehension or monitoring of a sound event counts as listening.[6] Musicologist Cormac Newark comes to a similar conclusion via a very different route, namely, a study of the nineteenth-century reception of spectacular scenes in grand opera, which he synthesizes with the—only seemingly—paradoxical formula, "listening to the music, but not hearing it," where "hearing" presumably refers to the purely physiological measure of the music's impact (a measure that, in Handel's

---

sensations": Ulrici, *Gott und der Mensch*, vol. I, part I, 289, cited in Steege, *Helmoltz and the Modern Listener*, trans. Steege (Cambridge: Cambridge University Press, 2013), 108.

[4] "The passivity of the ears," writes Michael Bull, "appears to be merely a historical effect, now technologically superseded through the development of earpieces, which empower users so that they can choose what they wish to hear, screening out the urban soundscape to create a private auditory universe": Bull, "Remaking the Urban: The Audiovisual Aesthetics of Ipod Use," in *The Oxford Handbook of New Audiovisual Aesthetics*, ed. John Richardson, Claudia Gorbman, and Carol Vernallis (New York: Oxford University Press, 2013), 632. Their impact notwithstanding, earpieces *magnify* the ability to filter out the sounds of one's immediate surroundings rather than creating it ab nihilo (think about the ability to isolate oneself or concentrate amidst a loud crowd). The iPod is in this sense the materialization of an impulse and a capacity as much as their sole enabling agent. On the cultural impetus behind the development of new technologies, see also Jonathan Sterne, *The Audible Past: Cultural Origins of Sound Reproduction* (Durham, NC: Duke University Press, 2003).

[5] "Listening is not the same as hearing. The physical pressure wave enables perception but does not force it. Listening is active; it allows age, experience, and expertise to influence perception": Handel, *Listening*, 3.

[6] Philosopher Fred Dretske, for his part, restates the equivalent distinction in the realm of vision, namely, the difference between "seeing" and "looking." Writing on the phenomenon known as "change blindness," he points out how, insofar as light reaches one's retinas, one invariably *sees* something; one just does not notice—he or she is blind to the fact—that it has changed. So-called change blindness, on this view, is therefore not a kind of blindness at all, unless one expanded the notion of seeing to encompass the ability to *recognize*. See Fred I. Dretske, "Change Blindness," *Philosophical Studies* 120 (2004): 1–18. On the relevance of perceptual blindness to image composition and continuity editing in film, see Murray Smith, "Consciousness," in *The Routledge Companion to Philosophy and Film*, ed. Paisley Livingston and Carl Plantinga (New York and London: Routledge, 2009), 41.

model, is purely theoretical).[7] Newark takes the paradox a step further, as he concedes that in grand opera, the music is not merely subsumed under the on-stage visual spectacle but may be ignored or even silenced—and yet without this causing a situation of "not paying attention, still less not understanding."[8]

I mention Newark's discussion here not only for its intrinsic interest but also because it offers what at first blush may seem like a striking parallel to music in the cinema but which in fact exemplifies, in my opinion, its opposite. To concede that music in grand opera may not be listened to is to contend with a bias that opera is a fundamentally musical genre; that film music is, on the contrary, listened to has been obscured in the culture at large by the equally strong bias according to which cinema is a quintessentially visual form. And yet, we not only hear music in cinema but also listen to it, in the sense that we pay attention to at least *some aspects* of it. Perceiving film music as "loud," recognizing it as music or even merely as "being there" is already to listen—unless, that is, we take a normative view of what counts as music listening by collapsing the term "listening," for instance, with contemplation. It follows that the lapsing of one's attention to certain aspects of a stimulus does not mark a failure of listening, either; rather, it is a state in which the full arsenal of tools and skills deployed to parse the auditory scene remains in a "standby" mode ready to be activated at will—as soon as the effort of recognizing a new event requires it.

Even when one gives the term "listening" such latitude, however, there remains the need to differentiate among many different levels of engagement with sound, as they reflect the work of the attention in all its different forms and gradations. Capturing such work or breaking it down into clear-cut stages is an arduous task. As Aldous Huxley noted in a comparison between visual and auditory perception:

> Ears have nothing corresponding to the fovea centralis, consequently the indispensable shifting of attention within the auditory field does not involve any parallel shifting of the bodily organ. The discriminating and selecting of auditory sensa can be done by the mind alone, and do not require corresponding movements of the ears.[9]

---

[7] Cormac Newark, "Not Listening in Paris: Critical and Fictional Lapses of Attention at the Opera," in *Words and Notes in the Long Nineteenth Century*, ed. Phyllis Weliver and Katharine Ellis (Woodbridge, UK: Boydell & Brewer, 2013), 49. For an early formulation of the ideal of absorbed listening, exemplified by instrumental music in an intimate setting cast against the context of its impossibility in "complicated opera," see Arthur Schopenhauer, *Parerga and Paralipomena: Short Philosophical Essays*, vol. 1 (Oxford: Clarendon Press, 1851 [1974]), 432.

[8] Newark, "Not Listening in Paris," 53. For an account of Wagner's rather different evaluation of listening habits in the Paris of the time, see David Levin, "A Picture-Perfect Man? Senta, Absorption, and Wagnerian Theatricality," *Musical Quarterly* 21, no. 3 (Summer 2005): 53.

[9] Aldous Huxley, *The Art of Seeing* (London: Flamingo, 1994), 44.

The difficulty of capturing attention to sound would seem to reinforce the old, Cartesian dualism of body and mind. Just because something is not observable to the naked eye, however, does not imply that it does not have a material—read, bodily—dimension. Huxley, moreover, is not altogether accurate. While it is true that we hear around corners, often we do turn our whole body in response to a new sound. The ability to move our head along the horizontal plane may explain the loss in the ability to move the ears themselves (the muscles in and around our ears are in fact a classic example of so-called vestigial—that is, no longer functional—features). The sensory organs of both the outer and inner ear, finally, do engage in adjustments as they prepare to process the sounds reaching them; it is just that they are hardly visible as such.[10] Huxley's point, in other words, is especially valid when it comes to how to detect, and hence *represent*, auditory attention.[11] This remains a challenge for the painter, stage director, or film director alike. To be sure, there is a whole coterie of visual signals and staging conventions, traceable in both painting and acting manuals as far back as the baroque era, giving tangible form, to quote Huxley again, to the "discriminating and selecting . . . done by the mind alone." They include bringing a hand close to the ear; turning the head slightly in the direction of the source of a sound or, should the latter be frontally located, looking intently at it; staring into nothing as if in a state of unseeing abstraction or closing one's eyes, as if the subtraction of one sense could enhance the potency of the other; and, finally, displaying signs of involuntary, automatic, or unconscious interest. But can "the movements of the body," to adapt Leon Battista Alberti's famous formulation to a new context, capture "the movements of the soul"?[12] Cleese's deportment and ostensive object of attention—the man at the cheese shop counter—conceal that he is, momentarily at least, very much aware of the music being played behind him. By the same token, the seemingly demonstrative posture of many a listener in a concert hall need not correspond to a disposition of genuine interest toward the putative object of their attention (be it the music, the performance, or the performer), for, as Newark has aptly observed, "inwardness . . . is not the same as receptiveness."[13]

[10] On the "efforts to construct aural attention as something evidently corporeal" in Germany in the 1860s, see Steege, *Helmholtz and the Modern Listener*, 110–14.

[11] Michel Chion touches briefly on this in *Film: A Sound Art*, trans. C. Gorbman (New York: Columbia University Press, 2009), 291–92.

[12] Leon B. Alberti, *On Painting* (New Haven, CT: Yale University Press, 1966), 77.

[13] Newark's observation comes, not coincidentally, at the end of his rereading of a famous image of listeners, Eugène Louis Lami's drawing, *Andanté de la symphonie en la*. The same image graces the cover of James H. Johnson's influential book, *Listening in Paris: A Cultural History*. See Newark, "Not Listening in Paris," 37.

The Varieties of Attention

Writing about the onset of a distinguished artistic tradition that prized psychological realism, Michael Fried has famously argued that the legacy of such eighteenth-century painters as Greuze or Chardin was the establishment of

> the supreme fiction or ontological illusion that the beholder does not exist, that there is no one standing before the canvas. It does this principally in two ways: through the persuasive representation of figures so deeply absorbed in what they are doing, feeling, and thinking that they appear oblivious to anything else, specifically including the beholder's presence before the canvas, and by means of an ideal pictorial unity according to which all the elements in the painting are perceived as motivated by a single dramatic imperative.[14]

Theatricality, or the acknowledgment of the beholder, can only be held at bay—not eliminated. Put bluntly, all a painter can do is to be more or less oblique about it. That is why Fried calls its erasure a fiction or illusion. Yet it is an illusion that has held sway across a vast field of representational practices. Fried is so sanguine about the dominance of absorptive modes of pictorial representation that, in contravening the modernist dogma of medium specificity, he detects their impact in contemporary photography[15] as well, while pushing the moment at which the absorptive paradigm emerged even further back chronologically (the previous citation, for instance, comes from his study on immersion and specularity in the art of Caravaggio—a subject I return to briefly in chapter 2). It hardly needs stressing that the "fiction that the beholder does not exist" is absolutely central not only to all manner of realistic genres, both novelistic and theatrical, but also to cinematic mise-en-scène and exhibition practices. Fried talks in this respect of the "self-forgetting darkness of the cinema."[16] Quite so. One in fact wonders whether the dominance of mainstream narrative cinema and TV dramas, where absorption in the narrative is often definitive and all-encompassing, is responsible for shaping twentieth- and twenty-first-century perceptions of older modes of realistic representations as well. Tracing the course of such "reverse" historiography is a subject worth pursuing in its own right but lies well beyond the confines of this study. In what follows, rather, I will

---

[14] Michael Fried, *The Moment of Caravaggio* (Princeton, NJ: Princeton University Press, 2010), 2.

[15] Michael Fried, *Why Photography Matters as Art as Never Before* (New Haven, CT: Yale University Press, 2008).

[16] Cited in Ken Wilder, "Michael Fried and Beholding Video Art," *Proceedings of the European Society for Aesthetics* 3 (2011): 305.

examine cinematic representations of listeners in a variety of contexts—their home, a concert hall, a club, and so forth. Through them, I will also attempt to bring to light the complementary and mutually fulfilling states of focused attention and inattention that characterize the attentive, engrossed, or, in Fried's preferred word, absorbed film spectator.

In their classic formulation in *Absorption and Theatricality: Painting and Beholder in the Age of Diderot* (1988), Fried's twin notions of absorption and theatricality are grounded in his interpretations of the "golden standard" espoused by Diderot's critical writings on art, on the one hand, and a rhetorically powerful close reading of the paintings themselves—in particular, their composition—on the other. To the extent that absorption is a foil to theatricality, the explicit acknowledgment of the beholder, it is of relatively little import whether attention is to this or that, two or more things simultaneously, or altogether feigned; what matters is that the depicted figure appears to be absorbed in something, and in this way the illusion of the beholder's nonexistence is sustained. It follows that, Fried's—and Diderot's—eloquent psychological descriptions notwithstanding, the actual content of the mental life of the characters depicted in the paintings is to some extent immaterial to the central argument. Of course, Fried's seemingly reductive strategy also has to do with the nature of absorption itself. Being completely occupied or engrossed in something, after all, is a disposition: more the premise or the consequence of than an emotion proper. Its representation, unsurprisingly, calls forth the "assimilation of expression to absorption."[17]

There is no reason to dispute the gist of Fried's findings, let alone the force of his examples. Two striking omissions are, however, worth observing. Only rarely does Fried examine paintings that depict absorption in sounds other than the spoken word of a character who is him- or herself prominently figured in the composition; nor, more important still, does Fried raise the possibility of failed, feigned, wandering, or at least divided attention.[18] Yet, is not this possibility the most tantalizing consequence of Huxley's point that "the discriminating and selecting of auditory *sensa* can be done by the mind alone"? The two omissions in Fried's account naturally reflect the historical conventions of the period he examines, as well as the limitations of painting as a medium. But they also tell us something about the inherent difficulty of representing the (in-)attention to sound. The use of music to inform the spectator about the disposition

---

[17] Michael Fried, *Absorption and Theatricality: Painting and Beholder in the Age of Diderot* (Berkeley: University of California Press, 1980), 22.

[18] Tellingly, the one example of a character making or listening to music is that of Vien's *Ermit Endormi* (The Sleeping Hermit, 1753), a figure caught, as implied by the title, in arguably the most unequivocal state of obliviousness—sleep. Ibid., 30.

of a character, whether in the theater or in the cinema, is to my mind a response to precisely this kind of difficulty. The development of a coterie of specialized musical techniques surely widened the gulf existing between figurative painting, the theater, and subsequently the cinema. But one should not underestimate the fact that those techniques are underpinned by the same impetus that drove the development of key aspects of the other forms as well, namely, the representation of character psychology.

In translating some of Fried's concerns in terms applicable to the use of music in cinema, then, my goal is twofold: on the one hand, I intend to stress not only the transparency but also the potential duplicity or unreadability of absorption; on the other, I wish to bring certain uses of music in film into line with the history of the representation of subjectivity (a history that predates the beginning of film by at least a century).[19] I am less interested in the relation between absorption and theatricality per se than I am in how a film goes about controlling, via the (absorbed?) character as *vector*, our response to a given stream of sound, and the surprising forms exerting such a control, or failing to do so, may take. It is a truism of film theory, and in particular the effort to define the new medium as against the theater, that variable framing and editing enable the director to control the attention of the spectator in a manner that is simply not attainable in other art forms. Alessandra Campana has rightly suggested that such opposition is too facile, especially when weighed against late nineteenth-century "devices that function appositely to position and align the audience – its viewing, listening, emotional connection to the staged events – by enacting a specific scopic regime."[20] I would go even further. The director, whether at the theater or at the movies, can control the attention even without such "devices" or explicit directives; all he or she needs is a particular orientation of the characters' own attention, as indicated by a particular choice of words, gestures, or the effective manipulation of the pace with which certain events will unfold. What variable framing and its auditory equivalent —the audio close-up—bring to the plate is an element of *coercion* (which is nevertheless obtainable at the theater, too, by manipulating lighting and sound, for instance). For this reason, I am especially interested in the extent to which it is

---

[19] While Charles Rosen has stressed the role of Romantic poetry in the representation of the act of remembering in the *lied* tradition, Luca Zoppelli has linked the musical representation of selective attention in opera to the modern novel. Karol Berger too has identified a preoccupation with the representation of different orders of being, the real and the imagined or remembered, in nothing less than Beethoven's piano sonatas. See Charles Rosen et al., *The Romantic Generation* (Cambridge, MA: Harvard University Press, 1995); Luca Zoppelli, *L'opera come racconto* (Venezia: Marsilio, 1994); and Karol Berger, "Beethoven and the Aesthetic State," *Beethoven Forum* 7 (1999): 17–44.

[20] Alessandra Campana, *Opera and Modern Spectatorship in Late Nineteenth-Century Italy* (Cambridge: Cambridge University Press, 2015), 144.

a *particular frame of reference*, not a textual element per se, that either enhances or impedes the availability of certain traits of musical sound (and the scene of which it is part). In charting this process, my observations follow from the gestalt principle according to which a given perspective brings certain elements of a scene into the foreground ("figure") while pushing the rest into the background ("ground"). My references from the literature on the psychology of perception, be they works by Rudolf Arnheim, Michael Polanyi, or Albert Bregman, reflect this methodological orientation. Within a complex dramatic situation, figure and ground are metaphors for aspects of sonic configurations whose condition of existence as objects of perception is the discriminating work of the attention.

In chapter 1 ("Music, Off Stage"), I take a close look at a number of examples of inattentiveness set in the most ideal environment imaginable: a concert hall. Architecture and design figure prominently in the discussion as pawns in a game of strategies through which to manage, or subvert the power of, the aesthetic attention. Inscribed in the dramatic arc of a film sequence is a prediction, no matter how explicitly formulated, about where the spectator's attention will fall. It is for this reason that, in chapter 2 ("The Listener in the Picture"), I turn to jokes or what elsewhere I also call "reversals."[21] Implicit in a conjuring trick is the confidence, akin to a magician's, to not only anticipate a certain kind of disposition but also guide the spectator's attention when the unveiling of the trick requires it. Reversals are an eloquent demonstration of Alfred Gell's theory of artworks as traps, and as such they lend credence to his insistence on the continuity between artworks and everyday objects.[22] A given film sequence will exploit its knowledge of the mind of the spectator, which it embodies in its very structure. "The trap is therefore both a model of its creator, the hunter, but also a model of its victim, the prey animal. But more than this, the trap embodies a scenario, which is the dramatic nexus that binds these two protagonists together, and which aligns them in time and space."[23] The virtuosity needed for the "trap" to work, moreover, lends the artwork a veneer of inscrutability that puts us in awe ("enchantment") of the artist, community, or institution that presides over it. In the third chapter ("The Radio Broadcast as Anamorphic Spot"), I move on to examples of how filmmakers use the radio as an agent in the chance encounter with music on the part of characters whose focus of attention remains to us opaque—whether because of the undemonstrative acting of the actors

---

[21] Giorgio Biancorosso, "The Harpist in the Closet: Film Music as Epistemological Joke," *Music and the Moving Image* 2, no. 3 (2009): 11–33.

[22] Alfred Gell, "Vogel's Net: Traps as Artworks and Artworks as Traps," *Journal of Material Culture* 1 (1996): 15–38.

[23] Ibid., 27.

or because of the ambiguity of the mise-en-scène. I discuss the implications of these "quasi encounters" between a character and a broadcast in terms of the specific, indeed idiosyncratic, nature of the built space in which the action unfolds and the significance of the radio in creating virtual communities across not only space but also time. This state of affairs does not merely result in a potential misalignment between character and spectator with regards to what is being attended to; it also frees up the music, as it were, allowing it to behave in ways that are not entirely predictable. The main argument of chapter 4 ("The Spectator as Situated Listener") revolves around Hitchcock's virtuosic, but ultimately unsuccessful, attempt to control or limit such a freedom in *Rear Window* (1954) and the proliferation of partially or wholly unintended sync points this failure entails.

Acting and mise-en-scène are necessary yet may not be sufficient—or sufficiently stringent—conditions to control the spectator's attention in such a way that it aligns with that of the character. This preoccupation prompts the use of a film score to restrict the range of sounds in the mix and sometimes usurp the soundtrack altogether. My main case studies are here drawn from two classical tropes of mainstream narrative cinema: "epiphanies" (chapter 5) and "love at first sight" scenes (chapter 6). In these two chapters, I also broach a theme that recurs throughout the book as a whole: the vying for attention between physical stimuli reaching us from the outside environment and internal emotional-sensorial processes, such as those triggered by the discovery of someone's betrayal or a feeling of repulsion (which may make us temporarily numb to our surroundings). While this remains a deplorably underappreciated subject in psychology, films have given eloquent musical form to it. I am especially interested in drawing out the significance of how and why inattentiveness to sound and music, at such junctures, is itself represented musically. As we witness the protagonist recover from the shock of what he or she sees or grasps, one or more sounds, be they voices, music, proximal sounds, or background noise, are substituted for another—the film score. The onset of the music, normally via an audio dissolve, is meant to convey a temporary suspension of one's awareness—a short-circuiting of the attention. We, the spectators, are given no choice but to partake in this drastically altered, indeed imploded, soundscape. A legacy of melodrama—this technique is as draconian as it is common. The familiarity of some of the examples, ranging from *Vertigo* to *The Godfather II*, will go some way, I hope, to restore a sense of its strangeness.

There is nothing strange about the musical selections themselves. They are either recurring, and thus already familiar, cues or conventional interventions with a clear expressive role. The audio dissolve thus registers a precious convergence between rhetoric, the effective delivery of story content, and mimesis or even immersion, namely, the phenomenologically fine-grained representation of the temporary breakdown of attention (which the filmmaker gives us access to from within the mind of the protagonist). The film score thus becomes a vivid metaphor for a paradoxical form of perceived silence, which I term *heterological silence.*

Music and the "View from Nowhere"

The listeners who make up the bulk of my examples are not symptomatic of a new era of "distracted listening." I resist the temptation to trace a teleological, and totalizing, trajectory that maps all too neatly historical changes with changes in media and expressive forms (besides, I am as interested in continuities as I am in change). By addressing the significance of what I call "situated listening," the larger aim of this book is theoretical rather than historical: namely, the rebuttal not of absorbed listening per se, but of the "view from nowhere" that has characterized much musicological work in both the distant and recent past. On this "view," perspective is hollowed out of the listening experience to confer legitimacy to the knowledge produced through one's scholarly efforts.[24] In rejecting this approach, my project is indebted to Thomas Nagel's philosophy, and particularly his insistence that subjective experience warrants the same kind of scrutiny afforded to other aspects of our physical and social reality.[25] My work also echoes reception studies and more recent work on music and identity, soundscape studies, and the sociology of the everyday.[26] Whether implicitly or explicitly, much of this scholarship values the study of situatedness, be it socially mediated or occasioned by unique circumstances, as a conduit toward a more humane musicology.

In what ways does film provide a vantage point from which to study situated listening? To be sure, traditional modes of musical analysis and interpretation have been superseded by new and sophisticated approaches that stress the production of meaning over formal properties, and the performative over

---

[24] Pertinent here is Helmholtz's proto-modernist critique of "everyday perception" and "everyday listening." The "hollowing out" of perspective, and the attendant "lapses" in attention perspective entails, underpins the ethos of the enterprise of music theory as a whole. For a reconstruction of the historical and intellectual context in which Helmholtz formulated his ideas on attention, see Steege, *Helmholtz and the Modern Listener*, esp. chap. 3. Inspired by the revolution in psychology initiated by J. J. Gibson, Eric Clarke endeavors to factor "perspective" into the discipline of music theory in *Ways of Listening: An Ecological Approach to the Perception of Musical Meaning* (Oxford: Oxford University Press, 2005).

[25] Thomas Nagel, *The View from Nowhere* (New York: Oxford University Press, 1986).

[26] For a recent example, see Lisa Gilman, "An American Soldier's iPod: Layers of Identity and Situated Listening in Iraq," *Music and Politics* 4 (2), http://quod.lib.umich.edu/m/mp/9460447.0004.201/--american-soldiers-ipod-layers-of-identity-and-situated?rgn=main;view=fulltext.

the textual. Yet for all this, one bias remains firmly at the heart of musical scholarship: the modeling of listening after the experience of the untroubled, reverential museum or gallery dweller, a figure stigmatized with unparalleled gusto and wealth of insights by Brian O'Dougherty in *Inside the White Cube* forty years ago.[27] It is a bias as pervasive and far-reaching as it is unspoken, and it crosses methodological boundaries whether one wishes to think of music as text, realization of an imaginary work, recording, or performance.[28] To give a recent and much-discussed example, Carolyn Abbate's revival of Jankelevitch's notion of the "drastic" in "Music—Gnostic or Drastic?"[29] substitutes the actual, moment-to-moment process of making music for the work as the main object of the listening experience. Abbate suggests this without fundamentally altering the scenario in which the encounter with music takes place, however. In verbally recording actual (i.e., personal) listening experiences, moreover, her examples suggest that the main question revolving around what she calls the "drastic" in music may not turn on the production of sound per se, but rather on point of view, and the viability of a "subjective musicology."[30] Her insistence on liveness suggests as much. The unique, irretrievable aspects of performance are not those tied to its physicality and materiality—themselves repeatable as such—but rather the uniquely situated position of the participating agents, be they performers (proprioceptively) or listeners (perceptively), as the physical dimensions of music manifest themselves to them in the unrecoverable here and now. First-person accounts such as Abbate's are of course immensely valuable insofar as they can be grasped as representative examples of the listening experience. For the purposes of a theory of musical reception, however, the form in which they reach us is not different from that of their fictional counterparts—hence my reliance on cinematic representations, which have the advantage of being instances of "distributed experiences" shareable across a vast cultural space.

---

[27] Brian O'Doherty. *Inside the White Cube: The Ideology of the Gallery Space* (Berkeley: University of California Press, 1999).

[28] For a critique of this model, see Cristopher Small, *Musicking: The Meanings of Performing and Listening* (Hanover, NH: University Press of New England, 1998). Recent explorations of listening contexts normally at the fringe of musicological inquiry include, among others, Tia De Nora, "Musicalizing Consciousness: Aesthetics and Anaesthetics," in *Music Asylums: Wellbeing Through Music in Everyday Life* (London and New York: Routledge, 2014), 97-120; and *Ubiquitous Musics: The Everyday Sounds That We Don't Always Notice*, ed. M. G. Quiñones, Anahid Kassabian, and Elena Boschi (Aldershot, UK: Ashgate, 2013).

[29] Carolyn Abbate, "Music—Drastic or Gnostic?" *Critical Inquiry* 30, no. 3 (2004): 505–36.

[30] On this, see also Elizabeth Le Guin, "One Bar in Eight: Debussy and the Death of Description," in *Beyond Structural Listening: Postmodern Modes of Hearing* (Berkeley and London: University of California Press, 2004), 233–51.

The Writer as Situated Listener

The bulk of the films sampled cover what one might call "international classical style" between World War II and the so-called New Hollywood of the 1970s, at the dawn of the so-called Dolby era. With Dolby, the dialectic that is central to this book—that between vectorization, via the actor/auditor, and coercion, via editing—gives way to a different and broader range of possibilities. In particular, the black-and-white, all-or-nothing representation of the selective attention is replaced by a more nuanced manner, one in which background and foreground coexist more seamlessly.[31] When revived, as it certainly is even today, the stark binary between the presence and absence of sound has something of the citation or the oneiric about it.[32] Not coincidentally, it is especially common in horror films.

The representation of aural subjectivity manifesting itself in recurrent—predictable even—form across films from different regions across the central decades of the century just past is but another confirmation that the fundamentals of film language have long been accessible to a global audience. Whether this is the result of universal patterns of cognition, the sheer influence of a few paradigmatic examples, or the commercial dominance of studio filmmaking—or any mix of the three in varying ratios—remains a difficult and controversial question that this book can only hope to acknowledge, but not answer.[33] Since the core theoretical questions drove the selection of the examples, the latter do not easily coalesce into a genre, nor are they a representative cross section of a circumscribed period of film history. What they do share, however, is a concern, at key junctures of their narratives, with capturing the world as seen and

---

[31] For an account of the impact of Dolby, see Gianluca Sergi, *The Dolby Era: Film Sound in Contemporary Hollywood* (Manchester: Manchester University Press, 2004). On the difference between mono and Dolby, see also Chion's analysis of the beginning of Spielberg's *Close Encounters of the Third Kind* (1977), in *Film: A Sound Art*, 346.

[32] Think, for example, of the party scene in David Lynch's *Lost Highway* (1997) in which Fred Madison meets "Mystery Man."

[33] For a view of film language as emerging from universal patterns of cognitions, see, for instance, David Bordwell, "Convention, Construction, and Vision," in *Post-Theory: Reconstructing Film Studies*, ed. David Bordwell and Noël Carroll (Madison: University of Wisconsin Press, 1996), 87–107. For a critique of "cultural exceptionalism," especially with regard to Japanese cinema, see David Bordwell, "Review of Noël Burch, To the Distant Observer," *Wide Angle* 3, no. 4 (1980): 70–73; and Eric Crosby, "Widescreen Composition and Transnational Influence: Early Anamorphic Filmmaking in Japan," in *Widescreen Worldwide*, ed. John Belton, Sheldon Hall, and Steve Neale (Herts, UK: John Libbey Publishing, 2010): 181–82. Jonathan Crary's work on vision in *Techniques of the Observer: On Vision and Modernity in the Nineteenth Century* (Cambridge, MA: MIT Press, 1990), and attention in *Suspensions of Perception Attention, Spectacle, and Modern Culture* (Cambridge, MA: MIT Press, 1999) may be seen as espousing the diametrically opposed position. My own position is that these two extremes, or ideal types, shed light on different, yet equally significant, *aspects* of the psychology underpinning the aesthetic experience.

heard by the character—a concern, in other words, with perceptually specific information. This is especially apparent in the two main Hitchcock examples, *Rear Window* (1954) and *Vertigo* (1958), both paragons of what Elisabeth Weis has called "the subjective film,"[34] and the Scorsese, Bertolucci, and Truffaut examples. The excerpts from films by Godard, Antonioni, and Hou Hsiao-hsien, to name three, are brought into play as a result of their striking disregard for, or original treatment of, the representation of aural subjectivity.

Historical and geographical diversity are a function of my own catholic taste, emerging from my peregrinations as a scholar across three continents—Europe, North America, and East Asia—in pursuit of the theoretical questions that shaped the project from its inception. The dramatic situations I examine, such as the trope of the evening at the theater, for instance, are common in narratives from different parts of the world. Their specific realization and meaning in the context of the films in which they are embedded, however, call for a fine-grained exegesis. For this reason, I have privileged close readings of a few select episodes over the review of large amounts of data. I celebrate the particular while simultaneously aiming at some degree of theoretical generalization in the hope that, in so doing, I may be able to point in the direction of the gray area between the generalizable and the unrepeatable, on the one hand, and the psychologically and the culturally situated, on the other.

Like any similar enterprise, then, this book bears the marks of its author—so much so, in fact, that he may well be mistaken for the "situated listener" himself. My first encounters with cinema took place via its historic nemesis—the television. While I was able to cultivate my passion for seeing movies on the big screen frequently enough, it was on the small one that my cinephilia was given free rein (I was aided in this by the appearance of the VHS tape and the generous and far-sighted programming of the Italian public television service in the 1980s and early 1990s). This will no doubt irk the purist and has at times led me to question my own commitment to cinema.[35] Yet it also enabled me to see that cinema as a medium and the fiction film as a form are not one and the same thing. The former begot the latter but could not prevent it from traversing the mediascape, bringing

---

[34] Elisabeth Weis, *The Silent Scream: Alfred Hitchcock's Sound Track* (Rutherford, NJ: Fairleigh Dickinson University Press, 1982).

[35] For a classic critique of the impact of television on film culture, see Gerald Mast, *Film/Cinema/ Movie: A Theory of Experience* (New York: Harper and Row, 1977). A striking, and much earlier, counterpart in the field of music is Theodor W. Adorno's "The Radio Symphony: An Experiment in Theory," in *Radio Research, 1941*, ed. Paul F. Lazarsfeld and Frank Stanton (New York: Duell, Sloan, and Pearce, 1941), 110–39. In the essay, Adorno argues that the very medium fundamentally alters the nature of what is being listened to. Needless to say, I part from Adorno's totalizing critique as I consider the listener, too, implicated in the creation of the imaginary entity that is the object of the listening experience. There is more, in a symphony, than meets the ear.

with it resilient modes of fruition. The transfer from one medium to another brings about an irreversible transformation, and indeed a loss in not simply information but also sheer physical impact.[36] However, this does not amount to a complete metamorphosis. Even on television, *Star Wars* is still a film, as some of its features resist being swallowed up entirely by their new host. Think of the nature and scope of the narrative—for instance, its editing patterns, the dynamics of the on-screen interactions between the actors or the aura lent to them by the complex marketing machine (not to mention the plethora of paratextual elements that surrounded its release, and long aftermath). Though commercial interests have driven many filmmakers to turn out work that "translates" easily into television, and now other formats as well, it goes without saying that features that may survive intact—or almost—through any such transfer nevertheless do not define the "essence" of a fiction film (to the medium purist, in fact, it will be quite the opposite). All the same, I have no doubt that in my case, the television, by muting the impact of the textural and spectacular dimensions of cinema, encouraged my interest in film as a species of dramatic writing. This bias has remained with me ever since, fed by a certain impatience, too, with the notion of music as "pure sound" that is implicit in the promotion surrounding high-fidelity, digital recording technology and various other kinds of sound enhancement systems (promotion that I have come to see as the "ersatz" version of the ideology of absolute music). Lest the reader think I am advocating some kind of stripped-down, ascetic rewriting of cinema, I hasten to add that in my analyses, I happily indulge in the melodic, textural, and timbral richness of musical sound, and the sound mix more generally. But I do so because I am convinced that a compelling dramatic situation enhances and indeed invests these parameters with a value they would not have otherwise, all the more so upon experiencing a film in the perceptually more sumptuous form afforded by the latest technology in a state-of-the-art movie theater.[37]

It may be argued that dwelling on details of mise-en-scène, musical texture, or sound design reflects a disposition that is at odds with my stated aim, namely, capturing the experience of the "situated listener"—particularly if one construes such a listener, as I do here, as a distracted character or a spectator too busy processing narrative information to really care about music per se. I offer two lines of defense to this, one that pertains to film music in particular, the other to the nature and goals of description in general. My explicit focus is dramatic action. If

---

[36] I am thinking, for example, of the impact an extreme close-up has on the large screen, and how this is muted on a television screen.

[37] For the (relatively) peaceful coexistence between an ever-expanding palette of visual effects and the traditional narrative values in recent Hollywood cinema, see David Bordwell, "Intensified Continuity: Visual Style in Contemporary Hollywood Film," *Film Quarterly*, 55, no. 3 (Spring 2002): 16–28.

I describe music in any detail, this is to reveal an aspect that I believe is perceptually salient in the context of the scene of which it is a constituent element. At no point do I engage in what, to paraphrase D. A. Miller, one might call "too close analysis."[38] By this I mean either the erudite, elaborate hermeneutic interrogation of a musical episode or close, technical parsing of a musical score.[39] I do not deny that the former can be a creative form of engagement with a film in its own right, nor that the latter brings out important dimensions of the musician's work. At issue here is not the adherence to a normative view of what the film experience is or ought to be, but rather the acknowledgment of the conditions under which music is apprehended. It isn't just that, to quote Murray Smith, "there may be aspects of perceptual experience beyond the reach of such types of analysis."[40] It is also that in practicing it, writers and scholars speak from a position of omniscience, in the process giving music a conspicuousness it simply does not have.[41] We musicologists, in particular, are keen to stress the presence of music whenever possible. This runs the risk of betraying the actual—read, intermittent, and often subsidiary—role music has in movies (and life more generally). The analyses that follow, then, reflect a mimetic impulse of sorts, one that situates music within a large field of visual and dramatic considerations. Only when subsumed under an enlarged field of experience does music assume the values we claim it possesses.

Offering a detailed description of what happens in a scene does not constitute a betrayal of the "average" or statistically most representative encounter with a film. It is not just that many films—unlike, say, the news—reward and indeed demand repeated viewings. It is also that even when solely interested in a "bare bones" representation of the action in the course of a single sitting, our eyes and ears take in far more than language can hope to capture. A film is a "take" on reality and as such a partial rendering of it. Despite the exercise of the selective attention that it simultaneously records and fleshes out, the resulting images and sounds open up, in turn, a potentially infinite number of foci for the attention. Reality, even when captured on film, is mathematically continuous, a fact easily brought home when playing a favorite scene in slow motion, carefully listening

---

[38] D. A. Miller, "Hitchcock's Hidden Pictures," *Critical Inquiry* 37, no. 1 (2010): 106–30.

[39] For an example of the former, see Lawrence Kramer, "Melodic Trains: Music in Polanski's *The Pianist*," in *Beyond the Soundtrack: Representing Music in Cinema*, ed. Daniel Goldmark, Lawrence Kramer, and Richard Leppert (Berkeley, CA: University of California Press, 2007), 66–85; for the latter, see David Cooper, "Film Form and Musical Form in Bernard Herrmann's Score to Vertigo," *Journal of Film Music* 1, no. 2/3 (Fall–Winter 2003): 239–48.

[40] Smith, "Consciousness," 49. The context of the cited passage is the discussion of the relative merits of "impressionistic criticism" and "technical analysis," respectively.

[41] I return to the question of how to interrogate the presence of symbolically rich musical citations in chapter 3.

to its soundtrack in isolation, or even contemplating a freeze frame from a single shot. New levels of detail continue to emerge, seemingly unstoppably. (Kenneth Anger's rescreenings of his own work at slower speed come to mind here, as does Douglas Gordon's *24-Hour Psycho*, a slowed-down version of Hitchcock's original film.) All of this is uncontroversial. Yet the act of rewatching and rehearing a film for the sake of capturing the contours of our experience in language need not be solely the occasion for noticing new sights and sounds (as guided, say, by the hand of the perceptive critic or new circumstances of reception). It is as much the occasion to fix on paper what one has heard the first time around, too.[42] To be sure, making what one sees and hears intersubjectively available is an enterprise marred by myriad pitfalls and a deep sense of inadequacy. It takes time and, on the written page, space (ask the readers of Proust). But one must be careful not to attribute the qualities that define the process of verbal description to that which this process seeks to describe. Like memory, and no matter how seemingly exhaustive, a description breaks down, simplifies, and curtails—it reduces one's experience to a sliver of what it once had been, redeeming itself only on those rare occasions in which it becomes the premise for someone else's.

A Note on Terminology

In what follows, I use the terms "source music" and "scoring" or simply "score" to refer to "diegetic" and "nondiegetic music," respectively. I hasten to add that I do not consider "source" to be an exact synonym of "diegetic," nor "scoring" of "nondiegetic." I opted for "source" and "score" to circumvent a number of possible misunderstandings as to the meaning of the more theoretically laden, if undoubtedly widespread, "diegetic" and "nondiegetic."[43] One such potential pitfall is the use of "nondiegetic" to indicate that the music exists outside a concurrent scene, as if "intruding" upon it from someplace else.[44] As I see it, the risk is the result of a misunderstanding. As used by Gorbman and others, the discriminating factor is not the position or status of music relative to a scene but rather whether it is perceivable—*as such*, I would add—by the characters in the story world. That so-called nondiegetic music can and does embody events and

---

[42] My thinking here is indebted to Richard Doty, *The Art of Description* (Minneapolis: Graywolf Press, 2010).

[43] For a full discussion of these terms, including compounds such as "source scoring," see William H. Rosar, "Film Studies in Musicology: Disciplinarity vs. Interdisciplinarity," *Journal of Film Music* 2, no. 2–4 (Winter 2009): 108–15.

[44] See, for instance, Ben Winters, "The Non-Diegetic Fallacy: Film, Music and Narrative Space," *Music and Letters* 91, no. 2 (2010): 224–44.

phenomena integral to a scene has in fact long been recognized, and is well in keeping with the history of music in the theater as well.[45] Even so, the terminology has contributed to the confusion. This is perhaps because it aims to *describe* rather than simply refer. If the goal is to simply point to something, as is my wish here, then "source" and "scoring," in my opinion, do a better job.

The difference between reference and description is relevant to my use of the term "spectator" as well. I am fully aware that "spectator" is associated with a long history of film criticism and scholarship that gave little or no consideration to the auditory dimension of cinema (and that it is etymologically linked to the Latin verb *spectare*, "to watch" or "to look at"). Despite this, I use "spectator" not only for the sake of convenience but also because I do not believe that the definition of a term necessarily follows from its etymology. Given its long history, the term is, to me at least, as much a proper name —or "rigid designator," in Kripke's words—as a description.[46] I see it as fitting that it should take a whole book to specify its referent, for spectatorship is so complex that no term can begin to capture its contours. I for a time contemplated adopting Anahid Kassabian's term "perceiver." Kassabian's proposal is to me triply interesting not only because the term immediately does away with a perceived—no pun intended—bias for the visual but also because it signals two more theoretical moves on her part: first, her use of "perceiver" as a "theoretical placeholder for audience members . . . that cannot be reduced to either textuality or an extratextual 'real' "; and second, the consideration of the personal and social histories of said "perceivers." Such consideration follows, I take it, from the idea that perception is historical and informed by memory.[47] For all the appeal of this choice, however, I have decided to use a term less tied to the senses. Being a spectator, after all, involves more than seeing and hearing; albeit embodied through and through, spectatorship is also a cognitive and affective experience, and continues well after a film is over in the form of discourse and memories. Like Kassabian, I have proceeded to theorize rather than describe a flesh-and-blood spectator, but I have stopped short of considering what Vivian Sobchak calls "particularized spectators" (whether theoretical, as in Kassabian's model, or empirical, as in reception studies). I have privileged instead the personal and social particularities of the characters as listeners that figure in the films I examine. As applied to film spectators, therefore, the term "situated" refers less to their personal and social identity than to the constraints posed on, and the opportunities afforded to, them as *listeners* by the perils and joys of sitting through a film.

---

[45] See, for instance, Bernard Herrmann, "Music in Film—A Rebuttal," in *The Routledge Film Music Sourcebook*, ed. James Wierzbicki, Nathan Platte, and Colin Roust (New York and London: Routledge, 2012), 120.

[46] Saul Kripke, *Naming and Necessity* (Cambridge, MA: Harvard University Press, 1980).

[47] Anahid Kassabian, *Hearing Film* (New York and London: Routledge, 2001), 110–11.

Part I

THE CHARACTER AS VECTOR

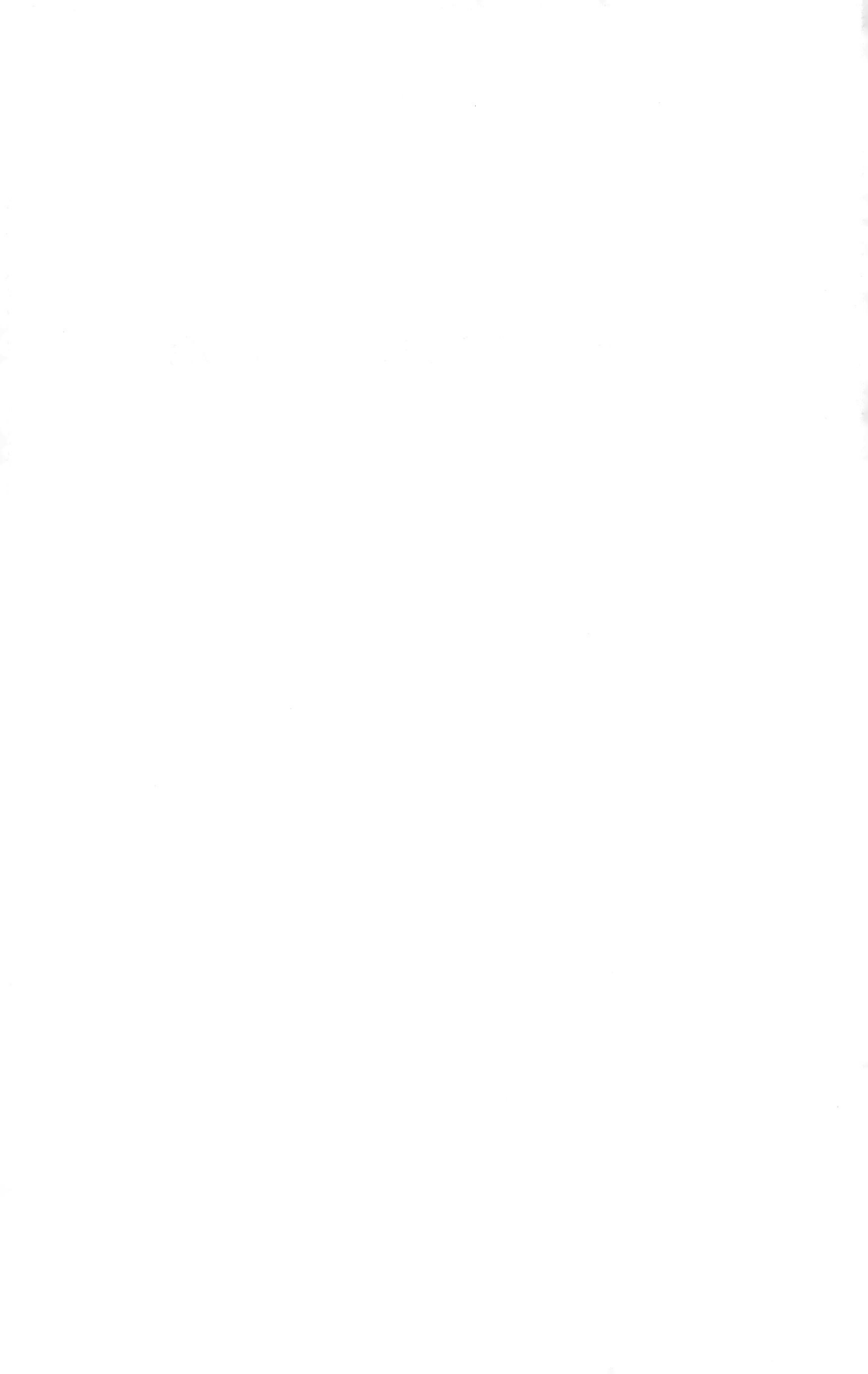

1

Music, Off Stage

Of the principles regulating the use of film music laid out by Claudia Gorbman in *Unheard Melodies*, one of the most far-reaching is also the least discussed. This is the principle of "subordination," according to which "music is subordinated to narrative meaning in the standard feature film."[1] Significantly, her central example of the latter is not background scoring but a performance attended by the protagonists of a decidedly *auteur* film, Eric Rohmer's *My Night at Maud's* (1969).

When we witness a film character engaged in listening, the music reaches us in the form of an audiovisual recording, and it naturally takes a back seat to story and character development. It is to the latter that we pay attention. This much is so uncontroversial as to be banal. It is for this reason, I suspect, that to illustrate her idea, Gorbman chose what she (rightly) considered a limit case, one in which "pure musical codes apparently dominate."[2] This is the episode in which the protagonist of Rohmer's film, Jean-Louis (Jean-Louis Trintignant), goes to a violin recital with his friend, Vidal (A. Vitez), whom he's serendipitously met in Clermont-Ferrand. One may want to quibble with Gorbman's adoption of a vocabulary wedded to formalist analysis and her lack of interest in the music as performance, but the important point is that the sequence is indeed striking for its length and the simple, laconic manner with which it is staged and edited. Its documentary quality contributes to the effort, apparent throughout the film, to create the impression that the camera is casually rendering a portion of the life of the educated middle class in a provincial city outside the spotlight of the Parisian stage. The bareness of Rohmer's approach also belies a fundamental ambiguity between *film as a recording medium and film as a dramatic form.*

---

[1] Claudia Gorbman, *Unheard Melodies: Narrative Film Music* (Bloomington: Indiana University Press, 1987), 14.

[2] Gorbman, *Unheard Melodies*, 13.

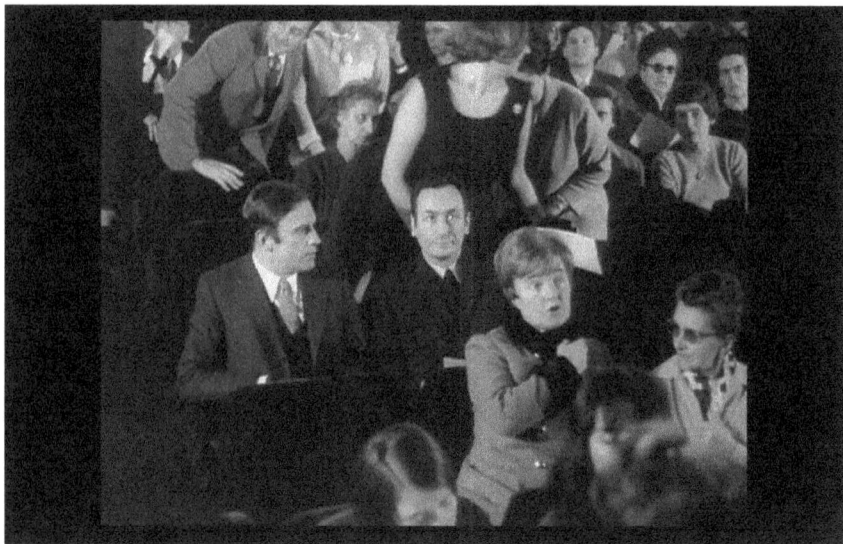

Figure 1.1 My Night at Maud's.

After a brief shot of the entrance of the theater from the street, a cut takes us to the interior of the opera house hosting the concert (Figure 1.1). From a position roughly equivalent to the stage, we see the audience members take their seats, the two friends among them. Vidal raises his head, ostensibly to look at the elaborate glass lamp and ornate ceiling lying above. By a combined tilt and pan, the point-of-view shot that follows shows the round contours of the ceiling and the upper boxes filled with people. The moving shot comes to a sudden close as a more tightly framed image of the lamp, held till the lights are off, signals the entrance of the artists. This is synchronized to the accompanying off-screen sound of the audience clapping. The sound continues across a cut to a *plan américain* of the duo standing onstage, and about to start (Figure 1.2).

In the absence of fades, the artificiality of the temporal compression is palpable. The avowed simplicity of the camera movements, elliptical editing, and demonstrative use of sound add to the impression of a strong stylistic signature; only it is a style that announces itself by subtracting rather than adding visual and sonic interest to the presentation of the event. The performance of Mozart's Sonata in B-flat major, K. 378, brings this approach to a culmination. The camera remains fixed on violinist Léonide Kogan and his pianist for nearly two minutes in the same, unedited shot. The view cannot be that of the protagonists—the shot is too close—but is nevertheless consistent with that of the audience facing the stage. Just as the duo is about to play the second theme of the exposition of the Allegro, a straight cut brings the music to an abrupt halt, taking us to a

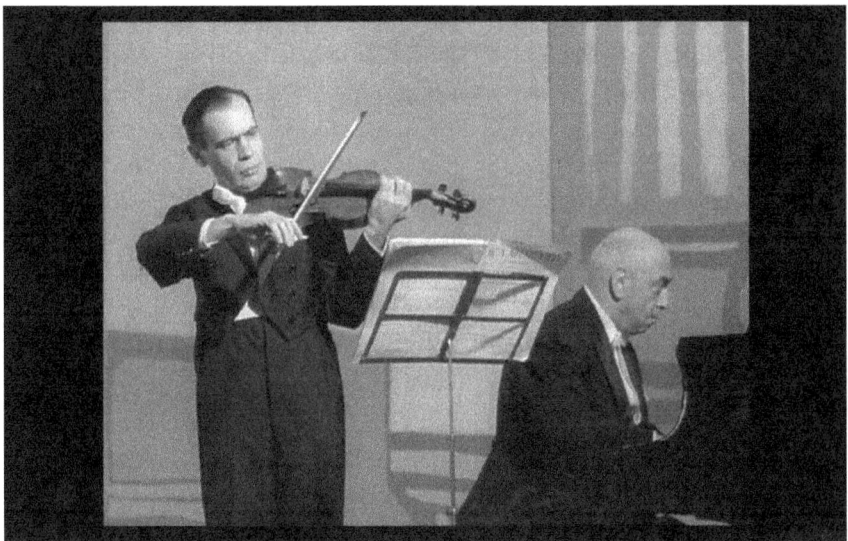

Figure 1.2 My Night at Maud's.

restaurant where Jean-Louis and Vidal are eating dinner. They hardly exchange a word on the concert. Their silence on the performance may have to do with Jean-Louis's initial resistance to attending (he says as much in the conversation at the cafe that immediately precedes it). We will never find out. Like the heated yet polite exchanges on chance and the meaning of life, the two friends' chance encounter itself, and the famous debate on Pascal's wager later in the night, the lack of rhetorical emphasis is an oblique invitation to understand the performance as something that simply happens, devoid of any special meaning and in no way exemplar.

Rohmer's strategy "interl[aces] documentary and fictional imperatives," in the words of Kent Jones.[3] The sequence is the recording of an actual performance— that is, one not staged for the film—featuring Kogan, who at the time was a well-known violin performer.[4] To quote Jones again, "Rohmer's meticulous preparation neither dispels the need for luck nor compensates for it. In fact, he creates situations, in his filmmaking and for his characters, in which preparation and chance go hand in hand."[5] This being a film, however, we know a selection

[3] Kent Jones, *"My Night at Maud's*: Chances Are . . . ," *The Criterion Collection*, accessed July 8, 2015, http://www.criterion.com/current/posts/436-my-night-at-maud-s-chances-are.

[4] In answering a question about his choice of Kogan's performance, Rohmer replied, "It's simply that he was playing in Clermont-Ferrand while we were shooting": in "Eric Rohmer, le son au plus vrai," interview by Bertrand Dermonourt, *L'Express*, January 13, 2010, http://www.lexpress.fr/culture/musique/eric-rohmer-le-son-au-plus-vrai_841713.html (translation mine).

[5] Jones, "My Night at Maud's: Chances Are. . . ."

has been consciously made as to what incidents to leave in the final edit. The concert, after all, is an occasion for Jean-Louis to catch sight of Francoise, with whom he is infatuated (he will later marry her). The municipal opera house and repertory, for their part, are symptomatic of Vidal's curiosity and fit rather nicely with his intellectual outlook. He is a philosophy professor, loves books, and takes a liberal, noncommittal approach to his relationships with women—as the remainder of the film will bear out. As *My Night at Maud's* veers decisively into an investigation of Jean-Louis and Maud's intellectual and sexual identities, however, the performance may slip out of the viewer's memory altogether. But, in a further twist, the ending makes it clear that even the putative subject of the film—Jean-Louis's "night at Maud's"—may not have been the harbinger of anything of consequence in the protagonist's life. A night is a night is a night: the unity of time, violated only in the flash-forward that concludes the film, is a function of an aesthetic, rather than dramatic, principle. Everything we have seen, including the performance of Mozart's violin sonata, is in retrospect the record of a night whose representativeness in the characters' lives we will never be able to determine.

Gorbman's choice of the film as an illustration of the idea of "subordination" is indeed apposite. The sequence features few or no subjective shots and appears unmotivated by the characters' will or agency; rather, the episode comes across almost as an accident in their lives, the result of unforeseen circumstances. This, as we have seen, was indeed the case as far as the inclusion of the performance in the film is concerned. The unscripted nature of its production lends a sense of the unscripted to the lives of the fictional characters themselves. None of this, however, precludes us from concentrating "as much on the fact of Paul's spectatorial presence as on the explicit content of the scene (musicians and music)."[6] Straitjacketed into such a seemingly restrictive frame, the sonata may well be said to be "subordinate" in the sense that its formal, technical, and expressive features fail to make a claim on the attention (or are set aside in the expectation, eventually frustrated, that we may be able to attach some kind of dramatic significance to them). It may be argued that, as Gorbman herself acknowledges, in *My Night at Maud's,* we are not so much listening to the sonata as we are watching the musicians perform.[7] Far from being a deviation or impoverishing the experience, witnessing the very act of music making with one's own eyes is an inescapable aspect of "the nature and meaning of music in performance."[8] This is naturally the case for filmed

---

[6] Gorbman, *Unheard Melodies,* 13.

[7] Ibid.

[8] Nicholas Cook, *Beyond the Score: Music as Performance* (New York: Oxford University Press, 2014), 293.

performances too, given the panoply of tools film directors have at their disposal to showcase the body in performance.[9]

Kogan's performance in *My Night at Maud's* is doubtlessly unlike the same performance experienced live at a public concert. This is not just because it is recorded on film; the difference also arises from its position, however unresolved this may be, within a narrative. Commenting on the film, Ben Winters observes that "Kogan is entirely divorced from the narrative . . . : the scene seems to exist primarily to allow an audience to marvel at Kogan's playing."[10] This is in one sense accurate, but, like Gorbman, I also read the disassociation between Kogan and the main narrative thread of the film as having a defamiliarizing effect, thereby drawing attention to the power of the standard narrative format to engulf even the most seemingly discrete, self-standing scene within a horizon of expectation. Channeled by the characters' own situation, if not their literal point of view, we are unlikely to experience that indeterminacy of listening modes, that fuzziness so often disavowed and yet so central to a more immersive experience of music (whether performed live or not).[11] Deprived of that moment-to-moment shifting of perceptual strategies, one feels that the music has been stripped of something fundamental and peculiar to it, recoverable only by rehearing it abstracted from a narrative or dramatic scenario. Just as we seem to be able to rest assured that the performance will go on, and we may even ease ourselves into a position of contemplation, there is a cut. Despite the open-endedness of the film's main episodes and its nondramatic rhetoric, the cut reminds us that the performance is glued to a syntagmatic chain that far transcends, in both scope and duration, the musical episode we have just seen. As part of a narrative, the performance is subsumed under an interpretive

[9] Ben Winters argues that a filmed performance may restore a sense of what Abbate calls the "drastic," which he interprets as the "appreciation of the physicality and perilous nature" in musical performance: Winters, *Music, Performance, and the Realities of Film: Shared Concert Experiences in Screen Fiction* (New York: Routledge, 2013), 71–72. But the counterpart to the "drastic" in a movie theater would be the appreciation of the unmediated object of perception, that is, moving images and a recorded mix or, to break this down to its elemental components, patterns of light on screen in various degrees of sync with sound waves emitted by loudspeakers. Translating the concept of the "drastic" for the film experience clarifies what makes it ultimately untenable or at least highly unpalatable in the sphere of music as well, if one is to hear more than just the physical substratum of music qua music.

[10] Winters, *Music, Performance, and the Realities of Film*, 27.

[11] "Music of any degree of complexity," writes Eric Clarke, "offers multiple parsings at almost every stage": see Eric Clarke, "Music Perception and Musical Consciousness," in David Clarke and Eric Clarke, eds., *Music and Consciousness: Philosophical, Psychological and Cultural Perspectives* (Oxford: Clarendon Press, 2011), 208. For the notion of "fuzziness" applied to the experience of instrumental music, and how narrative cinema drastically reduces it by channeling perception into preordained routes, see G. Biancorosso, *Where Does the Music Come From? Studies in the Aesthetics of Film Music* (PhD diss., Princeton University, 2002), 15. The idea inverts Gorbman's point about music "anchoring" the image the way a caption disambiguates the content of a photograph: Gorbman, *Unheard Melodies*, 32.

horizon that drastically redefines it as perceptual experience, preventing us, even in the context of a long, objective shot with a fixed camera, from enjoying dimensions of it we normally take for granted. Yet this is a scenario that also encourages the apprehension of aspects that are normally not allowed to emerge in our accounts of the listening experience. After all, the sonata does temporarily take center stage, both literally and metaphorically, but it does so under an aspect that is unfortunately not taken to be representative of music listening proper, namely, as the uniquely situated event in the lives of two individuals (whom the film, by insisting on them, has aligned us with).[12] Cast within a richly articulated chain of situations, the performance is not separable from the circumstances that give rise to it and the motives that underpin its occurrence. It is simply untenable to deem the music as a self-contained, autonomous perceptual object. Though the length of the shot makes it the sole focus of the undivided attention, the performance is not an immersive, "world-constituting" event. It is instead engulfed by a situation that, albeit equivocally, both encompasses and transcends it.

When the Music Stops

The history of cinema offers many clear-cut, eloquent examples of the reframing of the listening experience as part of a representation. The clearest, most obvious symptom of the status of the music in this context is the truncated form in which it often reaches us. Only rarely, in a play or film, does the performance of a given piece retain its integrity.[13] Whether the interruption is precipitated by one or more characters or is the result of an editing decision, interruption may be seen as an allegorical commentary on the intrusion of real-life concerns into the leisurely space of artistic contemplation. Life, like a story, must go on.

Often the interruption is itself an integral component of the story. The climax of Hitchcock's *The Man Who Knew Too Much* (1955), to cite a well-known

---

[12] I say "partially" since Rohmer's film leaves large aspects of the characters' interior life opaque or simply inaccessible. I use the term "alignment," after Murray Smith, to refer to "the process by which spectators are placed in [a privileged] relation to characters in terms of access to their actions and to what they know and feel": Murray Smith, "Altered States: Character and Emotional Response in Cinema," *Cinema Journal* 33, no. 4 (1994): 41.

[13] As a foil to her discussion of the Rohmer example, Gorbman introduces Jean-Marie Huillet-Straub's *Chronicle of Anna Magdalena Bach* (*Chronik der Anna Magdalena Bach*, 1968), a film replete with long takes of complete performances, one in which "musical rhetoric can once more be recognized by spectators and enjoyed as such": Gorbman, *Unheard Melodies*, 14. For an in-depth analysis of this important example of semifictional reconstruction, see Barton Byg, "Traces of a Life: *Chronicle of Anna Magdalena Bach*," in *Landscapes of Resistance: The German Films of Danièle Huillet and Jean-Marie Straub* (Berkeley: University of California Press, 1995), 51–70.

example, occurs during the performance of a cantata at Royal Albert Hall. The moment when the musically literate assassin fires the gun is signaled by a crash, notated in the score, of the cymbals. As Murray Pomerance has noted in his virtuosic, moment-to-moment account of the sequence, multiple perspectives of the music are built into this long sequence. They encompass a spectrum ranging from rapt to wandering attention, and from "musical appreciation . . . to a calculation."[14] Since we are in on the plot, however, the music is shot through from the very start with considerable suspense (the very structure of Pomerance's own reconstruction, cruising the music from beginning to end measure by measure, and even beat by beat, makes this plain).[15] When the feared passage arrives at last, a gun is fired, but the bullet is deflected as the killer is distracted by Jo's (Doris Day's) scream, "rending the musical tissue."[16] The performance of the cantata, already demoted to the unwitting role of stopwatch, must now stop altogether.

A less discussed but equally paradigmatic instance of interrupted music marks, in Stanley Kubrick's *Barry Lyndon* (1975), the most spectacular showdown in Redmond Barry's doomed quest to become a member of the British peerage (Figures 1.3 and 1.4). Set in a large room of the impeccably decorated Castle Hackton, the sequence is a re-creation of the eighteenth-century prototype of the modern concert hall experience. Under the auspices, one presumes, of Berry's sponsors, Lord Hallam and Lord Wendover, the performance features members of the extended Lyndon family—her Ladyship at the harpsichord, Reverend Hunt at the *traverso*—playing an arrangement of the Adagio from Bach's Concerto for two harpsichords in C minor with the accompaniment of a full orchestra. The camera is placed between the latter and the soloists. As if cued by the beginning of the music, it begins to pan gently to the right almost immediately thereafter, gradually affording us a view of the magnificent room filled by dozens of well-appointed, intent listeners. The occasion is formal but festive. The guests can be seen resting in their comfortably spaced armchairs. The motion caresses as it reveals this enchanting and ordered space, enhancing by contrast the sight of the absolute stillness of the audience of noblemen and noblewomen who have come to pay homage to the patrons, as well as the hopeful would-be peer, Barry himself.

Following this majestic introduction to the venue, radiating from within the heart of the music-making ensemble, a blunt transition to the medium

---

[14] Murray Pomerance, "Finding Release: 'Storm Clouds' and *The Man Who Knew Too Much*," in *Music and Cinema*, ed. James Buhler, Caryl Flinn, and David Neumeyer (Hanover, CT: Wesleyan University Press, 2000), 219.

[15] On this aspect of the sequence, see also Winters, *Music, Performance, and the Realities of Film*, 81; and James Wierzbicki, "Grand Illusion: The 'Storm Cloud' Music in Hitchcock's *The Man Who Knew Too Much*," *Journal of Film Music* 1, no. 2–3 (2003): 220.

[16] Murray Pomerance, "Finding Release," 241.

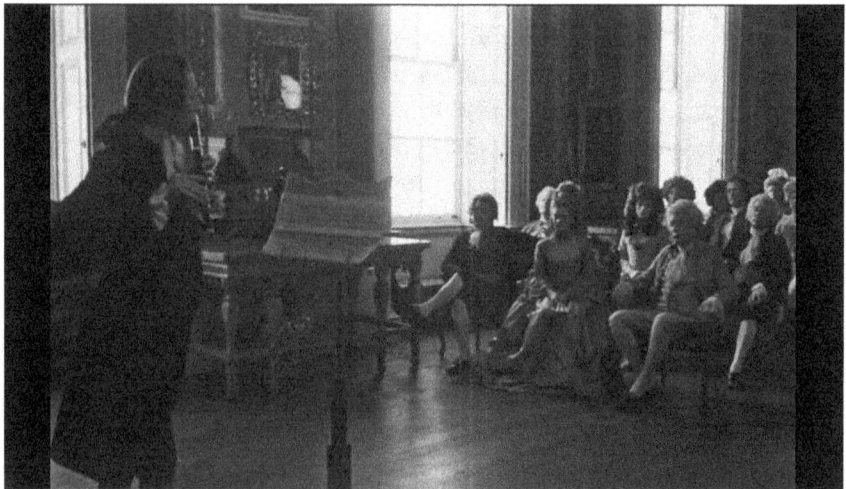

Figure 1.3 Barry Lyndon.

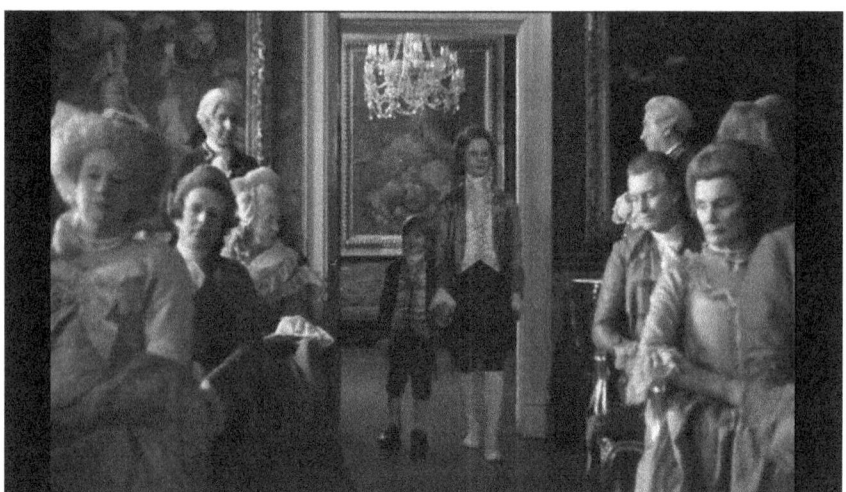

Figure 1.4 Barry Lyndon.

shot of the door at the other end of the room causes the first adjustment. The change in camera setup signals the beginning of a derailment. The door opens to Lord Bullingdon and his younger step-brother walking in, the latter wearing a conspicuous pair of outsized clattering clogs "making, in Kate McQuiston's words, loud, clunking noises against the orderly, measured pace of the music."[17]

[17] Kate McQuiston, *We'll Meet Again: Musical Design in the Films of Stanley Kubrick* (New York: Oxford University Press, 2013), 93. I have amended the original "peace" into what I believe to be the intended "pace."

The new sight and sounds cause a second, and more drastic, reappraisal of what is happening. As the two siblings approach the orchestra hand in hand along the aisle forming between the two halves of the audience, the camera stays on them and tracks backward in one long take. Shown in a characteristic close-up against the blur of the musicians behind her, a bewildered Lady Lyndon can no longer carry on with her solo. Soon the music begins to disintegrate. By the time her children are at arm's length from the instruments, the orchestra has stopped playing altogether. Bullingdon stops walking, there being no longer any need to sabotage a performance he has already so effectively killed. Yet the episode is only halfway through. There follows a famous speech in which he publicly denounces Barry and the even more notorious savage brawl, shot, significantly, with a hand-held camera. The latter draws us "into Barry's violence, . . . into the chaos of his situation while compressing the space so that there are no vistas of escape."[18] The ensuing chaos shatters the sense of order and control exuded by the beginning of the concert. The utterly unexpected unraveling of the performance coincides with the end of Barry's ambitions and the beginning of his inexorable, downward path toward personal and financial ruin.

Cantus Interruptus

A less drastic way of silencing or at least sidelining the role of an on-screen performance involves not its forceful interruption but the use of a distracted character as a vector. Woody Allen's *Manhattan* (1979) features just such a setup in the form of a joke played at the expense of the self-importance of classical music institutions and the music lovers who patronize them (Figure 1.5). The stage is Avery Fisher Hall in New York City, a prime example of the socially sanctioned, architecturally driven mode of attentive listening that is all but taken for granted in most discussions of music, and whose incipience, in the representative context of a major European urban capital, has been so eloquently chronicled in Johnson's *Listening in Paris*.[19] A performance of Mozart's Symphony in G minor, K. 550, is under way; yet instead of seeing the musicians and their conductor, we are made to ponder in a long, unedited shot the farcical antics of Isaac (Woody

---

[18] Michal Klein, "Narrative and Discourse in Kubrick's Modern Tragedy," in *The English Novel and The Movies*, ed. Michael Klein and Gillian Parker (New York: Frederick Ungar, 1981).

[19] For similarly enlightening accounts of listening practices in North America ca. 1900 and nineteenth-century London, respectively, see Emily Thompson, *The Soundscape of Modernity* (Cambridge, MA: MIT Press, 2002) and Roger Parker, "'As a Stranger Give It Welcome': Musical Meanings in 1830s London," in *Representation in Western Music*, ed. Joshua Walden (Cambridge: Cambridge University Press, 2013), 33–46.

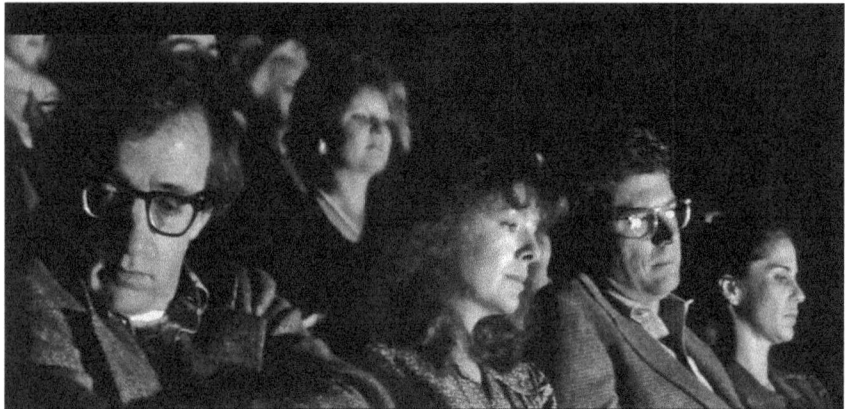

Figure 1.5 Manhattan.

Allen), Mary (Diane Keaton), and Yale (Michael Murphy) as they learn to cope, in an admittedly inconvenient location, with the difficult situation they find themselves in.

What is their predicament? Isaac and Mary have been seeing each other for some (screen) time. They owe their acquaintance to Yale, who dated Mary before introducing her to Isaac. The reasons for this are not clearly stated, but it is likely that, being married to Emily (Anne Byrne), Yale has all too expediently resolved to "offload" Mary on to Isaac to try to keep his marriage intact—a move, however, he now obviously regrets. Yale's wife, Emily, is herself visible in the penumbra of the theater, seemingly unaware of the comically virtual ménage-à-trois between her concert companions. She sits three seats to Isaac's left, along the diagonal of light that runs from the top left-hand corner of the frame and constitutes the true and only space of the action. That the situation reminds one of the self-inflicted entanglements found in Mozart's *Così Fan Tutte* only adds to the irony of the particular choice of repertory. Despite his pronouncement earlier in the film that another Mozart symphony (the *Jupiter*) "is one of the reasons why life is worth living," Allen seems intent on demonstrating the primacy of eros over artistic pursuits here. The fictional Mozart of Shaffer's play, and Forman's film, *Amadeus* (1984), would have concurred; and so would Sir Donald Tovey, who, in his essay on the symphony, heard it in the spirit of *opera buffa*.[20]

The setup and execution of the sequence is striking in its economy and directness. The two couples meet in Yale and Emily's apartment just before the concert. A straight cut takes us to the hall *in medias res*, as the orchestra is engaged

---

[20] Donald Francis Tovey, *Essays in Musical Analysis*, vol. 6 (London: Oxford University Press, 1935), 192–93.

with the recapitulation of the first movement (the tumultuous retransition, to be exact). This implies that we are seeing the climax of a process that has possibly been going on for quite some time, namely, the duration of the movement's exposition and development (possibly complete with a repeat). The camera is placed at an angle of the row of seats so that the four protagonists lie along a line whose receding point, like the orchestra, is off screen. It is a setup that, given the circumstances, ensures optimal visibility of the uncoordinated ballet of more or less concealed gesticulations and facial expressions on the part of the characters. Only Emily sits still in due diligence, respectful of the etiquette that regulates the attendance of classical music concerts. Whether she is absorbed in the performance is hard to tell; her glacial demeanor gives away little in the way of involvement in, let alone enjoyment of, the music. Then again, that she should be thought of as relishing the passage at hand precisely on account of her appearance is perhaps part of Allen's joke, too.

Within the narrow confines of the hall's chairs, seated in such a way as to invite trouble, and bounded by a strict code of silence, Isaac, Mary, and Yale enact a silent ensemble against Mozart's orchestra, delineating three different states of mind against the blur of the off-screen music. Isaac is all too mindful of Yale's past involvement with Mary and wonders about a rekindling of his passion for her (a fear that will turn out to be prophetic as the two will pick up the affair again). In a recognizably Allenesque manner, he is awkwardly trying to prevent what, in his mind, is Yale's inappropriate behavior toward her. Yale, for his part, looks on nervously, experiencing perhaps a pang of jealousy, or coming to regret having introduced Mary to Isaac in the first place. Sandwiched between her two neurotic male lovers, Mary does the best she can to disavow her own awareness of what is happening, managing to more or less limit the damages. The light source is directed pointedly at the portion of space occupied by the three protagonists, leaving Emily in the limbo of a penumbra. Despite its patently selective action, the light is soft and diffused enough to allow us a glimpse of Mary's eyes rolling and the angered expression on her face. All in all, it is a searing parody of a standard trope of narrative cinema, and especially romantic comedies—the concert-going sequence wherein two or more characters cement a relationship as reassuringly familiar music becomes the object of their attuned attention. In keeping with the parody, the familiarity of Mozart's symphony is inflected or, better, deflected, as if by a deviously placed mirror, in the direction of conflict and nonresolution. As per a long tradition in both the cinema and the theater—think of the play within the play in *Hamlet*, and dozens of others—the performance is a (musical) rite of passage: the moment at which, synchronized to the passing of music, the precarious balance of the three friends' situation is fatally exposed. Allen must have aimed at broad appeal and accessibility. Mozart's exceedingly famous theme, despite its fractured appearance in the retransition, still rings familiar in the context of the kaleidoscope of keys leading up to the equally recognizable second theme. The result is a pull in the spectator's attention between two opposite forces: appreciation of the comic pantomime on the one hand and recognition of the music on the other.

In his comprehensive guide to music in Allen's films, Adam Harvey praises the choice not just of the symphony but of its harmonically aggrieved, agitated recapitulation. The choice, according to Harvey, allegedly reflects the uneasiness of the protagonists.[21] Positing a relationship of reflection or even congruence between music and the action—as if the former were distinct from, or placed in some metaphorical outside of, the latter—is a common enough conceit in commentaries on film music. Allen may well have intended the music this way. We will never know. But his staging of the action speaks louder than what he may have said about it and begs for a different kind of interpretation. By understanding music as integral to the scene, rather than an "add-on" or "supplement," the impulse to read it as a mere tracing, or "rubbing," of what is already apparent on the screen may perhaps be more easily resisted.[22] Let me start by first considering the decision to plunge us into the performance *in medias res*. This is made clear not just by the lack of preliminaries—buying tickets, easing one's way into the audience, finding seats, hearing the orchestra tune up, and so forth—but by the place at which the symphony movement starts, that is, its tumultuous middle. It is not that the affective qualities and topical allusions of this particular passage call up relevant precedents of movie music. As film music, after all, the retransition of the first movement of the G-minor Symphony is not especially topical (except, perhaps, as a citation of itself). Its impact, rather, is contingent on something simultaneously simpler and more profound. Because it is the retransition, and not the beginning, that we're hearing, we are invited to entertain the disturbing thought that we are witnessing the climax of a process that has begun much earlier: not just the exposition of this particular piece but, possibly, the beginning of the whole program! If so, the retransition marks the latest, or at least a representative, station of what appears to be a sustained calvary at the sound of music, now creeping into observable—and for us, enjoyable—form. In this way, the scene rewrites the middle of the movement as akin to a state of "being in the middle of business well under way." This is first and foremost a matter of scope in that the excerpt implies, metonymically, a duration larger than

---

[21] Adam Harvey, *The Soundtracks of Woody Allen: A Complete Guide to the Songs and Music in Every Film, 1969-2005* (Jefferson, NC: McFarland, 2007).

[22] On the tradition of reading music and narrative this way, see Carolyn Abbate's critique in *Unsung Voices: Opera and Musical Narrative in the Nineteenth Century* (Princeton, NJ: Princeton University Press, 1991).

itself: a long "before" and, presumably, a just as excruciating long, if not longer, "after" (there are three more movements to go).

What we see on screen is what makes the music readable in this particular way. The scene is in this respect a classic instance of what Nicholas Cook calls, in the context of multimedia analysis, "emergent relationships."[23] The dramatic situation makes the retransition of a symphony movement acquire meanings and functions it would hardly possess otherwise. The concept of emergence exposes the logical fallacy, aside from the limits, implicit in reading film music—indeed, any instance of dramatic scoring, whether composed or embedded in a scene, as is the case here—in terms of similarity or reflection. The qualities we assume the music possesses, and that allegedly enable the process of reflection or the commentary to occur in the first place, are in fact emergent, and the impression that the music possesses them prior to its use in the film is a retrospective illusion. It takes no specialist knowledge to be aware that by the time we see the first image of the protagonists in Carnegie Hall, the music has long been under way. The transfer of certain qualities proceeding from certain aspects of the dramatic situation to the music, and vice versa, occurs independently of prior musical knowledge. But there is no doubt that awareness of certain musico-critical tropes creates a further element of interest in the scene, enabling one to hear its harmonic instability and thematic restlessness, for instance, as a sign of incipient disaster. The history of music criticism and theory is replete with programmatic interpretations of sonata form. To those familiar with this tradition, the synchronization between the visible distress of the male leads and the retransition in the symphony movement is the playful counterpart, the hilariously "ersatz" version—indeed, the debased reversal—of the ponderous allegorizations of the recapitulation as the sonic image of the resolution to a crisis.[24] As if stressing the unwillingness to nail the significance of music in the episode down to one unequivocal role, a straight cut takes us to a construction site in midtown Manhattan. The deafening noise of the new setting, rather like an acoustical blank slate, magnifies the change in locale and propels the story to what appears to be a new stage altogether (in fact, Isaac's strange mix of insecurity and self-aggrandizing sense of himself will soon be much in evidence there, too).

Mozart's symphony is too distinctive and striking a presence to be, as per the logic of similarity Cook rightly dismisses, merely reinforcing or, worse, duplicating what the spectator reconstitutes in his or her mind as "the action." This is not merely because the transfer of qualities mentioned earlier is predicated on "difference," however.[25] Notwithstanding its clever posing as a "mock" film

---

[23] Nicholas Cook, *Analysing Musical Multimedia* (Oxford: Clarendon Press, 1998).

[24] On this history, see Carolyn Abbate's comments on A. B. Marx in *Unsung Voices*, and Scott Burnham, *Beethoven Hero* (Princeton, NJ: Princeton University Press, 1995).

[25] Nicholas Cook, *Analysing Musical Multimedia*, 59.

score, the music is *integral* to the action, not a track running parallel to it. Its aesthetically most pertinent facet, as obvious as this may sound, is that it is both the unwitting occasion for a loosely choreographed pantomime and a performance the characters fail spectacularly to attend to. It would be that even in a silent film, or a novel, where its existence as sonorous medium would be out of the question.[26] Far from being paradoxical, the conceptualization of music as potentially soundless unveils its essentially dramaturgical nature, its raison d'être nested in its status as an event in the character's life (as posited by the imaginative perception of the spectator or, as in the case of a novel, reader). It hardly needs stressing that thinking of a film sequence in terms of literature or dramaturgy need not bind us to view film in terms solely borrowed from narrative theory or theater studies. There is, in fact, a distinctly cinematic manner of handling the situation at hand in this sequence from *Manhattan*, one that is channeled by the tools specific, so to speak, of the trade. The metonymic suggestion of duration through the use of a straight cut to a performance that is already halfway through would not be out of place in opera (nor in other forms of music theater). As to the conceit of leaving the source of the music outside the frame, this could be easily replicated on a theater stage or, for that matter, a painting. The satire of high art at work here, in fact, brings to mind that master of middle-brow cleverness, Norman Rockwell, as well as numerous precedents in the history of nineteenth-century illustration. But while fully capable of rendering any one expression of discomfort on the protagonists' part, no still image or theatrical representation could capture the pantomime in sustained form as Allen's long, unedited shot does, and down to the minutest—yet vitally crucial—detail of the actors' bodily movements. Despite its appearance as "canned theater," the sequence is in fact an exquisite demonstration that, as Malcolm Turvey has put it, "it is, for the most part, truths about human beings and their environments that are invisible in the sense of being concealed or overlooked that the cinema as an art, as opposed to cinema as technology, reveals."[27] The expedient, almost furtive manner in which the camera steals a glimpse of what lies hidden in the darkness of a concert hall, at a time when all eyes and ears are supposed to be focused on the onstage activities, could not be a better demonstration of Turvey's statement.

The derisory setup, complete with the revelation of something that would otherwise remain hidden, has precedents in both American and European

---

[26] On "silent" diegetic music, see Jeff Smith, "Bridging the Gap: Reconsidering the Boundary Between Diegetic and Non-Diegetic Music," *Music and the Moving Image* 2, no. 1 (2009), 1–25. and William H. Rosar, "Film Studies in Musicology," *The Journal of Film Music* 2, nos. 2–4 (Winter 2009), 113.

[27] Malcolm Turvey, *Doubting Vision: Film and the Revelationist Tradition* (New York: Oxford University Press, 2008), 130.

cinema. I am thinking of the Marx Brothers' send-up of operatic protocol in *A Night at the Opera* (1935), which Allen, a self-professed Marx Brothers fan, must have surely known by heart. Closer to the particulars of the example from *Manhattan* is the central conceit of Preston Sturges's *Unfaithfully Yours* (1944), in which a conductor—of all people—is all but distracted from the very music he is performing by dark revenge fantasies in retribution for his wife's alleged infidelity. We are privy to the turmoil in his mind as his dark ruminations unfold before our eyes in the form of extended subjective sequences. These are signaled by a peculiar conceit, referred to as "trick shot" in the screenplay: the camera, crawling across the orchestra toward the conductor's podium, inches closer and closer to his face all the way into his left eye. Following this metaphorical movement into his mind, we are taken to a locale where the visualization of his paranoid fantasies is presented in a plain, realistic style. All the while, the music he is conducting—the overtures to Rossini's *Semiramide*, Wagner's *Tannhaüser*, and Tchaikowksy's *Francesca da Rimini*, respectively—keeps on running in the soundtrack. The music reminds us of the initial frame of reference and acts as the accidental, and not infrequently reluctant, soundtrack to the improbable proceedings. The performance of Berlioz's *Symphonie Fantastique* in François Truffaut's *Antoine et Colette* (1964) comes to mind too. This celebrated episode is the subject of a self-quotation by Truffaut himself in *Love on the Run* (1968)— his summation of the Antoine Doinel series—and features both a cut in action from one movement of the music to another and a to-and-fro play of glances and feigned indifference between Antoine and Colette across several seats of the fully packed hall. If we think of Berlioz's work as an instance of what Goethe referred to as "invisible theater," then Truffaut's sequence will appear to be an irreverent realization of the drama implicit in the work's program (the unrequited love of the opiated artist).[28]

In the Allen, Truffaut, and Sturges examples, there is a suggestion of potential sync points between music and the actors' movements; in all of them, moreover, the music imparts its own rhythm to the onscreen action. In the case of *Antoine et Colette*, it plays off the rhythm of the editing as well. This need not require complex deliberations on the part of the filmmaker. John Cage was famously proud of the fact that the music he provided for Merce Cunningham's dances was written in blissful ignorance of the specifics of his partner's choreography.[29]

---

[28] On hearing symphonies, especially Haydn's, in terms of characters and situations, see Johnson, *Listening in Paris*, 206–12.

[29] On the Cage-Cunningham collaboration, see Carolyn Brown, *Chance and Circumstance: Twenty Years with Cage and Cunningham* (Evanston: Northwestern University Press, 2009) and Marjorie Perloff, *Lana Turner: A Journal of Poetry and Opinion* 3, accessed October 3, 2013, http://www.la-naturnerjournal.com/archives/constructed-anarchy. For Jean Cocteau's similar ideas on what he

He practiced what we may call "synchronization zero-degree," the minimum and only requirement for which is the simultaneity of a given action and stream of sounds, and their being coterminous. This is naturally in keeping with Cage's aesthetics and the radical expansion of the vocabulary of accepted forms of co-ordination between music and dance that this aesthetics entailed. Most of all, it perfectly captures the erasure of the difference between life and art that is at the heart of Cage's project. The burden of synchronizing is shouldered by the audience. Purely a matter of perception, synchronization ceases to be a technical operation decided upon during the creative process. As such, it is fuzzy, unpredictable, and dependent on the attentiveness and subjective circumstances of the spectator.

Underpinning the aesthetics of synchronization is not just the historical nature of perception but also a deep-seated impulse to read simultaneous events causally or at least as bearing some relation to one another.[30] Yet memory and knowledge of the accidental nature of the pairing between music and action also act as inhibitors. Familiarity with the conventions of film both encourage and discourage one from projecting sync points where none have, or so we are led to believe, been planned. If so, mutual implication gives way to the mere simultaneity of two ongoing events, each unfolding in respectful indifference to the other, and bringing into sharp relief the disconnect between the main action and the music. The result is an expanded scene, expanded not just in the sense of extending beyond what we see on the screen—the putative orchestra, lying off screen—but also in the metaphorical one of a single setting in which unrelated events take place simultaneously.[31] This also serves the film director well, for the point of employing a public performance as a background to a private drama taking place among the audience is precisely to leave the relationship of the former to the latter open (their sole connection residing in sharing the same locale). In *Manhattan*, the generous length of the shot allows for the spectator to hear sync points as he or she may see fit. But, let it be stressed, this is a case of synchronization not between music and the moving image but rather, as in ballet, between music and the actor-dancer. Less a tyrant than a benign prompter, Mozart's music opens up noncoercively a space for exploration of rhythmic correspondences between this bodily gesture and that motion

called the "mystery of accidental synchronization," see Frank W. D. Ries, *The Dance Theatre of Jean Cocteau* (Ann Arbor, MI: UMI Research Press, 1986), 112.

[30] Giorgio Biancorosso, "Sound," in *The Routledge Companion to Film and Philosophy*, ed. Paisley Livingston and Carl Plantinga (New York and London: Routledge, 2008), 266–67.

[31] Robert Altman was a master at capturing, by means of sound, the "cacophony" of the social world. On the soundtracks of Altman's films, see Sherwood Magee, *Robert Altman's Soundtracks: Film, Music and Sound from M*A*S*H to a Prairie Home Companion* (Oxford: Oxford University Press, 2014).

in the music, and somatic ones between a given display of emotion on the characters' part and the concurrent affect in the off-screen music. Whatever the shape this accidentally choreographed action may take, it is clear that the true show is taking place not on stage but among the audience. It is the camera that peremptorily states so, either by giving us glimpses of the performance, and thus intensifying our curiosity for the fate of Antoine's infatuation, as in *Antoine et Colette*, or denying us the view of the orchestra altogether, as in *Manhattan*. The role of the concert hall as a paragon of civic architecture, social etiquette, and channel for the aesthetic attention is thus not merely diminished but comically subverted.

When it languishes unattended because of an irresistible impulse that threatens its summoning power, even the most familiar piece of music undergoes surprising transformations. This reminds us that the interest and sensitivity of the perceiving subject are a vital component of the exchange between musicians and their audiences along the conduit of the aesthetic attention. The deliberately extreme examples of the failure of the aesthetic attention I have just surveyed bring into special relief an important corollary to this. Dedicated venues do not so much determine the pursuit of an ideal of focused, attentive listening—as a long tradition of theory and criticism of spectatorship would lead one to believe—as they *represent* such an ideal through the combined languages of architecture and interior design. Take the hall that more than any other, perhaps, epitomizes the modern obsession with the control of the spectator's attention. The *Festpielhaus* in Bayreuth is less than is usually adduced in that it could not literally remake the spectator's experience, as contemporaneous accounts, and contemporary theorists, have sometimes claimed.[32] The very features of the *Festspielhaus* that have drawn the most attention are the multiple proscenium arches, the "mystical gulf," and the contrast in lighting between stage and the rest of the theater, all of which creates a definitive sense of "dissociation between stage and audience."[33] These are effective devices, to be sure, but their existence also betrays a certain defensiveness about the ability to captivate the audience. Far from producing an ironic juxtaposition, the attempts at managing the attention implicit in the architecture of the *Festspielhaus* and Nordau's harsh dismissal of Wagner's work as "the form in which incapacity for attention shows itself in music"[34] not only

---

[32] Jonathan Crary, for instance, seems to take statements about the coercive nature of Wagnerian spectacle by Nietzsche and Adorno, among others, at face value. This results in a deterministic view of the relationship between technology, architecture, and the aesthetic experience: Crary, *Suspensions of Perception, Attention, Spectacle, and Modern Culture* (Cambridge, MA: MIT Press, 1999), 251–52.

[33] Ibid., 254.

[34] Ibid., 250.

belong to the same cultural climate but are different manners of responding to the same kind of anxiety.

Precisely because actual control lies beyond its reach, the *Festspielhaus* is also much more than a coercive machine. To borrow Hegel's phrase, it is a striking objectivization of a facet of human behavior, namely, the capacity for sustained, focused attention. As such, it is a "social agent," in Alfred Gell's sense of the word: an affordance and instrument of self-discovery as much as a reflection of a mental capacity.[35] By the same token, its "phantasmagoric" qualities, which Adorno interpreted as a denial and even mystification of the process of production, are more than a means to summon the attention to certain—and to Adorno, regressive— aspects of the operas.[36] To assume that the concealment of the orchestra automatically induces a trance-like neglect of its existence, to give one example, is not only to paint a caricature of the listener but also to miss the *representational* impetus that guides the creation of the mystic gulf in the first place. The *Festspielhaus* is a self-reflexive statement in that through its own design it celebrates, above and beyond its functional features, the very mode of listening it was built to facilitate. To be sure, good acoustics and design are enablers, but the sustained, engaged effort that underpins the aesthetic attention is an emergent phenomenon. Insofar as they encourage a certain type of behavior, the features of a concert hall do so rather indirectly, like illocutionary acts in languages and thanks to the considerable persuasive—and cohesive—power of social rules (the tacit acceptance of which implies a modicum of willing participation).

The physical makeup of the *Festspielhaus* and the new mode of spectatorship it inspired fulfilled the didactic mission of creating a new audience as much as if not more than the operas themselves.[37] The re-enactment of the Greek ideal of spectatorship, which Wagner derived second-hand via the German nineteenth-century reception of Aristotle and Greek tragedy, found expression less in his fantastical, allegorical epics than in the ritualistic re-creation of a new audience that took place in the theater itself.[38] As with Allen's gag in *Manhattan*, sacrilegious as the analogy may seem, the action in Bayreuth therefore also took place off stage, the willing practitioners of a new type of ritual playing the principals in a varied, international cast. "In Bayreuth, even

---

[35] See Alfred Gell, *Art and Agency: An Anthropological Theory* (Oxford: Clarendon Press, 1998), 17–21.

[36] Theodor W. Adorno, *In Search of Wagner* (London: Verso, 2005).

[37] On Wagner's ideas on the theater, see Dieter Borchmeyer, *Richard Wagner: Theory and Theatre*, trans. Stewart Spencer (Oxford: Clarendon Press, 1991), especially part 1. On the legacy of Bayreuth, see Juliet Koss, *Modernism after Wagner* (Minneapolis and London: University of Minnesota Press, 2010).

[38] For a study of the influence of Greek tragedy on Wagner's choice of themes and their subsequent musical elaboration, see Jason Geary, *The Politics of Appropriation: German Romantic Music and the Ancient Greek Legacy* (Oxford: Oxford University Press, 2014).

the spectator is a spectacle worth seeing," Nietzsche wryly observed.[39] That history and politics made of that audience the antithesis of the benevolent folk community Wagner had either delusionally envisioned or, as is more likely, disingenuously preached about is of course an important part of the history of Bayreuth.[40] But one should resist the facile equation of absorptive experience and fascist or authoritarian tendencies, for aside from being an abuse of common sense, that conflation denies what is specific to that history, and thus completely misdiagnoses it.

Outside the Black Box

With this in mind, it is revealing to contrast the failure to listen in a concert hall to the ability to carve out a space for contemplation in the most testing circumstances or improbable locales. Cinema has long exploited the (melo)dramatic potential inherent in this trope, bending it toward the effort to cast a character under a particular, and usually favorable, light. The arresting power of music is as much a sonic figure of the listener's desperate need for redemption or, to reassert his nobility of spirit, as a statement on the qualities of what is being heard. The aesthetic pull of the music, put another way, feeds a fantasy about personal affirmation. Appropriately enough, examples abound in the war and prison genres. The almost comically curtailed performance of a Chopin ballade in Roman Polanski's *The Pianist* (2002) is a case in point. The German general's obvious appreciation for the fugitive Szpilman's artistic talent and the resulting decision to spare his life express a goodness of spirit that, in the context of a year-long escape under the most oppressive and barbaric circumstances imaginable, takes on quasi-cosmic proportions. Its most memorable image remains, significantly, that of attentive listening. Mozart's *Le Nozze di Figaro* is similarly symptomatic of the resilience of moral character in a trying environment—a high-security prison—in Frank Darabont's *The Shawshank Redemption* (1994). Despite the somewhat contrived manner in which Mozart is made to voice a display of moral grandstanding on the hero's part and the expedient manner in which the film uses the music to raise its own cultural cachet, the homage has earned it a small cottage industry of learned and penetrating musicological

[39] Friedrich W. Nietzsche, "Richard Wagner in Bayreuth," in *Untimely Meditations* (Cambridge: Cambridge University Press, 1997), 198.

[40] A short but penetrating "biography" of Bayreuth is Millington, "'Bayreuth Idealism: The Catastrophe,'" in *Wagner* (Master Musicians) (Oxford and New York: Oxford University Press, 1999), 114–15. On the role of the theater as an instrument of both inclusion and exclusion and the attendant idea of spectatorship as "recognition," see Marc A. Weiner, *Richard Wagner and the Anti-Semitic Imagination* (Lincoln: University of Nebraska Press, 1995).

commentaries.[41] Most pertinent to my discussion is the broadcast of the Act I duet "Sull'aria" through the public address system of the prison where the protagonist, Andy (Tim Robbins), has been unjustly incarcerated. The infraction costs him solitary confinement but awakens his aspirations in front of an audience of stunned inmates who, gradually attuned to the strange music, listen attentively with knowing approval of his act of defiance and tacit understanding of what it entails.

Tales of classical music heard or played in the midst of Nazi persecutions or set against stories of justice gone awry rekindle in the musically literate filmgoer memories of actual events involving flesh-and-blood musicians. One such example is Olivier Messiaen's well-known *Quartet for the End of Time*, composed in a prisoner-of-war camp. Unwittingly, Steven Spielberg's *Schindler's List* (1993) features what is simultaneously a striking reversal and a dark parody of this episode of Messiaen's life. I refer to a sudden, almost fugitive appearance of the Allemande from Bach's English Suite no. 2, played impromptu by a German soldier who stumbles upon a piano during the final rounding up of the Jewish ghetto in Krakow.[42] As he miraculously carves out a time and place for a performance, he finds unlikely listeners in two fellow soldiers—and, given the circumstances, murderers—who end up arguing over what he is playing. The recognition must bring with it memories of an education in music, and thus of a life before the war. But while it provides the perpetrators an unhoped-for occasion to regain a sense of their residual humanness, the musical digression is for the spectator a moral trap of sorts, for the exercise of the aesthetic attention at this juncture would be nothing less than the indication of a callousness of truly Hitchcockian magnitude.

If such musical interventions ring didactic or, worse, suspect, this is not because of signing up the classical repertoire to the cause of the box office but rather because they themselves come across as high-handed attempts to revive its fading power. It is a risk that the final scene of Stanley Kubrick's *Paths of Glory* (1958) eschews on account not only of a stronger dramatic premise but also the employment of a folk song, "Der treue Husar" (a well-known "soldier tune" but one devoid

---

[41] Mary Hunter, "Opera in Film—Sentiment and Wit, Feeling and Knowing: The Shawshank Redemption and Prizzi's Honor," in *Between Opera and Cinema*, ed. Jeongwon Joe and Rose Theresa (New York: Routledge, 2002), 93–119; Pierpaolo Polzonetti, *Italian Opera in the Age of the American Revolution* (Cambridge: Cambridge University Press, 2011), 315; and Daniel Chua, "Listening to the Self: *The Shawshank Redemption* and the Technology of Music," *Nineteenth Century Music* 34, no. 3 (2011): 341–55.

[42] On this episode, and the relationship of *The Pianist* to *Schindler's List*, see Lawrence Kramer, "Melodic Trains: Music in Polanski's *The Pianist*," in *Beyond the Soundtrack*, edited by D. Goldmark, L. Kramer and R. Leppert (Berkeley: University of California Press, 2007), 67–68.

of the baggage of the classical repertoire).[43] Forced to perform before a brutalized audience of hostile and potentially threatening soldiers, a terrified young German woman finds the notes as she goes along, managing in the process to woo their attention first, and eventually also their sympathy. Because the music does not bear the marks of an acknowledged masterpiece, she overcomes the impasse through the sheer persuasiveness of singing as an ennobling form of behavior. The end of the episode brings home the point by having the entire cast of soldiers join the unwitting soloist in unison. Their heightened attention gives way to active participation as a consequence of not merely their emotional involvement but also the unspoken urge to erase thoughts of the imminent return to the battlefield.

Scripted versus Impromptu

Despite its focus on the performing arts and the significance of music in the history of the forms it surveys, Hou Hsiao-hsien's *The Puppetmaster* (1993) features only one genuinely musical episode. The stand-alone scene consists, characteristically, of one long, unedited shot of Li's newly formed theater group rehearsing a set piece from a Taiwanese opera in a room (Figure 1.6). The players are both actors and spectators of their own music making, and their performance is a blend of what W. H. Auden, in his essay on music in Shakespeare, calls "called-for song" and "impromptu song."[44] The latter is music occasioned by the genuine desire to express oneself in song rather than words, and without the trappings of professional standards, while the former is a paid performance by a professional. Introduced by a fade-in and brought to a close as the tune comes to its end by an avowedly symmetrical fade to black, the performance may seem like a discrete, self-sufficient tableaux of little import. It does, however, gain considerable momentum—hence, naturally, its inclusion—if one ponders its links to the episodes about Li's coming of age that both precede and follow it, the casual yet heartfelt demeanor of the characters and their tested partnership as they play and listen intently to themselves.[45] Their music making falls at the point in which Li has become fully conscious of his true vocation and foster family: the theater. In stressing the very becoming of the music all the way from their initially

---

[43] For a reading of this moment as symptomatic of Max Ophüls's influence on Kubrick's cinema, see Kate McQuiston, *We'll Meet Again: Musical Design in the Films of Stanley Kubrick*, 182–84.

[44] "Music in Shakespeare," in W. H. Auden, *The Dyer's Hand* (London: Faber, 2013), 511.

[45] Though these young men of the theater are proficient musicians, their unscripted singing exudes some of the power extolled by Claudia Gorbman in her "Artless Singing," *Music, Sound, and the Moving Image* 5, no. 2 (2011): 157–71.

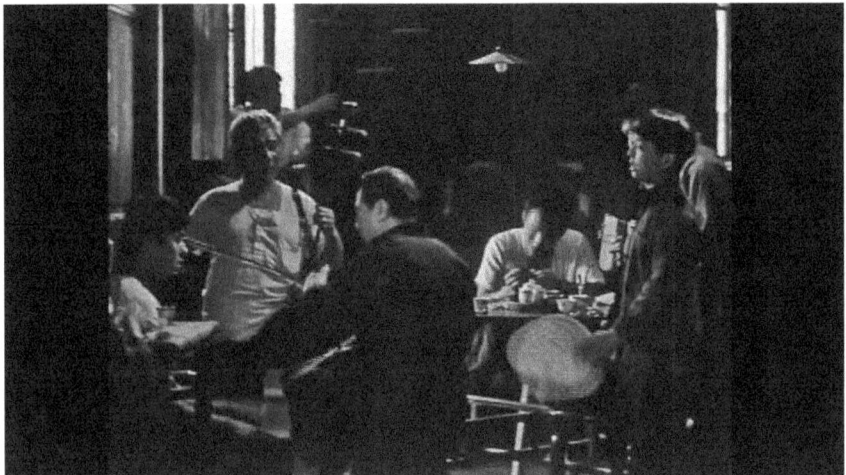

Figure 1.6 The Puppetmaster.

tentative through the more and more confident rendering, the rehearsal sanctions the forging of this new close-knit group of fellow artists.

A seemingly unscripted yet revelatory event, the performance does not merely bank on the intrinsic value of the music and its lyrics but earns its significance by playing a role in a particular chain of dramatic situations. In his essay, Auden provided something like a blueprint for an aesthetics of dramatic music along the lines exemplified in this episode from *The Puppetmaster*. Auden first summarizes the ancient theory, traceable to Pythagoras and still exerting its influence in Shakespeare's time, according to which "music is unique among the arts for it is the only art practiced in Heaven and by the unfallen creatures."[46] This theory, and its insistence on the proportions that regulate musical intervals, is of little relevance today, Auden says, except as a key to certain passages in Shakespeare that would otherwise remain obscure—notably Lorenzo's answer to Jessica in *The Merchant of Venice*. He offers one particularly memorable account—there exist many—of why such music cannot be heard. "What Campanella calls the *molino vivo* of the self drowns out the celestial sounds. In certain exceptional states of ecstasy, however, certain individuals have heard it."[47] Auden concedes that "when we now speak of music as an art, we mean that the elements of tone and rhythm are used to create a structure of sounds which are to be listened for their own sake."[48] Thus, conceived—and *experienced*—music is a "virtual image of our experience of living as temporal."[49]

[46] Auden, "Music in Shakespeare," 501.

[47] Ibid., 501.

[48] Ibid., 504.

[49] Ibid.

What is most striking about this admittedly captivating formulation, however, is how little purchase it has on our understanding of music in the Shakespeare dramas themselves (and drama more generally). There opens up, in other words, a rift between music as art and dramatic, or functional, music. Auden swiftly describes the essential difference thus:

> If one takes, say, a sea-shanty out of its context and listens to it on a gramophone the way one might listen to a lied by Schubert, one is very soon bored. The beauty of sound which it may have been felt to possess when accompanied by the sensation of muscular movement and visual images of the sea and sky cannot survive without them.[50]

In a nutshell, and again in deceptively plain language, Auden redefines what is normally referred to as the "extramusical" in terms not of meaning, but of situatedness.[51] It is the umbilical chord that ties music (a sea shanty) to a situation greater than itself, and the dynamic, "symbiotic" relationship between the two, that accounts for the value we perceive in it.[52] Note that despite his putative subject (Shakespeare's dramas), Auden refers here not to dramatic music, but to a functional song in what we might call a real-life situation. The inconsistency is a blessing in disguise, however, pointing as it does to a structural homology between the process by which music assumes value in a drama and the same process in real life. This value is not illusory, to the contrary; but it begs to be recognized and described in terms that must necessarily differ from those we use to elucidate the beauty and power of art music (or, as the misnomer often goes, "music in itself").[53] This Auden does, succinctly but very suggestively, in the second part of his essay. His most fundamental intuition carries echoes of the philosophy of language of his contemporary, J. L. Austin. The intuition is that music is a social fact, something done by people with and for other people: "Composing, performing, listening to music are things which human beings do under certain circumstances just as they fight or make love."[54]

---

[50] Ibid., 505.

[51] This point is also adumbrated in Irene Kahn Atkins's pioneering, yet by and large ignored, *Source Music in Motion Pictures* (Rutherford, NJ: Farleigh Dickinson University Press, 1983).

[52] The relation of symbiosis is not necessarily one of harmony. As literary scholar, and executor of the estate of W. H. Auden, Edward Mendelsohn writes, the essay points to the "failure of harmony in art to harmonize anything in real life (Prospero's incomplete forgiveness, etc.). Auden put his essay on music at the end of *The Dyer's Hand*, I think, in order to end the book with a gesture toward the superiority of silence over words": Edward Mendelsohn, personal communication.

[53] On "everyday music" (*lebensgebundene Musik*) as a challenge to traditional musical aesthetics, see also Heinrich Besseler, *Das musikalische Hören der Neuzeit* (Berlin: Academie, 1959), chap. 1, and "Grundfragen des musikalischen Hörens," *Jahrbuch des Musikbiblothek Peters für 1925* 32 (1926): 45.

[54] Auden, "Music in Shakespeare," 502.

From this seemingly banal observation, he develops a concise but forceful argument centered on the significance of music as a symptom of character, state of affairs, social hierarchy, or stage in the development of the action. He also sketches a gallery of the kinds of behavior often associated with music: the discharge of professional duty, self-expression, desire to conform, pursuit of pleasant distraction, or daydreaming.

The Shakespearian impromptu song, unmotivated by external circumstances and brought into being by a character's need to express him- or herself in song, takes pride of place in Auden's summary as the paradigm of music as behavior (as opposed to music as art, the domain of the professional, encapsulated in the contrastive term "called-for song"). In a tantalizing passage, Auden more or less declares the superiority of the spoken drama over opera in conveying the special nature of this particular form of musical self-expression: "No producer ... would seek to engage Madame Callas for the part of Ophelia, because the beauty of her voice would distract the audience's attention from the real dramatic point which is that Ophelia's songs are to the highest degree not called-for."[55] Two considerations immediately follow from this statement. Substitute for a moment Ophelia with, say, Verdi's Desdemona or Gluck's Orpheus. The century-old question about the dramatic justification of set pieces is approached afresh as one about how the beauty of a melodic line or artfulness of its delivery stands in the way of the appreciation of the drama. On this reading, singing is a thick, opaque glass that encases a character inside walls of beautiful sounds.[56] Second, Auden's insistence that the point of Ophelia's songs is that they are not called for is not a *post facto* argument but a recipe for the special type of appreciation he is invoking—a critical insight, put simply. Implicit in his position, however, is too stark a contrast between art and functional or dramatic music on the one hand, and called for and impromptu on the other. While one may agree with Auden that a sea shanty loses some of its sheen, and indeed its raison d'être, without the contextual factors that enshrine its presence and enrich its impact, this should not be held against it. A sea shanty should not be judged for not accomplishing something it does not set out to. For its part, a piece of art music, despite its intrinsic interest and presumed ability to hold the attention on its own, does benefit from being cast in a particular configuration of circumstances at a particular time. This indicates a far more blurry boundary between the terms in question and, in particular, the extent to which agency is shared between the artwork, the listener,

[55] Ibid., 522.

[56] Peter Kivy, "Speech, Song, and the Transparency of Medium: A Note on Operatic Metaphysics," in *Musical Worlds: New Directions in the Philosophy of Music*, ed. Philip Alperson (University Park: Pennsylvania State University Press, 1998), 63–68.

and a social situation in determining the impact of a musical performance, no matter how self-sufficient it may seem.

The dramatic situations examined in this chapter feature either the professional, "called for" delivery of a work derailed by entirely unpredictable circumstances of reception or an "impromptu" performance that stood to benefit from them. Like Hou's *The Puppetmaster*, Satyajit Ray's *The Music Room* (1958) combines elements of both scenarios. The film consists of long sequences showing characters doing nothing but listening undisturbed to scripted, paid-for performances by recognized virtuosos of Indian classical music and dance genres (Figure 1.7). Unusually for an Indian film, the music is not employed as interlude or background to a spectacular sequence. Instead, it is the avowed focus of long, realistically staged scenes during which the act of listening is as conspicuous an element of the mise-en-scène as the virtuosos' gestures themselves. The setting is the large but now decrepit home of Roy, an impoverished member of the Bengal landed gentry who cannot give up his expensive lifestyle nor, in particular, his taste for music. The costly indulgence brings him personal and financial ruin, paving the way for the two defining events of the story: the emergence of a moneyed commoner who challenges his primacy as a host of musical feasts, and finally the death of his only son and thus the extinction of the family line—and with it the silencing of the music.

The many musical sequences that form the spine of the film not only are valuable in and of themselves as a record of music making (the penchant for documentary that Ray shared with Rohmer, and perhaps acquired watching Renoir

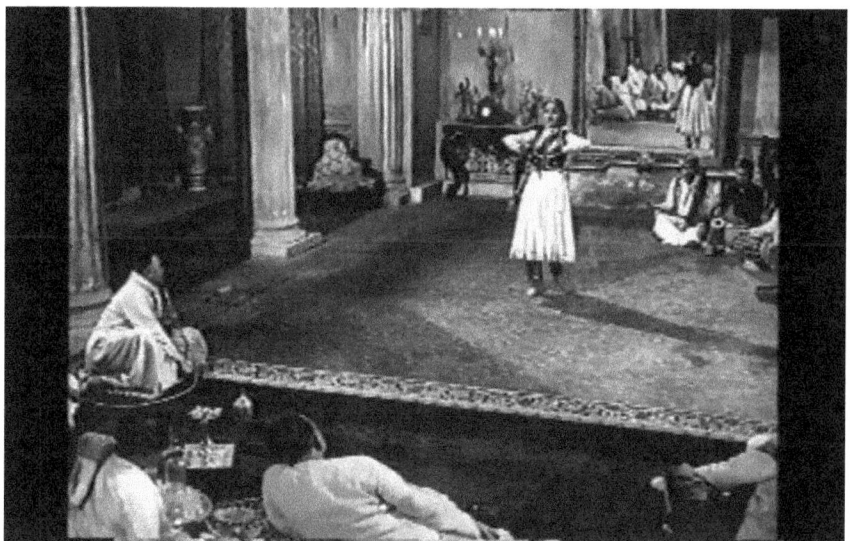

Figure 1.7 The Music Room.

and Rossellini's films) but also acquire an additional value through their complex relationship to the poignant circumstances that function as their premise. These must not be understood as "extramusical," nor do they make the music "subordinate" to the narrative for, to cite Andy Hamilton on gesture, "attending to sounds as part of the human and material world is a *genuinely musical* part of musical experience."[57] To fully bring out the human dimension of music, we need a more robustly expanded notion of listening than even Hamilton allows, however, one that encompasses longer time spans, multiple agencies, and rich, complex situations. Music does not stop at the doorstep of the "human" in the form of gesture but fully embraces it across a whole life cycle, which it both punctuates and reflects, as the stories of a Li or Roy so eloquently show.

[57] Andy Hamilton, "The Sound of Music," in *Sounds and Perception,* ed. Matthew Nudds and Casey O'Callaghan (Oxford: Oxford University Press, 2009), 151.

2

The Listener in the Picture

Staging inattentiveness to music not only requires a scene multifaceted enough to afford multiple points of interest, out of which the character picks one, but also presents another difficulty, one that makes inattentiveness potentially even more invisible than its foil. Consider the Monty Python "Cheese Shop Sketch" again. The spectator is confronted with an increasingly funny, utterly absurd exchange between customer and shop owner. Full-on engagement is by definition selective. It is only too natural that we filter out the bouzouki and focus our attention on the dialogue instead. Such parsing of the soundtrack is reinforced—indeed, guided—by the steady focus of the camera on the two comedians, as well as their demeanor. After all, the two characters are involved in an increasingly fraught exchange, and as such betray no interest in the music per se. Their inattentiveness to it soon seems so intuitive as to pass entirely unobserved, and so will ours—hence the brilliance of having John Cleese unexpectedly turn toward the dancers. Caught by surprise, we learn he was in fact aware of—indeed, annoyed by—them. We entered the picture, thereby obscuring it, in something like the way we obscure a floor mosaic by stepping on it.[1]

Whether the cheese-mad customer is conscious of the music all along is an unanswerable question both in the sense that other minds are inscrutable and in that as a fictional character he is a cipher, a projective screen for the spectator to fill in. Yet if we suspend our disbelief, the picture suggests a psychological trajectory that is not only plausible but also somewhat nuanced. Upon first entering the shop, he explicitly acknowledges the presence of the musician and

---

[1] In discussing the difference between looking at the ceiling and looking at a floor, Rudolf Arnheim observes that "the floor . . . is the base of much human action, so that, when used for visual decoration, [it] has to serve two conflicting functions. Our feet get in the way of our eyes. . . . There is a disturbing contradiction between the verticality of the viewer and that of the figures represented in the floor. In addition, the close physical relation *discourages detached contemplation*": Arnheim, *The Power of the Center: A Study of Composition in the Visual Arts* (Berkeley: University of California Press, 1982), 39 [emphasis mine].

dancers, if not without the slightest yet detectable indication of surprise or even bemusement. He appears to be in such a joyful mood as to be able to afford to boast, in characteristically pedantic terms, an appreciative ear for it ("I am one who delights in all manifestations of the Terpsichorean muse!"). Habituation then sets in and, we may assume, the music gradually recedes to the fringes of his consciousness as an odd but reassuringly consistent feature of the environment. What, if anything, causes his attention—and, following his outburst, our own— to eventually turn to the bouzouki, then? The verbal exchange between the cus- tomer and the shop owner is playful, surreal, and, for us, hilarious, but finally it takes a toll. He is a hungry man after all. As irritation at the lack of edible options paves the way for a fully confrontational mood, the presence of the ensemble appeals to his attention once again and causes him to react violently. The music now appears to him under a different, and much darker, aspect. As a symptom of the sheer strangeness of the titular cheese shop, the continuing performance spells out in mockingly abrasive tones his inability to master the strange situa- tion he's found himself in. He thus feels mocked twice over. Having registered the destabilizing presence of the musician and dancers from the start, he now re- alizes that he should have known better: there had to be something wrong about a cheese shop with a bouzouki ensemble in it![2] It is his drastically altered state of mind, in other words, that allows the music to seep back into the spotlight. No longer capable of shaping the environment through the force of his selective attention, his last resort is to stipulate, verbally, that the music cease altogether. Angry, he orders the musicians to stop. In this newly silenced space, he then shoots the man at the counter. With that shocking *denouement*, the sketch comes to an end.

"Can You Stop the Music First?"

Displaying annoyance at a musical performance or a broadcast is a common enough occurrence in movies. It is a well-known fact that music can have a deeply negative impact, especially when it is poorly performed or appears at the wrong time. On reflection, however, the trope is also a handy gimmick that read- ily provides a rationale for introducing it at key junctures of the plot. The char- acter's irritation is little more than the expedient disavowal of responsibility for its (calculated) appearance. The first episode ("Montmartre") of the omnibus

---

[2] Of course, to treat the music this way is to assume that it sounds "strange" or, worse, unattract- ive: a move that given today's sensibilities would raise more than a few eyebrows. The Greek financial crisis that began in 2010 and gives no sign of abating, moreover, has coincidentally given the sketch a dark subtext.

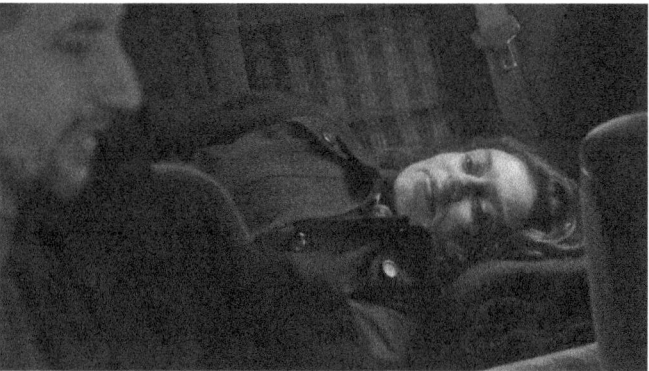

Figure 2.1 Paris je t'aime.

film *Paris je t'aime* (2006) features an especially subtle version of this situation, turning it into more than the mere setup for a non sequitur at the spectator's expense. Musing on his bad luck with women, an otherwise unnamed "car driver" has his unlikely break when a young woman faints on the sidewalk just outside his parked vehicle. Despite the awkwardly unfortunate circumstance, he rises to the occasion, relishing his long-awaited opportunity to display his wit, readiness to help others, and problem-solving skills—all the more so when the beneficiary happens to be an attractive woman roughly his age. After he promptly resuscitates and shelters her in his car, she awakens. The two strike up a conversation (Figure 2.1). The chemistry between them is soon apparent. Meanwhile, a theme treading ambiguously the major/minor divide, and combining the texture of Bach's *Goldberg Variations* with the angular contour and deadpan tempo of Mancini's "Pink Panther" theme, keeps on playing on the radio of the car. Chiming in discreetly like conventional underscoring, the music teases out the emotional nuances of the rapprochement under way, while it simultaneously insulates sonically the two protagonists (we barely hear the noise of the traffic outside). As such, it is a fully integrated element of a construct that encompasses music, sound, and moving images.

What name should one give to this construct? Michel Chion calls the cinema "a place of images and sounds" and refers to our experience of it as "audio-vision."[3] This is of course accurate insofar as its constitutive elements are concerned and applies to a wide range of forms and genres (including the documentary film). In addressing a specific instance of this ensemble of sounds and images in the context of a narrative film, I here prefer to talk of a *situation*. I use the term "situation" in the dramaturgical sense of "incident" and the

[3] Michel Chion, *Audio-Vision: Sound on Screen* (New York: Columbia University Press, 1994).

existential one of "predicament."[4] In a film like *Paris je t'aime*, the attention of the absorbed spectator will be guided by a hierarchy that reflects a dramatic sensibility, a clear sense, in other words, of what constitutes the main incident. Here, as in most dialogue scenes, such a spectator is focally aware of the dialogue between the two would-be lovers. Focal attention to the dialogue does not entail the parallel processing—or, worse, outright neglect—of the other elements of the mise-en-scène; to the contrary, it subsumes the subsidiary awareness of everything one sees and hears, be it the close-up of the lead character, a salient facial expression, the specific quality of the sunlight caressing the car's windshield, or the music filling in the interstices in the soundtrack. All this is brought to bear on the main incident as it unfolds and evolves in the course of the sequence. Driven by interest and the effort after some kind of narrative progression, we group certain aspects of the scene under a common umbrella. The irrepressible tendency to weave things together and adopt a perspective in which all elements of a scene stand in some kind of relation to one another, whether synchronically or diachronically, is a defining aspect of what it means to be an engaged spectator. The interdependence of focal and subsidiary attention bespeaks a holistic view of a scene that the character who is part of it cannot simply afford.

In summarizing Jerome Stolnitz's ideas on aesthetic distance, James Shelley writes that

> bearing an aesthetic attitude toward an object is a matter of attending to it disinterestedly and sympathetically, where to attend to it disinterestedly is to attend to it with no purpose beyond that of attending to it, and to attend to it sympathetically is to "accept it on its own terms," allowing it, and not one's own preconceptions, to guide one's attention of it. The result of such attention is a comparatively richer experience of the object, i.e., an experience taking in comparatively many of the object's features. Whereas a practical attitude limits and fragments the object of our experience, allowing us to "see only those of its features which are

---

[4] Jean P. Sartre, "For a Theater of Situations," in *Modern Theories of Drama: A Selection of Writings on Drama and Theatre 1850-1990* (Oxford: Oxford University Press, 1998), 42–44. On Jean Epstein's notion of "situation" as a "narrative event in which past and future become visible in the present," see Turvey, *Doubting Vision: Film and the Revelationist Tradition* (New York: Oxford University Press, 2008), 51. Victor Burgin refers to "situation" in yet another sense, namely, the perception of aesthetic objects from the phenomenological perspective of the minimalist artist. In elaborating a "situational aesthetics," he goes further than is my intention here in positing that "the specific nature of any object is largely contingent upon the details of the situation": Burgin, "Situational Aesthetics," *Studio International* 178 (October): 119, reprinted in, among others, *Art in Theory 1900-1990: An Anthology of Changing Ideas*, ed. Charles Harrison and Paul J. Wood (Oxford and Cambridge, MA: Blackwell Publishing, 2002).

relevant to our purposes," the aesthetic attitude, by contrast, "isolates" the object and focuses upon it.[5]

When we experience a reversal, the hierarchy and organizational principles that underpin the economy of the attention described by Stolnitz receive a subtle yet decisive jolt, however. In *Paris, je t'aime* (2006), for instance, at the driver's insistence that they tour the city together in his car, the young woman quips, "Yes, but could you please stop the music first?" Her question shows the music to be itself an incident and momentarily gives it a prominence it would not otherwise have by turning it into the subject of the conversation, if only in passing (once again, note that it only comes to prominence when a character decrees it must stop). The main action and a minor, supporting element of the setting enter into a momentary collision course. The reversal also tells us that to carry on with the conversation, the young woman was, much to her chagrin, trying to separate out the sound of the music from that of his words. The music and the conversation were from her perspective discrete, unrelated, and indeed mutually exclusive streams of the auditory scene. The difference between the spectator's integrating tendencies, as opposed to her sustained attempt at segregation, captures in psychologically vivid terms the different situations of character and spectator, respectively. The former, despite being putatively fictional, appears to inhabit a world much more bound by the laws of physical reality than we are. Faced with mutually exclusive choices, all of them in one way or another irreversible and with real and instantaneous consequences, she must make a choice. If she does not, the music will become a distraction, a deterrent to action even—a far cry from what for us is an integrated, if subsidiary, element of the scene.

Should we respond with surprise to her quip—which is scripted in the expectation that we will—we would have to acknowledge that we have made inaccurate assumptions about where her attention falls. The difficulty of staging inattention points to a fundamental instability that belies our own sense of mastery over the material, planting a seed of skepticism that one can learn to assuage but not altogether erase. Our own sense of distance will be dented, if not shattered. The self-forgetting darkness of the cinema gives way to what Michael Fried calls, with reference to seventeenth-century self-portraiture, "specularity."[6]

---

[5] James Shelley, "The Concept of the Aesthetic," in *The Stanford Encyclopedia of Philosophy*, ed. Edward N. Zalta, Fall 2013, http://plato.stanford.edu/archives/fall2013/entries/aesthetic-concept/ . In addition to reviewing twentieth-century analytical aesthetics, Shelley also offers a critical survey of the concept of "distance" in the philosophy of Kant and Schopenhauer.

[6] Michael Fried, *The Moment of Caravaggio* (Princeton: Princeton University Press, 2010), 39. Note that Fried is primarily interested in the representation of the relationship between "immersion" and "specularity" (not the specularity experienced by the spectators as they realize the work

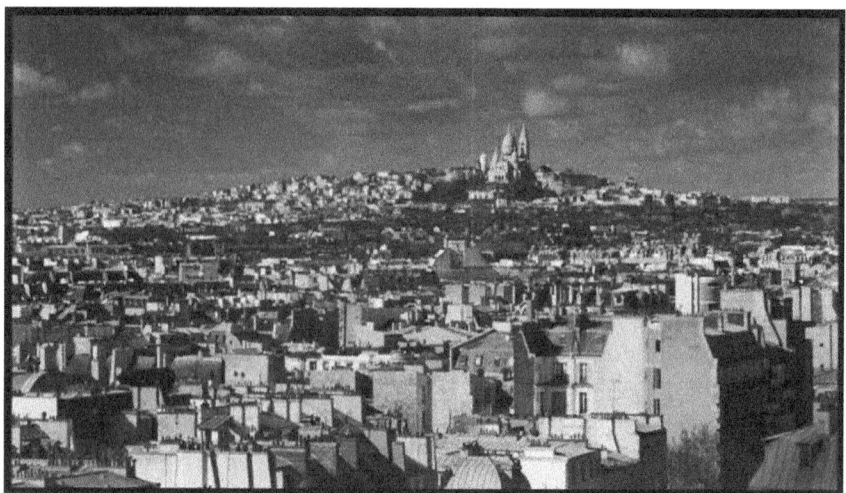

Figure 2.2 Paris je t'aime.

The film implicitly addresses us and we thus find ourselves to be "in" it or find that the film now exists in a space-time continuous with our own. At this crucial point, two moments overlap: "the first is a 'moment of extended duration,'" in which we are immersed in the action, while the "second is a 'moment,' notionally instantaneous of separating or indeed recoiling" from it.[7] We are no longer able to afford the ideal state of Schopenhaurean "will-less contemplation" we often strive to attain, even when considering events that, however grave or horrifying, are nevertheless fictional, and thus do not directly touch on our condition as flesh-and-blood spectators. Reversals are one way in which the protected, danger-free zone of spectatorship comes to resemble the more treacherous sphere of the everyday.[8]

In a mischievous defiance of the young woman's request, the music returns as "on the air" sound to underscore the two long, exterior shots that end the episode. First, there is a view of the building near where the story had begun, this time bathed in the shine of the late afternoon sun, and then a glorious long shot of the Quartier Montmartre (Figure 2.2). What happens when music goes "on the air"? Should we assume it is again playing on the driver's car stereo or the radio as the two of them drive to her tobaccologist, a journey during which, one assumes, their romance will be consummated? And, if so, are we hearing

addresses them). In particular, he refers to a genre of self-portraits in which the painter depicts him- or herself in the act of painting in front of a mirror.

[7] Ibid.

[8] Giorgio Biancorosso, "The Harpist in the Closet: Film Music as Epistemological Joke," *Music and the Moving Image* 2, no. 3 (2009): 11–33.

the radio with the characters inside the car while looking at the city from the outside?[9] The uncoupling of point of audition and point of view, if any, reveals the convergence of multiple perspectives across time and space. The music is a radio signal; its audibility marks the reach of the transmitter. It places the spectator in a position that simultaneously captures the story world as heard from the characters' point in space (inside the car) and seen from another location (outside). Whether the music is actually playing inside the car, in other words, whether we are "eavesdropping" on the characters, is in the end a moot question. Having been caught (no matter how fortuitously) in the current of their nascent romance, the theme has also become "their" music, ready to be activated anytime (like a recurrent motif, or a leitmotiv of a traditional film score). Similarly, the long shots of the city are not the representation of another perspective— that of an objective narrator, say—as much as a glorified version of the characters' own: the concrete projection of what they themselves experience as, in the wake of their nascent romance, they momentarily transcend the feeling of being bound to one place and feel the embrace of the neighborhood, and indeed the Paris of the title, as a whole.

The Feeble Sounds of a Record Player

Readers familiar with Hitchcock's *Vertigo* (1958) will recall the impatience, scorn, and even spite with which Scottie responds to a recording of the Sinfonia in E-flat, op. 9, no. 2 by Johann Christian Bach, playing softly in Midge's room:

MIDGE: "Have you had any dizzy spell lately?"
SCOTTIE: "I am having one now . . . from that music!"

Scottie's sarcastic remark comes near the end of a remarkably long dialogue scene and strikes Midge—and the spectator—by surprise, indicating, once

---

[9] In *Shoot the Piano Player* (1960), Truffaut playfully emphasizes the dissociation between point of view and point of audition by alternating between close shots of the protagonists inside their vehicle with long shots from outside the car, all the while letting their laughter continue at the same sound level. Later, in the same film, a more radical dissociation occurs. A young musician enters the room of a well-known, and notoriously abusive, agent for an audition. Unseen, from behind his door, we begin to hear her perform a solo. As the music continues, there is a cut not merely to a different place but also to a later point in time (we see her leave the building). The shift is jolting. No longer marking the passing of time, nor a uniquely situated event, the music becomes the architrave of a highly elliptical sequence compressing several lengthy events into a handful of relatively short shots.

again, that inattention cannot be taken for granted.[10] Engaged in a conversation on the pros and cons of quitting work following Scottie's near-death experience while chasing a criminal, Midge and Scottie are on close terms and unafraid of speaking their minds. We are made to understand that Midge loves Scottie but he does not seem to reciprocate. A few years before, in fact, he broke off an attempt at a relationship. Delivered to us by a small but unconcealed record player, the music helps establish a soundscape in striking, deliberate contrast to that of the preceding—and famous—chase sequence that opens the film (production notes have emerged in which Hitchcock states just that). Bach's Sinfonia does in fact add a fine touch of local color, but because the memory of Herrmann's ebullient music just heard over the vertigo shot still lingers, it also sounds lifeless, petty, and unglamorous. As such, it is quickly associated to Midge's milieu, which it subtly and unobtrusively helps to construct.[11] The juxtaposition between Herrmann's score and J. C. Bach's music is usually interpreted in symbolic terms as one between disorder and order.[12] But just as significant, it charges the difference between source music and Herrmann's score with a purely acoustical measure, exploiting the gap in absolute level of volume and resonance as experienced in the space of the movie theater (or the hi-fi environment of home viewing).[13]

Little does one know at this juncture of Vertigo that Scottie's irritation at J. C. Bach's music foreshadows his utter inability to respond to the sound of Mozart later on in the film. This occurs in another famous scene set in a sanatorium where, after Madeleine's alleged suicide, he is being cured from a devastating bout of depression (or, as it is euphemistically called in the film, melancholia). The music is the second movement, Andante in F major, from Mozart's Symphony no. 34. This time Scottie's inattentiveness is tragically apparent, reminding one of the pictures of sleeping or otherwise catatonically absent subjects that exemplify extreme examples of what Fried calls the representation of absorption.

---

[10] For a similar episode from Betrand Blier's Buffet froid (1980) having to do with birds singing, see Michel Chion, Film: A Sound Art (New York: Columbia University Press, 2009), 312.

[11] On the character of Midge and screenwriter's Samuel Taylor's role in creating it, see Charles Barr, Vertigo (London: BFI Publishing, 2002), 28–30.

[12] Royal S. Brown, "Hermann, Hitchcock, and the Music of the Irrational," Cinema Journal 21, no. 2 (1982): 14–49; David P. Schroeder, Hitchcock's Ear: Music and the Director's Art (New York: Continuum, 2012).

[13] The juxtaposition resonates in much more recent films as well. In Jonathan Demme's The Silence of the Lambs (1991), for instance, the aria from Bach's Goldberg Variations follows the nondiegetic cue that accompanies Lecter's savage murder of the prison warden. Carlo Cenciarelli describes it thus: "Against the carnage, the renewed piano seems smaller and flatter, its contrapuntal duet unfolding on the head of a pin, miniaturized by the vanishing blasts of orchestral sound": Cenciarelli, "Dr Lecter's Taste for 'Goldberg', or: The Horror of Bach in the Hannibal Franchise," Journal of the Royal Musical Association 137, no. 1 (2012): 121.

The two episodes of *Vertigo* are linked through not only the presence of Midge but also a striking stylistic similarity: in both cases the music is played on a gramophone whose sole mark of distinction is how poorly it projects sound. In both scenes, moreover, the music moves at a moderate tempo and begins in the middle-to-high register of the strings. This is markedly in contrast to the growls in the low register with which the preceding cue, playing in the "nightmare" sequence, ends. The closing low, long-held D in the lower woodwinds, strings, tuba, timpani, and Hammond organ is prolonged even further as it metamorphoses into the sound of a ship's fog horn coming from the bay (which is shown in a long shot just before the fade to black). Two similarly crafted transitions create a rhyming effect. The two musical episodes shed light upon one another. The Mozart gives the J. C. Bach a premonitory role one cannot divine upon first hearing it. The J. C. Bach, in turn, prepares the spectator to recognize a recurrence, as if stressing the significance of the choice of Mozart, whose music at this point in the film stands for a whole world making its last, ridiculously inadequate attempt to engage Scottie's attention. The world has receded to the role of an inane, barely audible symphony movement tied to a therapeutic mission doomed to fail from the start. What is remarkable is that such a rich coterie of connotations is not suggested in the abstract but given tangible, sensuous form as the perceptually striking contrast between Hermann's score and a preexisting, classical piece used as a prop within a highly distinctive setting. Within the short span of a transition between two sequences, the film recreates a situation similar to one we sometimes experience when different kinds of music, playing in different places at different volumes, compete for our attention, giving us a glimpse of what it is like for classical music to navigate a world that's already filled with other music, and a full range of sounds.

Auditory Scene Analysis

The "Cheese Shop Sketch" flaunts the bizarreness of the music as an element of the setting, only to eventually chastise us for not reading it as a symptom of things going awry. *Paris je t'aime* and *Vertigo* are in a sense more virtuosic in that they feature music that threads the boundary between the plausible and the implausible; the reproach to the gullible spectator is all the more pointed for being more subtle. My next example combines elements of both. It is taken from the disturbing yet compelling *Sauve qui peut* (*La vie*) (*Every Man for Himself*, aka *Slow Motion*, directed by J.-L. Godard, 1979, heretofore referred to as *Slow Motion*). Near the beginning of the film, a comically resolved ambiguity underpins another example of feigned inattention or, which comes to the same thing, the concealed awareness of a music found to be annoying (Figure 2.3). Paul

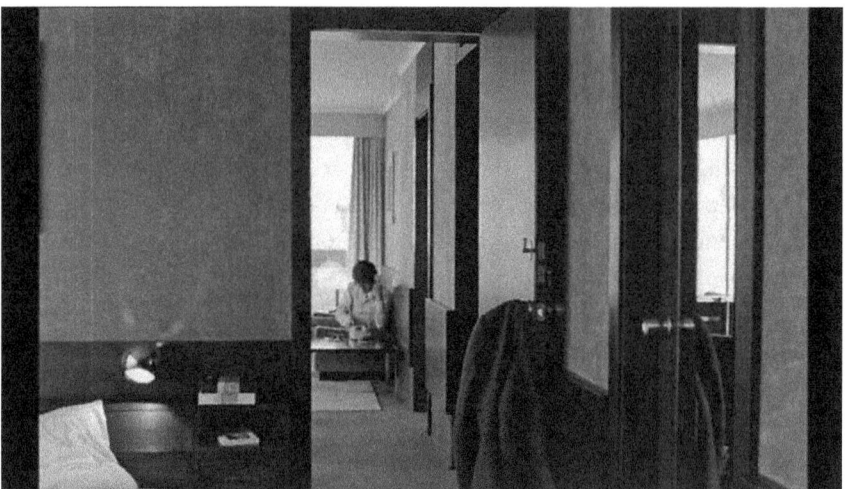

Figure 2.3 Slow Motion.

Godard, a video director who is an avatar of sorts for Godard himself, is readying himself for a day of work in the room of an expensive hotel. As he starts speaking on the phone while sitting on a sofa lying against the wall, we hear a loud, piercing voice intoning an operatic aria ("Suicidio!" from Ponchielli's *La Gioconda*, sung without the orchestral part). The intrusive sound is undoubtedly that of a capacious, professionally trained soprano voice. Judging from his demeanor, Paul seems all but oblivious of it. Yet the music does turn out to be the premise for a classic example of neighborly strife as we suddenly see him get up and bang the wall, asking for it to stop. Since the accompaniment is absent and the aria stops immediately, it is unlikely to be a recording but rather a flesh-and-blood singer. We learn that someone was rehearsing in the adjoining room. The distinctly professional quality of the voice adds a certain allure and prestige to the venue, confirming the impression of being in an expensive hotel frequented by globe-trotting performers. Just like the cheese shop customer in the Monty Python sketch, Paul was deeply annoyed and, unbeknownst to us, busy trying to ignore the music (so as to be able to carry on his phone conversation).

The episode is remarkably studied in its attempt to guide the attention of the spectator. Godard's manifold attention-controlling strategy, including the careful acoustical crafting of the voice, is aimed at setting us up for a reversal to begin with. How often do we chance upon a professional opera singer rehearsing next door? And what is an opera soprano to do with a familial drama set in a rich but provincial Swiss town? The very bigness of the voice, combined with the likelihood of living next door to an operatic soprano, makes the outcome utterly unexpected above and beyond Paul's own inscrutable demeanor (a demeanor that initially veers the spectator's attention away from the music despite its marked presence).[14] His sudden, almost hysterical reaction underlines the egregiousness of the trap. The mise-en-scène draws our attention toward him as he is the most comfortable focal point of the image and the subject of the only apparent piece of action (the phone conversation). All the while, the music has been not only sourceless but also arbitrarily placed. Nor are we given any evidence of its status as an event simultaneous and coterminous—the singer is next door—with what we see on screen. The acting only reinforces that assumption: it is almost as if the music did not exist for Paul at all (rather like a score or an instance of displaced diegetic sound). What we cannot suspect is that his is a clear example of hard-won inattentiveness or, put differently, distraction kept at bay—the equivalent, for the film spectator, of trying and mentally silencing a distracting noise that might otherwise detract from the appreciation of the film.

The instant Paul bursts out in anger, then, marks a liminal moment. In forcing his all-too-human need to segregate stimuli, that is, to keep the sound of the voice apart from that of his interlocutor on the phone, the revelation lays bare not only his predicament as a fictional character but also our incommensurably different vantage point of spectators. Before the anchoring, the voice, far from being a distraction, is for us an integral, significant—indeed, bizarrely conspicuous—component of the scene, brimming with potential meaning. Whereas Paul, who is on the inside, has to try to keep separate to minimize interference, we, looking in from the outside and enjoying the privilege of aesthetic distance, bring together the elements. As is common with Godard, however, the ensemble of sounds and images barely coalesces into a coherent whole. So utterly unlike a standard score or a plausible bit of source music, the music struggles to gravitate toward the traditional "center" of a film scene: the character in action. Rather, it injects into the scene a characteristically centrifugal force threatening to short-circuit our own ability to center and integrate—as opposed to segregate—different constituent elements. "Sound in general," writes Kristin Thompson, "plays a tremendous role in rendering the film illegible—that is, difficult to grasp in the time allotted for perception."[15] It is only after falling silent, ironically, that the music finds its natural place in the scene (as off-screen sound, that is). Pointing to an off-screen space continuous with that shown on screen and dutifully recognized as an element of the setting, albeit one no longer heard, the voice strengthens what Noël Burch called the

---

[14] Commenting on a later moment of the sequence, when the singer is shown continuing to sing as she leaves the hotel, Albertine Fox writes that "since the hotel guest-singer is not remarked upon by other characters, it is not difficult to entirely overlook her act": Fox, "Constructing Voices in Jean-Luc Godard's *Sauve qui peut (la vie)* (1979)," *Studies in French Cinema* 14, no. 1 (2014): 24.

[15] Kristin Thompson, *Breaking the Glass Armor: Neoformalist Film Analysis* (Princeton, NJ: Princeton University Press, 1988).

"diegetic effect," namely, the impression of a coherent and complete, if fictional, universe existing apart from us (and which we, rather like voyeurs, look into from a safe vantage point).[16] This space is normally unassailable from the outside in that it exists on a different order of reality. And yet because of the conjuring trick planted in the scene, we are in a sense also drawn into it, Godard's joke implicating us directly in its construction.

I use the terms "integration" and "segregation" in the sense assigned to them by psychologist Albert Bregman in his seminal work, *Auditory Scene Analysis* (1990). As Bregman suggests, integration can apply to different components of the same sound, as when we subsume the various harmonics of a single pitch under one fundamental, or to different sounds, as in hearing simultaneous tones as a chord. Segregation, on the other hand, allows us to perceive different parameters of a single sound event—semantic meaning and tone color, for instance—or separate sound sequences that carry crucially different information (integrating which would result in inaccurate perception). The parallel sequencing of strings of interlinked sounds is called by Bregman "streaming." In borrowing these terms, I also use them metaphorically. It is the integration and streaming—or segregation—of visual *and* auditory information, rather than the grouping of sounds alone, that the unorthodox exordium of *Slow Motion* invites us to ponder. Faced with a scene in a film, integration occurs when we perceive visual and auditory information as converging toward something like a coherent and meaningful, if composite, gestalt. The synchronization between a string of spoken words and a talking head provides perhaps the most intuitive instance of how such integration may occur in the cinema, and how it serves the effective delivery of narrative content in a fiction film by centering, as it were, the attention.

Integration need not refer to agreement, let alone redundancy, between the audio and video channels; rather, it is a relationship or, to use Claudia Gorbman's term, a form of "mutual implication."[17] The latitude afforded by this process is considerable, as is its force, for, as Chion observes in a crucial passage,

> in the presence of [the] image the relations of meaning, contrast, agreement, or divergence that speech, sound effects, and musical elements have among themselves are much weaker (and sometimes nonexistent), compared to the relations that each audio element has with a given visual or narrative element in the image.[18]

---

[16] Noël Burch, *In and Out of Synch: The Awakening of a Cine-Dreamer* (Aldershot, England: Scolar Press, 1991).

[17] Claudia Gorbman, *Unheard Melodies: Narrative Film Music* (Bloomington: Indiana University Press, 1987), 15.

[18] Chion, *Film: a Sound Art*, 491.

Chion may be overstating the case here. Syntagmatic and other kinds of sequential relations between sounds within the same shot or across more shots do matter a great deal (think about voice-over narration or the use of long cues over a montage sequence). He even goes as far as to say, in a statement now notorious, that "there is no soundtrack."[19] While indefensible if taken literally, the claim has the merit of drawing attention to the significance, depth, and complexity of the relation that matters perhaps more than any other in the cinema. The rhetorical exaggeration also underscores, to my ears at least, the scarcity of work on the relationship between the senses in the theory of film, and in the psychology of perception more generally. No work of Bregman's breadth and rigor exists on the relationship between seeing and hearing.[20] Its scope and internal consistency notwithstanding, moreover, the field of auditory scene analysis offers a somewhat truncated view of the auditory experience. This is because auditory scene analysis divorces hearing from the other senses on the one hand, and the listening experience from a concrete, situated, ecologically meaningful perspective on the other. As a heuristic, this is naturally justifiable. Scientists work by reduction to formulate testable hypotheses, assess their worth, and deliver measurable results. Expanding the scope of "scene analysis" to include the situatedness of the perceiver involves more than the consideration of the other senses. It would have to address a "scene" rather like a "situation," that is, a dynamic situation defined by human motives and interests. To do so would be tantamount to cross the proverbial Rubicon not just methodologically but disciplinarily as well, thereby acknowledging that even a bare-bones description of the perception of a scene is already an interpretation.

In addressing a phenomenon left languishing at the periphery of so many disciplinary areas for so long, Chion has coined a number of neologisms, or given new meanings to old words. He calls the cinema, as we saw earlier, "a place of images and sounds." He then continues:

> Let us insist on the indefinite, open aspect of the actual sound portion of a film, in that it is not united into a homogenous entity that one could call a "soundtrack." Because of the variable fluctuations in magnetization of sound by the image, which depends on what the latter is showing or not, and because of the diegetic link between sound and image,

---

[19] Chion, *Audio-Vision*, 40.

[20] The only instance of interaction between hearing and seeing that has received significant experimental and theoretical attention is the so-called McGurk effect. The effect was first described in the now-classic paper by Harry McGurk and John MacDonald, "Hearing Lips and Seeing Voices," *Nature* 264 (1976): 746–48.

or the elemental link created by synchresis, sound is, when it comes to its localization, in a constantly unstable state with respect to the image. Either it is included, or it includes, or in a third possibility it "roams over the surface." One could say that sound in the cinema is "that which seeks its place." And this seeking process is played out for each sound in a specific way—only rarely do all the sounds heard at the same time participate in the same emplacement.[21]

Chion's words vividly convey the multiplicity of simultaneous and qualitatively different relations—he mentions at least three—between sound(s) and the moving image. Yet if spectators and their continuing engagement with narrative films are any indication, what is striking is the resilience, not the instability, of synchronization and the ever-expanding latitude of what constitutes the acceptable, indeed productive, "mutual implication" between sound and the moving image. Two other key terms coined by Chion will help us examine this question in more detail. One is *concomitance*, which he defines as a "situation of simultaneous perception of sounds and images, which may or may not intentionally give rise to effects." The second, *synchresis*, refers to the perception of ". . . the concomitance of a discrete sound event and a discrete visual event as a single phenomenon."[22] Godard's cinema is a good example of the pervasiveness of synchresis precisely because it tests its limits. In *Le Mépris* (*Contempt*, 1963), for example, he brings to the foreground the physically independent status of the soundtrack by stopping and restarting the music almost whimsically (I use the present tense on purpose, as the procedure imparts a great sense of presence to the director). Godard does this knowing full well that the spectators, despite being reminded of their technical separation, will nevertheless continue to reconstitute or "group" the two separate channels—music and image—as one meaningful, coherent form. The resulting to-and-fro effect enhances one's awareness of the tendency to synchronize, making it appear almost Pavlovian in character.[23] Time and again, Godard's films present us with an instance of mere concomitance, in Chion's sense, which we, as if by an irrepressible instinct, reconstitute as an intentionally designed, fully integrated entity (*synchresis*). Even the most avowedly self-sufficient, recalcitrant musical selection will enter in some kind of cooperation with the image.[24]

---

[21] Chion, *Film a Sound Art*, 485.

[22] Ibid., 473 and 492, respectively.

[23] For an extended discussion of the Pavlovian nature of synchronization, see Kevin J. Donnelly, *Occult Aesthetics: Synchronization in Sound Film* (New York: Oxford University Press, 2015).

[24] Gorbman, *Unheard Melodies*, 15.

Hearing the Music While Thinking of Something Else

For all its innovativeness and poetic flair, Chion's work is still wedded to an analytical discourse predicated on medium specificity. Rather than thinking in terms of heterogeneous elements or separate and, in the case of *La Gioconda*, already constituted media—a piece of richly connoted music, say, pasted onto a loosely defined "image"—let me return to the beginning of *Slow Motion* as a dramatic situation defined by human agents and their motives. By "situation," I mean a holistically perceived ensemble that calls for an approach sensitive to its fictional, character-centered nature. On this heuristic, which I assume most spectators share as they sit through a film, no one element is aesthetically separate, let alone prior, except in the technical or genetic sense of the term (the soundtrack being naturally produced or, in a case of a preexisting track, edited at a later stage than, say, principal photography). Rather, the elements combine into a richly textured, richly connoted situation, which is given shape and relief by a hierarchy between focal and subsidiary.[25] This hierarchy cuts across the different individual components of the scene and is independent of their absolute physical values (size, decibels, or light intensity). The object of the focal attention, in other words, can be a combination of two or more components (a talking head, for instance, or a monster whose appearance is concurrently signaled by a moving image and the score). In *Slow Motion*, despite the intrusive sonic presence of the singing voice, the scene features another clear focal center around which a sense of witnessing a particular state of affairs emerges. This focus is Paul sitting on the sofa and talking on the phone, and it tilts the balance of the economy of the attention in the direction not so much of the "image" but the (nascent) action. The key to whether the music synchronizes with what we see and how lies in the possibility of mutual implication, but this, I argue, is itself contingent on the hierarchy between focal and subsidiary attention.

To demonstrate this relation, I would like to begin by drawing on Michael Wood's "Distraction Theory," a brilliantly "mischievous" application of Benjamin's old idea of "perception in distraction."[26] Benjamin's idea of perception in distraction is central to his famous essay, "The Work of Art in the Age of Mechanical Reproduction."[27] He coined the expression to describe what he saw as the state of continuous distraction the spectator was plunged into by the

[25] Michael Polanyi, *The Study of Man* (Chicago: University of Chicago Press, 1959), 30.
[26] Michael Wood, "Distraction Theory," *Michigan Quarterly Review* 48, no. 4 (2009): 577–88.
[27] See Walter Benjamin, *The Work of Art in the Age of Its Technological Reproducibility, and Other Writings on Media* (Cambridge, MA: Belknap Press of Harvard University Press, 2008), for

incessant cutting from one shot to the next (the rationale being that each change of shot provoked a change in the attention). Yet this cannot be the case if the subject of the attention, as I argue here, is something at once more immaterial and more encompassing than the images themselves: namely, a dramatic situation. At heart, Benjamin's interpretation is materialist not in the Marxian but rather in the formalist sense of the word. Of course, a change in shot, framing, or camera focus causes a change in what we look at. But, in narrative films at least, that is akin more to a redirection of the attention than to the engendering of a state of distraction.[28]

In adapting the idea, Wood retains little of its original meaning. He contends instead that an attitude akin to distraction or, at least, less than fully fledged absorption is of the essence to the recognition of genre or appreciation of broad stylistic features in literature (as well as film).

> There are moments, I want to suggest, when only something like the concept of distraction will catch the contours of our experience in all kinds of reading. . . . [W]e can't read genre of any kind, in film or in literature, without an element of distraction in our practice. . . . We could also think of style rather than genre, and distraction in this case might rescue a book that concentration could only condemn.[29]

Wood dubs his particular brand of theory "How to Read While Thinking of Something Else." Yet it remains unclear in Wood's reading what this "something else" might be—what, in other words, prevents one from becoming more than fully absorbed in the stylistic traps of "some kind of masterpiece that has more or less unreadable passages on every other page—or at least passages that are unreadable by concentrating readers" or "the audio-visual textures and intertextual references of an otherwise unproblematic genre film."[30] The ability to read past these potential hurdles, I would suggest, lies not in the exercise of distraction but is engendered by a certain *habitus* vis-à-vis the work itself. This is the distance that allows one to grasp the broad outlines of an action, character, or plotline without getting mired in myriad distracting facets. It is a form of mastery, or *sprezzatura*, that the knowing spectator can only earn by

---

a new translation of the second version, retitled for the occasion "The Work of Art in the Age of Its Technological Reproducibility."

[28] On the question of how to track the attention of the spectator, see also the beginning of the conclusion, later. A persuasive, and to my mind definitive, critique of Benjamin's application of the idea of perception in distraction to film can be found in Malcolm Turvey, *The Filming of Modern Life* (Cambridge, MA: MIT Press, 2011), 163–81.

[29] Wood, "Distraction Theory," 577 and 585.

[30] Wood, "Distraction Theory," 586.

"unlearning" the practice of what Wood calls "recuperative" readings—reading too much into or retrospectively projecting onto the experience dimensions it never had in the first place—and that the unknowing or naïve spectator, if such can be called, can quickly adopt by abiding by Rembrandt's old dictum, here paraphrased, to not "stand too close to the screen (or else its light will blind him)."[31]

When it comes to the music one hears in a film, assuming this disposition performs two roles simultaneously for the spectator. First, it makes it possible to keep on watching a film undisturbed despite, to paraphrase Wood, the "more or less atrocious passages of music" in the soundtrack (of which, protestations by film music aficionados notwithstanding, there are a lot in all manner of films). This is not to say that certain film scores, like incidental music, are not craftily written or cannot take on a life of their own as pop hits, souvenirs, or concert hall classics. Films have been vehicles for innovative, compelling work, and the greatest songwriters have seen some of their best work embedded in a film practically since the inception of the medium. But it does a disservice to film music to judge it by criteria developed around other, already established genres. No matter how original, infelicitous, or derivative as a stand-alone piece, in the context of a film the music must be judged by standards germane to a different economy of the attention.

Take a well-known example of representational film music. In the first shark attack in Spielberg's *Jaws* (1975), the richness or manifold aspects of the music—its materiality as sound, structural organization, performative dimension, and so forth—could well pass unnoticed. The viewer, his or her perception channeled through the images, might be too absorbed by the situation at hand to be able to dwell, say, on the quality of the performance. Perhaps the structural elements of Williams's score are not parsed by the viewer in the manner academic discourse often associates with music listening tout court, or what Nicholas Cook has termed "musicological" listening.[32] To hear the shark in the music is essentially a process of disambiguation underpinned by selective attention. This is not to say that alternative aspects of the music go unperceived; rather, our attention is fixed firmly on what the music represents (its "recognitional" aspect)—the "shark"—rather than on its formal (or "configurational") aspect—the motive qua motive. Short of embracing a rigid Hanslickian position, whereby only the formal elements of music count as music, insofar as the shark's attack is the object of the focal attention, the music can be said to partake of the scene's focal center. In the words of Michael Polanyi, we are "subsidiarily" aware of selected aspects of the

---

[31] "Don't stand too close to the canvas, or else the paint will poison you," cited in Ernst H. Gombrich, *Art and Illusion* (New York: Pantheon Books, 1960), 196.

[32] Nicholas Cook, *Music, Imagination and Culture* (Oxford: Oxford University Press, 1990), 152.

music while "focally" aware of its narrative import.[33] Polanyi compares this to the situation when we hear speech, in which we are subsidiarily aware of its phonetic, grammatical, and syntactical aspects while focally aware of its content.[34] That is why transcriptions from a film score should be taken as mementos—cues that can be used to call to mind particular moments in a film—rather than literal representations of the full experience. From this perspective, the phenomenology of musical representation turns on a central question: not whether perception occurs, nor whether it is of a "subconscious" or "subliminal" kind, but rather where focal attention falls. It goes without saying that music's structural aspects are fundamental to our grasp of the film's action, even if we attend to them subsidiarily. Altering a motive's basic shape, for instance, entails losing its designative function.[35] Alteration can also be a matter of performance or recording: if the music is recorded in a way that jars with its presumed location—say, in a tavern full of drunken men shouting—I will not be able to hear it as an element of the setting.

What is so instructive about Godard's practice is how close it gets to short-circuiting this economy, thereby pulling a brake on the seemingly unstoppable tendency to weld what we see and what we hear. In *Slow Motion*, the impertinent withdrawal of information about the soprano voice's whereabouts combined with the low odds of it figuring in a hotel room makes its presence as source music a remote possibility for even the most imaginative spectator. As scoring, it scarcely seems more plausible. This state of affairs may encourage us to think to have entered a momentary no man's land: a classic instance of "concomitance" (as distinct from synchresis). Yet I believe that "concomitance" remains no more than a theoretical possibility. The music is not "parked" in some corner of our processing brain in the expectation that more information will help us find a place for it (certainly not upon a second viewing of the film, at which point its trajectory will be known from the start). There is no time to contemplate alternative interpretations of the singer's voice while watching the film in one sitting, leisurely weighing the merits of different possible solutions

---

[33] Polanyi, *The Study of Man*, 30, and "Sense-Giving and Sense-Reading," in *Knowing and Being: Essays by Michael Polanyi*, ed. Marjorie Grene (Chicago: University of Chicago Press, 1969), 181–82.

[34] The work of psychologist Annabel Cohen also takes into account the limits of attention, in terms of both focus and span. For the latest iteration of her research model, see Cohen, "Congruence-Association Model of Music and Multimedia: Origin and Evolution," in *The Psychology of Music in Multimedia*, ed. Siu-Lan Tan, Annabel J. Cohen, and Roger A. Kendall (New York: Oxford University Press, 2013), 17–47.

[35] Justin London, "Leitmotifs and Musical Reference in the Classical Film Score," in *Music and Cinema*, ed. J. Buhler, C. Flynn, and D. Neumeyer (Hanover-London: University Press of New England), 88.

to a puzzle whose perspicuousness is far from certain. The music, rather, is the subject of the subsidiary attention. To paraphrase Wood, we "hear it while thinking of something else" (that is, attending to Paul speaking on the phone). This is not to say it has no impact. To the contrary, the unmistakable sound of opera lends the scene an air of slight absurdity, chaos, and sheer lack of control, partaking of an assault to the spectator's senses that is as destabilizing as it is compelling. As such, the information it affords is immediate and unequivocal (if possibly mistaken or in need of revision, as the final anchoring will reveal). The idea of "perception as hypothesis," which stretches back to Helmholtz, is a metaphor designed to convey the epistemological status of perception, not a description of the phenomenology of having one. Only rarely is one second-guessing one's own perceptions at the very moment one is having them. There is no threshold, no liminal space for us to inhabit, however briefly. The "gap," to cite a much-cited term introduced by Robynn Stilwell with reference to the diegetic/nondiegetic divide, can only be *reflected upon in retrospect* rather than experienced in the first instance.[36] To be sure, we experience the changes but do not conceptualize them in terms of formal categories. The alternatives of source/score, live/recording, and amateur/professional, to mention three, are presented to us *after* the anchoring. This is not simply because the music is at that point no longer sounding (remember that the singer stops when Paul starts banging on the wall, thus locating the source of the sound). It is also because it would be a mistake to project the process entailed by the revision, or discovery, back on to the experience just passed. It is "getting" the joke that brings to light a coterie of ambiguities we had not had a chance to contemplate. No longer a subsidiary element of the scene, at that moment the voice becomes, if fleetingly, the object of the focal attention.

Before the realization that it comes from the room next door, the voice need not be perceived as unanchored, let alone unanchorable to a source (whether literally or metaphorically). To lend it the status of the *acousmêtre*, as Albertine Fox does, is to lavish onto it an amount of attention it can hardly be said to command—unless one approached the film the way one looks leisurely at a sculpture or savors a poem in the intimacy of one's home.[37] This is of course not

[36] Robynn Stilwell, "The Fantastical Gap between the Diegetic and Nondiegetic," in *Beyond the Soundtrack: Representing Music in Cinema*, ed. Daniel Goldmark, Lawrence Kramer, and Richard Leppert (Berkeley: University of California Press, 2007), 184–202. For this reason, the notion of the "fantastical gap" remains at best a theoretical construct. For different responses to this particular aspect of Stilwell's argument, see also Smith, "Bridging the Gap? Reconsidering the Border between Diegetic and Nondiegetic Music." *Music and the Moving Image* 2, no. 1 (2009): 1–25; Biancorosso, "The Harpist in the Closet," and Tobias Pontara, "Bach at the Space Station: Hermeneutic Pliability and Multiplying Gaps in Andrei Tarkovski's *Solaris*," *Music, Sound, and the Moving Image* 8, no. 1 (2013): 1–23.

[37] Fox, "Constructing Voices in Jean-Luc Godard's *Sauve qui peut (la vie)* (1979)," 23.

only legitimate but also productive from the critical standpoint.[38] The question turns on what type of viewing experience one assumes as being normative or at any rate desirable. The conundrum Godard's *oeuvre* poses is that it exploits the format and circuit of mainstream cinema to distribute works that are also poetic in character.[39] Insofar as one approaches *Slow Motion* as a standard narrative film, Thompson's claim that the film runs the risk of being "unintelligible" is meaningful. Yet Paul's sudden fit of impatience toward the voice surprises us, causing the acknowledgment of a texture far too rich or at any rate beguiling for us to absorb in only one go. The reversal, put another way, weaves into the fabric of the film the suggestion of a second viewing, effectively upending the industry standard of one-off, dispensable experiences on which *Slow Motion* nevertheless depends.[40]

Synchronization and/as Intentionality

When the relationship between a sound and an image in the cinema is unclear or frustrates the desire for resolution, Chion suggests, there is at least an "elemental link" binding them together. It is this link that channels our perception of them as a meaning-making combination, making even the most intractable sound-image complex amenable to some kind of interpretation. Chion insists that the tendency to bring image and sound together is instinctive, and mentions in this respect inscrutable psychophysiological processes.[41] I would add at least one culturally induced reason to account for its power and pervasiveness. This is the habit to understand the copresence and combination of various elements of a representation as dictated by a rationale (such as assisting the construction of a setting or presenting story material). To assume the presence of such a rationale is to posit a relationship or set of relationships that, however tentative or subject to revision, allow us to engage productively with what lies before us. Different types of rationales will serve different expressive and representational goals. As played over images of the atomic bomb in Kubrick's *Dr. Strangelove*, for example, the song "We'll Meet Again" begins to make sense

---

[38] See, for instance, Fox's reading of Paul's subsequent chance encounter with the singer: "Constructing Voices in Jean-Luc Godard's *Sauve qui peut (la vie)* (1979)," 25.

[39] *Slow Motion*, it is worth noting, marked Godard's return to commercial cinema after several years of political filmmaking and video work outside the circuit.

[40] I address this question again in chapter 3.

[41] One example of the power of these forces is what he calls "spatial magnetization," namely, the illusion that a sound comes from a particular point in the scene despite the fact that the loudspeakers in the theater are not in a position consistent with such a reading of the sound. On the question of whether synchronization is innate or the result of cultural habits, see also Donnelly, *Occult Aesthetics*.

to me as soon as I consider it as a deliberately ironic juxtaposition. In the case of a scene featuring the same song as a radio broadcast in a downtown diner or a number in a variety show, the music will serve the needs of a different dramatic imperative. And so forth.

Judging the significance of the music in a film in terms of a plausible rationale that accounts for its presence betrays the belief that the latter is, at a minimum, intentionally constructed. Whether a film is understood as an expressive or communicative act, its sounds and images have been deliberately combined and deployed to achieve a certain effect. We cast an all-encompassing gaze onto this ensemble, adopting a holistic approach that does justice not only to all its components but also to their mutually binding relationships (even when none are intended). It is thanks to this binding effort on the part of the spectator that a scene, so to speak, "holds together." I am aware that intention is a charged topic in aesthetics. Intentionalism is mired in controversy and has been the subject of trenchant critiques. I should stress that the kind of intentionalism I am proposing here has little to do with "facts about the intentions that some artist or group of artists actually had,"[42] let alone any of these putative facts determining the meaning of a film or scene thereof. What I have in mind, rather, is that ascribing a rationale to the way in which sounds and images are combined is a *condition* for us to make the proper inferences and interpret the material in such a way as to complete the construction of the scene unfolding before us. We lend a willing eye and ear, and set our two senses to work together, so to speak, because we place trust in the fact that the exercise will be rewarded. Therein lies, in my opinion, the contract between filmmaker and spectator.

It is against this context that improvisatory or deconstructive practices acquire such significance. Of Godard's sound practices, for instance, one could say that the effects they produce are parasitic on his exploiting the institution of the mainstream cinema.[43] The good faith of the spectator can be counted on to match sound and image to best advantage, irrespective of how carelessly or arbitrarily they have been put together. Dada, Alea, and Minimalism take this scenario a step further. Key to John Cage's practice, for example, is not the renunciation of premeditated compositional logic per se, but rather his insistence that we, the audience, *be aware* of such a renunciation. This strikes me as exactly right, for it preempts the ascription of artistic intentions that he rightly saw as the defining element of the reigning paradigm of spectatorship in the performing arts (and, one presumes, the arts more generally). Such a situation is, however,

---

[42] George Wilson, "Interpretation," in *The Routledge Companion to Philosophy and Film*, ed. Paisley Livingston and Carl Plantinga (New York: Routledge, 2008), 167.

[43] On this aspect of Godard's early films, see also David Bordwell, *Narration in the Fiction Film* (Madison: University of Wisconsin Press, 1985), 311–338.

impossible to attain in practice. The use of "found objects" by Duchamp was, too, an attempt to give form to a practice defined by a complete, radical renunciation of artistic responsibility. But as Alfred Gell noted, "having 'no reason' to select something as an object of ready-made art is, of course, a reason, since it is motivated by the need to avoid selecting anything for whose selection some reason might be proposed."[44] Whether the paradox is the point or not, the net result of such strategies is equivocal. Cage endorsed all sounds as amenable to contemplation as "music," in a grand democracy unaffected by intentions, or the listener's discriminating interest. He subtracted the human element from music by collapsing the latter onto what preexists, or exists independently of, human consciousness. But such a vertiginously expanded musical field is a curious limit case that reinforces, rather than subverts, the cordoning off of the musical experience from the humanizing, enriching powers of perspective. In saying that every sound demands our attention, Cage did not so much take music out of the concert hall as re-envisioned the world as a virtual concert hall, a site for musical contemplation, to be activated by the aesthetic attention of the "attuned" listener. For such a compulsive contemplator, the whole world becomes a black box resounding with "purely musical" values.

The closest counterpart to Cage and Duchamp's examples in the realm of cinema are perhaps the minimalist films of Andy Warhol. Before 1968, Godard's films enjoyed some circulation at the edges of the commercial circuit and were a staple in the burgeoning "art house" one. Too radical to pass even as "art films," the natural home of Warhol's film work was the alternative, or underground, circuit and the joyfully anarchic setting of the happening.[45] Some of his films give the impression of almost complete withdrawal from authorial responsibility as concerns subject matter, staging, and elaboration of the material. The filmmaker was deemed responsible solely for the initial and often only camera setup, and eventually the speed of projection. Having decided on a setup, Warhol let the camera roll till the film stock at his disposal ended. Having mounted a new roll of film, he would repeat the exercise. The most egregious example of this practice is the single-setup, eight-hour film of the Empire State Building, shot from the roof of a Chelsea loft (*Empire*, 1964). As Branden W. Joseph aptly summarizes:

> Whether by reducing profilmic events to such an extent that the viewer's interest almost inevitably wanders—as in *Empire* and even *Blow Job*

---

[44] Alfred Gell, *Art and Agency: An Anthropological Theory* (Oxford: Clarendon Press, 1998), 30.

[45] On Warhol's film work, see Stephen Koch's classic *Stargazer: Andy Warhol's World and His Films* (New York: Praeger, 1973), and the more recent monographs by Douglas Crimp, *"Our Kind of Movie": The Films of Andy Warhol* (Cambridge, MA: MIT Press, 2012), and J. J. Murphy, *The Black Hole of the Camera: The Films of Andy Warhol* (Berkeley: University of California Press, 2012).

(1964)—or, inversely, by so multiplying the foci of visual attraction throughout the frame (and, eventually, across multiple screens)—as in *Haircut (No. 1)* (1963), *Couch* (1964), *Vinyl* (1965), and *The Chelsea Girls*—Warhol frees, or pushes, his audiences to investigate the visual field subjectively.[46]

In another telling recounting, Wayne Koestenbaum writes:

> Watching dozens of hours of these early Warhol films in which little or nothing happens, I couldn't take my eyes off the screen, lest I miss something important. I didn't dare look down at my pad, peer around, close my eyes, or leave the room. I could barely take notes, so entirely was I hypnotized by minute gradations of light and shadow, anger and lust.[47]

An inkling of Warhol's approach can be detected in earlier mainstream cinema, too. Think of the free-flowing mise-en-scène of an Antonioni, whose unwillingness to guide the spectator's attention at each and every turn is of a piece with the absence, to some irksome, of a dramatic imperative.[48] Like Warhol, Antonioni reveled in long close-ups of his stars, encouraging the viewer to explore a face as if it were a landscape. Warhol naturally goes further in redefining of the century-old contract between authors and their spectators. No longer engaged on a moment-to-moment basis and mesmerized or frustrated by the sheer duration of the films, spectators invariably report of finding themselves turning their attention self-reflexively inward. In so doing, they gain a renewed awareness of their own body and presence in the theater, or ponder the circumstances of exhibition themselves. Studies of the body in cinema have focused almost exclusively on pornography or extreme representations of violence.[49] Warhol's films suggest another way in which questions about the body of the spectator may be addressed. I would in fact argue that "the self-forgetting darkness of the

---

[46] Branden W. Joseph, "Factory Setting" [review of Douglas Crimp, "*Our Kind of Movie*" (Cambridge, MA: MIT Press, 2012)] and J. J. Murphy, *The Black Hole of the Camera* (Berkeley: University of California Press, 2012)], *Artforum* 51, no. 2 (2012): 59–60.

[47] Wayne Koestenbaum, *Andy Warhol* (New York: Viking, 2001).

[48] Welles, in a manner redolent of Fried's critique of minimalist artists, denounced Antonioni's practice as bogus, a renunciation of the duty of writing and directing coherent characters and a compelling storyline: Peter Bogdanovich, *This Is Orson Welles*, ed. Jonathan Rosenbaum (New York: HarperCollins, 1998), 104.

[49] See, for instance, Linda Williams, *Hard Core: Power, Pressure, and the "Frenzy of the Visible"* (Berkeley: University of California Press, 1999), or Theresa Anne Cronin, *Disciplining the Spectator: Subjectivity, the Body and Contemporary Spectatorship* (Doctoral thesis, Goldsmiths, University of London, 2011).

cinema," to use Fried's expression again, is an intensely *bodily* experience in and of itself, as is the accompanying condition of forced or at any rate socially conditioned stillness. Even though film theorists and critics may have treated them as such, the spectator's ears and eyes cannot not, in the end, be disincarnate.

> The perceiving subject is itself defined dialectically as being neither (pure) consciousness nor (physical, in itself) body. Conscious-ness . . . is not a pure self-presence; the subject is present to and knows itself only through the mediation of the body, which is to say that this presence is always mediated, i.e., is indirect and incomplete."[50]

"One consequence of the manner in which Warhol refused the standard interpellative procedures of mainstream Hollywood cinema," observes Joseph, "is his films' capacity to change quite dramatically depending on the circumstances of their showing and the viewer's attentiveness and subjective investments."[51] Nam June Paik's *Zen for Film*, also made in 1964, is even more radically minimal in its renunciation not merely of traditional film aesthetics but of the photographic process itself. There is no "film," only "celluloid." As Andrew V. Uroskie writes:

> One has the experience of simply being present in a particular space, watching light being projected through a moving celluloid strip. It is an experience diametrically opposed to that of the narrative film, wherein all sense of local space and present time are meant to be definitely negated by the spatiotemporal conditions of the cinematic narrative into which we have become absorbed.[52]

The film spectators thus become part of the work not in the sense of momentarily obscuring the picture but rather as the result of the work unfolding in a space coterminous and even congruent with that occupied by them. Their awareness of their own presence is of a piece with the artwork—the very turn to the "theatrical" that characterizes minimalist art, and that Fried decried as a denial of artistic responsibility.

---

[50] In Gary Brant Madison, "Did Merleau-Ponty Have a Theory of Perception," in *Merleau-Ponty and Postmodernism*, ed. Thomas Busch, cited in Vivian Sobchak, *Carnal Thoughts: Embodiment and Moving Image Culture* (Berkeley: University of California Press, 2004), 6. On the visual system as extending from the eyes to the body, and vice versa, finally, see James Jerome Gibson, *The Ecological Approach to Visual Perception* (London and Hillsdale, NJ: Lawrence Erlbaum, 1986), 218.

[51] Branden W. Joseph, "Factory Setting," *Artforum International* 51, no. 2 (2012): 59.

[52] Andrew V. Uroskie, *Expanded Cinema and Postwar Art* (Chicago: Chicago University Press, 2014), 19.

This is not the place to endorse or dispute Fried's rejection of minimalism. Rather than seeing the absorptive and the theatrical as polar opposites, I see a continuum running between them. Clearly, the artist cannot forsake the display of his or her responsibility entirely in setting up the conditions for the spectator's experience. Even the happening has one or more "masters of ceremony" whose role is to channel the energy and creative possibilities of the moment. On the other hand, highly structured works, such as a tightly constructed Hollywood film, do allow for a measure of freedom to explore their array of stimuli, not least in the context of repeated, ironic, or deliberately "deviant" readings (which recording, new technologies, and social media have made all the more common). As the examples examined in this chapter illustrate, reversals and puns have a way of addressing the spectator obliquely, that is, without giving the impression of openly acknowledging his or her presence. In keeping with their nature as jokes, one might say that they eat their cake (spectatorial address) while simultaneously keeping it (absorption). Having said this, I take Fried's point about the "fiction that the beholder does not exist" literally—namely, I believe it *is* a fiction. With Alfred Gell, I maintain that every work, like a trap, addresses a recipient, inscribing a scenario of his or her encounter. Setting aside the issue of theatricality, I interpret spectatorial address, no matter how oblique, as encoded knowledge about spectators' minds. If in the chapters that follow I espouse Fried's commitment to absorptive art driven by a single, clear dramatic imperative, then I do this on heuristic rather than aesthetic grounds—that is, as a window into the listening experience that has so far remained untapped in musicology and film studies alike.

3

The Radio Broadcast
as Anamorphic Spot

In this chapter I continue the exploration of situated listening in the cinema under a dual perspective: the fictive one of the character and that of the spectator. My focus is the equivocal use of radio broadcasts in three films that aim, each in its own way, to represent different faces of the inscrutability of in/attention. They are Jean Renoir's *The Rules of the Game* (*La Règle du jeu*, 1939), Michelangelo Antonioni's *The Eclipse* (*L'Eclisse*, 1962), and Akira Kurosawa's *High and Low* (*Tengoku to jigoku*, 1963). I say "equivocal" because while on the one hand the radio is buried deep into the setting and the characters ignore its presence, on the other its central role is reaffirmed in any number of ways: a striking choice of repertoire, a recurrence that begs for recognition or directorial sleight of hand. Whatever the method adopted, the way in which the radio is woven into the narrative entails a range of possible responses at the extremes of which stand, for the spectator, two starkly opposed scenarios: at one extreme one ignores the music altogether, the attention channeled by the demeanor of the characters themselves or drawn to what is patently more urgent business at hand; at the other, the music broadcast takes center stage not just as an element of the setting but as a deliberate intervention brimming with symbolic and even allegorical power.

"To understand movies figurally," writes Vivian Sobchak, "we first must make literal sense of them."[1] In heeding this dictum, I came to realize that subtending my discussion is a dichotomy between dramatic action and setting. If one attends to a detail of the latter, as in taking notice of a radio broadcast, the former recedes into something like the background and vice versa. The instances in which filmmakers employ preexisting music as symbolic presence or commentary in the guise of a casually presented element of the setting are too numerous

[1] Vivian Sobchak, *Carnal Thoughts: Embodiment and Moving Image Culture* (Berkeley: University of California Press, 2004), 59.

to even begin to rehearse here. In most cases the relationship between music and the on-screen action is either too obvious, in which case the music is divested of its temporal dimension and is used as a mere vessel of conceptual meanings, or it is simply too hidden, in which case the music floats unintelligibly beneath the surface of the narrative and the appreciation of its role becomes a mere intertextual game, a cerebral, ex post facto affair. What distinguishes the examples I examine here is that they betray an awareness on the filmmaker's part that a symbol planted in a realistically constructed setting may or may not be immediately available to the attention of the spectator. It is the very difficulty of accessing the meanings of that symbol that becomes a dynamic, signifying element (above and beyond the symbol itself). The dichotomy between action and setting, put another way, manifests itself as the simultaneous yet exclusive affordance of two perspectives on the same representation, and the significance of the radio broadcasts will be seen to reside precisely in that exclusivity. The conspicuousness of the music as construed in my analysis, therefore, will to some extent be seen as an artifact of exegesis—and that is precisely the point. The musical interventions I single out belie the widespread assumption that films are supposed to be one-time experiences; indeed, they bespeak a frankly auteurist approach to filmmaking at a time when music was not yet a vehicle for its expression—hence their paradigmatic role in the history of music in cinema.

My discussion will proceed in essence as an exercise in film appreciation. My method is, simply put, descriptive, and my focus will be one crucial scene of each film, examined in detail to bring out the almost extravagant richness of its visual and sonic textures and the director's control over them—richness of detail and control being of the essence of the three directors' art and also the main reason for privileging close reading over other kinds of analytical methods and expository styles. I will attempt to account for why a richly connoted sonic symbol has been planted at the heart of the film and, near the end of the chapter, offer some preliminary thoughts on how to go about interpreting buried symbols in film and other media and their significance for the theory of attention adumbrated in this book. The role of criticism as a way of drawing attention will, I hope, find here a fertile terrain, as does the idea of the spectator as informed, cultivated listener. The kind of musical connoisseurship I invoke here, however, is bound up with a dramaturgical sensibility, for it emerges from an appraisal of the conventions of film and the role music plays in it as much as the traditional givens of musical appreciation.

Music as Setting

The Rules of the Game begins with an open acknowledgment of the primacy of the radio in the (then) contemporary mediascape. Having just landed at Le

Bourget Airfield near Paris following an aviation feat, André Jurieux (Roland Toutain) uses the obligatory radio interview to express his grief at not seeing his beloved Christine (Nora Grégor) welcome him at the airport. A more egregious use of a public resource for a private purpose would be hard to imagine. The episode underscores how access to the media equals privilege and influence, a point rendered all the more tangible by the actual reach of radio signals into the most hidden recesses of the land.[2] When the radio appears again in the film in a later scene, the conditions of its functioning could not be any more different.[3] The characters are not in the position of determining its contents, let alone using it to their advantage, but figure at most as passive receptacles of a musical program that bears no relationship to them. I am referring to the elaborately choreographed sequence that introduces the cooks and servants working in the Chateau of the Marquis Robert de la Chesnaye (Marcel Delio). The setting is the kitchen downstairs, where the servants all share their meal around the same table. First we see the guardian Schumacher (Gaston Modot) on his way out, crossing gazes with Marceau (Julien Carette), whom he believes to be the poacher who has been trapping rabbits throughout the Marquis's property for some time. Much to Schumacher's dismay, the Marquis has not only pardoned Marceau but also hired him as a new servant. Figure 3.1 shows Marceau introducing himself to his new "colleagues." Next is the Marquis's cuisinier (Léon Larive), who comments on the owner's harshness but defends his being "a man of the world" despite his Jewish lineage. "Below stairs," writes Keith Reader, "is the only place, we may infer, that so delicate an issue can be broached. Such, at least, was the view of the extreme right-winger François Vinneuil."[4] At this point Chopin's "Minute Waltz" is cued in, underscoring the remainder of the sequence, "evocative perhaps of a certain closeness between the world of the servants and that of the masters."[5] Figures 3.2 and 3.3 telescope the nascent sympathy between Marceau and Schumacher's wife, Lisette (Paulette Dubost). Following a series of shots and counter shots of Marceau and Lisette, there is a cut to a long shot of Schumacher making

[2] On the radio as a political and cultural site, see Susan J. Douglas, *Listening In: Radio and the American Imagination* (Minneapolis: University of Minnesota Press, 2004); and Kate Lacey, *Listening Publics: The Politics and Experience of Listening in the Media Age* (Cambridge: Polity, 2013).

[3] See also my analysis of the same sequence in "The Harpist in the Closet: Film Music as Epistemological Joke," *Music and the Moving Image* 2, no. 3 (2009): 11–33, revised for the present monograph.

[4] Keith Reader, *La Règle du jeu: French Film Guide* (London: I. B. Tauris, 2010), 49. In his vicious review, Vinneuil wrote that "only the common people remember the Marquis's origins and judge them pitilessly. The salons, vain and distracted, have forgotten all about them," cited in Reader, *La Règle du jeu*, 49.

[5] Ibid., 49.

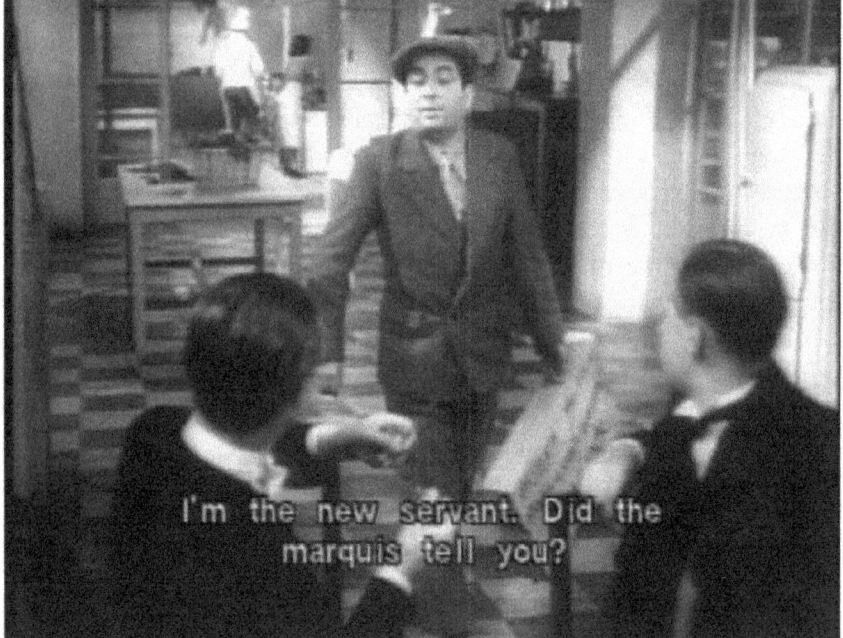

Figure 3.1 The Rules of the Game.

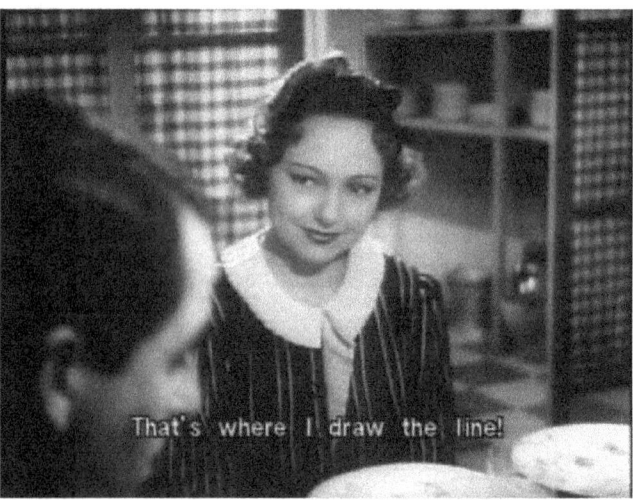

Figure 3.2 The Rules of the Game.

his way back downstairs, made suspicious by Marceau's flirtatious behavior toward his wife. Then the scene comes to a fastidiously coordinated close: just as the waltz is approaching the end on a triumphant final chord, there is a cut to the shot of a radio (Figure 3.4). The "countdown," as it were, is over. A dissolve into the shot of an elaborately ornate clock marking the hour and the

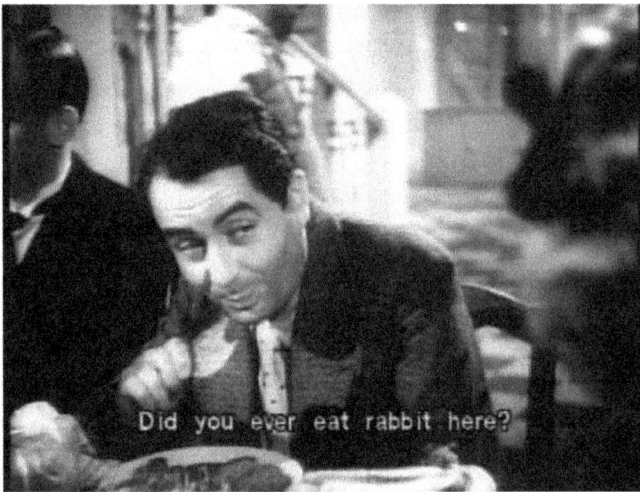

Figure 3.3 The Rules of the Game.

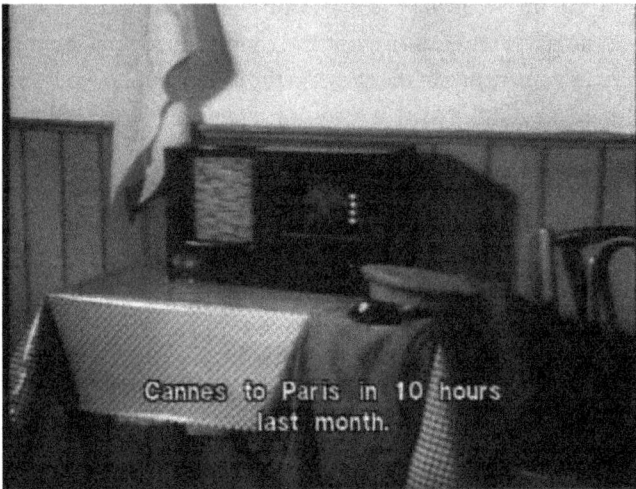

Figure 3.4 The Rules of the Game.

off-screen dialogue of the Marquis's guests bring the action back to the upper floor of the house.

Renoir timed the beginning of the music in such a way as to create a coincidence between the end of the piece and the end of the scene. It is the shot of the radio itself that turns out to be the ultimate destination point and nexus of meaning. Since the waltz is notorious for its short duration and since it turns out to function like a countdown, the ironies and double meanings of the dialogue are themselves contained within the irony of allowing the servants to talk, so to speak, for a mere minute (the piece lasts longer in fact, even when played at a fast tempo). Appearing at low volume halfway through the scene and with the conversation among the servants taking up all of our attention, the waltz hovers for its entire duration in a penumbra between attentiveness and inattentiveness, participating in the knowingly ironic and joyfully chaotic atmosphere of the meal but without calling attention to itself. The peculiar nature of this listening mode is perhaps best captured by the expression "global perception," employed by art historian Ernst H. Gombrich to characterize the perception of the regularity of decorative patterns.[6] We know the music is there and sense the appropriateness of its role in the scene but without bringing to bear on it the full extent of a complete, detailed scrutiny. Then, through a wonderful and paradoxical move, Renoir highlights the presence of the music—the shot of the radio—at the very moment it ceases to resound. An element of the ground suddenly becomes a figure, calls for our scrutiny, and disappears—all at once.[7]

"There are long passages," writes Victor Perkins, "where movement flows within and between shots, and where the sound is delicately engineered to hold everything together."[8] The continuous music does, indeed, "hold everything together." But the image of the radio also turns the broadcast into an element expressive of the psychological focus of the characters. By placing such marked emphasis on the provenance of the music—the same kitchen where the servants are having their meal—the final shot of the radio invites one to ask what the music sounded like and why. In particular, it makes the volume appear in retrospect as a sign of the fact that no one in the kitchen was listening. The servants' lack of attention to the music, of course, both mirrors and determines the attitude of the audience.[9]

---

[6] E. H. Gombrich, *The Sense of Order: A Study in the Psychology of Decorative Art* (London: Phaidon, 1984), 115–16. In a different vein, Stravinsky notoriously compared film music to "wallpaper." For a recent reappraisal of the idea of music as "wallpaper," see Ben Winters, "Musical Wallpaper? Towards an Appreciation of Non-Narrating Music in Film," *Music, Sound, and the Moving Image* 6, no. 1 (2012): 39–54.

[7] In discussing the related issue of foreground and background, Robynn Stilwell observes that "diegetic and nondiegetic are a matter of technical placement; foreground and background are a matter of perception, conditioned by a complex of factors, including dialogue, postures of attentiveness from the actors, and aural perspective": Stilwell, "The Fantastical Gap between the Diegetic and Nondiegetic," in *Beyond the Soundtrack: Representing Music in Cinema*, ed. Daniel Goldmark, Lawrence Kramer, and Richard Leppert (Berkeley: University of California Press, 2007), 189.

[8] Victor F. Perkins, *La Règle du jeu* (New York: Palgrave Macmillan, 2012), 89. On this aspect of the film soundtrack, see Alexander Sesonske, *Jean Renoir, the French Films* (Cambridge, MA: Harvard University Press, 1980), 438.

[9] A similar dynamic seems to regulate the perception of the foreground and background of the images. Except for the series of shots and counter shots of Marceau and Lisette in conversation, the sequence is shot with a deep-focus lens. Yet because the talking faces take up all of our attention, few, if any, will pay attention to the space of the kitchen behind the characters lined up in the foreground.

   As is the case with the spatial and acoustical characteristics of the music, the significance of its topical associations emerges only in retrospect. The music strikes a subtly odd note in terms of both placement and register. A century old by the time *The Rules of the Game* was filmed, Chopin's "Minute Waltz"—so called for its exceptional brevity—was conceived for the Parisian aristocratic salon. Its original aristocratic associations notwithstanding, the piece became a staple of the bourgeois home as well, encapsulating attitudes toward music, music making, and domesticity (it still does now). As a fast waltz, it is also appropriate to underscore the dalliance between the poacher and Lisette (Shumacher's wife). Though not as pronounced as they must have been a century earlier—think of the use of the waltz as stage music in nineteenth-century opera, above all in Verdi's *La traviata*—the sexual connotations of the waltz as an incitement to flirtation and openly sexual behavior must have been clear in Renoir's mind.[10] The final shot of the radio redresses all of this. Throughout *The Rules of the Game* the informal and cordial exchanges between the servants and the other characters would seem to imply that anyone in the film treat each other as his or her equal.[11] The anchoring reveals the falsity and impossibility of a truly equal relationship, of a "world without choices and painful consequences."[12] Since the music turns out to have been a radio broadcast, one realizes that it was not deliberately synchronized to the scene (as a standard score would have been). Instead, it simply happens to be an accidentally simultaneous event. The fact that the radio broadcast and the servants' dinner are shown as being simultaneous yet unaffected by each other is a figure of the pseudo-integration between irreducibly distant social classes. Renoir has chosen to represent the social gap through a lack of relation between the music and the action rather than an overt, all-too-easily recognizable dissonance or counterpoint. But as a result of this extremely subtle and sophisticated treatment, the point remains buried. Few, if any, will initially wonder what the status of the music is and whether it is performed somewhere in the house or broadcast through a radio. Even fewer will ask themselves why a Chopin waltz is playing in a scene set in the servants' kitchen. The

---

[10] Jean's father, Pierre-August, left behind some memorable paintings of dancers embracing in joyous abandon. Among them, *Dance at the Moulin de la Galette* (1876), at the Musée D'Orsay, is perhaps the best known. On the history and the social meanings of the waltz in the nineteenth century, see Rémy Hess, *La valse: révolution du couple en Europe* (Paris: A. M. Métailié, 1989). On the literary sources that inspired (Jean) Renoir's depiction of the love triangles and quadrangles of the film, see Sesonske, *Jean Renoir*, 389–93.

[11] Lisette is in many ways a sexually more fulfilled version of her mistress, Christine, and the latter treats her as such and admires her for it, confiding in her even the most intimate details of her private life. As Perkins has observed, "The Marquis addresses Schumacher as 'vous' but the poacher is straightaway a 'tu'": Perkins, *La Règle du jeu*, 106.

[12] Ibid., 40.

social commentary I see implicit in the use of Chopin's waltz is lost on the spectators as it is being uttered; it can only be recuperated in retrospect. The last shot of the sequence, then, does not so much allegorize a social situation as much as function as a figure of the critical, analytical gaze, one that revisits a film in search of meaning and in so doing creates an alternative temporal structure.[13]

If I have indulged in a somewhat extended exercise in critical interpretation, this is to show how ambiguity can be nested within structures that not only resist simplification but also suggest fresh approaches to our understanding of it. Let us return to the last shot. As Rick Altman has suggested, the timing and content of this shot are so deliberate as to lead one to ask whether it is meant to dispel a doubt, as if acknowledging that the scene had raised a question that needed to be answered.

> Is this music diegetic or not? It's certainly not on-screen music, but it could be wafting down from upstairs, where one of the guests might have just sat down to the piano. The suspicion seems confirmed when the camera follows Schumacher up the stairs – we seem to be using the waltz as a sound bridge to the next scene. But half-way up the stairs Schumacher encounters Marceau, whom we follow back down. As the scene continues, the camera proceeds to wander, as if continuing to seek out the source of the still unexplained waltz.[14]

Altman is correct in stressing how the uncertain status of the waltz may have shaped shot composition (and, I might add, the choice of camera setups). He is also convincing in adducing the dialectic between live and mechanical or technologically mediated performance as a further element of interest. Indeed, the radio is set up early on in the film as a visual icon, a locus for aural motifs, and a matrix for the tension between the old order (the Marquis's musical toys) and the new (mass media reports and their impact on gender and class hierarchies). In this light, the graphic match across the dissolve between the radio and that of the clock acquires symbolic connotations.[15]

But can we really assume that the status of the music is perceived as being in doubt, its status as undecided to begin with? True, the camera's dalliances jokingly withhold the moment in which the source is shown. Yet Altman

---

[13] Retrospectively, we also appreciate that Renoir is using the waltz to create tension about how long the sequence shot will last.

[14] Rick Altman, "Cinema as Ventriloquism," *Yale French Studies: Cinema/Sound* 60, no. 2 (1980): 72.

[15] I am grateful to Gina Marchetti and Jeff Smith for their observations on my discussion of this point.

seems to be reading the scene from the vantage point of an omniscient specta-tor.[16] Familiarity with the mechanisms of perception suggests that the music be perceived firmly under one and only one aspect, and that prior to the last shot no questions about its status interfere in any way with the interpretation of the scene, which is focally oriented toward the conversation. The image of the radio with which the sequence ends is less meant to elicit a clear-cut process of revision, let alone the answering of a question, than an invitation to take cognizance of an ambiguity that has been overlooked. Renoir's goal seems to be playing with the convention of always showing the source of the music following the introduction of recorded sound around 1930. The convention was obsolete by 1939, and not just in Hollywood (where films were lavishly scored without anyone fearing that the music be heard as unrealistic or incongruous).[17] The Chopin broadcast might just as well have stopped without anyone wondering what its status was—hence the need to show that it had indeed a source within the film's story world and specify in the clearest possible manner the nature of that source (a radio). Only at that point is the possibility of an ambiguity raised.

Music as Sonic Artifact

In *The Eclipse,* a seemingly accidental radio broadcast in the second half of the film provides the pretext for the placement of the title song, "Twist," written by Giovanni Fusco for the budding star Mina, one of Italy's greatest pop vocalists. It is a classic attempt at cross-marketing at a time when the placement of a music hit was beginning to be deemed crucial to the distribution of a film.[18] Yet it is also a surprising one given the proclivities of its director, Michelangelo Antonioni. The Kerim brothers, who produced the film, are known for having forced the director's hand over the notorious finale. They must have worked hard at persuading him to acquiesce to a procedure he must have balked at and was not to repeat ever again. In a surprising twist—pun intended—Antonioni eventually embraced, perhaps even relished, the opportunity. He not only contributed the text for "Twist" but also reportedly spent hours in the recording studio with Mina and his star Monica Vitti (Vitti and Mina would eventually befriend each other). For all this, and while the strategy to market the soundtrack worked

---

[16] For a note of caution against synoptic, atemporal readings, one that resonates powerfully in the context of this chapter, see Edward T. Cone, "Three Ways of Reading a Detective Story," in *Music: A View from Delft*, ed. Robert P. Morgan (Chicago: University of Chicago Press, 1989), 77–93. I would like to thank Su-Yin Mak for reminding me of Cone's essay while preparing this analysis.

[17] See Irene K. Atkins, *Source Music in Motion Pictures* (Rutherford, NJ: Fairleigh Dickinson University Press, 1983), 43.

[18] See Jeff Smith, *The Sounds of Commerce* (New York: Columbia University Press, 1998).

in Japan—where the film met with surprising success—over time yet another twist was to reverse the hierarchy between the title song and its later appearance as a radio broadcast.

Doubtless, "Twist" is embedded in the story to show that, as per the proverbial phrase, it was "in the air." But the passing of time, and with it the inevitable fading away of the aura surrounding the song and its performer, has stripped the music of its quality of living, resonating link between the film and the mediascape. No longer the paratextual element such marketing ploys normally are, the song has gained a second life as fully engulfed in the poetics of the film, subsumed under the chillingly rendered portrait of the physical environment encasing its two wandering protagonists. The director's own stylistic and staging choices naturally played a role. Whether as a reluctant concession to the producers—a throwaway of sorts—or calculated delay, the song reappears only near the end of the film as Vittoria (Monica Vitti) listlessly explores Piero's (Alain Delon) large and empty apartment in Rome's historic ghetto. The two of them have just kissed each other for the first time, in the process tearing the shoulder of Vittoria's dress. The awkward incident sets Vittoria on yet another walk through the house, including what appears to be Piero's old bedroom. She walks into the room to fix her dress but ends up inspecting the room instead, mildly captivated by a novelty pen that doubles as an erotically titillating device by showing a woman dress and undress at the tilt of the wrist (Figure 3.5). During this, the song is playing on a radio that must have been left on all day long by either Piero, one of his parents, or the housemaid. Or perhaps, as suggested by Chion, it comes from a transistor radio held by someone in the courtyard outside.[19] We shall never know. The place seems all but deserted and no indication is given as to whether Piero's parents are in fact alive. The close-up of this vulgar symbol of Piero's frank sexuality is held long enough for us to partake of Vittoria's ambivalent reaction to it. The image pulls the music into its own orbit, as if contriving a short, self-contained vignette of sorts. But it is too banal to be of interest. Vittoria is soon bored by it. Having forgotten about the need to fix her dress, and all but indifferent to the music, she leaves the room and continues her half-hearted exploration of the apartment.

Like the sound of the electric fan in the famous opening sequence, the broadcast is a reminder of the role of machines in our lives. Unlike the fan, however, the radio plays no apparent function, as no listener is there to pick up its signal (and if there is one, we do not know his or her identity). The unwitting unveiling of its presence on Vittoria's part is entirely coincidental, just like her stumbling onto Piero's novelty pen. For all we know, the radio may have been operating for hours, days even. It is the trace of an aborted plan, perhaps, or past intention (hearing

---

[19] Michel Chion, "What a Time It Was! An Essay on Antonioni's *L'eclisse*," trans. Alain Renaud and Don Siegel, *The Soundtrack* 3, no. 2 (2010): 7.

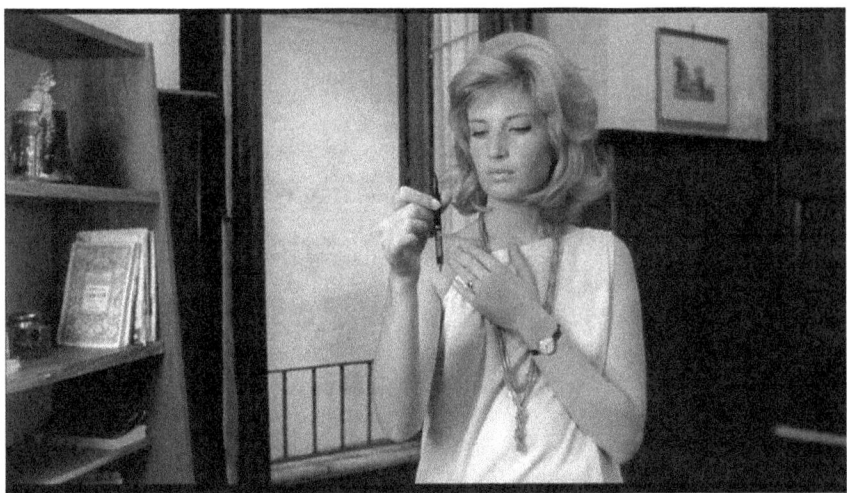

Figure 3.5 The Eclipse.

the news). What we are hearing is therefore merely a function of the program's schedule and the fortuitous convergence of a set of circumstances. In the absence of any incident proper, aside from Vittoria's wandering, the broadcast cannot even aspire to the status of what Chion has famously called "anempathetic music."[20] It is Vittoria who walks away from it, indifferent to its doomed fate as "song without a listener," chiming its acoustically impoverished tune to an empty room.

The deployment of the Mina recording at this point is a brilliant masterstroke in that it brings out, under the guise of a mere detail of setting, the uncanny concealed in mechanical objects when, independent of human agency, they partake of the senselessness of the world like a clock ticking away into nothingness. But for this meaning to emerge, one has to actually pay attention to it, and this is possible only through exegesis. In the context of a one-time sitting through the film, the combined effect of Vittoria's demeanor and the demands of the narrative make the appreciation of this subtle piece of sound work a remote possibility. Like other so-called film auteurs, Antonioni is using the resources of mass entertainment to create a work whose full disclosure is impeded by the modes of distribution and reception on which its very existence rests. It is the paradox that defines most auteur cinema of our time, and it poses a conundrum as regards the definition of our subject for, as I shall argue later, the appreciation of such details of setting does not simply augment but rather comes at the exclusion of the enjoyment of the narrative (however loose or meandering this may be, as is the case in *The Eclipse*).

[20] M. Chion, *Film, A Sound Art*, trans. Claudia Gorbman (New York: Columbia University Press, 2009), 467.

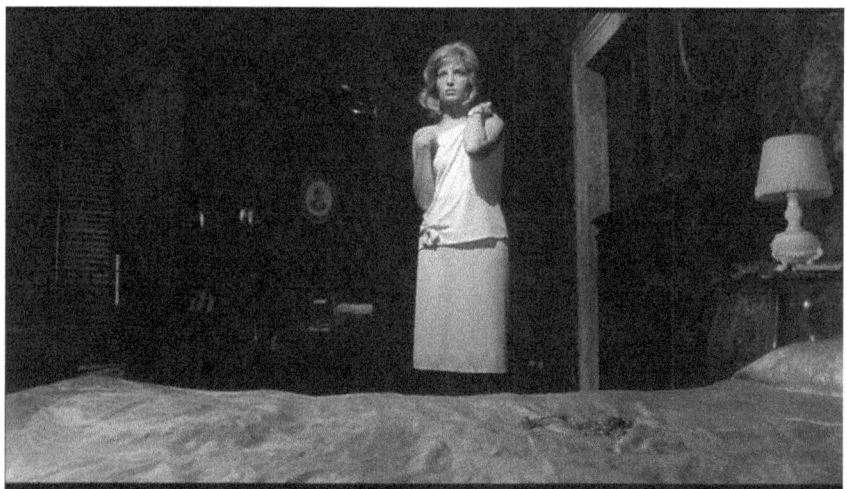

Figure 3.6 The Eclipse.

The Eclipse very nearly skirts presenting us with such a stark either/or scenario but only by virtue of its radical, indeed visionary, skirting of narrative
itself. As we see Vittoria irreverently enter what in a traditional Italian home is a
sancta sanctorum, the parents' bedroom, the music stops. On reflection, this is
somewhat implausible, given the proximity of the two rooms and the length of
the corridor she has just traversed. As is the norm in this and Antonioni's two
previous films, the sound mix is a representation of the position in space not
of the character but of the camera. The latter sits almost hidden across the bed
from her, at a level commensurate to someone lying on it, and looks at Vittoria
from below across what on the big silver screen is the vast area occupied by a
silk duvet (Figure 3.6). Traffic noise, meanwhile, sifts through the open window
on the left. Judging from her demeanor, we can be confident that Vittoria herself no longer registers the presence of the music in this new environment. To
her, the broadcast was just something "happening, over there," and as such ir-
revocably bound to one and one place only, incapable of lingering at the fringes
of the attention once she moves to a different location—despite what we must
assume was its continuing presence in the soundscape as measured in terms of
physical signal. Her indifference both mirrors and guides the perception of the
spectator; it is to her face, eyes, and the objects of her own somewhat wayward
attention—the pen, posters on the wall, the furniture, and eventually the somewhat morbid-looking new room she enters—that we are now drawn.[21]

---

[21] As a foil to this, consider another example of aimless wandering: the earlier sequence in which
Vittoria takes a walk outside her house in the middle of the night. Running into a row of flag poles,

The music has escaped critical scrutiny, too. Despite the many critical notices about this film, few have noted the reappearance of "Twist" as radio broadcast. Jonathan Rosenbaum makes much of the use of the song in the credits instead. He goes so far as seeing the final pulverization of the protagonists' affair at the film's end as a recapitulation of "the transition from a twist to anxiety-ridden modernist music behind the film's opening credits."[22] Rosenbaum thus sees the musical treatment of the credits as nothing less than the allegorical foreshadowing of the film's trajectory. This is naturally a big compliment made to the two tracks or, to be precise, their jarring juxtaposition. At the same time, the statement also betrays an all-too-common view of music as supplement standing outside of the film proper (which in one sense it is, but only if one considers the beginning credits). Fusco's "anxiety-ridden modernist music," as Rosenbaum calls it, does tint the ending of *The Eclipse* with quasi-apocalyptic tones. Shivers of electronically produced sound ominously pave the way for thunderous piano octaves just as the camera prepares to close in on the sun-like, burned-out core of light coming from a street lamp that constitutes the film's final image. But "Twist" was never associated with carefree romance and sexual chemistry in the first place, either. Its appearance in Piero's home, in fact, almost amounts to a parody of standard practice. Title themes often become sonic shorthand for a film or an exemplary event or main character thereof.[23] Their significance is cemented in the course of the narrative, meaning accruing over repeated and strategic appearances at key junctures, whether in the form of leitmotivic repetition or anchoring to a source. In this way the music does not simply represent the film from the outside in, but rather comes to embody, or be associated with, important events or characters very much from within. In *The Eclipse*, by contrast, the title song is tied to an insignificant event—Vittoria's disengaged wandering through an empty home—that is hollowed out of dramatic import altogether. This produces a novel, rather startling effect: less the setup for a significant recurrence, the title theme appears in hindsight like the foreshadowing of a randomly chosen piece of soundscape that does not impinge on the story at all. As such, it is much more representative than Fusco's "modernist" score of the way in which in *The Eclipse* objects engulf people and settings engulf their stories. In Rosenbaum's words:

she is enchanted by the sounds they make as the wing passes over them rather like, in Roberto Calabretto's words, an "aeolian harp": Roberto Calabretto, *Antonioni e la musica* (Venezia: Marsilio, 2012), 124.

[22] Jonathan Rosenbaum, "L'cclisse, A Vigilance of Desire," in *L'eclisse*, Michelangelo Antonioni, Criterion DVD, #278.

[23] A classic case is Otto Preminger's *Laura* (1944), where all three are conflated.

It's almost as if Antonioni has extracted the essence of everyday street life that serves as a background throughout the picture, and once we're presented with this essence in its undiluted form, it suddenly threatens and oppresses us. The implication is that behind every story there's a place and an absence, a mystery and a profound uncertainty, waiting like a vampire at every moment to emerge and take over, to stop the story dead in its tracks.[24]

The point applies, above all, to the culmination of the process Rosenbaum captures so poignantly, namely, the film's finale.[25] There, Antonioni shows images in no apparent order, except by following the transition from late afternoon to dusk of a singular locale in Rome's sparsely populated EUR district. The locale, a construction site, is ostensibly to serve as the meeting place for a rendezvous between the protagonists, one that, however, never occurs (at least not within the span of the screen time of the film). As the camera buys time to register seemingly irrelevant elements of the environment—irrelevant, that is, to the romantic interest that had till then more or less given the film its raison d'être—Vittoria and Piero are pushed further out of the world of the film and recede into the background of our memory. It is at this point that Fusco's music appears. Yet despite its "bruitiste" inspiration, the electronic score imparts a distinct veneer of suspense that seriously undermines the radical transformation under way in the patently nondramatic exploration of this space. The use of the radio broadcast of "Twist," despite its passing resemblance to a conventionally motivated, "in the air" title theme, instead serves Antonioni's defamiliarizing strategy much more effectively.

Anamorphosis

The instances in which filmmakers employ preexisting songs or instrumental music as cultural reference or commentary are too numerous to rehearse here. My goal in the last section of this chapter is to propose that the metaphor of

---

[24] Jonathan Rosenbaum, "L'eclisse, A Vigilance of Desire." Jacques Tati's *Playtime* (1967) is, too, an extended reflection on the status of a setting in narrative filmmaking. Devoid of a story proper, the film is held together by the identity of the setting—the areas in and around a newly built airport—and the focus on a single character negotiating this new and to him perplexing space. While the attention is centered on the putative protagonist, it is at the same time dispersed across the frame, as one is constantly on the lookout for an element of the setting perturbing the precarious balance between people, space, and the objects that populate it.

[25] For a detailed analysis of the soundtrack of the final sequence, see Calabretto, *Antonioni e la musica*, 125–35.

anamorphosis goes some way to suggest a different kind of yardstick with which to measure the use of preexisting music in film and indeed a wide range of sonic symbols planted in countless cinematic narratives. My central example is an enigmatic, seemingly functionless scene from Kurosawa's crime thriller, *High and Low*.

The English translation of *Tengoku to Jigoku* ("High and Low") is a somewhat tamed rendering of the original, "Heaven and Hell." But it is at least sufficiently suggestive of the binary opposition of high and low culture, fulfilled lifelong projects and shattered hopes, vast fortunes and abject poverty, beautiful imagery and deflated reality, heroic choices and base behavior, and luminous morals and bottomless corruption that lie at the core of this important and justly celebrated film. Kurosawa's film feeds off the tension created by these coexisting opposites while at the same time it shows how narrow the gap between them truly is. Sold to the producers as a genre piece, the film is an ambitious portrait of a complex moral universe, featuring a full range of human feelings and aspirations competing with one another in a stifling space. As an acknowledged masterpiece based on a long-forgotten, second-rate pulp police novel by Evan Hunter, Kurosawa's film is also a demonstration of the surprisingly narrow gap that separates commonplace storytelling from transcendental filmmaking, generic procedures from poetic gesture.

The film is a crime thriller in which a wealthy, conscientious, hard-working shoe manufacturer, Gondo (Toshirô Mifune), is the victim of a hideous crime: his chauffeur's son is kidnapped in mistake for his own. The kidnapper acknowledges the mix-up but wants the money nonetheless, thus forcing the entire family—including, of course, the chauffeur himself—into a moral dilemma. The time is the early sixties, as Japan prepares for the Olympic Games ready to showcase its economic miracle and recent successes in the fields of technology and manufacturing. Not coincidentally, Gondo's ultramodern house and a fast express train are two of the film's most important settings. They, however, are contained within the larger setting of Yokohama, then still a poorer relation to the capital, Tokyo. Yokohama is depicted as an industrial, heavily polluted city struggling to reap the benefits of the economic recovery enjoyed by Tokyo following the great Kanto earthquake of 1923 and the devastation of the Allies' bombings in 1945. The choice of the setting is significant, not to say proverbial, for other reasons as well. Yokohama shares strikingly similar features with other port cities in Japan—Kobe and Nagasaki; South Asia—Singapore and Madras; and especially China—Dalian, Qingdao, Shanghai, and, of course, Hong Kong. All these cities are in one way or another borne out of a traumatic encounter with Western forces—whether European or American—and have since become major actors in a shift of geopolitical balance of unprecedented proportions.

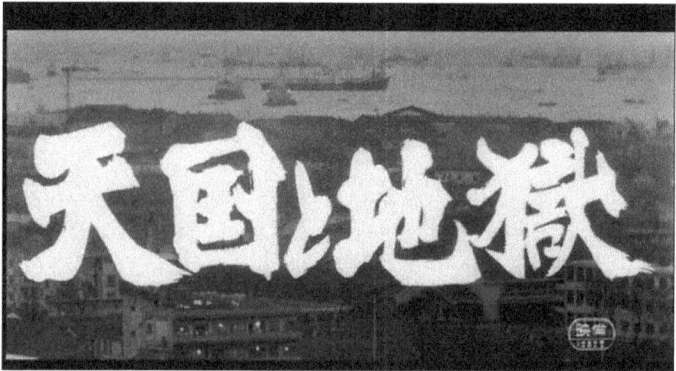

Figure 3.7 High and Low.

As raw material for an artistic re-creation, Yokohama held immediate appeal for Kurosawa, and the director and his collaborators offer up a portrait of the city starting with the title sequence. We begin with long shots of Yokohama in telephoto lens, a due reference to nineteenth-century representations of the port at the time of Commodore Perry's arrival (Figure 3.7). The use of the zoom flattens out the image, and the prominent titles further underline the bidimensionality of what we are seeing: mere images of the city. Sound adds both a third dimension and mobility to the viewpoint through which Kurosawa composes his panorama. Behaving rather like an extended stinger at the appearance of the title, the music continues as an intimation of the supernatural, the magical even: the residual of ancient rituals and epistemologies in the midst of a frantically modernizing urban experiment. We then hear a vocalise, a menacing motif played by a brass ensemble, and isolated cells at the percussions. As in the title sequence of Hitchcock's *Rear Window,* the collage-like, formally discontinuous, and jarring flow of motives and musical allusions come across as a stylized rendering of the city soundscape. Such a representation is, however, more naturalistic as the fragmentary nature of the musical discourse is explicit. Moreover, sound effects are added to the mix: the hum of the city port, ships' sirens, traffic noise, and the distant rumble of fast trains running across. While incapable of providing us with a coherent map of the urban sprawl displayed on screen, these sounds do at least convey a sense of distance of their sources from a point in space—is it a moving vantage point?—and thus imbue the images with a sense of depth. The music ends with the trumpet repeating the main motif heard at the beginning. It now dawns on us that it is a languid, exceedingly slow version of a mambo. The rhythm and especially the timbre of the trumpet call up images of jazz and film noir as important influences but also cue the spectator to the American presence in Yokohama—then still an important military outpost. Finally, and again, as in

Rear Window, at the end of the title sequence it is suggested that we may have been seeing through the eyes of someone—specifically, those of the manufacturer Gondo, whose silhouette emerges in the as-yet-unlit interior of the house as the film proper begins.

Whether they are point-of-view shots or not, the images of the credits sequence do show us what the city looks like from Gondo's beautiful, conspicuous house. The house is perched atop a hill next to the city slums and is shielded from the noise and dirt of the city below not only by its height but also by a super-modern air conditioning system and state-of-the-art glass panels protecting it from all sounds surrounding it. It is thus a strikingly insulated aural environment. The first part of the film takes place entirely inside this house—its living room, in fact—with Kurosawa choreographing the action rather like a stage director while taking full advantage of multicamera technology and widescreen format to flesh out relationships and create a visually entertaining spectacle. Several sounds punctuate the action, mostly carried forward through dialogue: the signature hush of the house's interior, the screams of the children playing, the ticking of the living room clock, and the voice of the kidnapper himself, heard first at the phone and then in playback recordings made by the police.

Following the fateful decision of paying the ransom, and after nearly an hour of screen time, the action moves at long last outside the house. Kurosawa jolts the spectator with an extremely dynamic sequence, shot partly with a hand-held camera and set entirely in the unusual location chosen by the kidnapper as the stage for the payment of the ransom—an express train. The reunion between Gondo and the driver's son, Shinichi (Masahiko Shimazu), is shot in an unusual way, with the police in the foreground and Gondo and Shinichi in the distance, down the receding line, near the right edge of the elongated frame. Credits aside, the brass peroration we hear as Gondo hugs the young boy is the only music in the first part of the film. It is rather like an exit off stage for Gondo who, from this point on, will hardly be seen (except in the very last sequence). The stage has been set for another film to begin, as it were, one devoted to the search for the criminal and the exploration of the Yokohama underworld (this will in turn be followed by an extended chase). Because the police feature prominently in all three, one could reformulate the content of the film as being about the relationship between the police and the victim in the first part, and between the police and the criminal in the second and third parts, respectively.

It is after the payment of the ransom and the reunion with the child that Kurosawa chooses to show us the kidnapper. As Noël Burch has observed, at this point the film breaks free of the restricted viewpoint that dominates the first

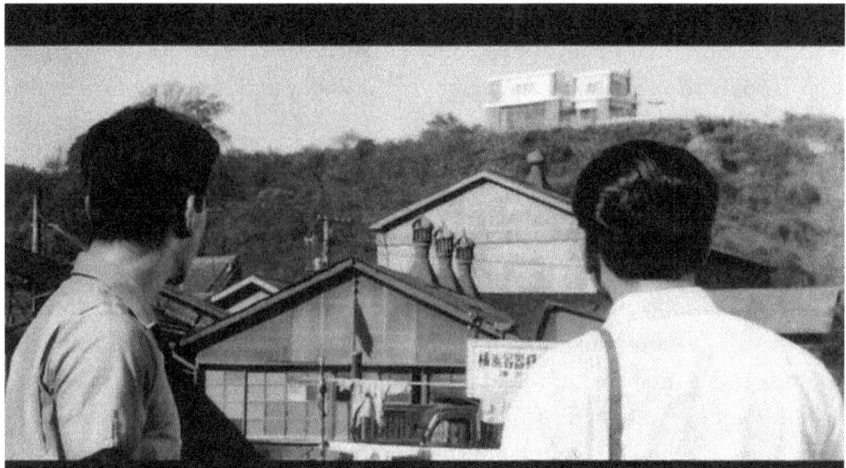

Figure 3.8 High and Low.

part.[26] The change consequently alters the almost exact alignment between audience and the police. The manner in which the kidnapper appears on screen is very studied and unusual, however. It is almost as if Kurosawa did not want us to recognize the man captured on screen as the criminal. We make our acquaintance with him initially by way of what he only distractedly hears—a radio broadcast of the last movement of Schubert's "The Trout." It is without a doubt one of the most original and puzzling appearances on screen of a villain in all of film history (Figures 3.8–3.11). The sequence begins with two investigators searching for clues near one of the many open-air sewers that plagued the city after the war. While looking at the house, they make a casual observation that resonates with the kidnapper's anger: "The kidnapper's right: that house does seem to look down its nose at you." Their comment stands in sharp contradiction to the last words uttered by the inspector just as the boy was being rescued at the very end of the previous sequence: "Now go get him. For Gondo's sake, be bloodhounds."[27] The contrast reveals a dilemma nested within the dilemma that drives the plot. Given his admittedly insensitive display of wealth and prosperity in the

---

[26] Noël Burch, *To the Distant Observer: Form and Meaning in Japanese Cinema* (Berkeley: University of California Press, 1979), 319.

[27] I note in passing that the rescue of Shinichi, and the brass peroration that accompanies it, may well have marked the point at which an intermission (*kyuukei*) started. While the shift in perspective would have been retained, the break would attenuate the impact of the contrast I am drawing attention to. The film is rather long (143 minutes). I speculate that another intermission might have occurred when we see pink smoke from one of the city incinerators (a moment also marked, not coincidentally, by fanfare). That is also the moment when the chase proper, as distinct from the investigation, begins.

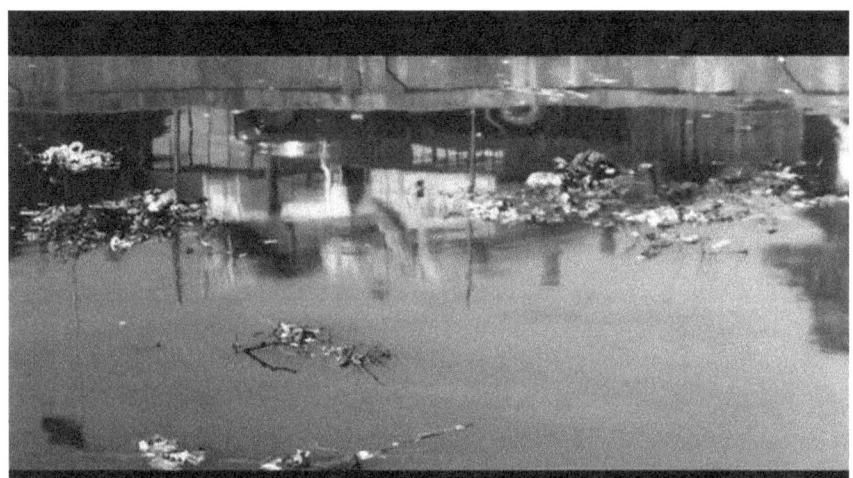

Figure 3.9 High and Low.

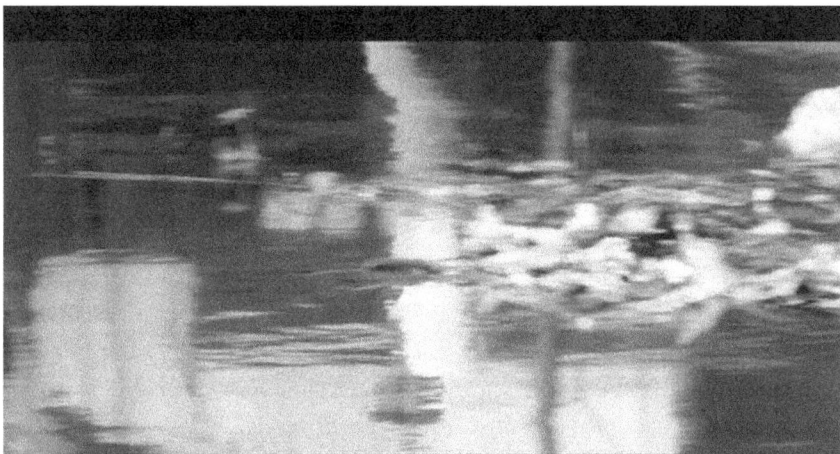

Figure 3.10 High and Low.

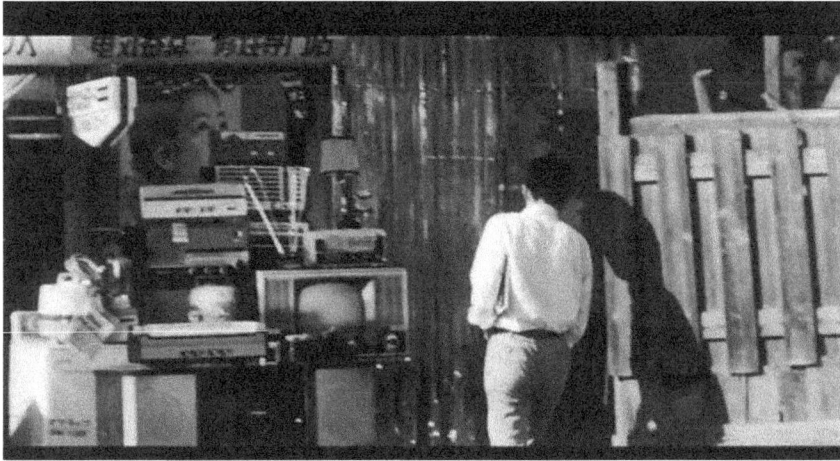

Figure 3.11 High and Low.

face of the inferno of the summer cauldron of the Yokohama slums, is Gondo in some way responsible, however unwittingly, for the kidnapper's anger?[28] As the investigators exit frame right, the camera tilts up, stops, and then reverses its course—from right to left—without cutting. A border is marked. The appearance of the kidnapper has by now already been signaled aurally first. It is a new sound that announces him. He quite literally enters the frame as an "ear," not a visible body. Soon thereafter we notice a human figure moving across the stream (and reflected in it). As another focal point of interest is introduced, the memory of the policemen vanishes from our consciousness. And yet they are only a few yards away (off screen). This is fitting, since the kidnapper is physically close but otherwise distant, unreachable, protected by the parallel world of the slums that are his curse but also his (temporary) reprieve.[29]

Since the sound of the music grows louder, point of view and point of audition are dramatically split. We are hearing from the point in space where the kidnapper is and yet are looking at him from a considerable distance (a fact stressed by the camera being still on this side of the canal). The tracking movement of the camera transforms the rubble and garbage floating on the water into elements of a beautiful abstract composition. Finally, the camera jumps across the filthy stream, affording us a closer, more accurate view of the squalor pervading the area. Meanwhile, the volume of the music rises and reaches a peak as the kidnapper walks by a hardware shop. In contrast to the flatness of the image resulting from the use of a telephoto lens, the changing sound of the broadcast creates a sense of spatial depth *along the horizontal axis* of the elongated frame. As the kidnapper turns at the corner and walks away, the sound level decreases. It is now obvious that we had been hearing through him all along. By the time he enters his shack, it can no longer be heard. Schubert's music will resurface, two variations later, as the kidnapper angrily changes the radio station having heard the news that he has made a hero of the man whose life he wanted to destroy. Now all but the most distracted member of the audience will know who he is. Again, he hardly pays attention to the music, its presence being the fortuitous result of

---

[28] Burch, *To the Distant Observer*, 320. While admiring the stylistic and formal qualities of the film, Burch sees nothing but conservatism and class bias in the narrative of the film. On the limitations of this schematic division between "form" and "content," see Mitsuhiro Yoshimoto, *Film Studies and Japanese Cinema* (Raleigh, NC: Duke University Press, 2000), 307. It goes without saying that my interest in the radio broadcast of "The Trout" and the subtle way in which it is presented is in part motivated by the wish to blur the boundary between form and content. A simple parsing of the narrative of the film, moreover, offers plenty of opportunities to question whether the film supports a Manichean view of its characters.

[29] Yoshimoto writes that the dichotomy of heaven and hell articulated by the film's original title (*Tengoku to jingoku*) "is somewhat undermined by the spatial proximity of the two": Yoshimoto, *Film Studies and Japanese Cinema*, 325.

his desire to silence the news station. Yet that is precisely what ties his fate to that of the broadcast.

Kurosawa had used Schubert before and will use it in later films as well, but never under such unusual circumstances and in such a sophisticated way (all of which makes the absence of a discussion of this episode in the large English-language literature on Kurosawa rather surprising).[30] Whether one associates it to the fresh and clear waters referred to in the poem by the same name set to music by Schubert, the Meiji period Westernization, the educational role of the radio in modern Japan, cultural refinement, or a hard-working, ambitious, and Westernized cross section of the Japanese population, "The Trout" is a striking and unexpected presence in Yokohama's shantytowns. As in Eisenstein's montage of attractions, seemingly incompatible images—or, to be precise, an image and a sound—are brought to bear on one another, but unlike Eisenstein's famous juxtapositions, image and sound are here simultaneous. Moreover, one term of the juxtaposition—the music—is disguised as an element of the setting. This allows scope for interpretation, creating the conditions for a positive act of interpretation of a detail whose symbolic significance is not announced but, at most, insinuated.[31] There is a parallel between the way in which Kurosawa uses a symbolic musical quotation in this context and the way in which directors compose an image in widescreen format by embedding visual details in a rich composition rather than parading their significance through editing or reframing.[32]

Of course, Kurosawa is constructing reality as much as documenting it. The radio broadcast is an element of the setting only to the extent that it is the accidentally simultaneous event occurring in a space contiguous to that crossed by the

---

[30] Consider, for instance, the redeeming message implicit in the use of a performance of the "Unfinished" in *One Wonderful Sunday* (1947), as well as the use of the lied "Heidenröselein," culminating in the apotheosis of the finale, in *Rhapsody in August* (1991). Regarding the former, Michael K. Bourdaghs writes how "Kurosawa has been accused of choosing the Schubert work for the film primarily for the connotations of its title": Bourdaghs, *Sayonara Amerika, Sayonara Nippon: A Geopolitical Prehistory of J-Pop* (New York: Columbia University Press, 2012), 28.

[31] Writing about a bundle floating in the water in Preminger's *River of No Return* (1954), Charles Barr argues that "the detail is placed in the background of the shot, and integrated naturally, so that we have to make a positive act of interpreting, of 'reading,' the shot. . . . The symbolism is in the event, not the visual pattern": Barr, "CinemaScope: Before and After," *Film Quarterly* 16, no 4 (Summer 1963): 11–12. In *High and Low*, the use of an arrangement of "O sole mio," also broadcast on the radio as the kidnapper is arrested and attempts suicide, is on the other hand more noticeably ironic. Its significance is picked out for us, as it were.

[32] *High and Low* was shot with an anamorphic lens in a standard film frame (to be subsequently stretched so as to be shown in a widescreen format). Though much could be written about Kurosawa's use of the widescreen format, I am not aware of any visual symbol functioning quite the way the radio broadcast of the Schubert quintet does. The tinted puff of pink smoke that precipitates the chase is a poignant reference to the silent era; yet in one sense it is the opposite of the Schubert broadcast in that it is impossible to miss.

kidnapper. A broadcast can, at least in principle, be heard in all neighborhoods and by members of all social classes. As such, rather like church bells and other such signals in older times, it convenes a large, diverse crowd to a virtual public arena, the confines of which coincide with that of the city, sometimes a whole country. It does say something about his sense of belonging to such a virtual community, then, that the kidnapper utterly ignores its content. Then again, his indifference also betrays an understanding of its presence and the significance of that presence. After all, the reach of the broadcast is often no more than a function of the technical capabilities of the machines that both transmit and receive its signal.

We, the spectators, are introduced to the music from the kidnapper's perspective—literally, through his point of audition. As he moves first toward and then away from the source of the sound, the sound level, timbre, and reverb of the broadcast change accordingly. This produces in the spectator the impression of being in someone else's ambit, of hearing through a consciousness—all the more striking here as it follows a whole, long section of the film in which the kidnapper was utterly excluded from our vision. Yet the kidnapper shows no visible sign that the music is having any impact on him. He seems utterly uninterested in what is around him, as if absorbed in his own thoughts, or perhaps intent on erasing the presence of the depressing surroundings that are the stage of his everyday activities. Perhaps the thought of the music crosses his mind. But in the absence of any visible response to its sound, and given Kurosawa's restraint in presenting it, the kidnapper appears to hear the music only insofar as it happens to fall within the range of what is audible from his point in space. It is a virtuosic representation of that state of absorption described by Fried with respect to eighteenth-century French realist painting—virtuosic on account of the fact that we are given an extraordinarily vivid impression of absorption in the form of the failure to attend to a stream of sound that is nevertheless within earshot. This stream of sound is registered by the senses without, however, being grasped with the full force of one's attention (and despite the absence of any apparent competing visual or auditory information).

To fully grasp the nature of the director's effort, it may be helpful to make a comparison to the theater. In the spoken theater and even more so in opera and the musical, inattentiveness to a sound is represented, somewhat more drastically, by eliminating it altogether or by replacing it with another sound or with the score. In fact, we could think of singing and the attendant orchestral sounds in nineteenth-century opera as means of constantly warding off sounds that threaten to intrude into the characters' solipsistic absorption in themselves. This is true of cinema as well, as when filmmakers cue in nondiegetic music to suggest introspection. I am thinking, for instance, of the sequence in which Captain Willard (Martin Sheen) watches his soldiers sing along with a radio broadcast of the Rolling Stones' "Satisfaction" in Francis F. Coppola's *Apocalypse Now* (1978). "The musical landscape," observes Rob Wright, "is largely a counterpoint between source music that punctuates the various, often bizarre, contexts through which the story moves and a somber, muted score that starkly illustrates the deepening unease within Willard as he travels deeper into the bush."[33] In one instance of the counterpoint described by Wright, the Rolling Stones' "Satisfaction," broadcast on the radio, accompanies the antics performed by members of the crew before Captain Willard's puzzled stare. The score written by Carmine Coppola soon takes over, however, replacing the broadcast altogether till, over the same music, a dissolve takes us to another point in the narrative. Reinforcing the effect of a close-up and the voice-over narration, Coppola's music signals that Willard's attention has turned elsewhere by gradually entering the sound space till it replaces the broadcast of the Rolling Stones' song entirely. The music simultaneously isolates Willard and gives concrete and sustained expression—in the form of a new sound that supersedes that of the radio—to his absorption in his own thoughts. His inattentiveness to the broadcast is expressed by denying the latter's right to exist as part of the scene. This procedure, as common as it is unexamined, would seem to be a tentative answer to the perplexing question of whether a sound, in this case a radio broadcast, can be drowned out by something purely mental, like intense concentration on another subject, given that physically a sound can be superseded only by another sound—hence, one suspects, the literalization of that process through music.[34]

The fact that in *High and Low* inattention is represented by leaving the unattended object in full view, as it were, does not merely imbue Kurosawa's solution with a greater degree of realism. It also creates the possibility of a split perception between character and audience. But this possibility and the manner in which it may be realized need to be qualified. True, the very presence of the music would, alone, seem to allow the audience to adopt an independent perspective on it. The timing and the content of the scene, however, make it hard for us to allocate any attention to the music and, therefore, for such an independent perspective to be gained. Film theorists study the way in which filmmakers direct attention almost exclusively by reference to visual composition (be it static or dynamic). What this misses is not only the power of sound in directing attention to certain events but also, and just as crucially, the extent to which in/attention to this rather than that is the result of our knowledge and horizon of expectations. In our example, the spectator is busy coming to terms with the startling realization that what he or she is seeing is, for the first time and after over an hour of film, the kidnapper himself. Having heard his voice on

---

[33] Rob Wright, "Score vs. Song: Art, Commerce, and the H factor in Film and Television Music," in *Popular Music and Film*, ed. Ian Inglis (London: Wallflower Press, 2003), 14.

[34] Of course, the procedure is also common in opera, where a play of mutually exclusive streams of music is also motivated by convention, as opera must feature music from beginning to end.

the phone only makes his appearance as visible form more captivating. It is the gradual realization of seeing him that commands one's attention, leaving little or no room for musing on a symbolic presence—Schubert's music—that is as potentially imbued with meaning as it is buried. The kidnapper's demeanor, too, is instrumental in channeling our perception in such a way that the music remains hidden, as it were, in plain sight. He is a focalizer, a force shaping our attention and sensitivity to what is featured in the scene. But he is also a double, his inattentiveness to the music a reflection of our own inattentiveness, his so-lipsistic absorption in his own predicament at the expense of the surrounding space a figure of our absorption in one aspect of the scene's construction at the expense of auditory information that is also part of that construction. By plant-ing a meaningful musical quotation that is bound to be overlooked by charac-ter and audience alike, only to be recuperated at the level of exegesis, the film suggests a disturbing alignment between spectator and fictional character: the kidnapper could be anyone, even you or me.

There are precedents for this phenomenon across a number of art forms. For the sake of convenience and to underline the poignancy of its effect, I would like to suggest an analogy between the radio broadcast in *High and Low* and an anamor-phic spot in a representational painting.[35] Think of Holbein's well-known painting, *The Ambassadors*. The painting shows Jean de Dinteville (lay power) and George de Selve (bishop, symbol of ecclesiastic power) at the height of their fame and success (the very existence of the painting itself bears witness to the stage in life they have both reached). There is a large art-historical literature on this painting. Yet existing interpretations, to my knowledge, fall short of accounting for the im-plications of the anamorphic distortion. The anamorphically rendered skull is un-derstood as a symbol of death whose presence transforms a celebratory portrait into an allegory of the futility of scientific knowledge, symbolized by the scientific paraphernalia displayed, and the frailty of human life, symbolized by the ambas-sadors themselves, depicted here in the full splendor of their vigor and confidence. This is fine as far it goes; after all, Holbein inherited a medieval exegetical tradition codified by Dante and others that sees the surface of a text or an image as but an entry point to theological, moral, and allegorical meanings. Even so, the interpre-tation of the anamorphosis as a traditional symbol fails to capture the extent to

---

[35] For a productive analogy between certain effects of cinematic narrative and anamorphosis, see John Belton, "The Space of Rear Window," in *Hitchcock's Rereleased Films: From Rope to Vertigo*, ed. Walter Raubichek and Walter Srebnick, with a Foreword by Andrew Sarris (Detroit: Wayne State University Press, 1991), 85. For a psychoanalytical, and in particular Lacanian, perspective on the meaning of anamorphic spots, see Todd McGowan, "Looking for the Gaze: Lacanian Film Theory and Its Vicissitudes," *Cinema Journal* 42, no. 3 (2003): 27–47. Elsie M. Walker adapts McGowan's ideas to film soundtracks in *Understanding Sound Tracks through Film Theory* (New York: Oxford University Press, 2015), 245–320.

which it short-circuits such a neat piling up of different kinds of meaning.[36] The anamorphosis is more than a suggestion of a hidden, deeper meaning; what it does is inscribe a narrative of the viewer's own encounter with it, the narrative of how something that is at first registered as a mere blot—if at all—upon a second viewing commands our attention as the key to the whole scene. Hanging instructions suggest that this was literally the case.[37] In so doing, the skull symbolizes not so much death but rather its opacity, unreadability, and unimaginability in the face of earthly success; what is more, it does so in terms of the viewer's experience. The result is a particular aesthetic trajectory that is itself symbolic of a shared quality between the viewer and the ambassadors—their obliviousness to death becomes a mirror image of our inability to read what strikes us at first as a blot.

In *High and Low*, the music is not literally distorted—certainly not to the point of being unrecognizable—but, like the skull in Holbein's painting, it is utterly unexpected and thus catches one unprepared. It is a foreign object in the slums of Yokohama and also an incidental, seemingly superfluous piece of information within the context of the narrative, in something like the way the skull is a foreign object in the lavishly ornate room where the two ambassadors are standing and the blot is an unexpected element in the viewer's encounter with the painting. What "smears" the music, turning it into a sonic "blot," is not the manipulation of the physical signal but our lack of attention to it (because of the timing of its occurrence and the pace with which the visual and auditory information of the scene unfolds). Inattention is here a matter, once again, of frame of reference.[38] Focusing on the music, as I am doing here now, causes the narrative to recede in the background in something like the way looking at the skull in such a way as to correct the optical distortion causes the rest of the scene to become blot-like, to disappear. Perceptually the two experiences are mutually exclusive; yet they are both integral parts of one and the same encounter with the work.[39]

Insofar as Kurosawa's treatment of the music acknowledges—indeed, encourages—the possibility that we may overlook it because of our absorption in the action, and because of the character's filtering role, the music stands as a reminder of the need to understand the film as more than just an action thriller. Like

[36] Recognizing this, Lacan wrote that the skull is a "trap for the gaze": Lacan, *The Seminar of Jacques Lacan, Book XI: The Four Fundamental Concepts of Psychoanalysis*, ed. Jacques-Alain Miller, trans. Alan Sheridan (New York: Norton, 1998), 89.

[37] See Jurgis Baltrušaitis, *Anamorphic Art* (New York: Harry N. Abrams, 1977).

[38] Anamorphosis lends support to the idea that picture or, to be precise, certain pictures must depict *from* points of view. For a discussion of this point, see John V. Kulvicki, *On Images: Their Structure and Content* (Oxford: Clarendon Press, 2006), 188–89.

[39] Focusing on the music, moreover, also puts us in a position toward the scene that, in Walker's words, "far exceeds its characters" and as such "resonates with McGowan's reading of the skull": Walker, *Understanding Sound Tracks through Film Theory*, 280. It is unclear, however, whether Walker considers the appreciation of the music as a symbol compatible with absorption in the

the anamorphically rendered skull in Holbein's painting, it creates depth along an axis different from the one dictated by standard conditions of spectatorship. Like it, moreover, the music bespeaks the pride of a highly self-conscious artist who, asked to produce a genre piece and financed to deliver one, creates something that far transcends it. Schubert's music is a symptom of a certain biographical trajectory on Kurosawa's part, a pedigree, and musical predilections—it is a mark of authorship. To be sure, Schubert's "The Trout" is not nearly as unambiguous and terrifying a symbol as a skull. Indeed, it may well be a sign of redemption—the inverse of a *vanitas* in a Renaissance painting. And, of course, it is a sound—and a peculiar one at that—not an image. The limits of our attention entail that its symbolic power may not disclose itself at first. The difficulty of accessing the meanings of that symbol becomes a dynamic, signifying element above and beyond the symbol itself. The question that the scene presents us with, in other words, is not so much what the music may mean in the context of the Yokohama slums but rather what is at stake in the fact that the meaning of its presence can be recuperated only through analysis. It is the question implicitly posed by all buried effects across the arts. Though this is still too rarely acknowledged, their meaning is phatic, not static; it lies, first and foremost, in their very buriedness, in whether and how they are made available to our consciousness of spectators above and beyond what they denote or connote. By virtue of being a paradoxical presence that calls for an interpretation and yet is likely to be overlooked, the music inscribes the possibility of a second reading that not only augments but also supersedes one's first encounter with the film. Such a second reading is not simply a slower, or more meticulous, one. More than velocity is at stake here.[40] The anamorphic spot is a dynamic element that mediates not only the relationship between audience and character but also that between plot and allegory, hence between two mutually exclusive yet ultimately inseparable experiences. The latter is not something outside our prereflective, unmediated experience of the film; what exegesis brings out upon a second viewing becomes an essential element of that experience, not an afterthought or an explication of it, so that experience and reflection upon that experience are collapsed, and a second viewing comes to be seen not merely as a more informed one but the inevitable fulfillment of the first.

---

narrative. Maybe the two perspectives are not as incompatible in the film she considers, Nicholas Ray's *Bigger Than Life* (1956), as I think they are in *High and Low*.

[40] Taking up with the question of the velocity of the reading experience, Peter Mendelsund argues that "if books were roads, some would be made for driving quickly—details are scant, and what details there are appear drab—but the velocity and torque of the narrative is exhilarating. Some books, if seen as roads, would be made for walking—the trajectory of the road mattering far less than the vistas these roads might afford. The best book for me: I drive through it quickly but am forced to stop on occasion, to pull over and marvel. These books are books meant to be reread": Mendelsund, *What We See When We Read: A Phenomenology* (New York: Vintage Books, 2014), 96.

4

The Spectator as Situated Listener

In *Rear Window*, L. B. Jefferies, recovering from a leg bone injury, is confined to a wheelchair in an apartment looking on to a large courtyard surrounded by tall buildings. Bored, he observes the comings and goings of his neighbors as framed by their own rear windows. In the process, he begins to piece together a murder plot on what appears to be flimsy evidence. Fantasy and reality eventually merge as a grisly murder turns out to have occurred after all, at which point he himself becomes an actor in the drama he has conjured.

Taking cue from Jefferies's immobility, and the mutually implicating notions of frame and window, many a critic and casual observer soon picked up on the analogy between Jefferies's position and that of a film spectator.[1] This eventually led to a large body of literature extolling the virtues of *Rear Window* as an allegory of the spectator experience. But if Jefferies is a spectator, is he also a situated listener? To answer this, I would like to turn first to another, and unanswered, question, one that ought to have been raised—by the characters, the audience, and above all the critics—and yet has remained buried under the hubris of the hermeneutic riot surrounding Hitchcock's unsurpassed dark fantasy. The question is the following: why is L. B. Jefferies reluctant to proffer what may be the only direct evidence of the struggle between Thorwald and his wife, a struggle that, as he goes to considerable lengths to suggest, points to murder?

The piece of evidence I am referring to comes in the form of sound or, better, two sounds. The sounds are clearly discernible: first a scream, then a

---

[1] The tradition began with Jean Douchet's 1960 essay "Hitch and His Public," in *A Hitchcock Reader*, 2nd ed., ed. Marshall Deutelbaum and Leland Poague, trans. V. A. Conley (Chichester, UK: Wiley-Blackwell, 2009), 17–24. On the window as frame, and vice versa, see Thomas Elsaesser and Malte Hagener, *Film Theory: An Introduction Through the Senses*, 2nd ed. (New York: Routledge, 2015), 14. The act of looking out of a window has an iconographical tradition that predates the cinema. Friedrich's 1822 painting, *Woman at the Window* (1822), is a well-known example. Friedrich invests the act of looking out with a strong sense of agency. This is less frequent in nineteenth-century painting than one would expect, however. For a representative survey, see Sabine Rewald, *Rooms with a View: The Open Window in the 19th Century* (New York: Metropolitan Museum of Art, 2011).

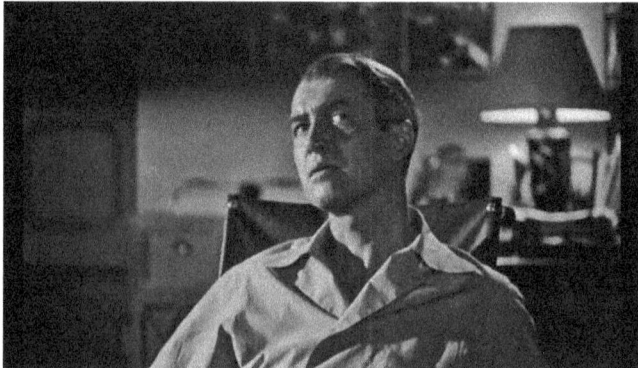

Figure 4.1 Rear Window.

glass shattering. Though their sources' exact location remains unidentified, they appear to originate from the same point in space. They follow one another in quick succession so as to be grouped together and betray a link, a causal chain: the glass breaks as a consequence of whatever provoked the scream in the first place. That Jefferies has heard them is beyond doubt. The expression on his face in the reaction shot, as Figure 4.1 shows, makes that clear enough.

The moment the sounds strike him is recorded by the quick acceleration and then jerky interruption of the otherwise smooth pan. The unorthodox camera movement and inconclusive ending of the shot enhance its anthropomorphic quality, lending it the character of a faithful transcription of eye movement (and causing the analyst to reassess just how anthropomorphic more orthodox point-of-view shots actually are). The manner in which the shot ends is jolting and amounts to a rupture, all the more so after the smooth crane and pan shots seen throughout the early stages of the film. The jolt marks a moment of unknowability, the point at which the courtyard begs to be examined by reason, conjecture, and speculation rather than plain observation.

The scream and the shattering glass are potentially significant as evidence of the murder, and many—though by no means all—critics have duly noted their occurrence.[2] Yet no one has attempted to bring them into line with the other leading motifs of the film. This is not surprising: rather like those hermeneutically

---

[2] "With no proof of the murder," writes Elisabeth Weis, "the only possible aural evidence is one scream, but its source remains unidentified": Weis, *The Silent Scream: Alfred Hitchcock's Sound Track* (Rutherford, NJ: Farleigh Dickinson University Press, 1982), 120. David Bordwell notes that they occur when Jefferies is "so eager for activity that he risks extrapolating too much": Bordwell, *Narration in the Fiction Film* (Madison, WI: University of Wisconsin Press, 1985), 41. Stefan Sharff points out the significance of the scream and the change in editing rhythm in the shots that follow, with fades indicating shorter-than-usual time deletions: Sharff, *The Art of Looking in Hitchcock's Rear Window* (New York: Limelight Editions, 1997), 43–45.

opaque passages in a Shakespeare play that puzzle and leave one uncomfortable, taking these sounds at face value calls for a readjustment of our frame of reference and a novel understanding of the whole. To tease out their special significance, I suggest that we return to my initial question and remind ourselves that Jefferies, upon piecing together his murder plot, fails to call up his memory of them. Given that he goes to extraordinary lengths to try to convince Stella, Doyle, and Lisa of the correctness of his intuition that a murder has been committed, and given that the corroborating evidence he puts forward is at best inconclusive, and at worst ludicrous, are we not justified in asking: why does he not mention the sounds? Only we never do. Just like Jefferies, we have forgotten them. Or have we?

The question hints at a theme central to the first part of this book: the channeling of the attention of the spectator via the character as vector. *Rear Window*, and Hitchcock's oeuvre more generally, is a paragon of the scope enjoyed by a film director in affording a full range of perceptions and emotions along preordained routes. The grip a Hitchcock film holds on the spectator's attention is famously summarized in the director's quip that

> the audience is like a giant organ that you and I are playing. At one moment we play this note on them and get this reaction, and then we play that chord and they react that way. And someday we won't even have to make a movie—they'll be electrodes implanted in their brains, and we'll just press different buttons and they'll go "ooooh" and "aaaah" and we'll frighten them. . . . Won't that be wonderful?[3]

Of this scenario of willful subjugation to the whims of the master-entertainer for the sake of an emotional roller coaster, *Rear Window* is the subtlest, and most virtuosic, consummation. In this film, I wish to argue, Hitchcock exercises control of the most indirect and insidious kind. He plants sonic evidence to precipitate a plot, only to withdraw it immediately thereafter, covering up his own traces as it were by having the protagonist throw himself into the investigation mind and body while conveniently forgetting what had led him to it in the first place. Judging from the enduring critical neglect of the sounds Jefferies hears on that fateful night, Hitchcock's gamble worked. This was not the only gamble he was to accept for this film, however. He employed a musical score consisting entirely of preexisting, rearranged, or newly composed source music (a classic example of "source score," in other words). This gave him an unprecedented degree of

---

[3] Cited in Donald Spoto, *The Dark Side of Genius: The Life of Alfred Hitchcock* (New York: Ballantine Books, 1983), 440. Hitchcock reportedly spoke these words while talking to the screenwriter of *North by Northwest* (1959), Ernest Lehmann.

control over what the music *sounded* like (with the significant exception, as we shall see, of "Lisa"). In all likelihood boosted by such knowledge, he and his collaborators graced the film with generous doses of source music (so much so, in fact, that the courtyard may seem like a prescient version of today's music-filled environments).[4] Such an arrangement would cost Hitchcock what was perhaps dearest to his mission—and very identity—as an artist: complete control over the audience's attention. Winning the attention of an audience to the film is one thing; drawing it to certain aspects of the finished product is quite another, rather like a prize sanctioning the dominance of whomever controls the work of a Hollywood studio.[5] We can think of a production team as working in harmony toward the completion of the best possible product while simultaneously allowing that actors, directors, writers, cinematographers, and musicians vie for attention to their own craft in one way or another (at times even undercutting the attainment of their shared goal). When the occasion arose, Hitchcock continued to exercise influence on the reception of the films he directed well after they were released (via spoken or written statements, for instance). Both Bill Krohn and David Schroeder have duly noted Hitchcock's unwillingness to spell out the credit he owed to screenwriter John Michael Hayes for the creation of the characters. In response to Truffaut's prompting that with *Rear Window* he was working with his "very best screenplay," Hitchcock laconically replied that Hayes was "a radio writer and he wrote the dialogue."[6] Terse as the statement is, however, it does also point to the radio as an ineliminable source of inspiration not only for how the dialogue was fashioned but also for the conception of the film as a whole—a fact borne out by the nearly constant presence of off-screen sound as a means to project a sense of the space of the courtyard.

---

[4] On the use of music in public spaces, such as malls and cafes, and the complex interactions that result from the more or less transient relationships dwellers entertain with it, see Jonathan Sterne, "Sounds Like the Mall of America: Programmed Music and the Architectonics of Commercial Space," *Ethnomusicology* 41, no. 1 (1997): 22–50; and Anahid Kassabian, *Ubiquitous Listening: Affect, Attention, and Distributed Subjectivity* (Berkeley: University of California Press, 2013). Writing about sound as artistic practice, Douglas Kahn places the beginning of a "revolution" driven by audiophonic technologies and defined by "ubiquitous recording" in the mid-1920s, some thirty years before Hitchcock's film: Kahn, *Noise/Water/Meat: A History of Sound in the Arts* (Cambridge, MA: MIT Press, 1999), 123–56.

[5] On the production process of the film, and especially the use of the storyboard "as the primary means by which Hitchcock articulated and maintained his authorial voice," see Scott Curtis, "The Making of *Rear Window*," in *Alfred Hitchcock's Rear Window*, ed. John Belton (Cambridge: Cambridge University Press, 2000), 27. Meticulous and insightful as Curtis's reconstruction is, it elides consideration of sound and music altogether.

[6] François Truffaut, *Hitchcock*, rev. ed. (New York: Simon and Schuster, 1984), 222; David P. Schroeder, *Hitchcock's Ear: Music and the Director's Art* (New York: Continuum, 2012), 130. Bill Krohn, for whom the visual aspect of the film takes clear precedence, also notes how John M. Hayes may have exaggerated his own role: Krohn, *Hitchcock at Work* (London: Phaidon, 2000), 135.

Absolute Transparency
and the Disavowal of Sound

Soon after hearing the scream, Jefferies falls asleep. The sounds and our memory of them swiftly dissipate in the hush of another quiet night in the courtyard. What happens to this memory? A number of alternatives present themselves. In a striking yet, frankly, improbable reversal of what is now received wisdom among psychologists, sleep would seem to erase rather than cement Jefferies's memory of them. Conversely, sleep may be said to have drawn those sounds into its own orbit in such a way that they are reconstituted as moments of a dream, and therefore unimportant to the waking ego. As such, the sounds would operate as a subconscious force and, rather like a childhood trauma, become the guiding factor in his subsequent behavior. This reading, however convenient, would fail to explain what is so disturbing about the sounds for their occurrence to be denied, and their memory suppressed. After all, Jefferies goes about parading the gruesomeness of the murder from the very start. A navigated photo-reporter, he is not the squeamish type. My own interpretation dispenses with the cumbersome topography of psychoanalysis. The scream and the sound of the shattering glass bring about a change in disposition or, to be precise, a *bias*. As such, they are not forgotten; it is at Jefferies's behavior, not his words, that we must look for evidence that he remembers them. Unlike active retelling, which often reduces past events into anecdotes, Jefferies's memory of the sounds is embodied in his growing conviction that a murder has occurred, and the particular course of action he takes as a result.[7] His conviction will be reinforced when another, and similar, off-screen scream is heard, that of a woman who discovers that her dog is dead. The episode, it will be recalled, helps persuade us that Jefferies is onto something. While many people come out and show their sympathy, Thorwald, the presumed killer, remains conspicuously inside his apartment.[8]

---

[7] On the difference between "declarative" and "representational" memory and the relevance of this concept to the film experience, see Murray Smith, "Consciousness," in *The Routledge Companion to Film and Philosophy*, ed. Paisley Livingston and Carl Plantinga (London and New York: Routledge, 2008), 43. See also Daniel Barratt, "'Twist Blindness': The Role of Primacy, Priming, Schemas, and Reconstructive Memory in a First-Time Viewing of *The Sixth Sense*," in *Puzzle Films: Complex Storytelling in Contemporary Cinema*, ed. Warren Buckland (London: Blackwell Publishing, 2009), 62–86.

[8] John Belton notes not only the significance of this episode but also the sonic resemblance of the scream to the one accompanied by the shattering glass: Belton, "Introduction: Spectacle and Narrative," in *Alfred Hitchcock's Rear Window*, ed. John Belton (Cambridge: Cambridge University Press, 2000), 14. In an earlier essay, Belton refers to how Jefferies's "position in space forces him to see something that has been, as it were, anamorphically encoded into a larger representation, like the death's head in Hans Holbein's *The Ambassadors*": Belton, "The Space of *Rear Window*," in *Hitchcock's Rereleased Films: from Rope to Vertigo*, ed. Walter Raubicheck and Walter Srebnick (Detroit, MI: Wayne State University, 1991), 84. Translated in terms that resonate with my focus on sound,

Insofar as Jefferies's protestations that a murder has occurred seem acceptable or even justifiable, the spectator too engages in behavior that shows that he or she remembers what Jefferies has heard that fateful night. It is for the spectator, too, that those sounds provide a background against which the visual clues acquire an additional dimension that makes them stand out from the other goings on of the courtyard. That such a spectator fails to notice Jefferies's own failure to mention what he's heard in mounting his case is not inconsistent with this. The murder narrative is tightly focalized through Jefferies. So his inability to bring up the sounds naturally affects our own attitude toward them, too. Moreover, by the time the visual clues and speculations begin to add up into a believable plot, that memory will become the distant catalyst of a process that has rendered their active recall—what psychologists call declarative memory—increasingly difficult. The more successful the sounds are in creating a bias that heightens the significance of what is seen subsequently, the less likely it is we will remember their role as catalyst, for the visual clues will supersede them: absorbed by ever novel pieces of evidence, Jefferies—and the audience—will simply lack the attention and the time to revisit the moment that has propelled the plot in the first place.[9]

That the scream and the shattering glass did not invite scrutiny before the era of playback technology seems fair enough; indeed, the way in which they function in *Rear Window* is a marvelous instance of Hitchcock's ability to control the audience's attention through one sitting of a film. But what about the advent of tape, let alone digital technology? What about all those who have seen the film repeatedly, the countless critics and scholars who have subjected it to detailed analysis? Let me reformulate, with a twist, then, the question with which I opened this chapter: what is at stake in the widespread amnesia of Jefferies's astonishing omission?

Leaving aside the oft-repeated mantra about the primacy of vision, this state of affairs can be attributed first to Hitchcock's own statements on the film and, second, to a long critical tradition associating *Rear Window* with voyeurism. Of the film Hitchcock said, among other things, that it "has as its basic structure the purely visual."[10] In the following, having first mistaken Pudovkin for Kuleshov, Hitchcock extols the power of montage in giving an expression to an actor's face:

Belton may be paraphrased as saying that planting sonic evidence is a way of both alerting Jeffries to the presence of something while simultaneously *concealing* it from the eye. I treated the issue of anamorphic encoding in the previous chapter.

[9] Note that unlike, for example, the "insect-like" noise recorded by the sound man at the beginning of De Palma's *Blow Out* (1981), what Jefferies hears is not indeterminate. We can infer at least *some* of the sounds' causes, and we are certainly aware of their sources. It is the complex network of motives underpinning their emergence that we initially ignore. For an analysis of the role of the recorded sounds in *Blow Out*, and the film's play on our memory, see Chion, *Film, A Sound Art*, trans. Claudia Gorbman (New York: Columbia University Press, 2009), 290.

[10] Alfred Hitchcock, *"Rear Window,"* Take One 2, no. 2 (1968): 18. On the bias for the "pure film" expressing itself "visually," see also Weis, *The Silent Scream*, 13–14.

For example, if Mr. Stewart is looking out into this courtyard and—let's say—he sees a woman with a child in her arms. Well, the first cut is Mr. Stewart, then what he sees and then his reaction. We'll see him smile. Now if you took away the center piece of film and substituted—we'll say—a shot of the girl Miss Torso in a bikini, instead of being a benevolent gentleman he's now a dirty old man. . . . [I]t's the piecing together of the montage which makes what I call a pure film.[11]

Insofar as it goes, Hitchcock's statement is unexceptionable. The film does link "pieces of film," in the director's matter-of-fact parlance, into meaningful syntactical units of three or more shots. This not only creates the illusion of spatial contiguity and temporal continuity—the bread and butter of montage, so to speak—but also boosts the actor's expressiveness (the famous Kuleshov effect). But when he says that "the story is told only in visual terms," Hitchcock is, wittingly or not, leaving out half of the truth. The aspects of cinematic technique he mentions are in *Rear Window* subsumed under a sustained effort at representing the workings of involuntary attention precipitated by sound.[12] *Rear Window*, put another way, is as much Münsterberg as it is Kuleshov; its across-the-courtyard close-ups are almost a textbook demonstration of the German psychologist's dictum that "the close-up has objectified in our world of perception the mental act of attention."[13]

The close-up, in Münsterberg's unmistakably Hegelian wording, "objectifies" the work of attention. It does so irrespective of whether it is justified by the situation of a character or not (by the same token, the flashback objectifies memory irrespective of whether it is occasioned by the presence of a character remembering or not).[14] In a close-up that is also a point-of-view shot, attention is both objectified in the general sense expounded earlier and *exemplified* in the form of a specific, if fictional, manifestation: namely, as someone's perception. Filmmakers translate the seizing upon of an object or person on the part of a character by increasing, sometimes implausibly, its size in the visual field. The enhanced and not infrequently enlarged image of that which captivates the attention is symptomatic of a heightened perception resulting from contemplation, desire, or, as is most often the case in action cinema, curiosity and fear. So,

---

[11] Hitchcock, "*Rear Window*," 18.

[12] John Belton, too, questions the veracity of the statement, albeit in a different sense. For him, *Rear Window* is "one of Hitchcock's most 'theatrical' films." Ibid., 77.

[13] Hugo Münsterberg, "The Photoplay: A Psychological Study," in *Hugo Münsterberg on Film: The Photoplay: A Psychological Study and Other Writings*, ed. A. Langdale (New York: Routledge, 2002), 87.

[14] For a fascinating history of the point-of-view shot and the ways in which it both emerged and differentiated itself from the close-up, see Elena Dagrada, *Between the Eye and the World: The Emergence of the Point-of-View Shot* (Brussels: Peter Lang, 2015).

in *Rear Window*, when L. B. Jefferies looks intrigued at the Thorwalds arguing across the courtyard, Miss Torso lying on her bed, or Ms. Lonelyhearts preparing for a date, the image of their window looks much larger than it would from his literal point of view.[15] In *North by Northwest*, when Roger Thornhill is frantically looking for Eve Kendall, following the failed attempt on his life by a cropduster, the image of the elevator floor display is disproportionately big relative to his distance from it. Yet we accept it as not only a measure of where Eve's room is, which is what Thornhill is desperate to find out, but also an expression of his intense interest in it as a piece of information on which his very life might depend. We have come to accept these technically inaccurate representations as working substitutes for the metaphorical "bigness" of what we are attending to because of habituation to conventions and the sensible acknowledgment of the need, on the filmmaker's part, to deliver narratively crucial information in a clear, effective, and at times emphatic manner. But the practice reflects ecological conditions, too, as anyone who has ever taken photographs will know. Attention to a detail of a landscape, for instance, produces the illusion that it is larger than it is in reality. That is why, upon looking at a photograph of the scene containing it, one is often surprised at how small the detail actually is in the context of a newly reconfigured visual field (even when, upon using a normal lens, the result approximates the scope of our own gaze). The photograph made by a device such as a camera, put another way, corrects the impression produced by our attention in something like the way a microphone recording reveals to us the extent to which we filter the sonic reality around us by processing sounds according to hierarchies dictated by our interests and inclinations.

The central role of the logic of involuntary attention in shaping both the narrative and stylistic trajectories of *Rear Window* is made clear right after the titles. As the title theme assumes the guise of a radio broadcast, the suggestion is made of its source occupying a specific point in space. The music now reverberates across a distinctly configured space (that of an enclosed courtyard; Figures 4.2 and 4.3).[16] The camera approaches the windowsill; then, there is a cut to the image of a cat running up the stairs below. This is not arbitrary: both the cut to and the content of the new shot are motivated by a novel element that captivates the attention: the

---

[15] Hitchcock used different lenses—50, 75, and 100 mm, respectively—to represent "naked eye" views from Jefferies's vantage point. Krohn suggests that the changing of lenses may have initially been motivated as a way of creating alternate takes. Since Hitchcock used both takes of the same view, we must infer he meant, in Krohn's words, to "br[ing] the action closer": Krohn, *Hitchcock at Work*, 146.

[16] Reverberation is key to the construction of the courtyard as a sonic space. On the use of echo and reverb in popular music and the deployment of reverberation in Hollywood, see Peter Doyle, *Echo and Reverb: Fabricating Space in Popular Music Recording, 1900–1960* (Middletown, CT: Wesleyan University Press, 2005).

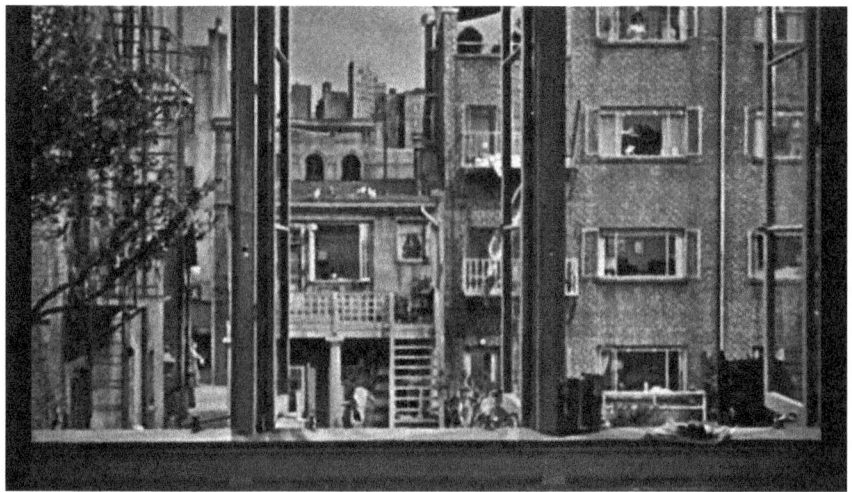

Figure 4.2 Rear Window.

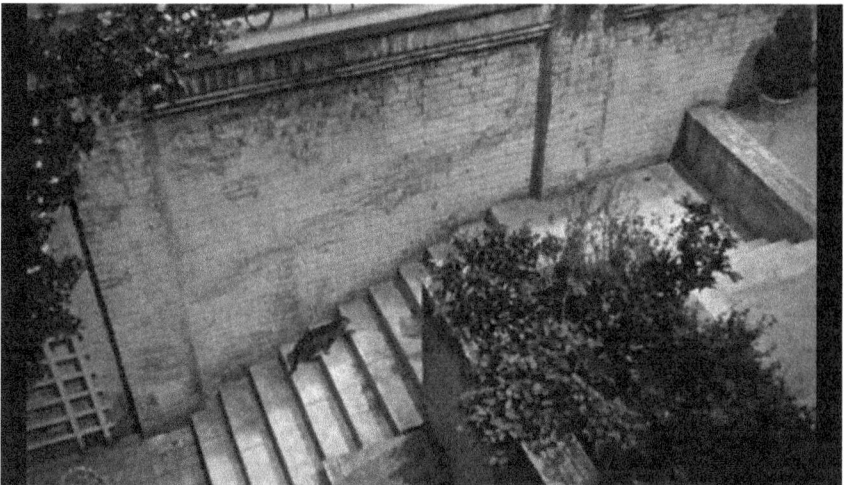

Figure 4.3 Rear Window.

presence of a moving cat (our brains being hard-wired to detect movement). Above and beyond the desire to give a meaning to the cut, the detail of the cat is important because it shows right at the beginning of the film that the gaze is not a self-motivating force, directed gratuitously at whatever falls in its range; rather, the gaze, albeit here belonging to no one in particular, is sustained by a logic that originates outside it, and this logic is the logic of involuntary attention.

In an elaborate variant of a classic establishing shot, the crane-mounted camera then goes on to introduce the viewer to the locale and its inhabitants. Though sufficiently suggestive of the arc a human head would trace in

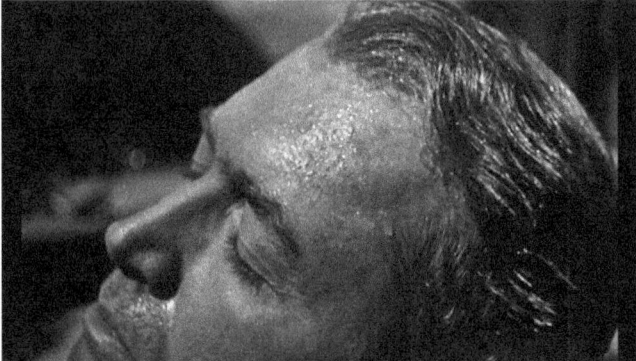

Figure 4.4 Rear Window.

scanning the yard, the pan turns out not to have been a point-of-view shot. This is emphasized by the image of the sleeping Jefferies (there is a hint, in other words, of an ambiguity, but one that can only be appreciated in retrospect; Figure 4.4). The anthropomorphic nature of this preamble cannot so easily be erased, however. Why do we learn about the courtyard as if seen and heard through his perceptual apparatus when he is in fact asleep? The film acknowledges a disparity between Jefferies and the viewer in terms of their respective knowledge of the locale. There is a past that predates the beginning of the film; accordingly, we are allowed to "catch up," as it were, with Jefferies, till the point at which character and audience are sufficiently aligned with one another. But this process of gradual alignment, as this and the following shots make clear, takes place in a manner that is consistent with the way in which Jefferies himself has experienced the courtyard: from afar and intermittently, unable to cast more than a passing glance onto the apartments across and the people living therein.[17]

As the camera begins its second tour of the courtyard, the leisurely scanning of a place signified by the continuous pan gives way to a more reactive, but equally instructive, mode of exploration, one that takes the form of sudden cuts to and from different portions of the space opening up before the window. To be sure, as was the case with the first long unedited shot, the primary goal of this

---

[17] Michel Chion, taking literal opticality as a criterion, interprets the beginning of the film as an "enlargement" of what he calls "the 'rule' of the *point of view of James Stewart*": Chion, "Alfred Hitchcock's *Rear Window*: The Fourth Side," in *Alfred Hitchcock's Rear Window*, ed. John Belton (Cambridge: Cambridge University Press, 2000), 111. In the same essay, Chion makes much out the voice of a female singer, which he locates somewhere in the "fourth wall": Chion, "Alfred Hitchcock's *Rear Window*," 114. While I concur that the representation of the fourth wall remains something of a taboo in *Rear Window*, I cannot see that much turns on the voice per se, nor the fact that its source remains hidden from view.

second run around the courtyard is to introduce new important elements to the viewers; but equally important is the logic that underpins its ebbs, flows, and jolts, and the stylistic figures that go with it. The cut to the image of the couple sleeping on the fire escape exemplifies this. It follows by a split second the off-screen sound of the alarm clock that awakens them; in fact, it is the sound that motivates the cut.[18] Involuntary attention is represented to the point of absolute transparency—its transparency renders it invisible, and we do not recognize the juxtaposition of the two shots, and the particular manner in which it is negotiated, as a representation of attention.

To be sure, attention is here disembodied. Yet the camera is anticipating the manner in which Jefferies will behave in the remainder of the film, as if proceeding to "seat itself" on to Jefferies's head. Throughout the first part of the film, at a point when he is either bored or idle, it is always either sound or music that titillates Jefferies's curiosity, thus initiating a perceptual cycle in which both hearing and seeing partake of one and the same process.[19] Typically, the camera will show something or someone—in one case the pianist's studio—dwell on it till after Jefferies's curiosity is exhausted only to be suddenly redirected by a new incident heralded, just as typically, by an off-screen sound or music. When Jefferies finds himself a "project" that rescues him from the boredom of his dependence on the wheelchair, the deliberate search for visual clues becomes paramount. Involuntary attention becomes voluntary, and on this difference hinges our interpretation of his motives.[20] And yet Jefferies's behavior in this new stage of the film, and the insistence on vision that is its most obvious manifestation, is not only consistent with the rules of the perceptual cycle I have

---

[18] The procedure has a distant progeny in what Barry Salt calls the "shock cut, which is a cut to a different scene accompanied by a sharp discontinuity in the accompanying sound—say from near silence to loud music." Salt argues it was "invented" by Hitchcock in *Blackmail*: Salt, *Film Style and Technology: History and Analysis*, 2nd expanded ed. (London: Starword, 1992), 216.

[19] Echoing Tania Modleski, Susan White writes that Jefferies "more closely resembles the invalid Mrs. Thorward than her murderous husband," going on to conclude: "his features register fear, amusement, irony, and desire—all in *reaction* to what he is seeing": White, *A Companion to Alfred Hitchcock*, ed. Thomas Leitch and Leland A. Poague (Chichester, UK: Wiley-Blackwell, 2011), 189. Such an account is accurate, but, as I hope to have indicated, it is incomplete without factoring in the role of sound.

[20] Tellingly, when at the end of the film Thorwald asks him, "What do you want from me?" Jefferies cannot provide an answer. This inability to justify why he is playing cop has naturally inspired a bevy of allegorizations. However we interpret Jefferies's motives, or lack thereof, the important point is that having been spurred onto the plot accidentally, as I claim, he then consciously decides to pursue it till its dangerous end. In this connection, one should remember with Armond White that "Jefferies and his police detective pal, Doyle, are both war vets whose resignation makes them suspicious and wary citizens": White, "Eternal Vigilance in *Rear Window*," in *Alfred Hitchcock's Rear Window*, ed. John Belton (Cambridge: Cambridge University Press, 2000), 125. Much of the US male audience of the film would have had memories of the wartime period, if not the war itself.

sketched but also originates with the unknown woman's scream and the sound of shattering glass.

The two sounds cut across the off-/on-screen distinction, for their sources hide deep in the dark recesses of the apartment complex. Jefferies's powers of localization through hearing alone are insufficient to anchor them with any degree of confidence. So he enrolls vision: a fine demonstration of the extent to which upon encountering a new sound vision does not merely confirm or recapitulate but rather completes what one has already heard. The movement of Jefferies's gaze quickly accelerates, as if gesturing toward a new target. We see a small portion of the yard in a blur—rather like a smear: a shot unique not only to this film but also, to my knowledge, to the whole of Hitchcock's oeuvre. Not knowing where to land, his eyes simply stop searching.[21] This is conveyed by having the camera stop, its focus hanging in midair. When the cut arrives, this is not to the image indicating the source of the sound but rather to a reaction shot of Jefferies. His face signals the temporary deactivation of the gaze; as the courtyard vaporizes before his eyes, he begins to ponder the nature and meaning of that sound.[22] It is a pivotal violation of the pattern established early on in the film. The norm, as we have seen, is that an off-screen sound calls attention to itself by either the dint of its volume or the fact that it is novel, unknown, or intriguing. We then see Jefferies look out at where it comes from. In turn, this is followed by a shot of the place where the source of the sound is presumably located, and with it the elucidation of the fact or event that has produced it. The cycle comes to an end with a reaction shot showing Jefferies's response, be it engaged, bemused, titillated, or irritated—sometimes all of the above, and in that order. After the glass shattering, the cycle is not completed. The exact location and identity of the sources of the sounds remain unknown. What is missing, put another way and to use Hitchcock's terminology, is that "center piece of film," the shot of what Jefferies is looking at. It is my contention that the remainder of the film is a fleshing out—a complete narrative told in dialogue, images, music, and sound effects—of what that "center piece of film" could have been. When Hitchcock talks about *Rear Window* being "purely visual" and expresses his satisfaction at the ability of montage to create the illusion of facial expression, he is neglecting to mention the first and refers primarily to the last of what I see as a four-stage process.

---

[21] Curiously, Sharff refrains from treating this pan as a point-of-view shot, whether in his analysis or shot-by-shot-inventory: Sharff, *The Art of Looking in Hitchcock's Rear Window*, 43 and 124, respectively.

[22] This is the point at which the original *Rear Window* comes closest to functioning like its quasi-remake, *Disturbia*, made in the digital surround era. Of the latter, Mark Kerins writes that it "substitutes a full three-dimensional geography for *Rear Window*'s unidirectional one and eliminates the boundary between voyeur and object": Kerins, *Beyond Dolby (Stereo): Cinema in the Digital Sound Age* (Bloomington: Indiana University Press, 2011), 224.

The role of Jefferies's reaction shot is not merely to confirm that we were indeed looking through Jefferies's own eyes. The point is also to show him pondering the meaning of what he has just heard. Staring into nothing, absorbed in thought, will not be Jefferies's preferred modus operandi. As he takes it upon himself to solve what he believes to be a murder case, he will instead enroll vision as a professional photographer whenever he can, coming to depend on visual clues and the technology to capture them (to the point of parody). But the relentless hunting for and gathering of visual evidence that take up the remaining part of the film is at heart a response—rather like an elaborately rehearsed counter shot—to the sounds he has accidentally just heard. The narrative may insist on vision and its various modes of deployment, but it is propelled by the attempt to answer a question that, as suggested by Rick Altman, underpins the perception of film sound tout court: where are those sounds coming from? The specific presentation this question receives in *Rear Window* brings out the often unrecognized complexity of what we normally refer to as a sound's "source": for it isn't so much the material source, or sources, that Jefferies needs to identify as much as a whole train of events and motives leading to their occurrence. By the same token, a piece of film showing a certain action occurring in a certain place is never just an image: it is the representation of an event that is, in turn, the outcome of a premise or the latest in a series of incidents linked by a complex thread of motivating factors and circumstances. As such, every shot depicting an action contains within itself a potentially endless chain of cause-and-effect relationships, as well as an infinite number of motifs that may or not be transparent to those who see it. Think about *Sunset Boulevard* and how the initial shot— that of a man floating on a pool, captured from under water—requires an entire film's worth of background information and digressions to be deciphered. Just as vision completes audition, so knowledge creates the conditions for a new perceptual cycle to take place, one in which we look again at the same image and see more, or differently.

Claiming a bigger role for sound in *Rear Window* is not merely a matter of redressing the balance between the moving image and the other elements of filmmaking, let alone one of corroborating tired narratives of voyeurism, repressed desire, and sadistic impulses. Rather, it is a question of reminding ourselves of the porous boundaries that exist between vision and hearing, the constant working out of one in terms of the other, and how prior knowledge underpins, and new knowledge results from, their deployment. It is in this respect instructive to consider the role that criticism and various other forms of commentaries have had on the reception of the film. Like a caption placed under a picture, a critical bias, whatever its source and merits, directs attention to certain aspects at the expense of others. Since the majority consensus in the literature is that *Rear Window* is an allegory of the gaze at its most voyeuristic and sexually disturbed, we are now in the position, I think, to answer the following question: "what is at stake in the critics' widespread amnesia of Jefferies's astonishing omission?" The scream and the shattering glass create a justifiable—sensible, even—bias, a bias, put another way, grounded in psychology and not psychiatry. Their significance must be denied because it is felt to threaten the view of the film as an allegory of the cinematic gaze in its voyeuristic and sadistic manifestations, a view hinted at by Hitchcock himself and repeated almost ad nauseam in most if not all critical interventions on the film.[23]

Now, I do not wish to deny that for Jefferies—and the audience—the murder plot may be not merely a plausible but a desirable development. Nor do I wish to deny that the incidents of the film could be interpreted as fantasy or delusion—a view supported by the near-omnipresent music, which gives a whiff of the fictional, and indeed the cinematic, to the space of the courtyard. Yet before giving in to the allegorizing impulse, we must put our own backyard in order, so to speak. To this end, it is crucial to take notice of the fine balance Hitchcock and his collaborators have attained in their representation of Jefferies's motives; this is, significantly, already detectable in the short story on which the film is based. Jefferies's position is extreme: he is almost immobile, confined to an excruciatingly repetitive routine.[24] Is he a pervert or is he simply bored? Is he voyeuristic or rather just nosy? Is he sublimating sadistically his hatred for Lisa or is he simply following through on what he has heard and seen? The antinomies can continue almost ad infinitum.[25] For every piece of damning evidence that Jefferies is a voyeur or a sadist, there is a mitigating factor—the scream and the sound of shattering glass being the biggest mitigating factors of them all and hence ones to be set aside, not without having awkwardly or, worse, begrudgingly noted their presence. But this is self-defeating. Allegory arises out of a play of the literal and the figurative, but when the allegorical supplants the literal, interpretation is stifled.[26]

---

[23] According to Robin Wood, for example, "What happens in the Thorwald apartment represents in an extreme and hideous form, the fulfillment of Jefferies's desire to be rid of Lisa": Wood, *Hitchcock's Films Revisited* (New York: Columbia University Press, 1989), 104. Slavoj Žižek, for his part, writes that what Jefferies "sees through the window are precisely *fantasy figurations of what could happen to him and Grace Kelly* [sic]": Žižek, "The Hitchcockian Blot," in *Looking Awry: An Introduction to Jacques Lacan through Popular Culture* (Cambridge: MIT Press, 1991), 92.

[24] "For a character to be physically immobile for the duration of a film is rare in commercial cinema. Yet that is precisely the fate of the seated spectator watching him on the screen. . . . [J]ust as viewers are immobile in watching, the technology of film usually does the opposite for the action viewed. It speeds up mobility": John Orr, *Hitchcock and Twentieth-Century Cinema* (London: Wallflower, 2005), 28.

[25] On this aspect of the film, see also John Fawell, *Hitchcock's Rear Window: The Well-Made Film* (Carbondale: Southern Illinois University Press, 2001), 7.

[26] In terms proposed by literary critic Davide Stimilli, my reading is an example of "criticism as 'transliteration' (which preserves the letter) rather than translation (which obliterates it)": From the book jacket of Davide Stimilli, *The Face of Immortality: Physiognomy and Criticism* (Albany: State University of New York Press, 2005).

Music at the Fringes

If, as I argue, the genius of *Rear Window* lies in the ineradicable ambiguity of Jefferies's motives, to attribute a specific and unambiguous motif to his behavior is to reveal one's own preoccupations, biases, or interests. Jefferies is both more and less than a vector; his perception is both more and less than the obligatory route through and with which we explore the courtyard and its dwellers. A striking precedent to some of David Lynch's characters, Jeffries has no agenda or personality, and as such he is a mirror, an empty cipher, returning the viewer whatever image he or she wants to see in him.[27]

Having said this, I must reveal my own interests and set of preconceptions. As may have been inferred already, I view Jefferies's trajectory as a textbook case in the psychology of attention, a survey of different modes of listening, and, not least, an exquisite demonstration of the roots of film music in the aesthetics of the everyday. It has been often remarked that Jefferies displays none of the sensitivity to music that Lisa does. While undoubtedly true, these remarks are, if anything, understatements. In Jefferies's world, music is the mere index of an event, one to be subsequently probed and understood in terms that often bear little or no relation to music's status as art, craft, or even mere pastime. It is as an index that, time and again, music guides his gaze across the courtyard: crucial in determining the course of his drifting and daydreaming but scarcely important, if at all, as an object of attention in and of itself.[28] The perceptual cycle I have outlined earlier, whereby an off-screen sound activates the gaze, applies to music, too (Figures 4.5 and 4.6). When the voice of Bing Crosby singing Burke-Van Heusen's "To see you is to love you" begins to sift through the blinds of Ms.

---

[27] "Characters are ciphers. And narratives are made richer by omission," writes art director Peter Mendelsund of novelistic characters in *What We See When We Read* (New York: Vintage Books, 2014), 31. The citation is given in incomplete form here for it is part of a drawing, taking up a full page, of a featureless, generically handsome male head (a head, incidentally, not unlike that of James Stewart ca. 1954). Mendelsund naturally is referring here to the physical features of a character of a novel, which in the case of a film character are spelled out instead.

[28] Contrast Jefferies's utilitarian understanding of the sounds of the courtyard, including music, to John Fawell's observation that the success of the soundtrack resides in "Hitchcock's 'musique concret' [sic], his careful attention (in the tradition of Jacques Tati and Robert Bresson) to the rhythm and arrangement of natural sounds": Fawell, *Hitchcock's Rear Window*, 5. As preached and practiced by its founding father, Pierre Schaeffer, *musique concrète* represents the most radical, if ultimately unsuccessful attempt to divorce sound from the network of causes that underpin it (what he derogatorily referred to as the "anecdotal" or "dramatic" aspect of sound). If this is at odds with the overtly referential nature of the soundtrack of *Rear Window*, this is not to say that the "rhythms" and "arrangements" heard by Fawell are wholly a figment of the critic's imagination. The acousmatic dimension of those sounds can be rethought of as one of their aspects (put otherwise, a function of the selective attention).

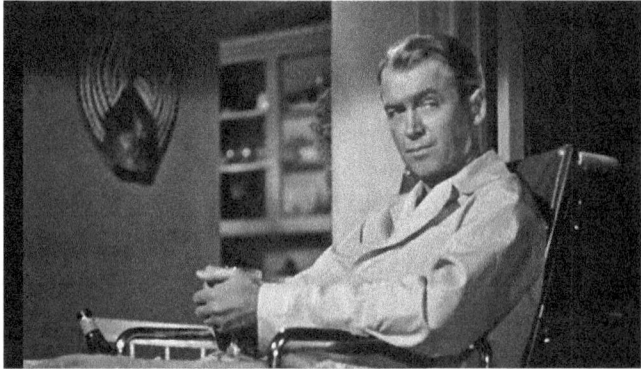

Figure 4.5 Rear Window.

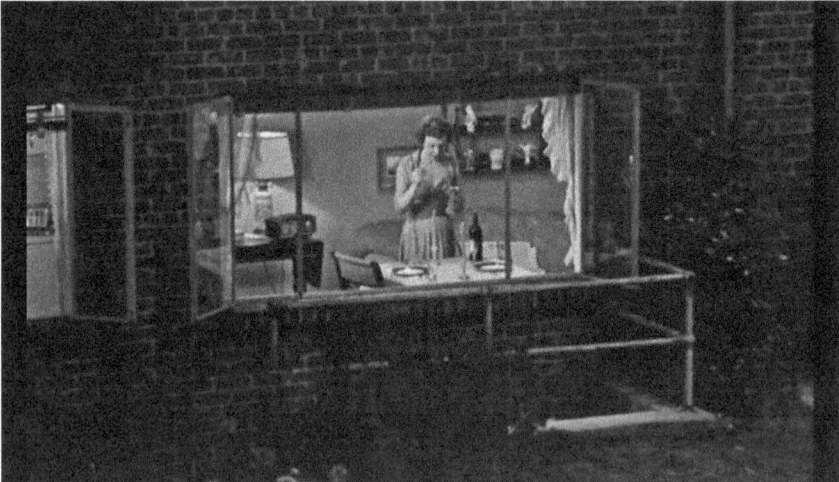

Figure 4.6 Rear Window.

Lonelyhearts's apartment, the volume and reverb tell him the music comes from across the courtyard. He turns to the building opposite his and scans it vertically, guided by his instinct—rather like feeling one's way through a dark room by tentatively touching the outer edges of the furniture or caressing its walls—till his eyes land on her apartment.[29] What he sees helps him anchor the sound: the plausibility of the music issuing from an apartment where someone is setting up

[29] The final realization of this transition matches exactly the description found in the extended memo sent to Richard Mealand, director of Paramount British Productions and written long after post-production had ended by Elinore Dolnick of the Music Department of Paramount Pictures ("Description of Manner in Which Music Was Used," July 6, 1954, *Franz Waxman Papers*, Special Collection Research Center, Syracuse University Libraries, Box OS 90, p. 2).

the table for dinner is as important as the information gauged through the sense of hearing alone.

So a novel stream of sound signals the onset of a new train of events. Appearing unannounced, it poses a question as to its provenance—and its meaning. Its grip on Jefferies's attention, however, ceases as soon as he localizes its source and understands its function. The song then continues its course, nearly undetected, till its rather unglamorous exit. Once Jefferies ascertains the nature and implication of what he has just witnessed, the music is relegated to the status of background noise. As such, to be sure, it continues to be heard and function as an index; it points, to be precise, to the continuation of the event whose appearance pulled Jefferies's attention back into the courtyard to begin with. However, the continuation of something is for the attention not quite tantamount to a new stimulus—and let me stress that what continues, what stays the same, is the very fact of music's happening, its sounding out. Habituation has cleared the floor for something novel to titillate his curiosity (and assuage his boredom). The music may be a recording Ms. Lonelyhearts is herself playing, and it is embedded in a complex—and, to Jefferies, interesting—course of action.[30]

Rather than drawing it to itself, in *Rear Window* music redirects the attention like a traffic comptroller or a warning system of sorts. Jefferies uses it as an oblique guide to parsing the dynamic field of action that is the courtyard. Yet unlike many sounds, music also tends to linger. Indeed, it is intuitive to think of music as a sustained stream of sounds coalescing into one continuous event unfolding over a period of time (a song, or the movement of a piece, for example). That is why forging relationships between different sound events so as to sustain the illusion of continuity and integrity is an important dimension of musical performance. Imagine, for argument's sake, a situation in which each note or motif of a piece were heard as a discrete event, say, in terms of the actions of the performers: this would result in a hopelessly fragmentary experience. Our attention glued to each stage of the production process of the music, we would be utterly unable to detect patterns let alone grasp a design. Jefferies, for his part, effortlessly ignores the unfolding of the music as an organized stream of sounds; he singles out just the beginning for perceptual intake. This is possible, it seems to me, because it is to the appearance of the music, not its unfolding, that he pays attention. The appearance, not the music, is what for Jefferies constitutes the perceptual object, one that is singular and self-contained at that, and expires within

---

[30] The source of the music remains unidentified, nor is it specified in the memo cited earlier, where it is dubbed, as per the shorthand characteristic of studio documents, "voc & inst bkg" (that is, vocal and instrumental background: "Description of the Manner in Which Music Was Used," 2). Fawell believes it comes from some other apartment and therefore comes to take on the role of "soundtrack" to Ms. Lonelyhearts's vignette only by accident: Fawell, *Hitchcock's Rear Window*, 31.

the span of an instant. His assessment is in a sense accurate: insofar as he listens to music as sound, and sound as an index of an event, the beginning of the music itself is all he needs to attend to. That is, to him, the event or, to be precise, the premise of a rich—and surprising—course of events. Ms. Lonelyhearts appears to be staging an imaginary dinner with a nonexistent partner, complete with atmospheric music. Having grasped the sense of what is happening, he turns over to the realm of the visible—he keeps on looking, and with some relish at that. Vision grants more plentiful, reliable, and detailed information about the rather astonishing scene taking place before him. What had begun as a reflex, a quasi-Pavlovian impulse to search for the source of the sound, has evolved into the fully conscious choice to dwell on what he is looking at. His attention is swamped with the image of Ms. Lonelyhearts moving to and fro in her long, narrow flat and gesticulating to the effect of welcoming and entertaining her ghostly guest. At one point he even engages in a mocking acknowledgment of Ms. Lonelyhearts's presence and their proximity as neighbors (this is when he returns the toast, embodying the guest, unbeknownst to her).

As a thing that moves, and a human being at that, Ms. Lonelyhearts commands attention over not just the music but the other—and static—visual elements of the scene as well. As the implications of what she is doing become clearer and clearer, her grip on Jefferies—and us—grows tighter and tighter. Yet Jefferies's distance from her apartment makes it impossible to observe the nuances of her body gestures, let alone the expression on her face. Even when real, and not staged by a delusional character, as is the case here, the dinner would come across as a pantomime, its protagonist a type rather than a fully formed character.[31] Throughout *Rear Window*, the absence of close shots translates for the viewer, who shares Jefferies's vantage point, into a form of stylization; our distance from her has the same effect as that of a mask. Inevitably, distance creates, too, a certain vagueness or lack of specificity to the portrayal of Ms. Lonelyhearts's emotions and with this the temptation to project one's best guess about what is really happening in that apartment (her nickname suggests as much). Such a projection will doubtless be tinged with a varying ratio of sympathy, fear, and anxiety, depending on one's own specific emotional and epistemic position. This in turn creates the possibility for differences in judgment to open up between Jefferies and us, the spectators.

In the absence of the two traditional targets of the spectator's attention—a human face to look at up close and dialogue around which to organize the other elements of the soundtrack—the song's lyrics eventually do emerge as a potential focus of attention in that they provide the linguistically most articulate, if

---

[31] Contrast this to the equivalent scene in *Hou Chuang*, the 1955 Hong Kong remake of *Rear Window*. There, the dinner does involve a real guest, and in place of music we overhear a dialogue.

vicarious, evidence of a human presence. Bing Crosby's voice is, at that point in the film, the only thing "speaking" to or for us. But his are the borrowed words of a well-known song sung by an equally well-known, and male, singer. Thus, while the lyrics undoubtedly help us identify Ms. Lonelyhearts's taste and assign to her a specific time and place in American history, they too partake of what is in the last analysis the construction of a type. This is, if anything, exacerbated by the irony of the text, casting rather implausibly Ms. Lonelyhearts as mocking her own inadequacies and hopelessness. The use of music to boost one's feelings or create the setting for a particular type of action involves a degree of self-deception, or at least the suspension of disbelief. Here, however, the particular choice of text comes across rather as overkill: more the cruel in-joke of the director or screenwriter than the necessary element in the portrait of a believable type.

The cruel irony of this particular choice of text notwithstanding, borrowed songs are shared elements of the culture at large rather than an individualized expression of a unique existential trajectory. As such, they play an equivocal role in the construction of a character. While they empower the director with an effective bridge to reach out to the world of the spectator—all the more so if the latter is familiar with the preexisting track or the persona of the performer—they also channel the potential for personal expression along ready-made tracks. If the song displays any sign of the character's own agency, this lies in its use as serendipitous soundtrack to Ms. Lonelyhearts's own staging of the dinner. Though symptomatic of a conventionally sentimental, petit bourgeois mentality—the clean tablecloth and kitchenware, candle lights, dim lights, and, of course, the music—the setting is at least her own creation, if one mediated by television ads and mail shopping catalogs. Upon stretching her own capacity for make-believe, she shows a certain resilience. When she is no longer capable of sustaining the illusion she herself has manufactured, she plunges back into desperation.

Despite or perhaps because of its limitations as the picture of an individual, Ms. Lonelyhearts captures a truth about collectivity. Her predicament is more common than we may be ready to admit. But its display is exceptional or, more to the point, implausible. Unless they are socially accepted, as when fans of a celebrity ritualistically gather for a concert or photo shoot in special gear, delusional self-portraits rarely go past the stage of mere imaginings. Such pitiful expressions of naïveté and self-deception are normally confined to the sealed-off, inviolable sphere of the self: representations by oneself for oneself. To gain access to these representations is a violation of one's privacy, a pornography of sorts.[32] That is why it is such a disturbing scene, one made all the more uncomfortable by

---

[32] In a poignant aside, Belton notes that Lisa's apartment is visible to us, "metaphorically displaced (and down-graded in status) in the apartments of Miss Torso and Miss Lonelyhearts": Belton, "The Space of *Rear Window*," 85.

Jefferies's seemingly unrepentant lingering on it. Jefferies's constant gazing about is less the chronic fixation of an inveterate pervert, as critics have maintained, than the justifiable response to a particular set of circumstances. It is occasioned by a plethora of aural stimuli and nurtured by a modicum of boredom. To deny this is to miss his peculiar evolution—or devolution, as the case might be—as a character. It is his lingering—the sustained, gratuitous, and willful attention of the gaze on display in this sequence—that makes him a voyeur.

The Accidental Score

Aside from being a voyeur, Jefferies is also a paradigmatic, if perhaps extreme, example of a poor listener. When he pays attention to music, he does so both involuntarily and "punctually"—that is, in short bursts of information-gathering efforts—rather than over time. Time and again, he displays a complete lack of musical sensibility. The film seems to want to make a point of it by contrasting Jefferies to Lisa, who, upon catching a whiff of the pianist's work, ponders what she's heard and exclaims: "It's enchanting!" To treat music merely as a source of information about his immediate environment, one to be discarded at will as soon as it successfully redirects his gaze to a new, titillating sight, does not merely betray a utilitarian attitude on Jefferies's part; it almost amounts to a denial of music qua music, for the role the latter plays in the film for him—waking him from his torpor, directing his attention to a portion of the courtyard, reminding him of the presence of this or that neighbor—could be just as easily fulfilled by any number of sounds. Unless, that is, we think of him as a spectator of dramas he cannot bring himself to take seriously partially on account of the music that accompanies them, and whose presence, however distractedly, he invariably registers. If physical distance turns a neighborly scene into a flat screen, the more or less accidentally synchronous music certifies, as it were, its fictionality (despite being, for their actors, all too real). But wouldn't this be too convenient a rationalization of Jefferies's callousness? And does it not dispense too summarily of one other important function of the soundtrack?

Rear Window is a revealing instance, within the Hollywood system, of the convergence between cinema and the theater under the aegis of sound; despite being based on a literary source, it wears its theatrical pedigree on its sleeve. Following on the heels of two experimental "chamber dramas," *Rope* (1948) and *Dial M for Murder* (1952), respectively, the film contains the main action within a circumscribed indoor space—Jefferies's apartment—thus creating countless occasions for the kind of dialogue-filled sequences that as early as the 1930s earned the epithet of "canned theater." The theatrically conceived domestic space is already an implicit representation of an attentional disposition, to the exclusion of the hum of the city outside. Yet the film's "source score" constantly threatens to puncture the sealed-off space of the house and draws the characters' attention outward. Such a soundtrack, moreover, is consistent with an important subsidiary function of both stage and off-stage music in nineteenth-century theater: the suggestion of a three-dimensional space around and across the stage. Compared to a hypothetical theatrical presentation of the same story, *Rear Window* enlarges the scope of what is visible by featuring images of the notorious courtyard, which the characters hardly trespass but, like the lone protagonist of the short story, repeatedly look into.

Jack Sullivan has described *Rear Window* as "Hitchcock's most daring experiment in popular music" and "the forerunner of *American Graffiti, Mona Lisa, After Hours*." Sullivan likens the film to a Shakespearian comedy in which "beauty and truth come together; the utterly beautiful saves a life."[33] The reference here is to the pianist's song, "Lisa," saving Ms. Lonelyhearts's life and bringing the two of them together, like an unwitting serenade. *Rear Window* is indeed Shakespearian in that, time and again, music appears in it as something people do, attend, or fail to listen to "under certain circumstances, just as they fight or make love."[34] Continuing a robust tradition in both literature and the theater, *Rear Window* reframes music as a quintessentially worldly affair and music listening as a matter of perspective. In displaying such Olympian disregard for the dimensions of music traditionally privileged by musical discourse, Jefferies delivers music back to the world of physical events, flesh-and-blood bodies, and concrete, material objects that give rise to it. His is admittedly only one extreme of a range of listening modes that lie on a continuum of possibilities activated by the incessant probing of his and the other characters' attention. So Lisa responds empathetically to the song the composer is crafting, while the latter, per Jefferies's speculation, composes to pay his bills; Ms. Lonelyhearts stumbles upon the same song as if by miracle, and it saves her life, while many other inhabitants of the courtyard willfully ignore it or, worse, casually take stock of its presence only to exercise their right to be indifferent to it. The courtyard is a metaphor of the casualization of music, precipitated by the excessive supply through the media, especially the radio (though in 1954, television would have also been a significant presence in a New York City block).[35]

---

[33] Jack Sullivan, *Hitchcock's Music* (New Haven, CT: Yale University Press, 2006), 174.

[34] W. H. Auden, "Music in Shakespeare." For an overview of source music in Hollywood cinema and the difficult question of narrative integration, see Irene Kahn Atkins, *Source Music in Motion Pictures* (Rutherford, NJ: Fairleigh Dickinson University Press, 1983). On songs in cinema, and especially the musical, see also the recent survey by Richard Dyer, *In the Space of a Song: The Uses of Song in Film* (New York: Routledge, 2012).

[35] Fragments of television shows constantly intrude into the main line story of Don DeLillo's novel, *White Noise* (New York: Viking Press, 1985). The novel is set in the 1980s, at a time when the role of television as a dominant cultural force in the United States was all but consummated.

Artfully integrated in an imaginary re-creation of worldly affairs, the import of the music is contingent on multiple, and sometimes mutually exclusive, perspectives—including that of the spectator. In technical terms, integration is a matter of spotting—deciding when to use music—and synchronization or, depending on the special needs of the situation at hand, lack thereof. The latter option is worth considering since it is important that the music, particularly when it is off screen or in the background, comes across as merely simultaneous, rather than intentionally synchronized to a particular moment of the main action. "Aural deep focus" makes possible the impression that we are watching an uncoordinated ensemble of people going about their lives in polite indifference to one another. Occasionally, music is also a fundamental ingredient to the occasional cacophony of simultaneities that is one of the film's greatest sources of poetry—and irony.[36]

Yet music also turns into an intermittently "accidental score," as the spectator forges imaginary sync points.[37] Here, the (musical) background fuses with the (visual, as well as aural) foreground. One of the best, and most likely deliberate, examples of this occurs at a pivotal moment of the film, when Lisa converts herself to Jefferies's belief that Thorwald has killed his wife. The music begins simultaneous with Jefferies unsavory comment about how Thorwald might have "cut up" his wife's body (which he delivers, significantly, while looking at Miss Torso lying in bed). Reaction shot of Lisa visibly alarmed by Jefferies's words, and with the pianist clearly visible in the background. As she draws down the window blinds, the rest of the scene unfolds at the continuing sound, off screen, of the song, "Lisa," played softly and tentatively, as if to suggest that it is being composed.[38] The acoustics place the piano far from the quasi-enclosed space of the living room where Lisa and Jefferies are discussing the plausibility of the murder plot. Having Lisa just finish scolding him for his "unhealthy" obsession with his plot, and just as we hear the descending fourth that is the opening theme's most recognizable feature, she sees something opposite Jefferies's apartment and rises up. The camera closes in on her. There follows a complete statement of the theme

---

[36] Weis, *The Silent Scream*, 111–113. Weis also stresses the difference between the mix of foreground and background sounds one hears in films of directors such as Renoir or Altman, and the same effect in Hitchcock. "The main function of Hitchcock's aural deep focus, she argues, is irony," 113.

[37] The intermittent, almost haphazard emergence of sync points, when they occur at all, makes them stand out. I follow here Chion's definition of sync points as "particularly salient, meaningful moments": Chion, *Film, A Sound Art*, 268.

[38] Technically, the scene features two cues. Correspondingly, in both the "Music cue sheet (feature)," and Dolnick's memo cited earlier, the music is broken down into two cues, both called "Lisa" and numbered "16" and "17," respectively. This is due to the pianist stopping to play for some time. While the first cue is shorthanded "inst vis & bkg," the second is only described as "inst bkg," meaning that the pianist is not seen ("Music cue sheet (feature)," July 6, 1954, and "Description of Manner in Which the Music Was Used," in *Franz Waxman Papers*, OS 90, 2 and 3, respectively).

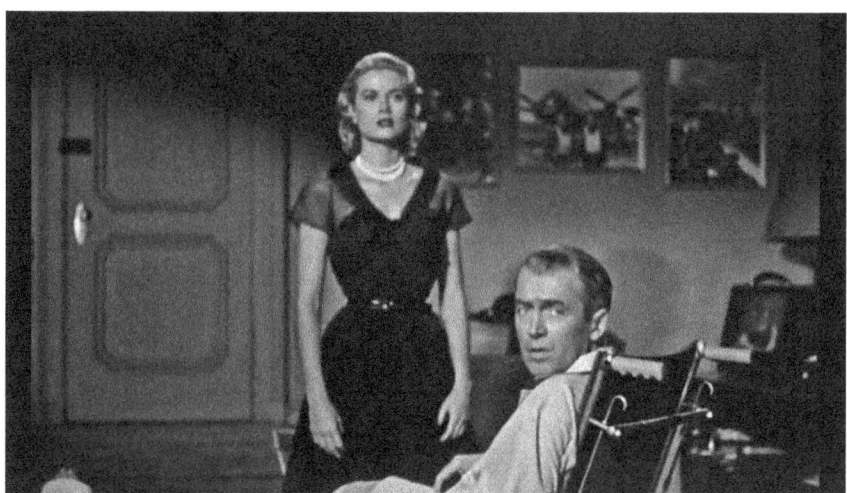

Figure 4.7 Rear Window.

and its sequential repetition. Lisa keeps on watching across the courtyard. The cue ends before we hear the transitional material that separates the two statements of the song's main theme but not without playing on the latter's final, three-note descending cell, which it repeats once in a clever harmonic variant that darkens the soundscape while paving the way for a silence that Lisa fills by saying, "Tell me everything you saw, and what you think it means" (Figure 4.7).[39]

Along with the careful, deliberate placement of well-chosen excerpts, key to the sudden emergence of such seemingly accidental sync points is the status of the music in the perceptual economy of the film. As a secondary motif of interest—secondary, that is, to the dialogue or visual action—"Lisa" often simply "hangs" there, floating unencumbered by the circumstances of its own production. Moreover, it keeps on repeating, which, if on the one hand is the reflection of its being a work in progress, on the other strikes one as if it were aping the recurrent themes or motives of more conventional film scores (the absence of a score proper conditions us to listen for one in the soundscape). This serves the film well insofar as we interpret the courtyard as the materialization of a cinematic fantasy. The convergence between the cinematic and the everyday that one observes in *Rear Window*, the richly musical character displayed by its locale, is in this respect exemplary—indeed, prescient. While the number,

[39] I use the term "theme" in the music-analytical sense of a recognizable melody or phrase upon which a piece is constructed. The tag "theme," in the studio sense of the most important cue of a film, applies to "Lisa" as a whole. While the cue sheet and Dolnick's memo refer to the song as "Lisa," the "Orchestra Chart," intended for internal use, dubs it "The Theme Lisa" (not dated, *Franz Waxman Papers*, OS 90).

diversity, and timing of the musical interventions stretch the limits of what is plausible, thus threatening their status as a believable representation of simultaneities, they also bring home the extent to which Jefferies has come to view the dealings of his neighbors in cinematic terms. Moreover, as Weis has observed:

> The ambiguity of whether we are listening to source music or music scored specifically for the film is appropriate to the thematic material of Rear Window and relates to the way we respond to the film visually. One of the major, unresolvable issues that Hitchcock dramatizes in the film is the audience's innate voyeurism. . . . [W]e cannot distinguish whether we are watching the neighbors because Jeff does so or because we are voyeuristic ourselves. This breaking down of the distinction between our actual behavior and our movie-going behavior is analogous to the blurring of the distinction between source music . . . and scoring.[40]

The suggestion of sync points, as much as if not more than the screen-like windows that frame the pantomimes enacted by Jefferies's neighbors, marks a trespassing into the cinematization of the everyday. But when we hear the courtyard music as a background score to Jefferies's own looking, panting, and ranting, we are framing him the same way in which he frames the people around him. In this way, we are simultaneously distancing ourselves from his epistemic perspective while reaffirming the similarity of our predicament to his.

Film soundtracks are constructed for the most part in such a way as to minimize the room to maneuver between alternatives. The music is "locked into" fixed configurations that control the proliferation of meaning and the assumption of new functions.[41] It is in refusing to use music in this way that *Rear Window*, sixty years after its release, still strikes one as, in Sullivan's words, a "daring experiment." Timing can propel the music into a region that is more germane to a conventional film score, if only for a split second. Since the awareness of sync points is contingent on personal disposition, knowledge of film history, and familiarity with the preexisting tracks, the behavior of the score thus remains unpredictable. Score-like effects are bound to be loose and intermittent, seemingly serendipitous sync points peppering the experience of the film from beginning to end without a predetermined, intelligible plan. The result is a joyously anarchic field of possibilities. By the same token, any

---

[40] Weis, *The Silent Scream*, 110.

[41] On the approach to scoring that minimizes "the ability for perceivers to shift positions within the fantasy scenarios offered," see Kassabian, *Hearing Film*, 45 and 108, and my "The Shark in the Music," *Music Analysis* 29 i/ii/iii (2010): 320.

given music will resist being assimilated to a score when it is patently incongruous or incompatible, by movie music standards, with the action we see on screen, or the content or tone of a dialogue. Sullivan notes how "the correspondences seem clear, then suddenly blur."[42] This is also true of what he, perhaps somewhat too confidently, calls examples of "counterpoint" between music and on-screen action. Counterpoint, too, after all, entails precise, deliberate synchronization.

Multipurpose Music: The Case of "Lisa"

Let us recall Auden's idea of music making or listening as kinds of action, something that people do. This aspect of the soundtrack is as crucial to *Rear Window* as it is to Shakespeare's dramas. Its handling in *Rear Window*, however, played a role in Hitchcock's notorious dissatisfaction with composer Waxman's treatment of "Lisa." The director told Truffaut that "it didn't work out quite the way I wanted it to, and I was quite disappointed,"[43] adding that he had "hired a film composer when what [he] needed was a songwriter."[44] Did Hitchcock mean that the song was poorly composed and unmemorable? This is doubtful, given the undeniable charm of the main theme, impeccable musicianship it displays, and (then) contemporary feel injected into it by the jazz-influenced arrangement in which it is skillfully clothed.[45] Might Hitchcock instead be referring to the fact that the song, as suggested by Jack Sullivan, and notwithstanding its inherent musical merits, was not marketable as a single?[46] That is in principle possible but strikes me as a remote possibility. True, the notorious falling out between Hitchcock and Herrmann took place precisely over a song intended for the single market that the composer failed, intentionally or not, to deliver. But cross-marketing of the sort that would become so common in the 1960s was not yet practiced aggressively in the early 1950s.[47]

David Schroeder points to at least two discrepancies between the shooting script and the final result with respect to "Lisa." Both involve the clash or cacophony, irritating to both Jefferies and the composer, between the latter's attempt

---

[42] Sullivan, *Hitchcock's Music*, 179.

[43] Truffaut, *Hitchcock*, 216.

[44] Cited in Weis, *The Silent Scream*, 115.

[45] On Waxman as a songwriter, see David Neumeyer and Nathan Platte, *Franz Waxman's Rebecca: A Film Score Guide* (Lanham, MD: Scarecrow Press, 2012), 11.

[46] Jack Sullivan, *Hitchcock's Music* (New Haven, CT: Yale University Press, 2006), 176.

[47] Jeff Smith places the beginning of this practice in the late 1950s, following Hollywood's arrival in the record business: Smith, *The Sounds of Commerce* (New York: Columbia University Press, 1998), esp. chap. 3.

at writing and the dance music coming from Miss Torso's apartment.[48] These are tantalizing cues, but they are hardly conclusive. Here is another possibility. The director was keen on creating the impression of the song as a work in progress: "I wanted to show how a popular song is composed by gradually developing it throughout the film until, in the final scene, it is played on a recording with a full orchestral accompaniment."[49] This is to me the most important clue, and it is in this connection that his dissatisfaction with Waxman's work arose. Hitchcock wanted the audience to attend to the act of composing "Lisa," as distinct from the song itself, in something like the way that, in Namuth-Falkenberg's film on Jackson Pollock, for instance, or Clouzot's documentary on Picasso, we are shown the action of painting rather than being invited to contemplate the finished product.[50] To be sure, detractors of Pollock's art will claim that in the absence of a detectable logic in his compositions, let alone a representational intent, one simply does not know when a Pollock painting can be considered finished. Others will insist that capturing the painter at work, as Namuth's film did, is tantamount to subtracting the main source of interest of his work, namely, the status of the painting as testimony or trace, ex post facto, of a process (hence H. Rosenberg's moniker, "action painting"). Yet even in the limit case of Pollock's art, it is undeniable that a process is rendered visible simply by showing the artist applying paint to his famously unprimed canvas.

This is not quite what happens with "Lisa." Yet what Hitchcock asked for was far from easy. What is the equivalent of a blank canvas, or a rough cube of wood, marble, or basalt, in music? Silence will not do, unless it is accompanied— indeed, captioned or explained—by the corresponding image of, or verbal reference to, someone engaging in the act of composing. Without supporting anecdotal evidence, in other words, it is hard to capture the coming into being of a piece of music. It is easier to observe the growth of a painting as an artist gradually fills out a blank canvas, or to track the emergence of a sculpture out of a formless chunk of material, than it is to document the shaping of a song as it develops from seemingly disconnected musical events, grapples of notes, and isolated gestures (and do so mostly by recourse to brief off-screen tidbits of music at that)—hence the images of the pianist ill at ease in his studio or plainly

---

[48] Schroeder, *Hitchcock's Ear: Music and the Director's Art*, 136 and 141. Schroeder also draws attention to the text of the recorded song, arguing that the Lisa described there "bears very little relation to the Lisa in Jeff's eyes": Ibid., 141.

[49] Truffaut, *Hitchcock*, 215.

[50] The trailer lends credence to the idea that the composer's daily practice is a thread of the narrative in its own right (the voice over refers to his "playing the same melody over and over again"). According to another memo, in the original trailer for the film "Lisa" is heard only once for ten seconds. Of the nine cues employed, it is the only one described "inst vis bkg," a description that implies the pianist is to be seen, as is indeed the case (the trailer is available on various internet repositories).

frustrated at the progress of his own work, as well as Jefferies's statement that "he is having so much trouble with [the song]." They are attempts to compensate for Waxman's difficulties in conveying, through sonic means alone, the labor involved in the compositional process.

Composition is often bound up with performance. The beginnings of the creation of a new musical work often coincide not with a fragment, let alone silence, but, derivatively, with another piece of music. The process through which the former emerges out of the latter, however, is often buried, rendered occult (this is especially true in the case of written repertories). Their overlap can be more easily detected upon hearing re-elaborations of a previously known work, controlled improvisation on a skeletal structure, or free improvisation. Jazz musicians privilege constant transformations against a stable background of already-existing, familiar chord changes or fully fledged tunes. Wittingly or not, this is what Waxman seems to have accomplished with the song that was to eventually become "Lisa." Its most important—indeed, memorable—feature, the main theme, often sounds indistinguishable in the mix or recedes into the background, driven to the fringes of our attention by more pressing information in the visuals or the dialogue. When one can attend to it as a separate, self-standing stream of sound, it hardly comes across as a fragment of a work in progress.[51] The only exception is, tellingly, one in which we actually see the composer at the piano playing and writing. What we hear then, however, is a staggered, unharmonized version of the arpeggio that follows the two-note hook opening the song. This cannot play any role in preparing us for the subsequent, and much more fully textured, versions of the same material: it is simply too fragmentary and amorphous to be remembered. The shot, put another way, provides us with general information about the identity of Jefferies's neighbor—he plays the piano, is a songwriter, and is at work on something—but fails to jump-start the process of following through the composition from the song's inception till its fully final version (which process Hitchcock wanted to weave into the plot). By the time we recognize the tune, it will sound fully formed, and as bearing no detectable linkage to what is heard here. Across the film, and to Hitchcock's chagrin, one does not hear progressively more complete as much as simply different, or at most differently scored, versions of the song. It is as if Waxman, like a jazz musician, were treating his own melody as a "traditional" to be subsequently harmonized or scored through ever-changing solutions. This is not to say that the song always sounds like jazz. Rather, Waxman adopted a jazz-inspired principle of

---

[51] In the sequence examined earlier, when Lisa sees something that finally persuades her of the correctness of Jefferies's intuition, the music does sound like the representation of a work-in-progress. But the information conveyed by the dialogue is far too significant for all but the most inveterate musician to notice the subtlety of Waxman's work.

transformation, coupled with a Brahmsian penchant for "developing variations," to explore a kaleidoscopic range of situations as he saw fit. The choice of musical materials to work with, if my interpretation is correct, must have stemmed from the need to devise a chameleon-like tune, one that allowed for maximum plasticity and adaptability to different dramatic situations. In doing this, Waxman acted like the film composer he was.[52]

Jazz does appear several times as an obligatory element term of reference of the New York downtown setting. But the only time a jazz ensemble makes a noticeable, indeed striking, appearance is when we hear a version of "Lisa" arranged for quintet. Its sounds allegedly save Ms. Lonelyhearts's life. Compared to the mock date at the sound of "To see you is to love you," this for her is a definite step—and three full floors—up, both musically and personally (the pianist lives on the fourth floor, she on the first). The moment she notices the song being played across the courtyard marks the most explicit suggestion of the parallel between her and Lisa. As Fawell notes:

> Just above Ms. Lonelyhearts, Lisa gravitates toward the [composer's] window. She has come to the window to show Jeff evidence she has gathered, some of Mrs. Thorwald's jewelry. But Hitchcock makes it clear that she has been temporarily set in trance by the music. Lisa's head is cocked in distracted reverie as she hears the music. She absentmindedly forgets to hold up the evidence for Jeff to see. For a few seconds, Hitchcock holds one of the most dramatic and striking shots in the film, Miss Lonelyhearts and Lisa, one above the other, in mathematical symmetry, each framed by their rectangular window, both hypnotized by the music.[53]

It is indeed not only a wonderful visual composition but also a rhetorically powerful staging of the involuntary attention. Fawell also notes that the idea is anticipated in Woolrich's story, albeit not in connection to music but rather as a function of mere serendipity. In the film, then, music synchronizes the emotional life of neighbors who know nothing of, yet are literally attuned to, one another.

Despite the instrumentation, and like the majority of the other musical items in the film, the track is a representation rather than an embodiment of jazz proper. This is in keeping with the compromise between the search for authentically

---

[52] The evolution of the music would seem less like showing how it is composed than watching its development, through more elaborate and expensive orchestrations, from piano version to record release—how a song becomes commercialized: Weis, personal communication.

[53] Fawell, *Hitchcock's Rear Window*, 96–97.

vernacular idioms and their translation for the predominantly white, middle-class audience for which the film was envisioned (a compromise that character-izes the soundtrack as a whole). Just as the giant set falls just short of standing in for the actual location, and despite the use of preexisting music, the soundtrack thus deserves the epithet pastiche.[54] The final version of "Lisa," complete with a string envelope, is sung by a crooning, suave tenor, taking us into the eponymous character's orbit as the sonic image of urbanity and sophistication. It is in this form that it fills the soundtrack as Lisa's own theme song at last, till it morphs, via a swift acoustical retrofitting, into the end-title theme. The evolution of the song marks Lisa's triumph, no doubt. But it is crucial to remember that the film takes a lengthy, circuitous route to endow the status of theme song on to it. Its vi-cissitudes allegorize the reverse "rake's progress" that culminates with Jefferies's reluctant acceptance, facilitated by a second leg break, of Lisa's presence in his life. That "Lisa" becomes Lisa's only at the very end exemplifies the serendipitous process by which a found melody seals its fate with that of a person, bringing the analogy of real persons to film characters full circle.

Music as Process

In the last analysis, one wonders whether the work of a popular songwriter, as distinct from a film composer of classical extraction like Waxman, would have pleased Hitchcock more. Songwriters often write without the support of nota-tion and leave behind even less evidence of their work than a classically trained composer (evidence that Waxman could have instead used, though apparently he did not). Much of the "sculpting" of a pop song goes on in the recording studio and involves instrumentation, acoustics, and nuances of vocal delivery (consider the alternate or premature takes by the Beatles that have emerged after the release of *The Beatles Anthology*, for instance). But most important to the evolving identity of a song, perhaps, are its roots in the text—a symbiotic rela-tionship that emerges in the course of composition and would have been hard to illustrate off screen, and intermittently at that. So an instrumental song of the

---

[54] Armond White similarly recognizes a tension between the pursuit of a vernacular setting and the constraints of studio aesthetics. He writes: "Hitchcock experiments with Hollywood's glossy, de-tailed stylizations while approximating Renoir's varied, shifting views of real life. Such a stylistic and philosophical *hybrid* influences film makers to this day": White, "Eternal Vigilance in *Rear Window*," 120 [emphasis mine]. In another statement that partially resonates with my reservations on the ve-racity of the reconstruction of the city block, Murray Pomerance writes that films like *Rear Window* "deploy townscapes and cityscapes still culture-bound to the nineteenth century": Pomerance, *Alfred Hitchcock's America* (Cambridge: Polity, 2013), 19. One will have to wait for the 1960s, and especially the films of Jack Smith and Andy Warhol, to enjoy an unadulterated picture of New York City's bohe-mian scene. Warhol's *Chelsea Girls* (1966) might well be seen as a parody of *Rear Window*.

kind Waxman wrote was not a bad call after all. An easier way of staging the evolution of a piece of music is the polyphonic treatment of a single line; alternatively, Waxman could have shown the process of instrumentation—from solo piano to full-blown quintet—in a more explicit, demonstrative fashion. Why this was not done, and why Waxman decided not to use sketches of his own work in progress, is not known. The impression remains that poor coordination and diverging goals, rather than the choice of a classical composer per se, were the causes of Hitchcock's dissatisfaction.

The final outcome vindicates the director's widely reported claim that he had little control over the work of the composer. But there is more at stake in Hitchcock's desire to show the evolution of "Lisa" as a musical composition. What is behind this seemingly innocent dramatic ploy? First, there was a need to complete the portrait of the neighbor-musician by showing what he does for a living—composing as distinct from merely performing. This could naturally be done, if less satisfactorily, by visual means alone (sure enough, at one point we do in fact see him scribble on music paper). The second goal of making composition per se palpable is to anchor music in the sphere of human action. The question is not to do so in the abstract; there is no doubt that we do know what the composer does and what the music is evidence of. The question goes beyond what we believe and impinges on how we experience the music, and this turns on attention. To be able to represent compositional effort as such directs the attention toward music as the product of work, and a chain of—for the most part invisible or plainly occult—bodily and mental operations.[55] Unfortunately for Hitchcock, this is hard to achieve if, as is often the case in *Rear Window*, the music reaches the audience in long, seemingly complete stretches and, what is more, off screen, that is, without visual corroboration that it is being composed.[56] In fact, as we have seen, "Lisa" veers away not only from the state of work in progress but also that of performance tout court, levitating instead toward a gaseous, floating state that enables it to engage at almost every turn in potential sync points with images, other sounds, and bits of dialogue. This flight from the anecdotal, as Pierre Schaeffer might have put it, is what underpins the phenomenology of much film music (and, needless to say, results in a complex gestalt, informed by a dramatic sensibility, that is worlds apart from acousmatic music as Schaeffer himself conceived it). The familiar sound of the composer at work, a mark of the knowability and predictability of the courtyard, no longer functions

---

[55] The stress on composition as paid work tallies with the characterization of the composer as a "solidly working-class type . . . persistently hacking away at that sweeping tune": Pomerance, *Alfred Hitchcock's America*, 104.

[56] For an instructive contrast, consider the scenes detailing the composer at work in *Amadeus* (1984), or Kieslowski's *Three Colors: Blue* (1993).

like a territorializing refrain, to borrow Deleuze-Guattari's formulation; instead, it has a destabilizing, "deterritorializing" effect as it suddenly and somewhat anarchically connects with other elements of the scene.[57]

The field of synergies that music finds itself part of, when it behaves like a score, is less a matter of subordination than of integration; music may well be the harbinger of the most important information of a scene or even a whole film. But there is no question that the transformations "Lisa" undergoes ever so often are all-encompassing in eradicating it from the performing bodies and the network of causes and circumstances that give rise to it, and in depriving it of its individuality as a spatially and temporally situated event. For "Lisa" to engage in score-like behavior, it must not only relinquish its eventhood but also become one with another body—the primary dramatic situation. How it can accomplish this involves so many factors subject to cultural pressure, historical circumstances, and personal taste as to preempt the possibility of a comprehensive taxonomy; luckily, filmmakers and composers have a strong enough sense of when source music "clicks" with a specific situation so as to perform the role normally allotted to a score. Waxman's chameleon theme allows for precisely that. Spectators, for their part, are willing enough to strike compromises and meet halfway, as it were, so as to render abstract legislation superfluous. Underpinning the metaphorical cooperation of music with the moving image is the *actual* cooperation, grounded in the social acceptance of conventions and the assumption of communicative motives, between filmmakers and their spectators. The conventions regulating our understanding of a pattern may be termed, after philosopher David Lewis, a form of "nonexplicit contract," and their effectiveness the result of "coordination behavior and games."[58]

Whether performed or broadcast, "Lisa" is first and foremost an element of the setting. Yet to be part of the setting is, in a sense, to recede in the background. This means not only that the music is off screen but also that something else is in the foreground that, and here lies the conundrum, inevitably makes the attempt to represent it as a type of action or event difficult, for that requires its being of a piece with the action (which it most often is not as it is simply heard as off-screen sound while something else is happening on screen). Quite aside from our knowledge that the music is scripted into the film by the director and his writer—we would conclude as much even if we heard the music just once—the increasing familiarity of the theme imparts to it the character of a strategically timed appearance. Consequently, just as often as one hears it casually and intermittently as "something, happening over there," one also takes it in, conditioned

---

[57] Gilles Deleuze and Félix Guattari, *A Thousand Plateaus: Capitalism and Schizophrenia* (Minneapolis: University of Minnesota Press, 1987), 299–300.

[58] Thomas Pavel, *Fictional Worlds* (Cambridge, MA: Harvard University Press, 1989), 119.

by years of experience with film music, as partaking of the construction of whatever it is he or she is focusing on, all the more so if it appears to be finished (that is, not a work in progress). In the worst case, the one that Hitchcock must have perhaps dreaded the most, "Lisa" distracted the viewer from the matter at hand—be it dialogue, across-the-courtyard action, or expository material—by morphing into a cue carrying an unintended effect. It is this state of affairs, in my opinion, that Hitchcock sought to address. And an intelligent attempt it was, too, for it comes to terms the best it can with the off-screen status of the music. How else was one to avert the possibility that "Lisa" might distract the viewer by jarring with a poorly matched scene or, conversely, turn into a running musical commentary of sorts, even when the director deemed it inappropriate? Hitchcock's request envisioned what was in essence a highly original—and difficult—representation of musical sound strictly as a form of physical action and type of work.[59] Naturally, he must have been aware of the risk, perhaps even reveled in it. If Hitchcock's sole interest had been to convey the active presence of an off-screen space, he would have reverted, quite simply, to sound or noise of the most mundane nature. This he patently did not do, knowing full well the potential a rich source score had in store for the film. On balance, it was a risk well worth taking, for the score-like moments are among the greatest in *Rear Window* and impart the entire soundtrack a reflexive ring that not only is in line with but also deepens its allegorical vision.

---

[59] Schroeder interprets Hitchcock's motives differently, arguing that the song should run "parallel to the unfolding of the film . . . taking on an essence that can be the underlying urge behind the structure of the film, and also prompt the tone of the film": Schroeder, *Hitchcock's Ear,* 130. If I understand this correctly, Schroeder is seeking to establish a relation of mirroring, or allegorization, between the compositional process (that never was) of the song and the film.

Part II

HETEROLOGICAL SILENCE

5

Epiphanies

In the examples surveyed in the previous chapters, the filmmaker marginalizes a stream of sound by encouraging the adoption of a certain frame of reference—primarily via the character as vector. Under no circumstance was the sound itself eliminated or cancelled out by the onset of another (the lone exception was the scene of the radio broadcast in *Apocalypse Now*, which I used as a foil to the other examples). In describing the admittedly virtuosic episode from *High and Low*, I raised the possibility that despite its fully fledged presentation, the radio broadcast of Schubert's "The Trout" risks falling under the threshold of one's attention altogether due not to the weakness of the signal as such but rather to the incongruousness and timing of its appearance. The resulting inattention is less a matter of capacity than the conflict between mutually exclusive frames of reference. The episode, and others like it, calls to mind the phenomenon known as "inattentional blindness." The term refers to a well-known experiment in which a man clad in a gorilla costume joins a team of players on a basketball court, yet very few spectators reported seeing a gorilla.[1] The data is striking. Yet we must remember that, to paraphrase Fred Dretske, one can be "blind" to the gorilla and still see everything that is visible.[2] The blindness, as Dretske argues, consists of a failure to *do* something—recognizing what one sees as a gorilla—not a failure to see tout court. By the same token, in *High and Low*, one can be "deaf" to the appearance of the broadcast and still hear everything that is audible.

The examples with which I open this chapter present a different scenario in that they coerce the spectator into sharing a subjectively reconfigured soundscape to which no alternative, however theoretical, is given. The unattended stimulus may not be attended to but is nevertheless heard by the character; yet it is simply wiped out of the soundtrack, with the result that the spectators are

---

[1] Daniel J. Simons and Christopher F. Chabris, "Gorillas in Our Midst: Sustained Inattentional Blindness for Dynamic Events," *Perception* 28, no. 9 (1999): 1059–74.

[2] Fred Dretske, "Change Blindness," *Philosophical Studies* 120, no. 1–3 (2004): 15.

not even in the position of being deaf to it (as there is nothing to be heard in the first place). It is in one sense a less subtle and less democratic approach to the representation of selective attention, and the inattentional deafness that is its foil. At the same time, it has given rise to an extremely common and yet somewhat overlooked state of affairs. The need to clarify that the character is no longer paying attention to a sound is itself given sonic, and more specifically *musical*, form.[3] "In cinema," writes Roman Jakobson, "it is not silence but music that announces the exclusion of the auditory object."[4] Writing in the early 1930s, Jakobson was responding to the advent of sound and the recognition that in the new context, silence had earned the status of "auditory object" in the sense of an "actual absence of sounds." In silent cinema, the presence of music did not indicate silence but a dimension apart from sound, since for Jakobson, "auditorily a silent film is entirely 'nonrepresentational' and for that very reason demands continuous musical accompaniment."[5] Music performed what Jakobson calls a "neutralizing" function. As he reports Bela Balázs's remark: "we instantly notice the absence of music, but we pay no attention to its presence, so that almost any music whatever is appropriate for virtually every scene."[6] In the second part of this book, I appropriate Jakobson's striking idea that "music announces the exclusion of the auditory object" to examine a different phenomenon, one justified by the representation of subjectivity and associated to a later stage of film history (though it can be traced back to certain moments of operatic representation as well). I am referring to the use of the score to suggest that the protagonist—for it is invariably the protagonist who warrants such treatment—is, literally, "tuning out." Chapter 6 will turn to several paradigmatic examples

---

[3] On music that is construable as a form of "sounded silence," see the analysis of Charles Ives' *The Unanswered Question* and *Central Park in the Dark* in William Brooks, "Pragmatics of Silence," in *Silence, Music, Silent Music*, ed. Nicky Losseff and Jenny Doctor (Aldershot, UK: Ashgate, 2007), 97–126.

[4] Roman Jakobson, "Is the Film in Decline?," in *Language in Literature*, ed. Krystyna Pomorska and Stephen Rudy (Cambridge, MA, and London: Harvard University Press, 1987), 461.

[5] Ibid. As it turns out, films were sometimes one hundred per cent silent. On the question of film exhibition in the United States in the so-called "silent" period, see Rick Altman, "The Silence of the Silents," *Musical Quarterly* 80, no. 4 (Winter 1996), 648-718.

[6] Ibid. These and other similar statements go some way in suggesting how the popular notion that film music is best when "unheard" came about. And yet they also indicate that the experience they invoke applies to one specific scenario, one in which we hear "music or sound whose logic is not dictated by events within the narrative space": Ben Winters, "The Non-Diegetic Fallacy: Film, Music and Narrative Space," *Music and Letters* 91, no. 2 (2010): 237. Winters calls such music "extradiegetic." His example is Samuel Barber's Adagio used by Oliver Stone in *Platoon* (1986). It goes without saying that the music Jakobson and Balázs refer to is far more disengaged from the narrative it concurrently accompanies than Barber's Adagio is from the moment of *Platoon* in which Stone deploys it. The latter's elegiac nature does in fact respond, if from an omniscient perspective, to the events just witnessed onscreen.

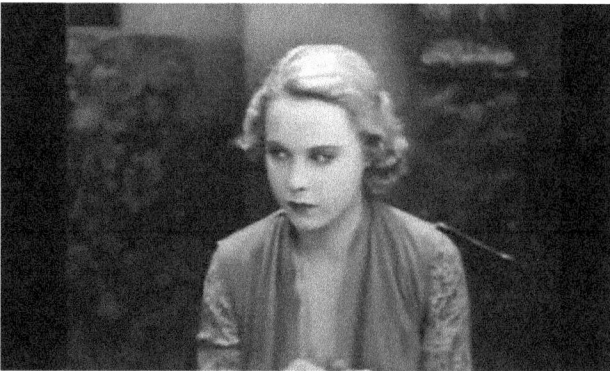

Figure 5.1 Blackmail.

of this form of *heterological silence*. Before that, however, I intend to consider another coercive—and paradoxical—representation of the selective attention by looking at scenes where a pivotal epiphany occurs. The emotional impact of a devastating insight, as we shall see, is rendered not as a flight from reality but rather as a complete submission to it. Sound overwhelms the mind of the character, and with it the final mix. Far from signaling a special gift or the mastery of one's environment, *hyperacousia* marks the breakdown of one's defenses against the sensorial assault of the outside world.[7]

I begin with an example that does not feature music but foreshadows key elements of the narrative trope I am interested in. This is the best-known sequence in Alfred Hitchcock's *Blackmail* (1929), set at the family breakfast table in the shop of Alice White's (Anny Ondra) parents (Figure 5.1). Listening to the speech of a customer who has stopped by, Alice keeps on picking out the word "knife." She hears the word as an indirect indictment over the murder she has just committed (the stabbing of a man who attempted to rape her). How is Alice's increasing sensitivity conveyed to the spectator? Visually, Hitchcock first pans from Alice to the gossip, then cuts back to Alice as the word is uttered, and finally closes in on her.[8] Aurally, everything her neighbor says other than "knife," to the extent that it is perceived at all, begins to sound like incomprehensible blabber. Delivered first in

[7] I borrow the term from Michel Chion, *Film, A Sound Art*, trans. C. Gorbman (New York: Columbia University Press, 2009), 308. In borrowing it, I also adapt it. Chion uses it to describe the permanent condition of an especially endowed character (his examples are little Anju in *Sansho the Bailiff* [1954] and Karin in *Through the Glass Darkly* [1961]). I use the term "hyperacousia" to describe a situation that is symptomatic of the functioning of attention, or its breaking down, in general. Given certain circumstances, "hyperacousia" can affect anyone.

[8] Elisabeth Weis, *The Silent Scream* (Rutherford, NJ: Farleigh Dickinson University Press, 1982), 44.

plain and then in gradually sharp, even sardonic tones, the word "knife" usurps the soundtrack, enacting in the process a restriction in the range of perceivable sounds in her—and our—proximal environment. The import of this coercive strategy is, in a sense, forced upon us. Yet it is precisely its coerciveness that ensures its rhetorical efficacy. Alice's reaction reinforces her culpability, which has been known to us since we saw the murder happen in an earlier sequence. But it also betrays her feeling of guilt, anxiety, and possibly also terror reawakened by the Pavlovian association of the word "knife" to the gruesome scene she must still be remembering so vividly. Only we are privy to this, however, as we hear what she hears in a way that is not possible—indeed, conceivable—to the other characters. This suddenly changes when, visibly stirred, she drops the knife with which she is slicing some bread; at that moment, the fourth wall is temporarily lifted. The spectators, her parents, and the neighbor all turn their attention to Alice's awkward—and to her parents and the customer, finally, suspicious—display of nervousness.

Film sound in a realist film responds to several imperatives at once.[9] On the one hand, filmmakers draw on a fund of well-known facts about sound to create a plausible or at least recognizable setting; on the other hand, they craft a soundtrack that negotiates effectively the conventions of the genre one is working in, the need to present narrative information as clearly as possible, the physical constraints of the medium they are using, and the exhibition space(s) where their work will most likely be experienced. These imperatives do not necessarily tally with one another, which is why even the most self-described realistic film in surround sound cannot claim to reproduce the conditions of a real-life setting. As spectators, we are confronted with and are constantly negotiating between two aspects of a twofold situation. The sounds we hear in the actual space we are in as we sit through the film must be subsumed under another space, the imagined one of the story world. In that space, different rules apply.

Think about the treatment of dialogue, for instance. The volume and clarity of the actors' voices in a dialogue scene are often implausible when compared to their values to an observer of the same scene in real life. To paraphrase Nick Browne, a basically dramatic account of such a scene would have it that the actors should sound essentially the way they would to a spectator following the action on a stage, as if at each moment he or she had the best perspective on the action (one that dispensed with potentially distracting noise, for example).[10] Yet this does not make dialogue scenes unrealistic, unless we equated realism with

---

[9] I employ the term "realist" as a specific reference to Hitchcock's style, and particularly the reception of his early films. On this aspect of the reception of Hitchcock, see Bill Krohn, *Hitchcock at Work* (London: Phaidon, 2000), 15 and 146.

[10] Nicholas Browne, "The Spectator-in-the-Text: The Rhetoric of *Stage Coach*," *Film Quarterly* 29, no. 2 (1975–76): 27. Note that Browne ignores the operations of the soundtrack altogether.

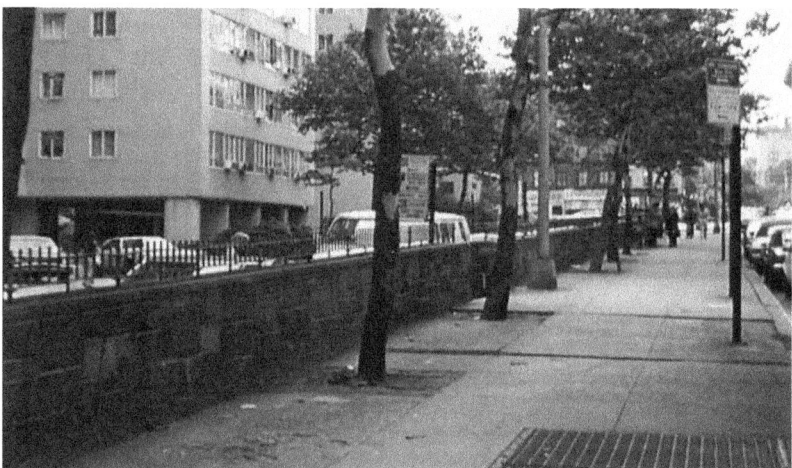

Figure 5.2 Annie Hall.

recording. Moreover, to alter this modus operandi is to run the risk of either less-ening dialogue intelligibility or engaging in (un)witting parody. Woody Allen's *Annie Hall* (1977) features a revealing example of the latter (Figure 5.2). In a single-shot sequence set in a street of Manhattan, while the stationary camera shows an empty sidewalk seen at an angle, we hear a conversation between Alvy (Woody Allen) and Max (Tony Roberts). The exchange centers on Alvy's perceived—Max implies "paranoid"—anti-Semitic innuendos he hears on a daily basis (the notorious "jew eat" joke, among others). Their voices are loud and clear, but Alvy and Max are nowhere to be seen. One does not quite know what to make of the image till we realize that it is in fact an extremely long shot of the two of them. Their figures begin to register visually ten seconds or so into the conversation, walking toward the camera from the top right-end corner of the frame. As they walk by the stationary camera, the latter does not even attempt to acknowledge their presence with a simple pan. As they exit frame left, the scene comes to an end. The reflexive gag pokes fun at the sometimes-egregious mismatch between sound and image scale.[11] But it also points to the widespread resistance to "traveling dialogue" and the significance of the radio as a commanding presence in the aesthetics of dialogue in the cinema.[12]

[11] Chion refers to the frequent "uncoupling of point of view and point of audition" in Allen's urban comedies and defends the practice as a means to guarantee dialogue comprehensibility. He also writes that the closely miked voice is more "realistic" on account of the mechanisms of the selective attention. See Michel Chion, *Film, A Sound Art*, 296–97.

[12] For a discussion of "traveling dialogue," the perceived "artificiality" of stereo sound, and the tension between realistic impulses and the inertial force of conventions, see John Belton, *Widescreen Cinema* (Cambridge, MA: Harvard University Press, 2012), 206–10.

The absolute preeminence of the actor's voice is of course also the theater's most profound, most pervasive convention (as is, in opera, the preeminence of the singing voice). As knowing spectators, we condone the lack of fidelity because we understand the scene *not as a recording, but a re-creation of human situation.*

There are countless conversation scenes in cinema—too many too enumerate, let alone examine here—in which a decrease of the volume of the ambient sound combines with an increase of the sound level of the words spoken, sometimes in noticeable contradiction to the distance of the characters from the camera.[13] The goal of this procedure, which may or may not include a framing musical background, is dialogue intelligibility or, more generally, the effective communication to the spectator of all narratively salient information. But another rationale is, as should by now be clear, the representation of an auditory perspective—typically, that of one or more characters. Rick Altman has termed this perspective—in a clear gesture toward the long-established term "point-of-view shot"—"point-of-audition sound."[14] Altman has also documented how sound engineers seemed to have struggled between the seemingly contradictory requirements of projecting a dialogue intelligibly on the one hand, and a "natural" and "acoustically faithful" rendition of the original on the other.[15] We need not be so concerned ourselves. Fidelity is a slippery notion, one that makes sense only to acousticians measuring the physical properties of a sound. In the real world, no sound is perceived in and of itself but always from a certain perspective, by which I mean not only a point in space ("point-of-audition" sound) but also a certain degree of cognitive and emotional investment. Cognitive and emotional investment drive both the selection and the highlighting of certain stimuli at the expense of others (*situated listening*). It is only too natural, then, that given the appropriate narrative context, increasing the volume of certain sounds at the expense of others results not only in greater fullness, clarity, and narrative emphasis but also the impression of a subjective, character-filtered selection of the auditory data and with it the representation of a certain psychological state.[16]

[13] On the discrepancy between image scale and sound scale as a function of dialogue intelligibility, see Rick Altman, "Sound Space," in *Sound Theory/Sound Practice*, ed. Rick Altman (New York: Routledge, 1992), 58–59.

[14] Ibid., 60.

[15] Rick Altman, "The Technology of the Voice," Part 1, *Iris* 3 (1985): 3–20; Part 2, *Iris* 4 (1985): 107–19.

[16] As Altman has indicated, the notion of fidelity can only apply to a sound as heard in the pro-filmic context anyhow, not the narratively constructed one: Altman, "Cinema Sound at the Crossroads: A Century of Identity Crises," in *Le son en perspective: nouvelles recherches*, ed. Dominique Nasta and Didier Huvelle (Bruxelles: Peter Lang, 2004), 26–28.

Consider, for argument's sake, a counterexample from Jean-Luc Godard's 1962 feature *Vivre sa vie*. The first conversation between Nana (Anna Karina) and her husband, Paul (André S. Labarthe), set in a café, is shot with direct sound and does not appear to have been dubbed or retouched in postproduction. That is, Godard did not adjust the levels and quality of the sounds present in the scene, nor did he decrease the volume of such competing sounds as one hears in a typical urban café: the chatter and occasional laughter of other customers, the roar of the off-screen traffic, the noise made by the barman as he cleans coffee cups and operates the coffee machine, and so forth. The seemingly haphazard use of fragments of Michel Legrande's plaintive title theme, rather than drawing us into the characters' ambit, further enhances the presence of ambient sound. The result, I would argue, is not merely a loss in dialogue intelligibility; there is also a distinct lessening of the impression that we are perceiving through the filter of a discriminating consciousness.[17] I am not claiming that clear, intelligible dialogue implicitly—and invariably—posits a perceptually specific perspective (whether that of a character or an invisible observer). Such a sound, simply by virtue of being intelligible or even foregrounded, is not the representation of a perceptual experience any more than a camera shot is the representation of a visual perception simply by virtue of being perspectival. Most techniques and figures of style in cinema are a function of presenting narratively salient, as opposed to perceptually specific, information.[18] Yet it is undeniable that in certain specific cases, the presence of a sound expresses the way in which the characters themselves experience it and that as such is "faithful" to the psychological reality of perception as selection (if not the physical reality of the sound as recorded).

Anesthesia/Hyperacousia

Alice's reaction in *Blackmail* is a clear case of stimulus-driven focusing of the attention. No longer engaged in the low-demand, mundane tasks associated with the consummation of an uneventful meal with her parents, she is made alert and starts amplifying the word "knife" in her mind (in a bit of admittedly

---

[17] The impression is strengthened by the visual presentation, as wife and husband are given each a separate shot, their back to the camera. For an interpretation of Godard's use of sound as a legacy of Brechtian theater, see Alan Williams's essay "Godard's Use of Sound," *Camera Obscura* 8 (1982): 194–209, and also Annette Davison, *Hollywood Theory, Non-Hollywood Practice: Cinema Soundtracks in the 1980s and 1990s* (Aldershot, UK: Ashgate, 2004), 80–81.

[18] On this, see David Bordwell, *Narration in the Fiction Film*: (Madison: University of Wisconsin Press, 1985), 9–12; and James Lastra, *Sound Technology and the American Cinema* (New York: Columbia University Press, 2000), 95–98.

contrived mise-en-scène, she is encouraged in this by the all-too-willing shop customer herself). This is not merely a case of selective attention. Put more precisely, *anesthesia*—Alice's inability to hear anything the older lady is saying, and presumably her obliviousness to the sounds of the environment around her as well—is a foil to *hyperacousia*, that is, her almost manic focus on, and greatly exaggerated susceptibility to, that incriminating word. The episode remains famous, and much commented on, partly on account of its distinctiveness (and, consequently, lack of a progeny). The Hitchcock of *Blackmail*, made at the dawn of the sound era, was experimenting with new solutions as much as complying with established conventions. In what remains the best analysis of the film, Elisabeth Weis argues that "Hitchcock's challenge was to find techniques for externalizing the heroine's guilt. The solution, which entails stylization and distortion, is the aural equivalent of visual expressionism."[19] Despite this, the intuitiveness of the dramatic situation and the rhetorical clarity of its handling made it instantly understood. We understand the scene because the psychology of Alice's reaction is grounded in everyday, ecological conditions. In particular, the scene is consistent with the impression—or, as I will argue later, the retrospective illusion—that upon focusing on a stimulus one is literally not hearing anything else. Nevertheless, at least two more dimensions of the soundtrack contribute to its communicativeness. First, the customer's gibberish is a sonic invention and a twofold metaphor at that, pointing as it does to her annoying presence on the one hand—an element of characterization—and Alice's being at a loss as to what she is saying on the other. The volume at which "knife" is uttered enhances its clarity, yet it also functions metaphorically. It tells us that Alice's attention is exclusively focused on that and *only that* word (which keeps replaying frantically in her mind at the expense of everything the old woman is saying). In music recordings, volume is sometimes varied to create the illusion of proximity or distance from the source of the sound. In this scene, volume functions as a metaphor for the attention in something like the way a point-of-view shot or the use of selective focus translates a character's interest in a particular portion of the visual field into a closer—or sharper—view of it than is actually the case. Alice's unusual degree of focus makes the clarity and intensity of the sound of the word "knife" inextricably tied into one another so as to make them almost seem indistinguishable aspects of what is being heard. These metaphorical dimensions are key to the oft-mentioned "expressionistic" quality of Hitchcock's use of sound and contribute to the "spectacular" dimension of the filmmaker's engagement with the then-new tool of recorded, in-sync sound.[20]

---

[19] Elisabeth Weis, *The Silent Scream*, 43.
[20] Ibid., 31. On the display of film technology as spectacle, see Belton, *Widescreen Cinema*.

Attention as Consciousness

In a seeming foil to this argument, Rick Altman has claimed that, to the contrary, the representation of perceptually specific information has played a major role in effacing the technological apparatus of the cinema.[21] By subsuming the sights and sounds of a film under the logic of subjective representation, so the argument goes, the operations of filmmaking are effaced since they appear to motivated by, indeed are collapsed out with, the position in space and specific circumstances of the character herself. "We are asked not to hear," writes Altman, "but to identify with someone who hears for us."[22] Unlike Altman and other scholars who have followed in his wake, I see sound technology as a resource, not something that needs "effacing." The relationship of film sound to real-life settings is not one of recording or one of greater or lesser fidelity to an aboriginal moment in which a given sound is uttered or generated through supposedly natural means. The relationship, rather, is one of *substitution*, one in which construction, interpretation, and reinvention are part and parcel of both the filmmaker and the audience's horizon of expectation. The representation of subjectivity possesses enough intrinsic interest for filmmakers to pursue it for its own sake, rather than playing second fiddle to some conspiratorial attempt to distract filmgoers from the artificial, highly mediated nature of the sounds they hear in a film.

This is not to say that subjectivity in cinema does not merit closer scrutiny. The subject remains shrouded in a curiously old-fashioned version of Cartesian dualism. For example, David Bordwell and Kristin Thompson distinguish between "perceptual subjectivity" on the one hand and "mental subjectivity" on the other.[23] The latter term refers to "purely internal" events such as the onset of images, memories, and hallucinations, while the former describes sights and sounds as perceived from a specific point of space and under specific external circumstances (such as the descending of a thick fog, for instance, or the deafening noise of gunfire in a battlefield). A moment's reflection tells us that the representation of selective attention falls in neither camp. When applied exclusively to sound, Bordwell and Thompson's term "perceptual subjectivity" approximates the meaning of what Rick Altman, as we have seen, calls

[21] Rick Altman, "Sound Space," in *Sound Theory/Sound Practice*, ed. Rick Altman (New York and London: Routledge, 1992), 61.

[22] Ibid., 60. The tenor of Altman's argument reminds one somewhat of Laura Mulvey's critique of subjectivity (a subject I touch on in the next chapter).

[23] For their latest work on the subject, see Kristin Thompson and David Bordwell, "Categorical Coherence: A Closer Look at Character Subjectivity," 2008, retrieved from http://www.davidbordwell.net/blog/2008/10/24/categorical-coherence-a-closer-look-at-character-subjectivity/.

"point-of-audition" sound. Now auditory perspective is undoubtedly central to film, but it measures physical circumstances such as relative or changing distance of the source, volume, acoustics, or certain physiological conditions affecting the hearer—none of which, again, accounts for selective attention.

Let us briefly return once again to the character of Alice in *Blackmail*. Neither "perceptual" nor "mental subjectivity" account for the contents of the scene. The long stretches of unintelligible blabber are not the result of sudden changes in distance from the dining table, the position of the speaker relative to her, or, more improbably still, her impaired speech. What they indicate is the focus of Alice's attention and the impact this focus has on her. It is the refocusing of her attention toward the incriminating word and its overwhelming emotional impact, not some kind of hallucination, that the "distortion" in the soundtrack is charting. To quote James Batcho, the particular treatment of the soundtrack signals not a flight into fantasy but "the objective world coming to the consciousness of the subject in a particular manner."[24] In Akira Kurosawa's *Ikiru* (1952), when Watanabe-san (Takashi Shimura) is diagnosed with an incurable stomach cancer, he leaves the doctor's study in a state of muted shock and near numbness. As he walks out, aimlessly, nothing can be heard till, suddenly, the sounds of the busy thoroughfare make themselves manifest. The sudden shift telegraphs not the dawn of reality following an "unreal," fantastical silence but, more simply, a change in perspective.[25] In Merleau-Ponty's words:

> To pay attention is not merely further to elucidate pre-existing data, it is to bring about a new articulation of them by taking them as *figures*. They are preformed only as *horizons*, they constitute in reality new regions in the total world. . . Thus attention is neither an association of images, nor the return to itself of thought already in control of its objects, but the active constitution of a new object which makes explicit and articulate what was until then presented as no more than an indeterminate horizon. . . . This passage from the indeterminate to the determinate, this recasting at every moment of its own history in the unity of a new meaning, is thought itself.[26]

---

[24] James Batcho, "The Sonic Lifeworld: A Phenomenological Exploration of the Imaginative Potential of Animation Sound," *Journal of Sonic Studies* 6, no. 1 (2014): sec. "The Hearing Subject," par. 2, http://journal.sonicstudies.org/vol06/nr01/a05. On the notion of subjectivity as a "mode of experience where self and world are difficult to distinguish," see Michael P. Steinberg, *Listening to Reason* (Princeton: Princeton University Press, 2006), 7–8.

[25] I owe this example to Claudia Gorbman.

[26] Maurice Merleau-Ponty, *The Phenomenology of Perception*, trans. Colin Smith (London: Routledge and Kegan Paul, 1962), 30–31, cited in Vivian Sobchak, *The Address of the Eye: A Phenomenology of Film Experience* (Princeton, NJ: Princeton University Press, 1992), 71–72.

The process captured by Merleau-Ponty encompasses both an affirmation and a withdrawal, a presence and an absence. Admittedly, the sometimes drastic, all-or-nothing form this takes in the cinema does put to a severe test the notion that the focusing of the attention merely restricts the scope of our consciousness, for such a restriction often involves so profound a reconfiguration of the world around us as to border on a misperception (or even hallucination). Yet Batcho's fundamental point stands: falling as it does between the foil concepts of auditory perspective on the one hand and inner re-creation—be it recall, dream, or fantasy—on the other, the representation of aural subjectivity in the cinema remains undertheorized. Missing from most accounts is how the cinema gives tangible form to subjectivity understood as consciousness or, put another way, the *listening of someone (not) listening*.[27]

In a move that is in my opinion unwarranted, however, Batcho goes on to claim that "the distinction between the objective and the subjective is more clear with images than with sound."[28] To buttress this statement, he uses the example of a high-angle, static view of a vehicle passing by a camera (the latter being placed on a crane). While clearly not a point-of-view shot, Batcho writes, the trajectory in the dynamics of the sound, from soft to loud, as the vehicle moves closer to the camera, introduces an element of aural subjectivity. The argument rehearses the fallacy of the invisible observer in the realm of sound.[29] To be sure, filmmakers have time and again flouted the requirements of sound perspective. They assume that the spectators will imagine the changes in the sound themselves or make up for the missing information by recourse to other cues. But this does not mean that when a finely calibrated sound perspective is crafted, this invariably translates into the representation of perceptually specific information. To hear it as such, the spectator has to be made to feel that the sounds partake of the life of a sentient being in a given predicament.

The use of sound perspective is so widespread, I would argue, because it makes sound *intelligible*. Sound perspective is a trace not of perceptually specific

---

[27] As I did in the introduction, here I appeal to Thomas Nagel's belief in the significance of the subjective character of experience and its compatibility with realism (as opposed to idealism). For a classic discussion, see Nagel, "What Is It Like to Be a Bat," *Philosophical Review* LXXXIII, 4 (October): 435-450. Edward Branigan offers the following definition of cinematic subjectivity: "Subjectivity, then, may be conceived as a specific instance or level of narration where the telling is *attributed* to a character in the narrative and received by us *as if* we were in the situation of a character": Branigan, *Point of View in the Cinema: A Theory of Narration and Subjectivity in Classical Cinema* (Berlin: Mouton Publishers, 1984), 73. Branigan's definition of subjectivity differs from mine in that it places a strong emphasis on narration and especially narrative agency (as if the latter were by default a salient aspect of the moviegoing experience). I prefer to think of a character as a perceiver rather than a narrator.

[28] Batcho, "The Sonic Lifeworld," sec. "The Hearing Subject," par. 1.

[29] See note 17.

information per se but rather of the particular manner in which we, as a species, interpret the sounds produced by one or more moving sources, in either a stationary or moving position. What would count as an "objective" sound in the case observed by Batcho anyway? A sound from no point in space at all? Or the recording produced by a microphone installed on the moving vehicle? That, too, would hardly count as "objective," as recording technology is itself highly mediated by existing biases and interests and therefore geared toward specific goals, not to mention that the unchanging nature of the sound would in itself count as the marker of a recognizable perspective (that of someone riding the vehicle, for one).

Aural subjectivity is of course possible and often also central to a filmmaker's concept of a scene (as the *Blackmail* example makes abundantly clear). But the sense of hearing through a consciousness must be established explicitly first, or at least suggested through some appropriate, context-specific cues. In Alfred Hitchcock's *North by Northwest* (1959), the famous crop-dusting sequence begins with a high-angle shot of a deserted crop field across which vehicles are seen driving by at irregular intervals—a situation, incidentally, not unlike the one described by Batcho in the example cited earlier. As the bus on which Thornhill (Cary Grant) travels approaches the stop, unloads its unlikely passenger, and then leaves, the sound of the engine changes in dynamics. Yet at no point does one feel the presence of a consciousness behind the stationary camera. It is when we see and hear cars and trucks drive by from Thornhill's own vantage point that an element of subjectivity is finally injected into the representation. As in the shots of McKenna (James Stewart) walking to the taxidermist's shop in Alfred Hitchcock's *The Man Who Knew Too Much* (1956), the impression of hearing what Thornhill is hearing is strengthened by the surreality of the situation and the sense of menace by which it is pervaded.[30]

Three limit cases illustrate the gray area that exists between the fully realized representation of a subjective perception and one that merely resembles it by virtue of the use of a certain technique.[31] One is the shot of a conversation taking place on a dinghy, just off the shore of the island where Anna gets lost, in Michelangelo Antonioni's *L'Avventura* (1959). The shot is in many ways the reverse of the example from Allen's *Annie Hall* examined earlier. A fixed camera shows two characters leaving the shore on a dinghy. The scene is completed by a carefully presented sound perspective, which is further emphasized as the sound

[30] I refrain here from considering whether the shift results in empathy for the character. I am content to claim, after Murray Smith, that we are perceptually *aligned* with Thornhill: Smith, "Altered States: Character and Emotional Response in Cinema," *Cinema Journal* 33, no. 4 (1994), 34–56.

[31] For a complete taxonomy of more unambiguously constructed point-of-view shots, centered around a "character," see Branigan, *Point of View in the Cinema*, 103–11.

of the human voices thin out as their owners move farther and farther away from the shore (and with it the fixed camera). Not having been prepared for it by preparatory material, however, we are unable to project a consciousness through which the sounds are being heard. The result is uncanny.[32] In another Antonioni film, *La notte* (1961), there is a dialogue scene taking place in a car during a rainy night. The voices are inaudible on account of no better reason, it seems, than that the camera is outside the vehicle. Only the sound of the rain and the windshield wiper can be heard. The effect is once again uncanny because despite the clearly anthropomorphic nature of the shot, we are hard put to feel the presence of an actual character behind the camera. The representation of a perception as if from the perspective of a conscious, sentient being is unsupported by the sense of there being a person through whose consciousness we are seeing and hearing (nor does the film warrant the positing of a missing one, as might be the case, however hypothetically, in *L'Avventura*). The possibility of subjectivity, finally, underpins a very unsettling articulation of the uncanny in Stanley Kubrick's *2001: A Space Odyssey* (1968). I am referring to the episode in which Hal 9000, the futuristic computer, closely observes—and reads—the movement of David Bowman's (Keir Dullea) and Frank Poole's (Gary Lockwood) lips as they decide to discontinue its operations (thus in effect "killing it"). Here the inability to hear sound and overcoming this put us in grave doubt as to the nature of the machine, which we feel is endowed with all the traits of human consciousness.[33]

---

[32] The image can be productively linked to two more episodes, the combined effect of which is to intimate, without openly acknowledging, the presence of the missing Anna (Lea Massari). One is the shot of the steep, rocky cliff where Sandro (Gabriele Ferzetti) is looking for her. Endowed with a sense of subjectivity, the image is in fact emphatically not a point-of-view shot, as clarified by Sandro entering the frame from the right. The second is the episode in which Sandro and Claudia (Monica Vitti) stop in a deserted town, which they initially mistake as the baroque city of Noto (and where they think Anna might be found). The town, one of the many abortive attempts to revitalize the Sicilian inland in the 1950s and 1960s, is absolutely empty, silent, and lifeless. After realizing that no one lives there, Sandro and Claudia get in their car and leave. Now, while most directors would have followed the two protagonists with a cut to a closer shot of the car, Antonioni has the camera roll without changing setup instead. As the shot continues, the camera begins to track forward. While we hear the sound of the car engine dissipating in the distance, the camera continues to move. One not only appreciates the better view of the church and the square in front of it but also appreciates the camera movement in and of itself. Is the shot conveying the point of view of an unseen character?

[33] Chion calls the shot "subjective," qualifying the adjective by the use of quotation marks: Chion, *Kubrick's Cinema Odyssey*, trans. Claudia Gorbman (London: British Film Institute, 2001). See also his observations on Hal at pp. 101–3. At the other end of the spectrum, a more recent film like Tarsem Singh's *The Cell* (2000) features sounds that are strongly marked subjectively but cannot always be attributed securely to a character or a position in time (we may see a character in the here and now of the story but hear someone else's or a past perception, unsure of whether it is a memory). In her fine analysis of the film's soundtrack, Anahid Kassabian writes that *The Cell* poses a challenge to theoretical paradigms predicated on narrative and narrativity: Kassabian, "Rethinking Point of Audition in The Cell," in *Lowering the Boom: Critical Studies in Film Sound*, ed. Jay Beck and Tony

Heterological Silence

The use of a film score to silence the sounds of the environment, while accepted by convention, is overtly metaphorical in its tonally articulated evocation of the selective attention.[34] Attaining the same goal via the manipulation of speech and sound effects is, on the other hand, a more covert strategy. This is because speech and sound effects play the indisputable role of naturalistically rendered elements of the setting as well (sounds surround us at all times, and people speak as a matter of course).[35] This "anchor" in the everyday world of the characters mutes the metaphorical dimensions of sound—so much so that often we do not even wonder whether the soundtrack is a representation of a subjective reconfiguration of the sound space in the first place. I have mentioned the case of muted environmental sounds in dialogue scenes. Another significant class of examples is the intimate kiss between two lead characters. One recent example, from Wong Kar-wai's *My Blueberry Nights* (2007), is the kiss Jeremy "inflicts" on an unsuspecting Elizabeth who is drunk and still asleep on the bakery's counter. Like the "blueberry-cum-ice-cream-shot" inspired by Lynch and Godard, the kiss, too, has a precedent: the famous episode in Hitchcock's *Rear Window* in which Lisa gently kisses awake Jefferies (till then asleep in his wheelchair). Lisa first appears as a shadow over Jeff's face. Then, in a daring camera setup, Hitchcock shows her luminous face in soft focus from below, approaching him as if from his point of view. Jefferies is asleep, however. It would be tempting to interpret the shot as an image from a concurrent dream (or at least colored by it). Yet this would discount the duration and peculiar trajectory of the shot. What we are presented with is a process, not just an image. In particular, we are made to witness the first few moments in which the waking Jefferies opens his eyes and begins to register the muffled sounds of his surroundings. Lisa's face is initially cast in a dark shadow. Only gradually do her features become visible, most

---

Grajeda (Urbana: University of Illinois Press, 2008), 304. Given historical precedents like Resnais's *Last Year in Marienbad* (1961) and Teinosuke Kinugasa's *A Page of Madness* (1926) on the one hand, and the continuing interest in traditional explorations of subjectivity in contemporary cinema on the other, I am more inclined to believe that we will continue to see a plurality of approaches to the definition of the boundaries of subjectivity.

[34] Paul Théberge coined in this connection the term "relational silence": Théberge, "Almost Silent: The Interplay of Sound and Silence in Contemporary Cinema and Television," in *Lowering the Boom: Critical Studies in Film Sound*, 51–67.

[35] An exception is the use of "sound montages," sometimes referred to loosely as *musique concrète*, as if they were a film score. On this practice, see Joseph G. Kickasola, "Kie´slowski's *Musique concrète*," and Danijela Kulezic-Wilson, "Gus Van Sant Soundwalks and Audio-Visual *Musique concrète*," in *Music, Sound, and Filmmakers: Sonic Style in Cinema*, ed. James Wierzbicki (New York: Routledge, 2012), 61–75 and 76–88, respectively. On the use of sound as "overdetermined, *both* realist and metaphorical," see Chion, *Film, A Sound Art*, 209–10.

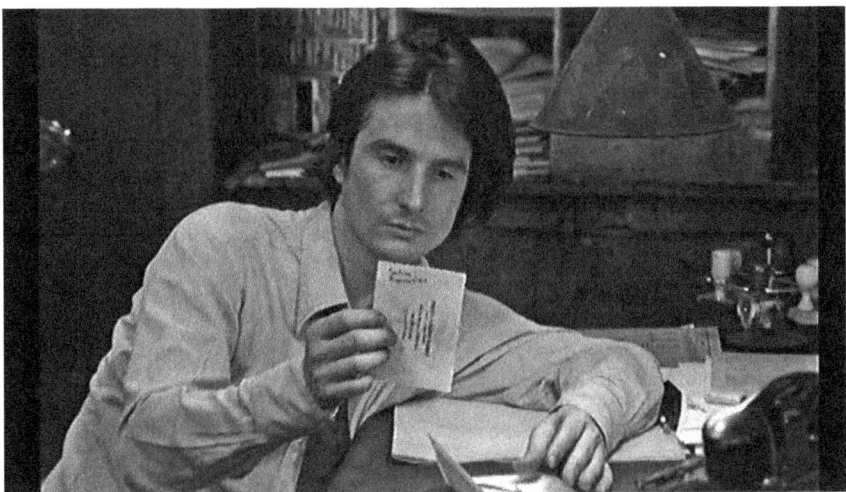

Figure 5.3 Love on the Run.

clearly as Grace Kelly enters the cone of an off-screen light source and nearly touches the lens (that is the moment immediately preceding the kiss). Kelly's movement toward the camera translates into a trajectory from opacity to clarity. A clear view of Lisa is the objective correlative of Jefferies's coming, literally, to his senses. Following a cut, finally, the camera "caresses" Lisa with a horizontal shot to highlight Kelly's exquisite profile just as her lips touch his. Jefferies is by now fully awake. As in *My Blueberry Nights*, the kiss is also singled out soni-cally. The scene begins in complete silence. Then, we hear the subtle traces of the rubbing of the fabric of her clothes against his, and perhaps the sound of their kiss (or is it imagined?). Wong Kar-wai and his team, too, created a fine piece of sound design to go with the kiss, the soundtrack consisting of nothing but tiny vibrations in the air and the sonic residue of microscopically small objects—the slight quiver of an erotically charged space, as it were, captured in a moment of extreme absorption. Because environmental sound is *subtracted*, however, the scene does not appear to be a representation of a perception.[36]

A more explicit case of a realistic sound morphing into a complex metaphori-cal nexus signaling the work of the attention occurs in François Truffaut's *Love on the Run* (*L'amour en fuite*, 1979; Figure 5.3). Antoine (Jean-Pierre Léaud), finish-ing his day shift in a newspaper room, is reading a letter sent to him by Sabine

---

[36] Writing about *Rear Window*, for instance, Chion states that Hitchcock "closes freely the noises from the courtyard . . . to 'close' the dramatic space on the little theater of the living room and on the intimate domesticity of Lisa and Jeff": "The Fourth Side," in John Belton, *Alfred Hitchcock's Rear Window* (Cambridge, MA: Cambridge University Press, 2000), 115. Chion writes about this scene also in *Film, A Sound Art*, 281–87.

(Dorothée), with whom he is in love. Sabine's rejection catches Antoine unaware and breaks his heart. Stung, he is consumed by a pain that encroaches upon him like a dark fog, a process Truffaut conveys by sound. The scenario mirrors, by a telling symmetry, what I refer to in the next chapter as the breakdown of one's alertness following the sight of the love object. As Antoine deals with the blow, instead of a more conventional music cue, the film adopts a solution that, though parasitic on the use of scoring, is at once more novel and subtle: the printing machines from the next room grow louder and louder, till their repetitive, harsh, and deafening sound can be said to inhabit him. Whether Antoine actually zeroes in on the sound is a moot question, for he is incapable of attention at this particular moment. In drowning out all other sounds within earshot, rather, the machines signal the letting down of his guard. It is a withdrawal that takes the form not of numbness but its opposite. Hyperacousia at this moment suggests that it takes an effort not to let the sounds of habitual surroundings intrude into the sonically insulated "space" of our routines. Antoine is now incapable of such an effort.

The Sound of Betrayal

In keeping with the example from both *Blackmail* and *Love on the Run*, the central epiphany of the *Godfather* trilogy features a heightened, expressionistically distorted sound. The film, however, also deploys a subtle yet critical intervention of the film score. The premise of the episode is Fredo's (John Cazale) betrayal of the family. As if to underline the unspeakable ugliness, difficulty of fully grasping, and ultimately attendant difficulty of *representing* the betrayal, its precise date is difficult to determine. Coppola lets the news of Fredo's involvement in the attempt on Michael's (Al Pacino) life seep ever so imperceptibly into the viewer's mind by carefully placing hints of his dealings with Roth's (Lee Strasberg) best man, Johnny Ola (Dominic Chianese), across a long stretch of the narrative. These range from a phone call to Fredo at night before the attempt on Pentangeli (Michael V. Gazzo) to a quick exchange in which Michael probingly asks his brother whether he knows Ola (in response to which Fredo lies). Among the hints is the moment when Michael himself realizes his brother's indirect involvement in the attempted assassination. Michael's epiphany is but one step in the meticulously calibrated uncovering of his brother's link to Roth, however. The last, most explicit, and most conclusive piece of the puzzle is the notorious "kiss of death" scene, during the New Year's party held in Batista's lavish residence. Michael's words, "I know it was you, Fredo: you broke my heart," serve the primary function of conveying the news to the spectator not yet aware of it; at the same time, to those in the know, they are indirect enough to preempt the impression of overexplicitness. The explicit address has a strong dramatic justification in the fact that Michael felt the need to let Fredo know he knew, without thereby making him feel threatened. Because the epiphany functions as a premise to this swift yet crucial change in the relationship between the two brothers, both the process leading up and Michael's initial response to it had to be suitably subdued—hence the choice to set the scene in public and articulate its onset through music and Pacino's body language alone.

The episode is placed at the beginning of the last third of the film, as his "business trip" to Cuba is about to come to a close. This will turn out to be an appropriate placement for such a momentous plot development, falling as it does at roughly the midpoint of the trilogy as a whole (if fortuitously at that, since at the time of filming *The Godfather II* Coppola had as yet no plans to make a third installment of the family saga). In a brilliant stroke of operatic irony, the setting is among the most counterintuitively lurid imaginable: a strip joint in Havana. We are only a few weeks away from the overturning of Batista's regime, and Michael is in Cuba to finalize a deal with long-time partner/rival Hyman Roth, with whom he has an intricate, devilish bond defined by huge business interests and an equally large dose of profound mistrust. Both are ostensibly there to deliver cash to the Cuban government in return for casino licenses; in fact, feigning undying friendship till the very end, they are in the process of carrying out an assassination attempt on one another (both, as it turns out, botched). Michael is still reeling from the earlier attempt on his life in his very home, which he traces back to Roth. He is therefore also simultaneously on a mission to excavate information on who might have betrayed him. It is at this juncture that he entrusts Fredo with shipping the necessary cash to Cuba and showing a "good time" to the business representatives and politicians flown in to endorse the agreement with Batista.

And a good time is being had by all (Figure 5.4). Fredo first introduces the guests to predictably standard fare only to bring them, as the evening edges into

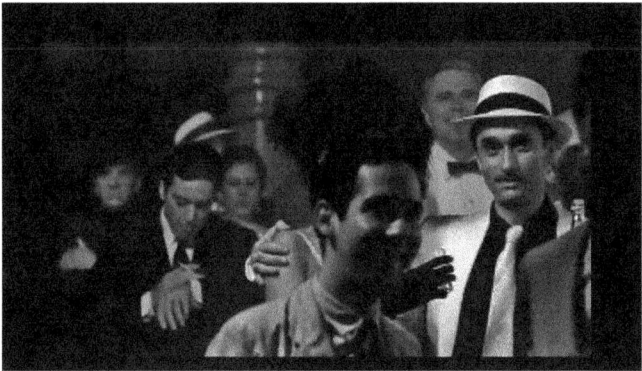

Figure 5.4 The Godfather II.

the night, to a notorious "adults only" club (in which he appears to be entirely at home). In the club, more than a bit inebriated, he plays master of ceremony of sorts to the group as a whole, guiding attendees through the various stages of the sadomasochistic ritual being enacted on stage at the expense of a tall, curvaceous, mixed-race girl tied to a pole. The cast is completed by the appearance of a tall, and ostensibly extraordinarily well-endowed, male, dubbed "superman." The latter is clearly as much an exhibit as the beautiful girl is, and he proceeds to perform a sexual act on her (not without being manhandled by the three threatening-looking female attendees who are clearly in charge of the proceedings). In the audience, the spectrum of characters and dispositions could not be wider. Fredo's guests make for a bemused audience. His female companion merrily goes along, as does Senator Geary's (G. D. Spradlin) girlfriend du jour. Geary himself, hard at work at mending his relationship with the Corleones after a harsh attack on the family followed by an even harsher put-down at his expense, feigns surprise and a certain amount of undisguised excitement about the display of human flesh. We of course know he is no innocent in sexual matters; indeed, his presence lends a degree of continuity between the sordid scene under way here and the equally sordid circumstances in which he was implicated earlier in the film. Michael, standing behind the group, is unimpressed. Further back, his bodyguard is his shadow and protector at once. His cool gaze encompasses the space as a whole, without betraying any engagement whatsoever. Temperamental differences aside, he and his boss are preoccupied by thoughts far graver than the other members of this ill-assorted group. As Roth has engineered the murder of Michael, the latter has, in turn, prepared a counterplan of his own, and he is only moments away from sending the bodyguard a cue. His awareness of the acute political crisis about to befall Batista, moreover, dresses up his nerve-breaking state of suspense in an aura of impending doom.

The camera setups follow from the psychological orientation of the characters, while the rhythm of the editing underlines each character's importance in the dynamics of the action. Medium-long reaction shots of the party include Fredo, Geary, and their companions in the foreground. Michael stands behind, to their right, and out of focus. The deployment of close-ups of Pacino, off-center, accentuates his distance and separateness, verging on impatience and frustration with the group. The bodyguard is visible in the background of the frame. He is also out of focus yet imposing, as if drawing Michael toward his ambit, and away from what lies in front of him. His role is to suggest an alternative line of action; as such, he is also featured in tighter cut-ins. His self-willed disengagement from the titillating show, while adding a touch of comedy, reminds us of what occupies his and his boss's mind. Michael occasionally turns toward him as if in open acknowledgment of the silent agreement taking shape between them. The arrangement and distribution of shots does not simply reflect but foreshadows the

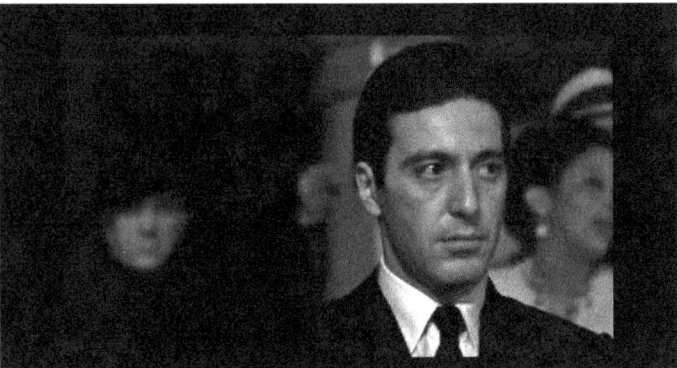

Figure 5.5 The Godfather II.

final destination of the scene, and with it the meaning of its inclusion in the film. It is Michael who, despite not occupying the literal center of any of the compositions, commands the setup, casting a shadow in two directions at once. Close-ups of Fredo, moreover, signal that he is first among peers; they, too, function as a premonition that he is soon to be the unwitting harbinger of change.

The sound mix reflects the raucous situation. The club is full and the audience responds to the antics on display with loud cheers and jeers. The show is accompanied by percussions and alto saxophone, the latter improvising suggestive slurs over an endlessly repeating rhythmic pattern circling around the chosen victim.[37] Following standard practice, the main characters' voices are artificially enhanced and thus emerge, with predictable clarity, from the crowd noise. Yet it is through the razor-sharp editing, Michael's silent reaction, and the appearance of a music cue, rather than any overt manipulation of Fredo's voice, that the most important utterance in the sequence—and arguably the whole saga—is framed. Geary asks Fredo how he has heard about the club. As Fredo replies that Johnny Ola took him there, there is a cut to a close-up of Michael overhearing (Figure 5.5). The cut is doubtless precipitated by the sudden shock provoked by his brother's off-the-cuff remark. As in *Blackmail*, "one frequent purpose of the offscreen dialogue is to contrast [Michael]'s emotions with the unawareness of other characters."[38] Next there is a cut to a medium close-up of Fredo, who continues to talk. At his mention of how "the old Roth" would never patronize such digs, Fredo's voice continues off screen as another shot shows Michael turning to his left and prompting the bodyguard to leave. The combined effect of the cut

[37] Written by Carmine Coppola, the cue is called "Danza esotica (Rumba di Amor)" and was recorded on location in Santo Domingo: Franco Sciannameo, *Nino Rota's The Godfather Trilogy: A Film Score Guide* (Plymouth, UK: Scarecrow Press, 2010), 128.

[38] Weis, *The Silent Scream*, 33.

first and then Michael's signal is to shift our attention away from Fredo's words without, however, altering the volume and quality of the sound of his voice. It is a shift that simultaneously also frames the casual remark he has made when still on screen, in retrospect, as an unwitting admission of guilt.

The confirmation of Michael's suspicion that Roth was the instigator of the attempt on his life is of a piece with the realization that Fredo betrayed him. As the bodyguard makes his way to kill Ola first and then Roth, the camera remains fixed on Michael, capturing, albeit partially, his coping with this unexpected piece of knowledge. I say partially because the representation of Michael's state is completed by a version of Nino Rota's so-called "The Immigrant," scored for the bass clarinet. Rota's score cuts an unusual figure against the sounds of the club, including, most prominently, the music being played on stage. Cacophony is here the sonic image of heartbreak. The cue begins exactly at the point when Michael turns toward the bodyguard after hearing Fredo's reference to Roth. The clarinet at first tentatively intones three Es, as if trying to find its bearings. Only after this tentative beginning does the instrument outline a recognizable statement of the theme, whose antecedent ends as Michael turns again toward the camera. The consequent of the first phrase completes the portrait of the daze Michael has suddenly found himself in, and the momentary desensitization to his surroundings that follows from it. In a classic image of the abstraction we fall prey to following a piercing revelation, Pacino's face wears an expression of despair, his eyes gazing into the void.

The sequence ends with a reprise of the long shot of Fredo and his guests. Fredo appears unaware of the false step he has just made. Michael is in the frame still, recoiling in pain, and throwing his head into his right hand (Figure 5.6). The sound of the saxophone, meanwhile, becomes more and more prominent till it nearly drowns out Rota's score. Michael, weakened by the sheer weight of his realization, bends forward. The gradual, finely calibrated, yet seemingly inexorable rise in volume of the sound of the saxophone would seem to

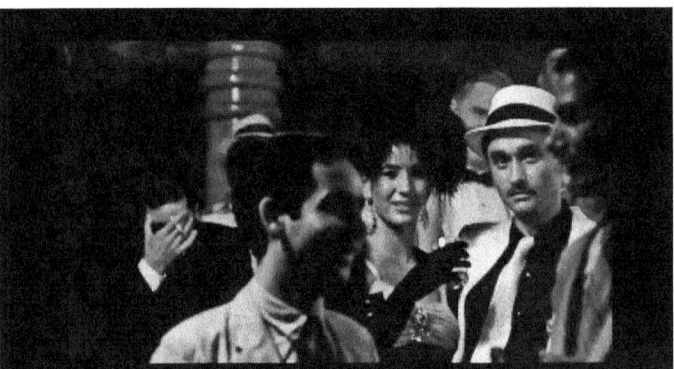

Figure 5.6 The Godfather II.

contradict the work just done by Rota's music; in fact, it is well in keeping with the psychological state Michael is experiencing. The vivid, grating, expressionistically reverberated sound of the saxophone bespeaks what is now his all-too-oppressive awareness of where he is and with whom, and his utter discomfort at not being able to erase their presence. A straight cut to the silent image of Johnny Ola standing in the balcony of Roth's hotel room puts an abrupt end to the scene. The sudden withdrawal of sound produces something like the acoustical equivalent of a smear. The echo of the club lingers but briefly in the new environment, and segues into a ponderous, slow-paced thump at the sound of which Michael's bodyguard quietly strangles Ola from behind.

Initiation

The enhancement of a sound to underline a character's isolation from his proximal environment is a technique redolent of Tennessee Williams's "plastic theater," a style of drama in which "setting, properties, music, sound and visual effects—all the elements of staging—must combine to reflect and enhance the action, theme, characters, and language."[39] An eloquent example of Coppola's embrace of this approach is yet another pivotal scene involving Michael: the killing, in *The Godfather I* (1972), of Sollozzo (Al Lettieri) and McCluskey (Sterling Hayden) (Figure 5.7). This is the episode that jump-starts Michael's career as a mafia boss. The three meet in an Italian restaurant in the Bronx to discuss an end to the feud over the need for protection of the drug dealing business that is holding sway as the biggest new source of money making in the underworld. As if foreshadowing the significance of sound in the climax, the space is strikingly silent. The characters sit down and exchange silent, interlocutory glances first. The only thing we hear is the sound made by the waiter pulling the cork of a bottle of wine. The resistance the cork offers to the waiter's upward pull strikes an appropriately uncomfortable, if slightly ironic, note. Sollozzo proceeds to talk to Michael in "Italian" (an impoverished, diluted version of Western Sicilian, in fact). This puts a degree of acoustical stress on the spectator who, like McCluskey, is at once excluded from the main conversation.[40] The move also clarifies for all parties involved, as well as the audience, the hierarchy in place between Sollozzo and the corrupt policeman

---

[39] Alice Griffin, *Understanding Tennessee Williams* (Columbia, SC: University of South California Press, 1995), 22. I am indebted to Feiwan Ho, currently a music major at the University of Hong Kong, for drawing my attention to Tennessee Williams's theater.

[40] On Coppola's choice, see Walter Murch's observations in Michael Ondaatje, *The Conversations: Walter Murch and the Art of Editing Film* (New York: Knopf, 2002), 121.

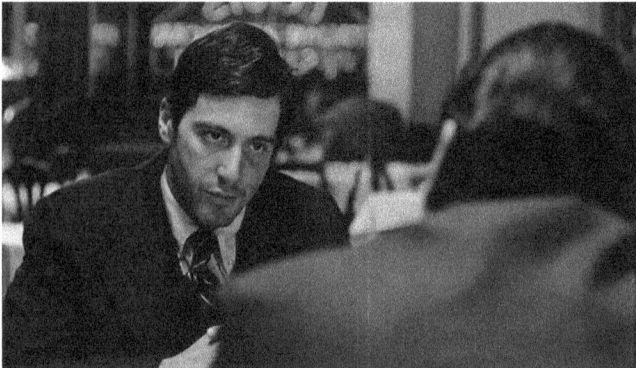

Figure 5.7 The Godfather I.

(who by virtue of being corrupt has debased himself even in the eyes of the criminals he works for). Michael, seen in repeated, sustained close-ups, listens on. The conversation being perfunctory, the switch to another language soon begins to underscore the futility of the verbal exchange. What it does manage to establish is the respective position of the three characters in the ensuing confrontation. McCluskey, in his role as law enforcer and keeper of appearances, is little more than an observer. The long shots of the restaurant interior capture his awareness of the need to come across as having a civilized conversation with his two dinner companions, just like the civilians dining a few tables away. Sollozzo, though obviously unaware of Michael's plot to kill him, appears to be in control since he is convinced that, short of being eliminated, he has the upper hand. Michael occupies the most complex situation of all, as he has to feign willingness to negotiate while preparing himself to strike.

Mindful of the plan, we watch the scene in a position of suspense. This intensifies the perception of time passing and prompts questions about when Michael will make his way to the restroom, where a gun has been planted. The conversation continues to be punctuated by long silences and glances. Meanwhile, the steel wheels of the elevated trains of the New York metro make a noticeable, screeching noise; the restaurant, one surmises, must be near a sharp turn or a stop.[41] The noise creates more than just an awareness of what lies outside; it also invites our contemplation of the rhythms of life in the world outside, a world indifferent to the terrifying knowledge that a double murder is about to be consummated. Such knowledge is naturally terrifying to the would-be executor, too. His sensitivity to this seemingly irrelevant sound, not coincidentally, grows as the decisive moment inexorably nears.

---

[41] On the use of sound in this scene, see the exchange between Walter Murch and Michael Ondaatje in Ondaatje, *The Conversations*, 120–24. Sciannameo reports that Rota had originally intended a cue to go with this scene: Sciannameo, *Nino Rota's The Godfather Trilogy*, 86.

With Mike back from the restroom, gun in tow, Sollozzo switches to speak dialect again after a few words in English. The camera tracks ever so slightly toward Michael, hinting not at the focusing of his attention, as the technique normally indicates, but rather at its drifting away. As in Puzo's novel, Sollozzo continues to talk but his words are at best merely registered.[42] It is to the sounds of the train's steel wheels that Michael has been turning again, rather like a ready-made mantra that allows him to remain cold and sane as he gathers the energy and cold blood to go ahead with the execution. By a gradual transformation, the sound of the train becomes at last an unwitting stopwatch, reminding Michael, on account of the assumption of regularity—trains run on a schedule—that time is passing, and that he has to honor the promise to act, and do so in a timely fashion. As the metaphorical countdown is over, the noise is at its loudest. But rather than simply marking the fateful moment at which he will finally spring to action and coloring it in predictably harsh tones, the intensity of the sound also tells us that Michael wishes he was not there. The implausible volume places him near the tracks. The presence of the off-screen metro noise is an expression of his nagging desire to be pulled outside that soon-to-be hellish scene.[43]

When he finally gets up and shoots, all off-screen sound promptly disappears. He regains his sense of being in the here and now of the restaurant, his mind one with the body. The gunshots take center stage against the silence—soon glacial—of the restaurant. The once-sitting bodies collapse backward, taking down the table with them. Coppola insists on the aftermath of the shooting long enough to show the scope of a novice's perception of the circumstances surrounding his initiation into murder. That these circumstances are eerily prosaic does not make them any less remarkable. A patron makes off as fast as he can while the restaurant staff looks on. A small group of diners at a different table remain seated, as if petrified. The furniture, tablecloths, silver, and food leftovers glow in their reassuring banality. After hesitating for a moment, Michael does what he had doubtless rehearsed many times. He runs out, but not without dropping his weapon first. A deactivated object, emptied of significance, the gun makes an aptly dull sound as it falls on the tiled floor.

The Sense of a Recurrence

Michael's initiation is capped by a fanfare-like version of "Michael's Theme," here appropriately redolent of a funeral march. "It's a classic example for me

---

[42] Mario Puzo, *The Godfather* (New York: G.P. Putnam's Son), 152.

[43] For a similar use of sound, albeit in a lighter vein, see also Curt's "initiation" to the Pharaohs gang in George Lucas's *American Graffiti* (1973). Murch rerecorded and edited the sound of Lucas's film, too.

of the correct use of music," says Walter Murch, "which is as a collector and channeler of previously created emotion, rather than the device that creates the emotion."[44] By now immediately recognizable, the cue is retrospective and prospective at once, lending a sense of inevitability to the outcome of Michael's "progress" as a mafia boss. The leitmotivic web intimates that he had always been destined to become a criminal. The future will bear this out in no uncertain terms, though, in fact, Michael *becomes* a criminal by *acting like one* in something like the way Gondo, in *High and Low*, also becomes a hero by acting out the part. Franco Sciannameo calls the musical intervention a "peroration" marking his "successful transformation into the new Godfather."[45] Sciannameo's choice of terms is apt; however, strictly speaking it is neither Michael nor the family but the operations of the narrative that the music self-reflexively "celebrates," with the film having successfully negotiated a difficult passage into a new stage of the saga.

Traditional leitmotivic analyses of film scores insist on the meaning attached to a theme and the latter's relationship to the other main themes of a score (as either parody, transformation, or development thereof). Nametags often assist in one's interpretive work, opening up new and sometimes unpredictable associations. One published score of the music for *The Godfather*, for example, calls the original version of the clarinet theme heard in the strip club sequence "Ethnic Longing Theme."[46] More commonly, the cue is referred to as the "The Immigrant Theme." To color the realization that Fredo betrayed the family with an evocation of a young Corleone arriving at Ellis Island creates a complex nexus of meaning.[47] Yet we run the risk of underestimating the impact of the music if we read too much into a nametag. Such tags apply to all variants of the same theme, irrespective of where they appear, and may well have been devised for practical and filing purposes (and in retrospect at that).[48] To think of recurrent themes in terms of semantic meaning, if not a verbal tag, is of course a long-standing topic of contention in musicology, with a ponderous literature to match. Far more interesting than any "meaning" Rota's theme may have is the way in which it endows

---

[44] Ondaatje, *The Conversations*, 122. Marcia Citron calls the cue "cathartic": Citron, "Operatic Style and Structure in Coppola's 'Godfather Trilogy,'" *Musical Quarterly* 87, no. 3 (2004): 445.

[45] Sciannameo, *Nino Rota's The Godfather Trilogy*, 86.

[46] See Citron, "Operatic Style and Structure in Coppola's 'Godfather Trilogy,'" 443.

[47] Sciannameo reads the use of the theme primarily in terms of the dark timbre of the bass clarinet, which he describes "as an excellent psychological brush stroke to express Michael's glacial inner feelings of contempt toward his brother": Sciannameo, *Nino Rota's The Godfather Trilogy*, 58.

[48] In this particular case, the name of the cue in the printed score speaks to its affect ("longing") as much as the placement in the narrative. Rota refers to it in the autograph score as "Gli emigranti" ("The Emigrants"), while the CD of the soundtrack refers to it as "The Immigrant." For a complete analysis of the score and the primary sources relating to its composition, see Sciannameo, *Nino Rota's The Godfather Trilogy*.

presence and gives a distinctive, indeed unique, shape to something that is, by definition, invisible or at any rate extremely difficult to detect: the veil of absorption that temporarily clouds Michael's perception of the space around him. Without such an understanding of the appearance of the music, it would be difficult to understand Pacino's body language as the outward symptom of the most momentous event of the scene (namely, the epiphany that so shocks and throws him off balance in the first place).

Marcia Citron has noted how the pickup pattern that opens each phrase and its characteristic dotted-quarter rhythm link this particular theme to the "Love Theme" and the "Trumpet Motive" that open the film, respectively. She also points out that there are harmonic similarities among them—the insistence on the first and fourth degree, among others—and comes to the conclusion that "just . . . as the story of *Godfather II* fills in *Godfather I*, so do Rota's thematic arrangements amplify the music's motivic material."[49] To be sure, the thematic relationships are striking—a case of "family" resemblance, indeed. Yet the case for a parallel between music and narrative development is weaker (whether intended, as Citron's reference to Coppola's interviews imply, or not). The significance of thematic relationships can be imputed to the need to create a tightly woven, cohesive sonic tapestry to sustain the impression of the coherence and interconnectedness of the world inhabited by the characters, and a sense of their evolving perspective on it. Leitmotifs have in this respect more than just a structural or rhetorical function. Thematic relationships make manifest the continuities in the characters' sense of their selves and their places in the world, which they flesh out in perceptually salient form. Citron's point about parallelism, moreover, seems to imply a separation between music and the narrative, as if the score were something that existed outside of or apart from the world of the characters. To the contrary, as I hope to have shown, Rota's theme *embodies* a moment of Michael's inner life and is thus, in more than one sense, *of* and not about—let alone outside of—his world (only not *as* music).[50] That Michael is not hearing the theme as music is in a sense obvious, and yet worth observing if only to stress that the outward appearance of something that he experiences from within, and is therefore invisible, is symptomatic of

[49] Citron, "Operatic Style and Structure in Coppola's 'Godfather Trilogy'," 443.

[50] On music "jumping the diegetic gap . . . 'seeking out' and uncovering the turmoil in Marion's mind," see Nicholas Cook, *Analysing Musical Multimedia* (Oxford: Clarendon Press, 1998), 66 (Cook is here writing about Hitchcock's *Psycho* [1960]). Note that Cook is not describing the process by which "nondiegetic" music becomes "diegetic," in film music studies parlance, for that would involve Marion hearing music in her head—a patently absurd idea. What Cook is referring to, rather, is how "music reveals the essence of the images—the truth that lies beneath their surface": Belton, "The Phenomenology of Film Sound: Robert Bresson's *A Man Escaped*," in *Lowering the Boom: Critical Studies in Film Sound*, 26. On the same question, see also Giorgio Biancorosso, "The Shark in the Music," and Kevin Donnelly, *Occult Aesthetics* (New York: Oxford University Press, 2015), 106.

a highly communicative narrative register.[51] In turning something that is intimately bound to a first-person perspective into an intersubjectively available form, film music simultaneously disavows and acknowledges the gulf that separates not only self from others but also fictional characters from flesh-and-blood spectators. The appreciation of this gulf, which is central to the experience of fiction, is muted if we posit too literal a process of identification between spectator and character. Ben Winters's claim that the characters hear the score of a film just as we do is a case in point.[52] The idea might apply to a musical or a Fellinian fantasy. But I do not think it can account for a much broader range of examples. Source music is transparent to its subject, as it were. This stands in clear contrast to the symbolic mediation involved in music embodying, representing, expressing, or at any rate pointing toward something else instead (a mode of functioning also performed by source music, incidentally, though it is normally shouldered by the film score). This is a distinction that matters a great deal, particularly if we are to grasp not only the panoply of ritual and syntactical functions music plays in a film but also its role in the effort after the representation of the invisible, immaterial, and even inaudible. Such effort was precipitated, among other things, by an interest in the representation of interiority, and the role music has played in this effort since the early nineteenth century is in this respect impossible to underestimate. Winters, moreover, seems unwilling to concede that music can further the goals of a realistic agenda, since its mere presence would be proof of the alternative reality or, to use Morin's term, "unreality" of cinema. Again, this is certainly valid for certain film genres, but not others. What makes (some) films realistic is not the degree to which they constitute a record of reality but rather how convincingly they construct situations that trigger self-recognition on our part (which is why even operas, to an operatically literate listener, can be realistic).

The "Immigrant Theme" appears at several points in the trilogy, punctuating key moments in the history of the Corleone family, as well as underscoring a sense of their familial bond. Why does the film convey Michael's intensely private experience in the strip joint in terms of a theme we have already heard? This is a question that touches not simply on the semantic meanings opened up by this particular scoring choice but also on the very interpretive strategy one is to take. The synoptic view of the distribution of recurrent themes and the interpretation of their meaning as accruing and evolving over time is common in operatic, symphonic, and now also film-musical analyses. In this vein, reading the film like a text, and with the benefit

---

[51] On communicative narration in cinema, see David Bordwell, *Narration in the Fiction Cinema* (Madison, WI: University of Wisconsin Press, 1985), 57–61.

[52] Winters, *Music, Performance, and the Realities of Film* (London and New York: Routledge, 2014), 181.

of hindsight, the reprise of the theme traces a lineage of blood and shared displacement from one's surroundings (be they a strip club, the city of Havana, Las Vegas, or even the Corleones' new home, the United States—all of them pale substitutes for the family's ancestral home in Corleone, Sicily). What I am interested in pursuing here, however, is the effect of repetition itself. This, despite or perhaps thanks to its seeming obviousness, remains underexamined in the enormous literature on leitmotifs (and the field of thematic analysis in general).

"The Immigrant" first appears in the climactic sequence of Vito's arrival by ship at Ellis Island in the company of hundreds of other hopeful immigrants. Citron rightly calls this presentation of the theme, as the new immigrants salute the Statue of Liberty, "unforgettable."[53] This is not merely apt praise but an apt description of what I see as the condition—recognizability—of its successful deployment in subsequent presentations. Later, upon hearing it and recognizing it as being the same, one need not call up the date or the specifics of the context in which it has already appeared. The point of recognition is to draw attention to how the theme is transformed, if at all, by a different balance in the mix, new acoustics or changes in texture, harmony and instrumentation. Recognition is as much a function of the appraisal of these changes as an encouragement to build connections between points lying at different stages of the narrative. Any such appraisal, moreover, will convey a sense of time past.[54] In the Havana strip joint, the minimal texture and sober, indeed sinister, timber of the bass clarinet mark a different station of the story (independent of what the theme may be referring to prior to this particular statement). What is so striking about this scene is the lengths to which Coppola and his team went, in a classic case of cinematic *sprezzatura*, to construct a piece of storytelling whose wealth of details and subtle inflections are in excess of the attentional span of the first-time viewer. The indirectness with which Michael's breakdown is staged is in keeping with the fact that at no point in the film is Fredo's "unspeakable" betrayal explicitly articulated. Rota's variant of "The Immigrant" is a key element of the staggered yet ultimately inexorable unveiling of Fredo's position in the plot to kill his brother. Coppola must have agreed that in the absence of too overt an expression of surprise and shock on Michael's part, some music was needed and yet it too, unlike more conventional fact-conveying recurrent themes, should insinuate rather than declare. It does so, as we have seen, as much by virtue of its own physiognomy as by creating a jarring dissonance with the sounds of the live performance. This is

[53] Citron, "Operatic Style and Structure in Coppola's 'Godfather Trilogy,'" 443.

[54] On creating a "past in music," see Carolyn Abbate, classroom lecture overheard at Princeton University, November 1993, in Richard Taruskin, *The Oxford History of Western Music*, vol. 3 (New York: Oxford University Press, 2005), 496.

achieved primarily through the extraordinary decision to maintain the volume of the latter constant throughout, in a cacophonous play of diegetic music and nondiegetic cue that has few peers in world cinema (though the Minghella of *The English Patient* comes close, and the precedent of Mizoguchi's films cannot be discounted). The low register at which the theme is played, as well as the relative rarity of the instrument itself, mutes its recognizability. The first note at the clarinet hardly registers as music; rather, it strikes one as yet another element of the crowd noise. It is only by insisting on the same note and the increasingly distinctive timbre that the cue begins to assert its presence as a separate, indeed discrete, element of the mix. Playing a tune at the extreme range of a sound source has long been a means of blurring the clarity of the line, and Rota exploits this fact brilliantly here. The continuing presence of the onstage music, finally, threatens the very comprehensibility of the cue as a melodic line at all. Whether one hears the melody or not, the cue manages to create a perceptible rift between Michael and the scene around him. This is its most important function, and one that is emergent in the specific context at hand.

We still have not answered the question, why employ a motif we have already heard? Few will deny that repetition and a new context are somehow responsible for investing it with a new and highly distinctive role (new, that is, in the context of *The Godfather*). The question is, how? Imagine, for argument's sake, that instead of using a variant of "The Immigrant," Coppola had insisted on a different cue; let this cue, moreover, be in roughly the same style, and scored for the same instrument. Given the context and the actor's body language, the gist of the scene would come across just as clearly: a veil of shock and distress is descending upon Michael. What is gained, instead, by deploying a variant of the theme heard at least four times already? As mentioned earlier, a standard answer would invoke the calling up of associations to places and situations "visited" or "touched" by the music on previous occasions. The answer would have some merit insofar as it elucidates how a composer—in this case, Rota—has responded to the needs of scoring key narrative junctures or moments in which the director seeks to build a character. After all, who but the composer knows exactly which music is heard at what moment of the film? Even when the composer acted intuitively, as was often the case with Rota, researching or speculating about his choices has an undeniable historical value. A synoptic view of a film's cues, however, tells us precious little as to why we respond to recurrent themes the way we do. Short of an extraordinary feat of memory, the web of associations is not perceivable. Their conception, and possibly perception, is really possible only upon a post facto, textual analysis of, or extreme familiarity with, the film.[55]

---

[55] See Jerold Levinson, *Music in the Moment* (Ithaca, NY: Cornell University, 1997) on the difference between perception and conception of form.

There is another way to answer the question about how recurrent themes work, one that does justice to the scope of the attention in the here and now of the film viewing experience. This is to posit the intention of a maker, or at least an "intelligent design," as a perceived property of a film. With this I do not mean the director as deus ex machina but rather the belief that the sounds and images presented to us have been laid out by a controlling intelligence whose use of recurring musical motifs—or, in the case of a new theme, generically recognizable features—begs for interpretation in that it is both deliberate and strategic. Recognition, in other words, cues us to search for meaning. Because of this, to recall a motif is not merely to recognize specific features of the music as being the same or a variant thereof; it is also to grasp the *sense* of a recurrence by detecting a pattern and reckoning the presence of a communicative intention.[56] This creates the leitmotif's reference. In this situation, memory is much more than a retrieval mechanism, for it is bound up with the very coming into being of the correspondence between the theme and the event it points to. It predisposes us to forging one in the first place. A leitmotif is not a floating capsule whose associative content simply awaits downloading, like a shipped good upon arriving at a dock. Recognizing it as being a recurring element deliberately dispatched to us is a constitutive stage in the activation of that very content. Without such recognition, the ship will moor at another port. It is a musicological truism that the basis of leitmotifs lies in the ability of music to make us recall the circumstances in which it was first heard.[57] I would put it the other way around: upon hearing a motif or theme a second, a third, or, as in this case, a fourth time, and recognizing it, the concurrent circumstances, specific to the drama's "here and now," attach themselves to the music.[58]

The fact that the crucial role played by Rota's theme in the Havana strip club sequence hardly figures into any of the writings on the film would seem to lend credence to Gorbman's idea of "unheard music." Narrative cueing of the sort heard—or barely registered—in the strip club sequence unquestionably calls upon habitual responses and skills acquired too early on in one's filmgoing life to register as exceptional or worth attending to. But one does not have to attend to the operations of meaning creation themselves to be said to be paying attention. The import, not the process by which it is acquired, is what matters. Michael's

---

[56] I use the term "sense" as defined by Gottlob Frege in the classic essay "Über Sinn und Bedeutung" ("On Sense and Reference"), *Zeitschrift für Philosophie und philosophische Kritik* 100 (1892): 25–50.

[57] An early, stimulating articulation of this truism is Leonid Sabaneev, "Remarks on the Leit-Motif," *Music and Letters* 13, no. 2 (1932): 200–6.

[58] There is something like the adumbration of a similar point in Dahlhaus's claim, with regard to the motives of Amfortas and the "fool" in *Parsifal*, that "the exposition of a motive [*sic*] is not necessarily the first time it is heard, but only when it is represented on the stage in some way": Carl Dahlhaus, *Richard Wagner's Music Dramas*, trans. Mary Whittall (Cambridge: Cambridge University Press, 1979), 149.

epiphany, however, poses a special problem. What is the saliency of, if not the music, at least the epiphany that the music plays so subtle yet crucial a role in conveying? In the popular art known as "the movies," simplicity and transparency serve the ideals of clarity and accessibility.[59] These ideals have been appropriated by the industry so as to enroll ever larger slices of not just the national but also the international markets, and to instill a constant desire for new products. Most films are made to be watched just once. While partaking of this modus operandi, *The Godfather*, like most other films examined in this book, works at different levels of comprehension simultaneously, exhibiting complex textures that betray the self-consciousness, pride, and pleasure of the filmmaker working for his peers and for an audience willing to engage in repeat encounters with his films.

At stake in the refusal to stage Michael's epiphany in all-too-explicit, easily accessible terms is also a question of tone and register, in particular, the understanding of the mafia culture as pervaded by a wariness of confrontations and the open display of one's knowledge. This explains, for instance, why Sonny (James Caan) exits the drama relatively early on. With him at the helm, the saga, or the route to the uncovering of a similarly plotted betrayal, for that matter, would have been very different indeed. *The Godfather* is unquestionably a character-driven as much as a topic-driven drama. Mike's own handling of the situation—silent, discreet, and oblique—determines how it appears to the spectator. This applies to the entire process that leads from his initial suspicion to his becoming absolutely certain about his brother's case. No step in the process of unveiling Fredo's betrayal is buried or hidden; yet each step is, in and of itself, insufficient for us to be able to tell where it leads. Only through repeated cues, and the mounting evidence they present, can the viewer grasp the gravity of what the hints have been pointing to all along. The result is that we come to know something without being aware of us learning about it at any one stage of the process. In this way, the open acknowledgment of the betrayal remains beyond—or, better, beneath—representation.

---

[59] Noël Carroll, *Interpreting the Moving Image* (Cambridge, MA: Cambridge University Press, 1998).

6

Love at First Sight

Intense attachments to particular individuals, especially when the attachments
are of an erotic or romantic sort, call the attention away from the world
of general concern.
—Martha C. Nussbaum, *"People as Fictions: Proust and the Ladder of Love"*

"Love at first sight" offers a particularly significant articulation of the irony of
representing through music the failure to perceive sound. When the proverbial
bolt of lightning strikes, the senses are temporarily numbed and the physical
world recedes in the background of one's consciousness—or, at least, so one
would surmise from all manner of literary, televisual, and cinematic representations thereof. As re-elaborated at the hands of filmmakers and musicians, the
love-at-first-sight scenario has profusely incorporated music, the use of which—
stingers, lush strings, and all—has indeed become proverbial (or, depending on
one's proclivities, notorious). A common feature of films both old and new is
the restriction of the visual field, the camera focusing on the face or at least the
upper part of the body of the lovers seen either in separate, alternating shots or
in the same frame. A stinger or other significant change in the soundtrack—a
new theme, the varied presentation of a previously heard one, or a sudden surge
in volume—may signal the moment love "strikes," temporarily pushing ambient
sound aside. If music is an element of the original environment—as in Zeffirelli's
paradigmatic *Romeo and Juliet* (1968), for instance—the composed score will
take its place in the mix. The music will invariably be languid, euphonious, and
scored for melodic instruments such as the upper strings supported by the warm
timbre of the woodwinds (and occasionally the orphic harp).

The use of music in love scenes harks back to both opera and the popular theater (especially melodrama). Common to all three forms is a concern with giving a
tangible presence to the most uncontrollable emotional impulses.[1] This led to the

---

[1] Peter Brooks, *The Melodramatic Imagination* (New Haven, CT: Yale University Press, 1974).

development of an extremely communicative form of presentation of the action, one in which nothing was to be hidden from view. The generous employment of music for just such a purpose also meant that the invisible, or undetectable, now revealed itself—somaticized, as it were—in musical form.[2] The language of "love at first sight" in the cinema is more than a rhetorically effective way of signaling the onset of a feeling, however. The close-ups, cross-fades, and music also tell us, often in lovingly executed detail, that the characters no longer see or hear what is around them; put another way, they sketch not only a symptomatology but also a *phenomenology* of what it is like to fall in love. While love at first sight may well be a myth, robust anecdotal and experimental evidence indicate that strong emotions do impair the attention, drastically narrowing the scope of our perception.[3] By an ironic form of mimesis, in the movies anesthesia is often sublimated into musical plenitude—a classic instance of heterological silence.

The evolution and, in some cases, increasing sophistication of "love at first sight" scenes has doubtless been facilitated and even encouraged by technology. Editing, synchronization, and analog, multitrack, and finally digital recording have proven to be powerful and sophisticated tools in the hands of the filmmaker interested in the fine-grained representation of the attention through the calibrated use of the different components of the final mix. Yet at the heart of the trope there also lies a difficulty. A discontinuity or gulf, crossing which is akin to leaping into a void, seems to mark the path that from the phenomenon takes us to its representation. If not an irreconcilable contradiction, the representation of perceived silence by its virtual opposite comes across at least as a desperate measure. The reason for this is that the representation of subjectivity is by its nature paradoxical, forcing us into the strange position of being party to a first-person experience of which we are simultaneously outside observers. Its history, moreover, is shaped by forces pushing in opposite directions. The exigencies of communicating effectively the perspective of a character must appeal to some intuitive sense of "what it is like" to be a person in that position, above and beyond the codes and conventions that have regulated the representation of love at first sight. Given its traditional role as the "language of the emotions," music was in a sense destined to play a role in this effort. This is ironic, however, for it coincided with a time in which a wide range of social, institutional, and creative agendas conspired to stress its status as the nonrepresentational art par excellence (culminating in the ideology of absolute music on the one hand and its

---

[2] Emilio Sala, *L'opera senza canto* (Venezia: Marsilio, 1995), 17–18. On the history of mélodrame, see also Jacqueline Waeber, *En musique dans le texte. Le mélodrame, de Rousseau à Schoenberg* (Paris: Van Dieren Editeur, 2006).

[3] For a classic interpretation of the findings, see Daniel Kahneman, *Attention and Effort* (Englewood Cliffs, NJ: Prentice Hall, 1973).

shallower, institutional version, formalism, on the other). Among the German Romantics, music could embody the subject, but only in a much more abstract and universalizing sense not ascribable to a concrete subject position.[4] Later in the nineteenth century and especially the twentieth century, a new, naturalistic sensibility emerged that deemed music used in such a fashion a redundant and, indeed, melodramatic intrusion into the toolkit of the realist artist.[5] This sensibility is still with us today and informs not only the visual and sonic language of many films from around the globe, which renounce music as a matter of principle, but also the reception of films that do feature music as a matter of course.

In a soap opera, one need not watch the screen to know what is happening: the music bares it all. It is a rhetoric that would seem to acknowledge not only the legacy of radio dramas but also the intermittent or distracted mode of television consumption (as in multitasking or doing chores away from the screen).[6] Modes of television viewing have changed, approximating, in the case of fiction, those of the cinema.[7] In certain genres, however, music still functions like a flag, a means to draw or prop the spectator's own slumbering attention, or to advertise the film's own sense of self-importance or gravity. But while it may be redundant, it is at times also an inescapable element of disambiguation. Love does not have a facial expression to match, which has made psychologists, and Darwin before them, think of it not as an emotion but rather a drive.[8] In this respect, the use of music partakes of the effort to attract and enthrall but also conjure plausible types and situations, all the while preserving the audience's absorption in the drama playing out before them. Despite what some commentators see as its irreducible "irreality," film music can in fact be enrolled to further the agenda of psychological realism.

The heterology "music equals silence" points to another difficulty. This follows from our understanding of what attention narrowing is. That the onset of a feeling should cloud perception, after all, is less intuitive than it seems, and makes for a decidedly intractable subject. This is not a simple case of what psychologists think of in terms of allocation as when, for instance, they consider the competition between stimuli in the same modality (for example, two sounds) or

---

[4] Michael P. Steinberg, *Listening to Reason* (Princeton: Princeton University Press, 2006), 9.

[5] Discomfort at the "irreality," "intrusiveness," or patent "sentimentality" of music in cinema reminds one of Diderot's distaste for the theatricality of eighteenth-century acting.

[6] John Ellis, *Visible Fictions: Cinema, Television, Video* (New York and London: Routledge), 128; Rick Altman, "Television Sound," in *Studies in Entertainment: Critical Approaches to Mass Culture*, ed. Tania Modleski (Bloomington: Indiana University Press), 50.

[7] Carolyn Birdsall and Anthony Enns, "Rethinking Theories of Television Sound," *Journal of Sonic Studies* 3, no. 1 (October 2012) [http://journal.sonicstudies.org/vol03/nr01/a01].

[8] Charles Darwin, *The Expression of the Emotions in Man and Animals*, 3rd ed., with an Introduction, Afterword and Commentaries by Paul Ekman (New York and Oxford: Oxford University Press, 1998), 83.

two or more modalities (a sound and the gazing upon of an object or a scene). Nor is it a case of a stimulus in one sense modality affecting another sense modality. Nor is it, finally, a type of mind wandering. Whether blissful or traumatic, a strong emotion is rather like a short circuit of the senses, the momentary failure of a sentient body whose mental life vaporizes into pure feeling as a result of, and in a sense coerced by, coming to terms with the emotional impact of a fellow human being. Whether films are accurate gauges of how attention works or not, the myriad ways in which they stage love at first sight are a stab at how to picture and talk about such a failure of the attention, one that scientific psychology has so far been unable to provide (whether for want of interest or imperviousness to experimental testing). Films invite us to think of attention in novel ways, that is, not simply as a resource to be allocated but as a capacity that breaks down—a passage that the irruption of music in the mix, despite flouting the most elementary rules of verisimilitude, conveys with unquestionable efficacy.

Music as Prosthesis

Do people fall in love at first sight? Insurmountable difficulties conspire to make the question virtually unanswerable. More a pointer than a descriptor, the expression itself is shorthand for a much more complex and nuanced situation. It isn't just the senses, let alone sight alone, that are responsible for the seemingly irresistible attraction between two strangers. Would-be lovers, moreover, are often cued up about one another, or at least in a state of "readiness" well before their first encounter. Reaching a consensus on the veracity of the scenario would have to overcome the hurdle of how to know what goes on in minds other than one's own: what philosophers refer to as the epistemology of other minds or, more colloquially, the "other minds problem." Disentangling personal history from self-mythologizing on the one hand, and lived experience from self-fulfilling prophecy on the other is not only difficult but also futile. Works of fiction shape our experience as much reflect it. Love at first sight, after all, makes for a good story, whether in an epic poem, novel, film, or real life. What we can be sure of is the reality and extraordinary longevity of its representations, and how these have provided us with a descriptive kit, a pool of gripping, powerful—if at times also stale—metaphors with which to make sense of our emotional life. Films play on the seemingly inexhaustible desire for romance by their audiences. Whether by exploiting generic expectations or planting along the way signs specific to the narrative at hand, writers and directors have steered the love-at-first-sight scenario decisively in the direction of suspense. Besides being feted, the two leads of a love story are invariably also *fated*, their encounter less a surprise than a fulfillment, however delayed, of what one had been expecting all along.

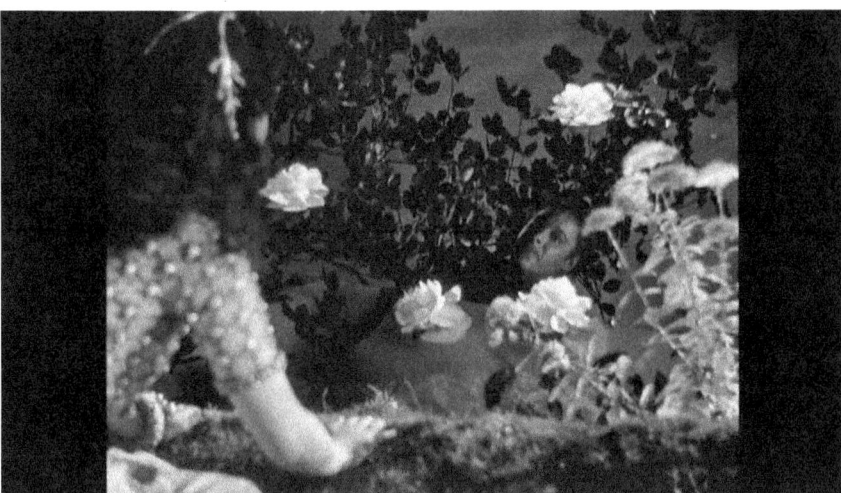

Figure 6.1 The Thief of Bagdad.

Whether as a crossroads, pivot, or crisis, love at first sight has inspired end-less elaborations, variants, and reinventions—hence the sense of competition, as much as respect for tradition, that pervades the history of its realizations in the cinema. The Technicolor, Alexander Korda–produced *Thief of Bagdad* (1940) offers a fine variant of the classic formula—close-up + eyeline match + music = love at first sight—that characterizes so many versions of the situa-tion (Figures 6.1–6.3).[9] The Princess (June Duprez) is alerted to the appearance of a "genie"—the disgraced King (John Justin) in disguise, as it turns out—by her coterie of attendants (who play in this context a role akin to that of Cupid). Though the part of the Princess is played by an actress older than her putative age, her reaction betrays the confused sexuality of the teenager. Erotic impulse, desire for play, and a sense of mystery drive her to uncover the genie's presence in the magical garden of her palace. She first sees Ahmad, with whom she falls in love, as a reflection in the water (the myth of Narcissus, here cleverly referenced by inversion, is a famous, indeed revealing, instance of the love-at-first-sight motif). It is not until the genie jumps off the tree and surprises her from behind that the two meet "in the flesh." At that point, he finally sees her, too, and swiftly reciprocates her feeling. As the camera gradually closes in on the two would-be lovers talking and looking intently into each other's eyes, the scene culmi-nates with a passionate kiss in a close-up against an idyllic, quasi-Disneyesque, background. Here the use of variable framing is not so much shorthand for felt,

[9] The film was famously directed by a "committee," as it were, the baton being shared by Michael Powell, Ludwig Berger, and Tim Whelan, and the additional contribution of Korda's own brothers Zoltán and Vincent.

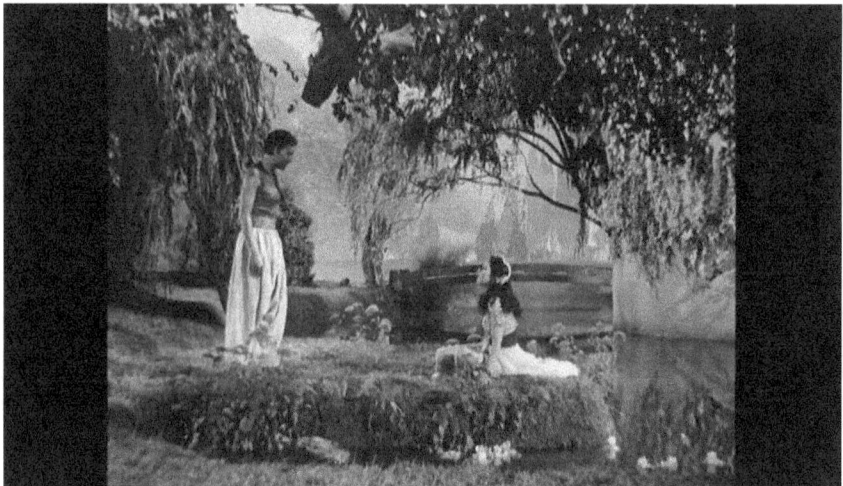

Figure 6.2 The Thief of Bagdad.

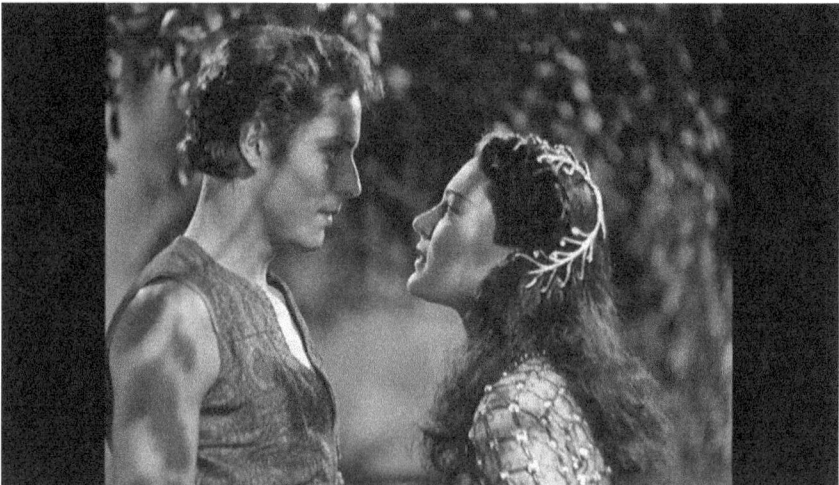

Figure 6.3 The Thief of Bagdad.

subjective experience as it is a tool at the service of clear, unambiguous exposition. As in *Romeo and Juliet*, it is the almost excessive wordiness of their exchange, rather than the narrowing of the visual field, that tells us that they are utterly absorbed in one another.

The fact that the music plays uninterruptedly, for its part, is a legacy of the silent era. In responding to the emotional ebbs and flows of their encounter, verging at times on Mickey-Mousing, the score also demarcates and gives the tempo to the different stages of the rapprochement between the Princess and her lover. It is a classic instance of music laying out a syntax of affects. She first hears about the genie over a lightly scored, bright, and fast-paced orchestral theme. "Giocoso" gives way to "misterioso" as the appearance of a celesta, the thinning out of the texture, and finally the coloring of the second theme with an augmented fifth make way, in a harmonically suspended context, for a harp figuration bookending the Princess's sighting of Ahmad in the pond. Subdued violins and cellos, at a perceptibly slower tempo, underscore their witty conversation with an expansive pastoral melody reminiscent of scenes of domestic love in westerns. In this way the music reinforces the impression of a decidedly nonconfrontational—indeed, almost flirtatious—exchange. As Ahmad's reflection dissipates in the ripples of water caused by the Princess's reaching hand, she voices her disappointment in descant with a plaintive cadenza, in a characteristic free tempo, played by a solo violin. Having safely landed on the ground from the tree where he had been hiding all along, Ahmad surprises her from behind, at which point we hear a variant of the theme already heard during their first exchange. This strikes the appropriate note since they are now taking up from where they had left off at the time of his mysterious and seemingly final—yet in the end only temporary—disappearance. As they now face one another, the music, set to a jaunty tempo and scored for full orchestra, sets the scene for the predictable climax of the kiss—the only moment in which, as the two leads at long last stop talking, the score takes center stage in the soundtrack. Along with the sets, costumes, and saturated color cinematography, Rosza's score constructs a wholly bucolic, indeed fairytale-ish, frame. But it also stands for environmental sounds, which it transfigures into musical tapestry (thus denying the spectator an independent perspective on the soundscape). The ambiguity between semiotic and immersive functions, between signifying a certain state of mind and representing it from within, arises precisely because in having the two leads talk so much over a musical score that drowns out all other sounds, the film recreates a scenario of ecological validity.

For its time, Rosza's music was in many ways standard, if doubtless highly proficient, fare. And yet the moment of the kiss poses a question that, because of the representativeness of the film, is well worth revisiting. How to account for such an openly intrusive score? The rise in volume, swelling strings, and unabashed lyricism are in retrospect so noticeable that one is invariably surprised at just how used audiences were to them, and to some extent still are, a fact that the dearth of scholarship on the subject well into the 1980s only went to, forgive the pun, underscore. As is well known, it is partly in response to this neglect that Claudia Gorbman coined the term that has come to define a whole stage of film music scholarship, "unheard music." In coining the notion of inaudibility, however, Gorbman also meant to refer to the scores themselves: subtle, unobtrusive, and placed at key junctures so as to combine maximum efficacy with minimal intervention. These are not terms that apply to Rosza's music. Habituation de-sensitizes us, and the focus on the sight of the lovers kissing in a loving embrace is a distraction. But this begs the question: why is such demonstrative orchestral crescendo there in the first place? And how does it serve the rhetoric of the film at that particular point? Would it not defy logic but also the economy of the scene to place a musical climax solely for the purpose of it being overshadowed by the seeing of something (the kiss) or, worse, ignored altogether?

To be sure, one need not assume representations are well-oiled machines in which all parts contribute harmoniously to a common goal. The ideal of opti-mization is a recent one—think about Baroque or Rococo art—and has always flown in the face of the uncertainties of the production process, dominant taste, and individual proclivities. But what strikes one as excessive, exaggerated, or merely unmotivated may in the last analysis respond to an underlying logic when considered across multiple instances of a genre, and from the perspec-tive of what Martha Feldman has called, with regard to opera seria, a *rhetoric of exchange* between artists and their audiences.[10] Within the reigning conven-tions the film abides by, melodramatic flourishes of the kind exhibited by Rosza's score follow both from the inertial force of compositional practices inherited from both operatic and cinematic precedents and the logic of representation ap-propriate to the dramatic situation. Implicit in this choice of scoring is also a cue as to how the audience, as a group, will think and feel.[11] Now whether one *actu-ally* "sighs," "cheers," or even "melts" at the sight of the kiss—whether, in other words, the setup actually persuades us to respond in a certain way—remains of course an open question (one whose answer will depend on the vagaries of reception). The odds that an old film like *The Thief of Bagdad* will inspire a spec-tator to react in just such a way are today low. The film is more likely to inspire a detached, historically informed, or even slightly condescending disposition, its style having jelled into a mark of an older era of filmmaking. What matters here, however, is less the empirical spectator than the position inferable from the film's own special, historically determined type of address. The kiss between Ahmad and the Princess is the apex of an emotional and cognitive trajectory that holds the attention captive. As they kiss one another, one is simply supposed to "emote" in sympathy with them. The music, like the laugh tracks in television shows, functions at this moment as a chorus, a proxy for the audience's puta-tive, and nowadays concealed, response. Rosza's cue is "somatic" not—or not

[10] Martha Feldman, *Opera and Sovereignty: Transforming Myths in Eighteenth-Century Italy* (Chicago: University of Chicago Press, 2007), 45 and 51–63.

[11] Anahid Kassabian refers to this phenomenon as "assimilating identification": Kassabian, *Hearing Film: Tracking Identifications in Contemporary Hollywood Film Music* (London and New York: 2000), 107–16.

only—because it brings to light in the body of the film the otherwise invisible emotions felt by the protagonists, as is the norm in the melodramatic tradition. The cue is somatic also, and just as importantly, because it functions prosthetically as the expression of the audience members' own emotional situations in light of what they see unfold on the screen. Herein, I would argue, is the most potent distractor to the appreciation of the music qua music, here transubstantiated into erotic feeling.[12]

Love Unrequited

Often a character responds not to the sight of the would-be lover but to something he or she hears (be it music, sound, or their soothing, menacing, or otherwise disturbing absence). In Max Ophuls's *Letter from an Unknown Woman* (1948), Lisa (Joan Fontaine) falls for Stefan (Louis Jourdan) by a cleverly staggered process that involves imagining, then hearing, and only in the last instance seeing the love object. First, she notices a moving company deliver to a neighboring flat the "precious objects"—books, fine pieces of furniture, a harp—of what promises to be a young, well-to-do man of taste and status (Figure 6.4). The event sets the story into motion. Leslie Hunt tellingly dubs the movers as "stage hands" delivering the props that will provide the background to the narrative about to unfold.[13] Moves are indeed metaphors of the arrival of much-awaited-for or at any rate timely change, and they are invariably presented as disrupting the routine of a dull life. In melodramas, and *Letter from an Unknown Woman* proves no exception, they are the harbinger of tormented love affairs. Truffaut's *A Woman Next Door* (1979) and, more recently, Wong Kar Wai's *In the Mood for Love* (2001), both of which begin with a fateful move, bear witness to the transcontinental reach of the genre and appeal of this specific narrative premise.

Most prominent among the various items delivered to the soon-to-be-occupied flat is a grand piano. Sure enough we soon see Lisa listening to it intently as her new neighbor rehearses the third of Liszt's Three Concert Etudes, "Un Sospiro." By a pointed reversal of conventional practice, the music does not

---

[12] Given the restrictions imposed by the Production Code, the kiss lasts only a few seconds. A crossfade subsequently takes us to the lovers strolling about in the garden and talking to one another (at which point Rosza's music changes register in keeping with its more muted role of underscoring). On the history of the kiss in the cinema, see A.O. Scott, "A Brief History of Kissing in Movies," *New York Times*, December 13–4 (2015), 17 and 19.

[13] Leslie H. Hunt, "The Paradox of the Unknown Lover: A Reading of *Letter from an Unknown Woman*," *Journal of Aesthetics and Art Criticism* 64, no. 1 (Winter 2006): 58.

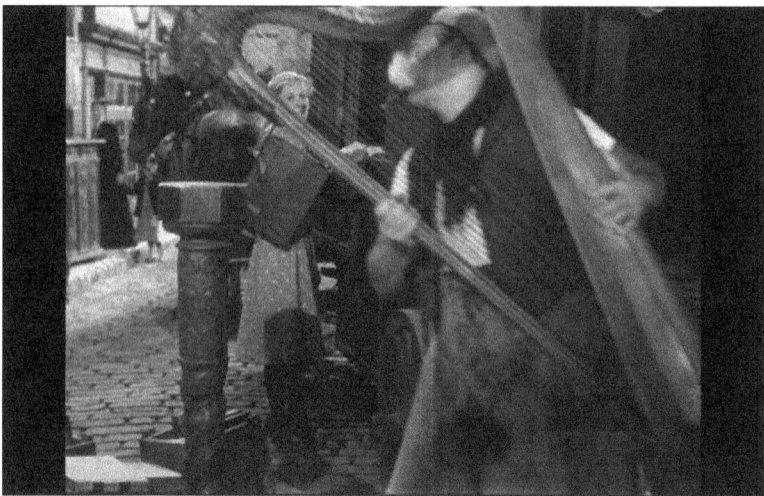

Figure 6.4 Letter from an Unknown Woman.

mark her falling for the as-yet-unseen love object by narrational sleight of hand;
rather, as an event that plays out—literally—at the hands of the love object,
music is the force that, at the supple tempo of the Liszt etude, draws her into his
orbit in the first place. It is a clever parody of the serenade: the male figure, from
the floor above, delivers musical sounds to the ground floor where a hopelessly
naive girl relishes them like many rose petals. Stefan is not deliberately serenad-
ing her, of course, as much as providing the unwitting confirmation of what his
budding female lover had wanted to hear all along. Lisa is predestined to find
herself mired in the throes of unrequited love by decree, as it were. Her character
is more complex, mercurial even, than the strictures of the genre would seem to
imply, however. She is the active seeker of the sounds of Stefan's piano, not the
unwitting victim of a chance encounter.[14] The film insists on showing her find
ever new opportunities to listen to and eventually see Stefan in ways that neither
he nor his endearing servant, both of them new to the place, can fathom. This
makes her the master of the only microcosm to which her age and gender con-
fine her, namely, the apartment complex where they both live.

Soon after the credits and the extended prologue, Stefan is at work, rehearsing for a recital in his new lodgings. The windows of his study room are conveniently open, letting the sounds of his piano permeate the morning atmosphere.
Lisa is in the courtyard riding a swing and listening in with gusto to what to her is
a wholly private concert. It is perhaps the only point in the whole film where she

[14] On Lisa as "dedicated listener and self-styled muse," see Heather Laing, *The Gendered
Score: Music in 1940s Melodrama and the Woman's Film* (Aldershot, UK: Ashgate, 2007), 77–97.

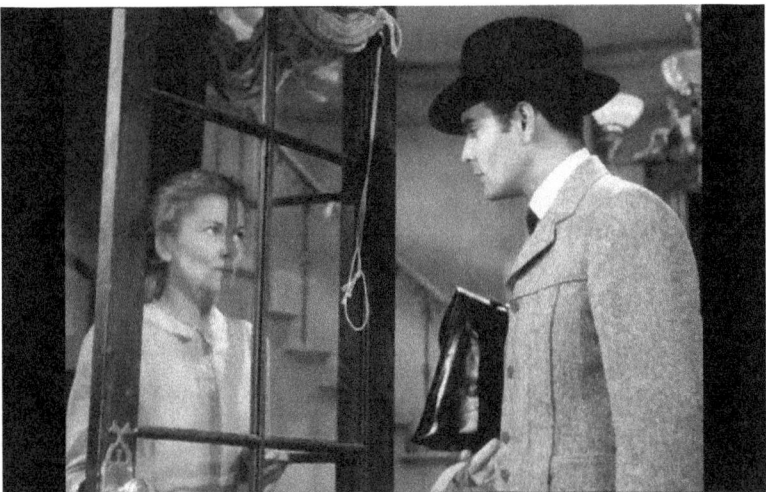

Figure 6.5 Letter from an Unknown Woman.

cuts the figure of a joyful, carefree, sexually playful young woman.[15] The camera crosscuts to his study, and we see him before she does. On the face of it, this runs the risk of spoiling the two central conceits of this initial segment of the film: her inability to see him on the one hand, and on the other the use of props and other oblique pieces of evidence—his furniture, his books, the butler, and of course his playing—as carefully timed signs of his encroaching presence. Yet so sure are we that Lisa is set on a collision course with Cupid that the images of him playing come across as visualizations of her fantasy or, for that matter, prescience (the rules of the genre tell us as much, too). That Stefan is predictably handsome, dignified, and stylish, moreover, creates suspense as to what will happen when she does set her eyes on him at last.

Lisa's longed-for encounter with Stefan is exquisitely staged. Knowing he is about to leave the building, Lisa waits in the lobby on the ground floor till Stefan finally appears rushing down the stairs. He is impeccably dressed for an evening out, hat and stick in tow. Reaching the front door only a moment before he does, she opens it for him with a dexterous and graceful sideways pirouette, all the while effacing the fact that the encounter has in fact been planned. Looking at him from below through one of the glass panes of the door, she waits for him to acknowledge the courtesy (Figure 6.5). This he promptly does, quickly taking stock of her charm. Lisa is hooked but need not express it; we are already in the know as to her feelings for him. We imagine how she feels inside, and the Kuleshov effect ensures that our knowledge also imparts nuances of physiognomic expression on to

[15] For an important iconographic precedent, see the suggestive paintings by Fragonard.

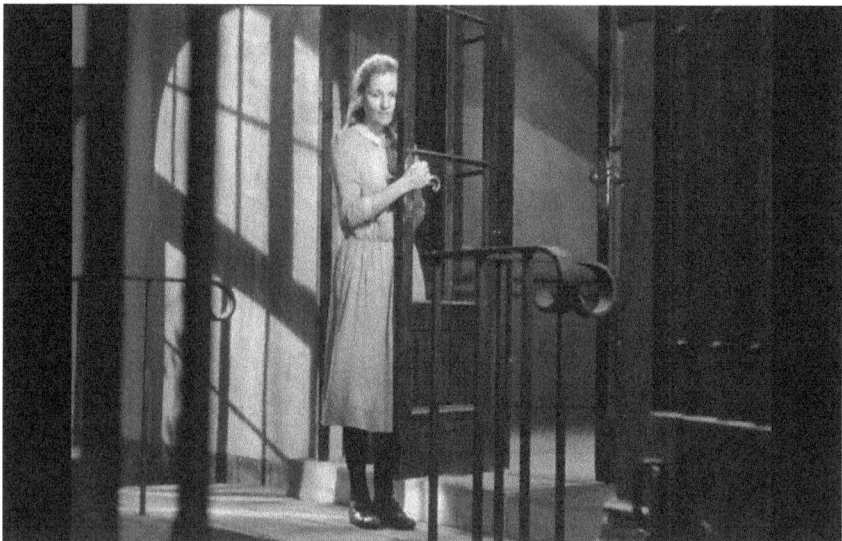

Figure 6.6 Letter from an Unknown Woman.

her relatively blank stare. Significantly, given the abundance of music in the film, no music is heard at this point. The sound of chirping birds notwithstanding— the residual vestige of a more explicit manner—it is a sensible choice. Better to allow the simple shot/countershot structure to communicate a remarkable balance of perspectives and a clear sense of the gulf that separates the two characters. A music cue would have obscured the pointed disparity between the two characters' position. When Stefan turns around to give her a second look, she is lost in reverie (Figure 6.6). This is the image that will come back to haunt him at the end of the film, pushing him to the brink of desperation.

After the sequence of the move, and that of his morning practice, this meeting marks the third stage of what will continue to be an inexorably asymmetrical relationship. The music adds considerable interest to what would otherwise be a rather stultifying course of events. Its status as a dimension of Stefan's everyday work means it is publicly accessible to whoever happens to be within earshot (Lisa's friend, for instance, or her mother). And yet despite this, it is precisely the public dimension of his playing that channels her secret, hidden-in-plain-sight passion. Lisa obviously relishes her ability to indulge her passion in broad daylight yet away from prying eyes, including those of the love object himself (for whom music is just work, however satisfying). The shot of a reverential Lisa looking up toward Stefan's flat captures a dynamic that is not only reinforced but also sanctioned in another, and even more famous, shot: that of an adoring Lisa squatting at his side, her eyes transfixed, while he is practicing. The image has come to symbolize the film, gracing the covers of subsequent releases of the film in various formats. The image also captures a condition of sustained attention, but attention to what, exactly? Lisa cannot see Stefan's hands. Her eyes indicate she is focused on his face instead. Stefan's practice session provides the occasion to gain both physical proximity to and a screen to protect herself from him: the enjoyment of utmost intimacy clothed under the appearance of distance and decorum. The train of perception moves from the music to his face, sights and sounds, in turn, subsumed under her loving—and covert— embrace.

Since her focus turns out to be delusional, the film casts a decidedly dark light on Lisa's capacity for sustained attention, however. The cognitive and emotional "unison" that blesses her elated state near the film's beginning turns out to be a screen that fogs her vision and the premise to a fantasy that proves for her nearly fatal. This is foreshadowed, albeit in a comical vein, as Lisa surreptitiously visits his flat. There, she quickly makes her way to his study, delighted at being able to give her fantasy a concrete, tangible form at long last. As she feels her way, cat-like, through his space, a paraphrasis of Liszt's etude appears in the soundtrack reworked like a reminiscent motif in opera. Caught inside a bubble of her own making, she caresses the piano and his books not without bumping into a harp, which she barely rescues from a calamitous fall, and eventually hitting a whole pile of scores. As these tumble to the floor, the music suddenly stops. No longer oblivious to her surroundings, she barely finds the time to regroup and quickly find her way her out before Stefan's lenient butler feigns a menacing look.

From Rhetoric to Phenomenology

Be it a series of long cues, "canned music," or wall-to-wall scoring, music in a film is historically overdetermined, performing several functions at once: frame, noise-canceling device, mood inducer, spectacular intervention, syntactic element, symbol, marketing gimmick, and so forth. Given this plethora of functions, it should come as no surprise that the practice lasted for as long as it did, and even shows strong signs of resurgence today (spurred, one suspects, by the aesthetics of video games). What I am most interested in examining here is the way in which a score acts as a frame across a film and how this, in turn, morphs into an "object," bleeding over into the representation (as much as stabilizing or containing it from the outside). Often the recognition of this transformation occurs, ironically, at the moment the music stops. During Lisa's visit to Stefan's flat, for instance, it is when the music suddenly comes to a halt and she reawakens from her reverie that we, in turn, realize it was giving tangible form to her rapt absorption into Stefan's possessions. The film exploits the audience's habituation to the presence of a continuous score as a framing device, or element of the environment, only to refit it into a highly specific representation of a specific psychological situation.

The greatest example of this functional convergence remains perhaps Hitchcock's *Vertigo* (1958). As is well known, the film features a large number of very long music cues. This gives it the veneer of a standardly packaged and, given the date of release, already somewhat retrospective Hollywood product. Herrmann's expansive score compensates for the absence of dialogue while at the same time erases the presence of ambient sound for an inordinately large amount of screen time. The length of the cues, however, is not merely generically appropriate but also highly specific in its representation of the state of mind of Scottie as he follows Madeleine meandering about town. *Vertigo* is operatic less for its alleged intertextual references to Wagner's *Tristan* than for the way in which the score restricts the spectator's perspective so that it almost comes to coincide with that of its solipsistic hero. Such a restriction is both sonic and visual. The key moment, a true rite of passage, is in this respect the sequence set at the restaurant Ernie's, where Scottie—and the audience—sees Madeleine for the first time. It is there and then that, upon sighting Judy aka Madeleine, Scottie takes permanent leave from the every day and plunges into an abyss. Hitchcock stages the fateful passage via an unsurpassed visual metaphor and, just as crucially, a movement that takes us from ambient sound to Herrmann's music.

The sequence at Ernie's is also striking in that, while following quite logically from a premise and being the necessary preamble to the car perambulations up and down the San Francisco hills that follow, it is perfectly self-contained. A "cavatina" in disguise, it transfigures what is after all a prosaic stage of the detective plot—his sighting the target of the investigation—into an elaborate presentation piece. Its pivotal role as the catalyst of Scottie's peculiar journey into the underworld is obvious. Hardly announced and matter-of-factly set aside after the fact, what happens at Ernie's sits in splendid isolation, like a set piece whose impact is not so much worked out logically as felt via a process of reverberation. The auditory metaphor seems especially apposite as much of the film's score derives from the music cue—dubbed "Madeline"—heard at precisely this juncture.[16]

We begin just outside the restaurant in the late evening, at a point when diners are nearly through with their meal (Figure 6.7). The street is silent, and an ominously anthropomorphic tracking shot smoothly takes us to the front door of the restaurant at eye level (and a speed similar to that of a person walking toward it). The image is transitional, a miniature establishing shot meant to introduce us to the new locale and commensurate with the length and scope of the sequence

---

[16] On this aspect of the score, see Graham Bruce, *Bernard Herrmann: Film, Music, and Narrative* (Ann Arbor, MI: UMI Press, 1985), 178–81; and David Cooper, *Bernard Herrmann's Vertigo: A Film Score Handbook* (Westport, CT, and London: Greenwood Press, 2002), 87–90.

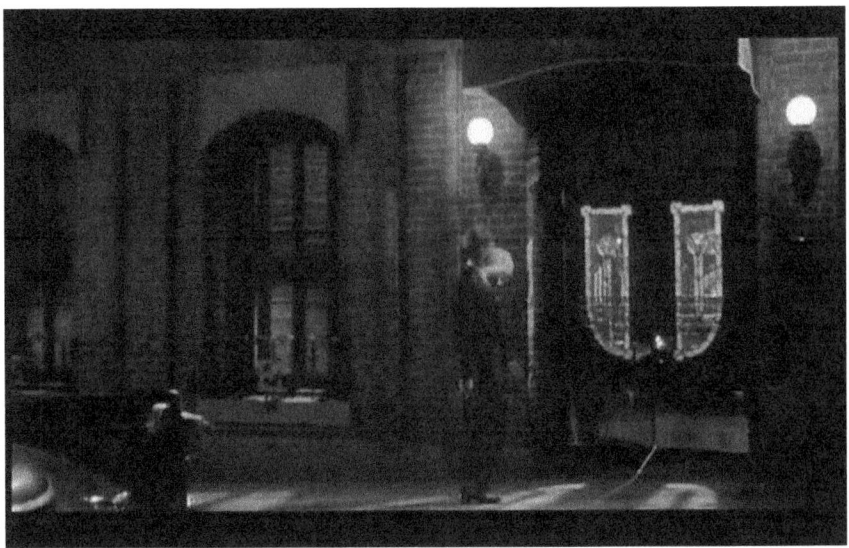

Figure 6.7 Vertigo.

about to begin. That Hitchcock thought Ernie's merited an introductory shot underlines the significance of what is to follow. The shot is not merely eluci-datory but suggestive of a perception, as tracking shots at eye level sometimes are. It is an implicit reference to Scottie's clandestine presence in the premises (as well as his sense that the restaurant is beyond his means, since he is not a member of the moneyed crowd that frequents it). Without seeing the face of the person whose point of view this is, however, the image remains unanchored to a specific character. Even so, the desolateness of the area immediately outside the restaurant is indicative of Scottie's condition of lonely hero set on an unlikely mission. Only a lonesome male figure crosses the field from left to right at a brisk pace. He is a passerby, possibly heading home after work. Yet another passerby walks behind the camera, in the same direction—frame left to right. We see his reflection on a plaque near the restaurant entrance. The anamorphic rendering of this anonymous city dweller is tiny yet animated, and thus titillates our atten-tion. It is an extraordinary detail, well worth the amount of planning and coordi-nation it must have entailed at the time of shooting. Moving along a parallel line to that of the other passerby, this male figure appears to draw a tiny segment of a circular orbit around a center located at the point opposite the frame's receding point (that is, far behind the camera). Sturdy and rectilinear, the entrance wall of Ernie's touches these ideal circular orbits like a tangent. To enter it is to defy the gravitational pull of the world Scottie is leaving behind, and to do so on account of a force whose propelling force Scottie will soon be able to appreciate. Ernie's is a solar system of its own. What happens inside the restaurant subverts, with the benefit of hindsight, the sense of agency and willfulness implicit in that tracking shot, for it is the restaurant that is drawing us in, like a magic cave. The point of having the passersby, while indisputably consistent with the need for a realistic setting to an establishing shot, is also to show that Scottie is at the threshold between two social spaces, themselves the metaphorical stages of two mutually exclusive ways of playing out one's destiny.

Transitions in *Vertigo* are swift and make no use of sound bridges. The silence of the office in the aftermath of the two friends' conversation gives way to the cold din of the deserted street at dusk, enlivened only by the subtle "click clack" of the two passersby. This, in turn, is followed by the hushed chatter of the people inside the restaurant. Three different soundscapes follow one another in quick succession without the need to smooth over their differences (a process facilitated by their relative quietness). It's the equivalent in the language of Hollywood soundtracks of creating one long, syntagmatic unit—rather like holding one's breath in preparation of a pivotal event. Once inside Ernie's, Hitchcock wastes no time in showing us Scottie plunge into Elster's trap. The action displays a velocity that is not merely metaphorical nor simply the result of the temporal compression of the narrative. The speed of the dollying camera becomes the speed at which the gaze—and hence, the action—happens. But whose gaze is it?[17]

Via a dissolve, the tracking shot leading to the restaurant entrance morphs into an image of the interior. Drink in hand, Scottie is in the bar adjacent to the dining

---

[17] Following a now-established tradition in film studies spearheaded by Laura Mulvey's work, Charles Barr identifies not one but at least three gazes: that of the camera-director, that of the audience for whom the camera acts as a facilitator, and finally the character's: Barr, *Vertigo* (London: BFI Publishing, 2002), 10. It is for this (male) triumvirate that the female figure exhibits herself, displaying all the cliched attributes of the case (sexually enticing, mute, mysterious). This setup is such that "in Hitchcock . . . the audience does see precisely what the hero sees": Laura Mulvey, "Visual Pleasure and Narrative Cinema," in *The Audience Studies Reader*, ed. Will Broker and Deborah Jermyn (New York and London: Routledge, 2002), 140. The target of Mulvey's critique, in a nutshell, is dual. The relentless display of the sexualized female body is not only deplorable in and of itself but also symptomatic of the partial view of the audience (as it appears to address only those interested in such a display to begin with). The pervasiveness of the point-of-view shot structure, in making the character a surrogate of the audience, moreover, creates the occasion for such relentless display, and thereby justifies it, making it "respectable," as it were. Now there is no denying the force of Mulvey's argument and the way in which it resonates across many of the examples presented here. Merits of Mulvey's main premise notwithstanding, a lot hinges on both the meaning of that "precisely" ("the audience does see precisely what the hero sees") and the meaning of her exclusive focus on vision. Taking Mulvey at face value, for example; Barr contends that her argument "is true of much of *Vertigo*, but not of the crucial scene that introduces Madeleine": Barr, *Vertigo*, 10. The point of contention is not only the frontal view of the dining room, technically impossible from Scottie's vantage point, but also the two emphatic close-ups of Kim Novak offered to us just "when Scottie has to look away": Ibid., 10. Barr's qualification is welcome but, as we will soon see, too literal. It also ignores the role of the music altogether.

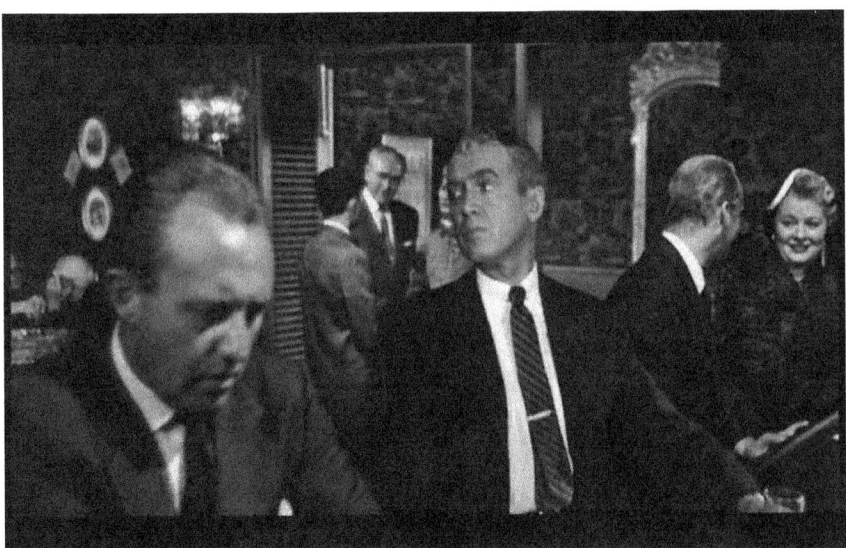

Figure 6.8 Vertigo.

room, sitting at the counter. In keeping with the ultimate destination of the setup, the focus changes immediately. He turns and looks off to his right; as if propelled by his gaze, the camera moves accordingly. With a stunningly sinuous move, and at a speed consistent with the tracking shot toward the restaurant's front door, the camera both pulls back and pans to the left, proceeding to offer a full view of the dining room (Figure 6.8). While impossible to attribute literally to any one character, the shot partakes of Scottie's desire to scan the new space he's in. It is a movement that mirrors the motion of his gaze and magnifies its reach. The vantage point afforded by the camera registers a perspective that transcends Scottie's optical point of view. But this, I would argue, is not to momentarily abstain from, let alone contradict, his epistemic and emotional position. As is the case with the musical score, it is, rather, a faithful measure of his—and hence, the film's— aggrandizing, mythologizing perception. The camera movement does not simply follow from his turning rightward but seems to prosthetically enhance his intoxicated gaze, and with the significant benefit of a view of the restaurant's guests (whom Scottie may not be able to see from that exact viewpoint but is certainly all too aware of). With the camera settled into the dining room at the height of the seated patrons' shoulders, the gradual emergence of Madeleine involves such a markedly different technique that it seems impossible to have occurred without a cut to a different shot. Following a gentle downward tilt, the camera simply changes course instead, making its way through the crowded room at a speed slower than that of the backward dolly. The target of this new movement is the corner at the opposite end of the room (Figure 6.9). The change in both direction

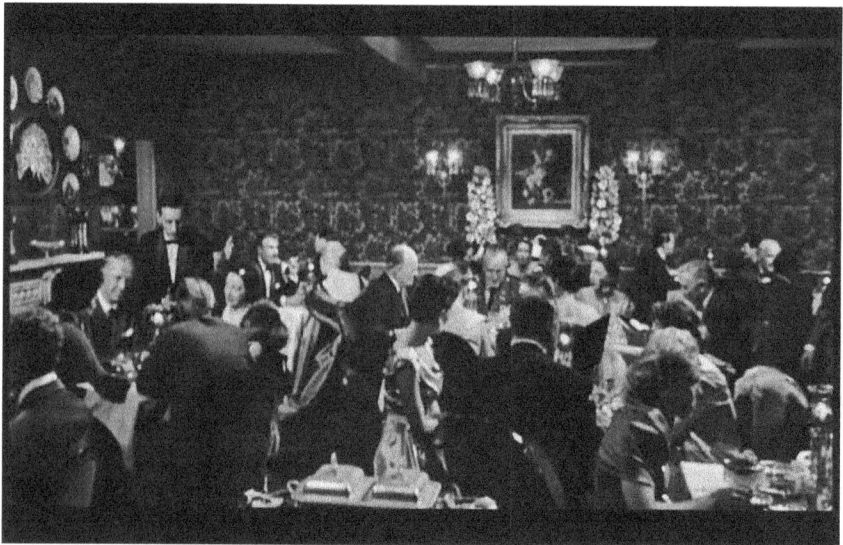

Figure 6.9 Vertigo.

and speed is almost precisely synchronized to the beginning of Hermann's cue, marking a new stage in Scottie's acquaintance with Madeleine. Having thrown a line out into the room, so to speak, he now begins to probe the space in search of her with understandable care, and not without a certain difficulty. The image is not merely anthropomorphic but also aligned to Scottie's perspective in that it tallies with the process of isolating a figure in a crowd (motivated by both professional duty and, we soon learn, desire). Madeleine is as yet unidentifiable to us. The new camera movement signals a distinctive focusing of the attention, but the moment at which our eyes land on target is impossible to date. For viewers familiar with the film, and thus mindful of the camera's ultimate destination from the start, it is difficult to recover a sense of just how masterfully Hitchcock not only delays the moment at which Madeleine is identified but also surrounds that same moment in a haze of indecidability. While she is the receding point of the image, first-time viewers need to wait till Elster becomes recognizable in the far left and subsequently infer that the blond woman next to him must be Madeleine. Of course, Scottie has located her before we did, having been warned of the seating arrangement beforehand. But while he knows who she is and where she stands, he—like us—cannot really see her (except for a sliver of her profile). Madeleine finally becomes fully visible—a majestic platinum blond, draped in green—in the first optical point-of-view shot of the sequence (the first point-of-view shot, in fact, following the vertigo shot in the film's prologue). She stands up, makes her way toward the exit, and, following a strategically timed stop near the unsuspecting detective, leaves the premises (Figure 6.10).

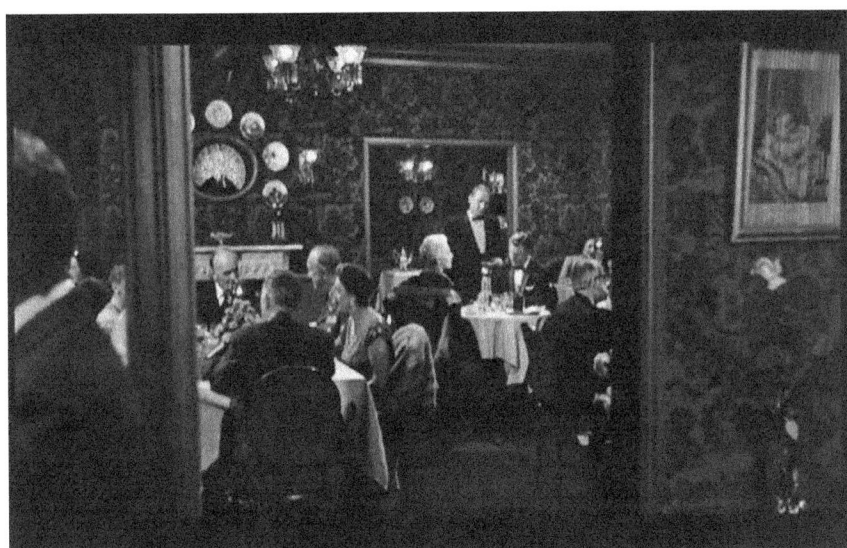

Figure 6.10 Vertigo.

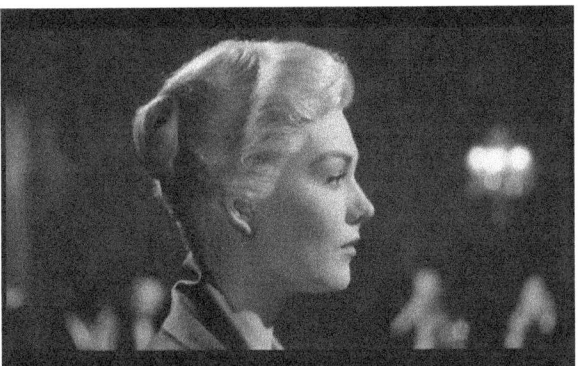

Figure 6.11 Vertigo.

Slavoj Žižek says of the two close-ups of Novak that they are "subjectless sub-jective shots" (Figure 6.11).[18] That love at first sight brings Scottie to imagine the space he's in from multiple perspectives, see things he cannot literally see, and paint them in shapes and colors so overwhelming as to seem unreal is perhaps too obvious a gloss on Žižek's paradoxical quip. Less obvious is the observation that what the seeming paradox refers to is in fact standard fare in much fiction. One need only think of first-person narration disguised as free indirect discourse

[18] Slavoj Žižek, "The Talking Heads," in *Organs without Bodies: On Deleuze and Consequences* (New York and London: Routledge, 2012), 154.

in literature, for instance, and its equivalents in film.[19] Careful consideration of Herrmann's score, too, as must by now be clear, sheds a great deal of light on the vexed question of subjectivity in this sequence (and many others of a similar ilk). Of course, Scottie cannot see the dining room from where Hitchcock's camera is; nor can he see Madeleine standing behind him as she waits for Elster. But should we, by the same token, claim that Scottie cannot hear Herrmann's music, and that therefore it cannot convey his perspective? And yet there is no doubt that the music is doing precisely that.

Scottie, let us recall, is at work. He is at Ernie's to sight a person his "employer" has assigned him to shadow to gather evidence about her and her increasingly "strange" demeanor. Yet by the time we see, with Scottie, Madeleine in all her grandeur and stereotypically albino beauty, the music has already inflected— some will say irreversibly sabotaged—the investigative line of the plot. It does this, come to think of it, even *before* we have sighted her. As already mentioned, Hermann's cue appears at the point in which the camera, having stopped to track backward, reverses the direction of its movement and sets its gaze, like a cat slowly prying on a prey, on something that is as yet unidentifiable. Scored for muted strings and moving rather like a slowed-down, melancholy dance, the music begins like a plaintive lament. Tonally ambiguous, it initially comes across as a long, continuous, yet open-ended melody in the violins. On close inspection, it consists of three separate versions of an elaborate lyrical phrase built from four 4-note motives whose main features are a regular, arch-like contour in various configurations, and a suspension on the third note. These features remain more or less in place as the second phrase explores a higher register. As the third phrase begins, at an even higher register, the melody-generating mechanism "jams." The four-note cell loses its head and in this reduced form it repeats twice till a rising major seventh marks the climax as Madeleine purposefully poses—"to best advantage," in Jerrold Levinson's words—near an unsuspecting and by then already smitten Scottie.[20] The seventh is as much a dynamic and textural climax—an arpeggio at the harp is heard at precisely this point—as it is a melodic one. As Scottie steals a furtive glance through the corner of his eye, she stands next to him, waiting for the conveniently delayed Elster, and aware of being watched. Rather than capturing it at a distance, Hitchcock filmed this

---

[19] On free indirect discourse in cinema, see Pier Paolo Pasolini, "Comments on Free Indirect Discourse," and "The Cinema of Poetry," in *Heretical Empiricism*, trans. Ben Lawton and Louise K. Barnett (Washington, DC: New Academia Publishing, 2005), 79–101 and 167–86, respectively; and P. Adams Sitney, *The Cinema of Poetry* (New York: Oxford University Press, 2015), 15–34.

[20] Jerrold Levinson, "Film Music and Narrative Agency," in *Post-Theory: Reconstructing Film Studies*, ed. David Bordwell and Nöel Carrol (Madison, WI: University of Wisconsin Press, 1996), 267.

most equivocal encounter as a briskly paced ballet of close shots that syncopate against the meter of the score. Following this climax, a release of both visual and musical tension follows. Scottie turns slightly to his left to track Elster and Madeleine's swift exit. The music returns to the register of the beginning and an exquisite, "domesticated" version of the lyrical phrase evenly split between the violins and, diminuendo, by a lone cello. Such "return" is hardly a closure, however, and not simply because the cue remains open-ended harmonically. As Madeleine disappears from sight, we know Scottie is hooked. He will be seen following her in a car immediately thereafter enveloped in a sonic bubble that follows directly from the cue just heard.

Though they have focused primarily on the title music, the notorious "Vertigo" chord, and the lengthy "Scene d'Amour," music scholars have duly— and admiringly—noted the thematic associations between the "Madeline" music and the film's other cues. The germination of the score from a handful of "primal" elements, the triplet figures of the title theme among them, and the obvious references—or unconscious borrowings, as the case may be—to Wagner's *Tristan* have evinced a great deal of commentary. Following a spectacular restoration of its master tape on the occasion of the 1996 rerelease of the film, and having now been recorded and performed as a work for the concert hall, the score now openly welcomes approaches that acknowledge its status as an autonomous piece of music.[21] Listening to the music of *Vertigo* as a symphonic poem or incidental music playing off the afterlife of the film in the listener's imagination is a fascinating prospect. Re-creations such as visual artist Douglas Gordon's *Feature Film* (1999), moreover, have drawn attention to Herrmann's music as a dynamic element of our heritage, one surprisingly emancipated from the film-as-text (which it evokes as musical memory or citation). Yet these are revivals and appropriations that the tools of formalist analysis are unlikely to shed much light on. While undoubtedly valuable in recovering a sense of the composer's craft, traditional analytical approaches reinscribe the music in the score-as-text paradigm, thereby functioning as the perfect, if unwitting, foil to the (many) critical studies that ignore the contribution of the music altogether (or justify the omission by claiming ignorance of the specialized tools of musical analysis). Feeling they cannot quite afford to ignore the substance of the film, scholars such as Bruce or Cooper punctuate their analyses of the score with acknowledgments of the narrative and character development it accompanies. Yet these references to what happens "in the film" are little more than programmatic tags and make the score seem like a repository of musical counterparts to motifs, themes,

---

[21] While Bruce's comprehensive survey of Herrmann's work was and remains a pioneering work, Cooper's analytical monograph is in part a reflection on the new status acquired by the music as a result of the revival of the film.

and stages of character development that are much more fully rendered through acting, photography, and editing. Conventional musical analysis, in other words, reconfigures a film score as a duplication of what is captured by dialogue and principal photography in the first place.

A different line of investigation takes the music to be actively contributing to, as opposed to merely shadowing, the unfolding of the action. "The intrinsic interest and sophistication of Bernard Herrmann's score has been much discussed," writes Jerrold Levinson, "but what is most striking about it in the context of the film is how significant a burden it bears for limning the mental states and traits of characters."[22] To bear out his observation, Levinson considers the sequence at Ernie's as a successful instance of characterization through music and buttresses his point by citing Graham Bruce, who observes how "it is the music that conveys most fully the sensual mystery of the woman."[23] How does it do that? Madeleine's appearance at Ernie's is an elaborate case of what Chion calls "added value." The synchronization between Herrmann's music and the elaborate visual presentation of the Kim Novak character forges a relation between sound and image that amounts, via a synthesis of the qualities of both, to nothing less than a fully fledged audiovisual portrait. Chion is keen to stress that when sound—or music—adds important dimensions to the visual image, as when, for instance, a certain tone of voice makes a face expressive of anger, added value may create the illusion that "sound is not necessary," that it is a mere supplement.[24] The qualities brought into play by sound are in such cases attributed to the image. Upon considering the scene at Ernie's, Bruce, and consequently also Levinson, err perhaps in the opposite direction. They are a bit too sanguine about the ability of music to "convey" the sensuality and mystery of Madeleine, rather like a fully formed "adjective" or "modifier" to the featureless "noun" of Novak's on-screen appearance.[25] Talking about Herrmann's music as if it possessed certain qualities, ready to be "dispatched" at the desired moment, is, too, a form of retrospective illusion. Such qualities as the music may be said to possess and, what is more important, lend to the image are, to the contrary, *emergent*. Of course, this is not to say that, given a certain dramatic situation, any music will perform the same task. Herrmann's cue appeals to the viewer's familiarity with certain generic markers and builds on a long history of precedents in both opera and the symphonic repertoire. But no amount of compositional effort or good will on the listener's part will endow the music

[22] Levinson, "Film Music and Narrative Agency," 267.

[23] Bruce, *Bernard Herrmann*, 173.

[24] Chion, *Audio-Vision: Sound on Screen*, trans. Claudia Gorbman (New York: Columbia University Press, 1994), 5.

[25] On the notion of music as modifier, see Nöel Carroll, "Notes on Movie Music," in *Theorizing the Moving Image* (Cambridge: Cambridge University Press, 1989), 139–45.

with the highly specific valences Bruce and Levinson hear in it; only the synchronization to the image of Madeleine will.

Levinson finds the import of the music, as well as the distinctive manner of presentation of Madeleine's profile, to be evidence of the need to posit the existence of a narrator (as distinct from the director, in this case Hitchcock, who, in his words, can only be doing "certain parallel things to Kim Novak and the set").[26] Turning thus to the question of narrative agency, he suggests that responsibility for the music goes to "the cinematic narrator, in order to indicate something about Scottie and the overwhelming psychic effect she has on Scottie on first encounter."[27] But isn't it imprudent to consider narrative agency—"who is narrating?"—a relevant aesthetic dimension? Often certain things are shown, and in a certain way at that, for the sake of clarity, narrative emphasis, or, say, display of virtuosity. The gratuitousness of positing narrators and narratees notwithstanding, it must be admitted that the sequence at Ernie's, and indeed the film as a whole, does invite scrutiny in the terms set forth by Levinson—only in a different sense. First, the sequence is an especially complex and layered instance of narration in that it combines, as is so often done in love-at-first-sight scenes, the work of characterization and the presentation of dramatic action collapsed into one. Moreover, the action is twofold. A dinner is taking place, during which Scottie becomes acquainted with Madeleine and, if not more significantly, falls for her ("the overwhelming psychic effect" mentioned by Levinson). Second, as Cooper has succinctly stated, *Vertigo* is "a film which is, as much as anything, about directorial control—for both Gavin Elster and Scottie adopt this role with Judy, fabricating and refashioning her as Madeleine."[28] This accounts for what is now almost a truism in *Vertigo* lore, namely, that the film, and this sequence in particular, is programmed to be seen twice, the second time to better enjoy the feigned spontaneity of the setup, Elster and Judy's consummate skill at timing their exit, and Judy aka Madeleine's awareness of her dual role. At Ernie's, it is Elster who chooses the stage of the encounter, its pace, and its choreography, and it is Scottie who, by casting glances across the room and responding so emotionally to what he sees, in a sense controls the unfolding of visual information and the affect it exudes.[29] Even the close-up of Madeleine registers a pose decided upon by Elster and the impact this has on his unsuspecting detective friend.

Who controls the music? There is no doubt that the music contributes to the audiovisual portrait of Madeleine. The music "makes fictional" a whole range

---

[26] Levinson, "Film Music and Narrative Agency," 267.

[27] Ibid.

[28] Cooper, *Bernard Herrmann's Vertigo*, xiiii.

[29] The camera searches with him, states the screenplay. Bruce implicitly follows this when he says that "the camera movement toward Madeleine lets us experience the physical nature of Scottie's immediate attraction to her": Bruce, *Bernard Herrmann*, 143.

of fictional truths about Madeleine and the situation that her appearance insti-
gates. It does so, moreover, to an extent that may seem beyond Elster's reach
(let alone Scottie's), or so it would appear from Levinson's observation that it
is the narrator who is responsible for it. Yet to think that Elster exploits a given
locale like a scenographer, a paid stand-in like an actress, and a costume to dress
her in but not a soundtrack to present her with would be to apply different standards to equal partners in crime, so to speak. Of course, a character is built across
separate stages in the filmmaking process—writing, casting, acting, costuming,
choice of sets and locales, scoring, and so forth. Correspondingly, each aspect
or dimension of the final product is traceable to a different agent responsible for
different stages of the filmmaking process, be it the director, costumist, editor,
make-up artist, or composer. As Elster's creation, Madeleine is not unlike a cinematic character, and her role at Ernie's the subject of study, choreography, direction, and so forth. But that Elster can buy a dress in a San Francisco store for
Judy to wear does not make him a plausible costume designer. His responsibility
for the scene presented to us goes beyond what an empirical director would be
able to conjure. To follow Levinson's own reasoning and terminology, a narrator
is not the physical "crafter" of the representation but rather its imagined perceptual guide—all of which makes it just as plausible to think of the music, too, as
an ingredient in Elster's creation of Madeleine. This is further facilitated by the
fact that, far from being against-type, the music works in concert with his magnificent cheat, thus making it intuitive to claim that the music follows from what
he, as the eminence gris from within the world of the story, has been conjuring
all along.

But music is overdetermined. Aside from defining their traits, Herrmann's
music also "limn[s] the mental states . . . of characters."[30] If so, the music may
be said to flesh out Scottie's arousal and adrenalinic shock following Madeleine's
appearance, painting an image of her in terms suggested to him not only by what
he is seeing in the restaurant but also the cues cleverly planted by Elster during
their conversation. Elster's manipulation is Scottie's perception. One is folded
into the other, and this makes both characters simultaneously responsible for
what we see and hear (only at different, indeed incompatible, ends). It would
be uninformative, as well as implausible, to claim that the music springs from
Scottie's mind; if that were the case, we would hear it as the memory of a performance and not as a representation of a mental state. The music, rather, makes
Scottie's response palpable for us. It is his emotional situation that justifies its
presence and allows it to permeate the whole environment in something like
the way, in La traviata, Violetta's emotional state is responsible for the music she

---

[30] Levinson, "Film Music and Narrative Agency," 266.

sings just as she is about to die (despite the fact that as a person whose lungs are devastated by tuberculosis, she cannot realistically sing).

Thus, characterization and the embodiment of Scottie's mental life are two sides of the same coin. Not only is the music accomplishing two tasks at the same time but also the two functions are interdependent. Because it partakes of the construction of Madeleine as a beautiful and mysterious, if fragile, woman, we can hear it simultaneously as the sonorous manifestation of Scottie's fascination with that construction. It is impossible to hear the leap of a seventh as voicing Scottie's anxiety and excitement as Madeleine stands closest to him if we were not persuaded by Elster's words, the camera work, the music, and the complex iconography of the scene that there is a reason for him to feel that way. The sight of Madeleine rehearses the capitalist ritual of star gazing. Her appearance generates considerable suspense, suspense that our awareness that the detective plot is bound up with romance will only exacerbate. It is along with Scottie, and in a sense guided by him, that throughout the film we will be piecing together an explanation for Madeleine's behavior. Following the episode at Ernie's, we are "taken on a ride"—in his own car, famously—and it is "his" Madeleine we keep on seeing in subsequent articulations of the plot (both in the sense that she is unfailingly portrayed as inscrutable and impossibly attractive and in the sense that she exists as Madeleine at all). We are caught in a trap along with him because, as so often occurs in focalized narratives, two stages of the plot—the introduction of a new character and the hero's visceral response to it—are collapsed into one. "In a subjective film," writes Elisabeth Weis, "Hitchcock may never bother to provide an objective alternative to the way things are presented."[31] This is, in the case of *Vertigo*, almost comically the case, since Madeleine exists for Scottie, and him alone. An objective shot of Madeleine would be nonsensical, for it would deliver us no more than Judy getting herself ready to play her.

Technically, the onset of Herrmann's music at Ernie's is somewhat akin to the audio dissolve, which Altman sees as central to the "blurring between the real and the ideal" in the musical.[32] In what to Altman is its most representative form, the audio dissolve involves the passage from source music to the score through the mediation of a realistically motivated song. As this transition unfolds, the character begins a sung or danced number, and fantasy reigns supreme. This is naturally not the case in the sequence at Ernie's. The plausibility of the setup makes it abundantly clear that the sequence is not the fleshing out of a dream or delusion. Scottie may be duped, but he is neither dreaming nor fantasizing nor, for that matter, hallucinating. Both the absence of a mediating element and the

---

[31] Elisabeth Weis, "The Sound of One Wing Flapping," February 2, 2015, http://www.filmsound.org.

[32] Rick Altman, *The American Film Music* (Bloomington: Indiana University Press, 1987), 63.

different narrative context differentiate the use of music in *Vertigo* from paradigmatic examples of the audio dissolve in ways that might conceal a fundamental similarity, however. Just as there is an element of unreality in Scottie's construction of Madeleine, and this unreality is enhanced by the employment of music as an essential element of her characterization, so there is a considerable dose of reality in the "irreality" of a musical number in a musical. Besides staging the idea that fantasy is a rewriting of reality, musicals also capture an element of its phenomenology: the feeling of what happens when, lost in reverie, we take leave of absence from our surroundings. While the specific realization flies in the face of what is plausible, it captures the gist of a relation between levels of reality that we grasp as intuitive. That the sounds of the environment are disavowed to the point of disappearing altogether is tantamount to saying that to attend to something at the expense of everything else is a form of reverse hallucination: the temporary denial of the world around us. To fully appreciate the significance, and irony, of the extent of Scottie's delusion in *Vertigo*, it is useful to recall two prominent, and already discussed, uses of source music: the recording of J. C. Bach's music in Midge's apartment and the Mozart heard at the sanatorium. The transitions in and out of these two tracks achieve precisely the opposite effect to the audio dissolve in the musical. Indeed, the distance Hitchcock creates between realistically justified sound and the score reinforces our sense of the quotidian in Scottie's life almost to the point of caricature.

Music and Variable Framing

In fleshing out Scottie's response to the sight of Madeleine, Herrmann's music partakes of a long tradition (in both the cinema and the theater). It does so through the deliberately paced play of themes and motifs; the manipulation of harmonic and melodic tension and their resolution; dynamic and textural contrasts; and instrumentation. As we have seen, the specific, as opposed to generic, qualities of the music are crucial in delineating both the trajectory and range of Scottie's emotional journey. However, two of these qualities—the timing of the cue and the balance in the sound mix—fall somewhere in between not only the generic and the specific but also the composer and the editor's art. As such, they are rarely discussed in the literature, and yet they are absolutely crucial to an understanding of how the music changes our relationship to the scene. As I observed earlier, the appearance of "Madeleine" is precisely timed to the onset of a new camera movement, along a straight line, toward the distant corner of the dining room. The sync point conveys a communicative intent. The goal seems to draw attention to the new status of the camera, thereby encouraging us to direct our gaze toward the unchanging vanishing point of the frame. It is rather like getting on board of the camera along its newly found trajectory as opposed to exploring the entirety of the frame. At that same point, too, ambient sound begins to thin out till, by a simple twiddle of the dial, it disappears entirely. The chatter of the restaurant patrons is glossed over by Scottie's singularly focused perception, a force so overwhelming that it eventually silences them all. Music, to use Jakobson's phrase again, announces the exclusion of the auditory object. The need to foreground the character's absorption in the object of his attention entails that, whether by design or not, inner life takes precedence over exterior reality. It is not the kind of effect that invites detailed, close musical analysis. As a function of mixing, moreover, it can be said to fall outside the sphere of composition proper. To make matters worse, it can be produced irrespective of the nature and individual features of the music cue itself. And yet the cross-fade is a prime example of how the cinema provided fertile ground for a new, expanded, and collaborative type of musical art, one in which the writing of the score is not the only important, let alone the only, stage.

In Luchino Visconti's *The Leopard* (1963), the impact of the score is so bound up with both mise-en-scène and camera work as to frustrate any attempt to weigh its merits in isolation. Tancredi's adrenalinic rush as he sees the resplendent Angelica for the first time is initially evoked through visual means alone. In a moment of eerie silence, the camera moves closer to his ecstatic face and, pointedly, in doing so it pans to the left as well (Figure 6.12). The meaning of the narrowing frame is unequivocal, yet we do not know what has drawn his attention until a cut to a long shot of Angelica about to enter the living room of the

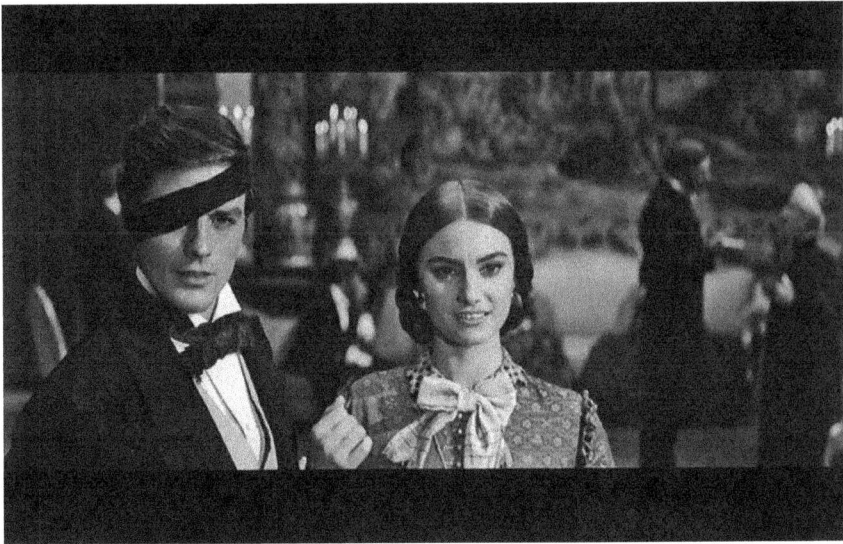

Figure 6.12 The Leopard.

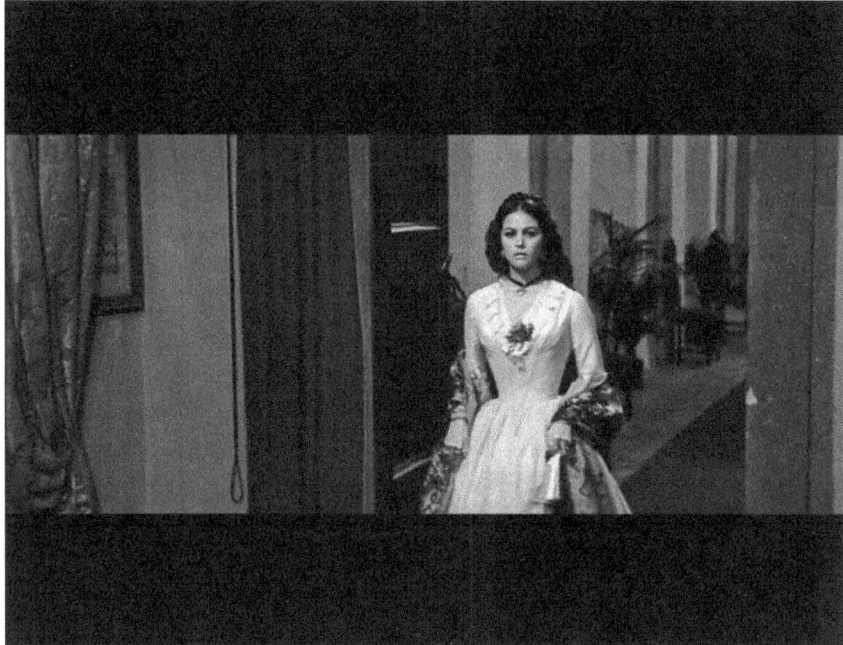

Figure 6.13 The Leopard.

Salina family palace (Figure 6.13). We hear a soaring melody ("Tema d'amore")
at the unison in the strings as she crosses the door, followed by a tender solo by
the violin that begins just as, having rehearsed in her mind the order in which to
greet her aristocratic hosts, she walks toward the family matriarch. By the time
Count Salina greets her, the strings have capped the impassionate, long main
theme. Yet the music goes on. The woodwinds intone a secondary theme in the
relative minor ("Tema sensuale"), repeated sequentially a minor third below,
thereby continuing to project a sense of her radiance, as well as the attention of
her stunned audience, while adding a note of melancholy to the evolving situation.[33] Angelica's entrance is an elaborate ritual in the course of which she is
introduced to a large number of people. There are as many different responses
to her, all of them in one way or another unspeakable, as there are people in
room. Concealing, in an aristocratic home, is a matter of etiquette. The obviousness of Angelica's youth and striking beauty is such that it cannot be articulated verbally. Only the family mother allows herself to praise her appearance (in
suitably measured, and slightly equivocal, almost resentful, tones). It is Rota's

[33] For a detailed reconstruction and commentary on the composition of the score to the film,
and especially its derivation from Rota's *Sinfonia sopra una canzone d'amore*, see Roberto Calabretto,
"La *Sinfonia sopra una canzone d'amore*. Per *Il Gattopardo*," *AAA/TAC* (*Acoustical Arts and Artifacts/
Technology Aesthetics, Communication*) 5 (2008): 5–125.

music that tells us that Tancredi's own appreciation of her beauty is echoed by all the members of the extended family. Private feelings are otherwise subsumed, indeed sublimated, in a string of public pleasantries—the sole exception being the unguarded, horrified gaze, akin to a silent scream, of Salina's jealous daughter as she first sees the woman who will take her place in her beloved cousin's heart (Figure 6.12).

When the feeling of love is one-sided or not reciprocated, the use of variable framing enables the director to reveal something that would otherwise remain concealed, bringing to light the separation—alienation, even—of the love-struck character from those around him (including, of course, the love object him- or herself). The lover is thus cast against an indifferent and at times hostile world. The music, for its part, aligns us with his or her predicament, making us privy to a secret knowledge. When, in Bertolucci's *The Conformist* (1970), Marcello catches sight of Anna, we instantly realize he is hopelessly in love (ludicrously, he proposes that she leave with him for Brazil only minutes after) (Figure 6.14). The director makes a subtle point of the ability of the cinematic medium to represent the anesthesia experienced by the lover stung by an unexpected, and overwhelming, sight. A dog figures quite prominently at the beginning of the sequence. Its sudden appearance has a frightened Giulia reach for the stairs and run all the way down to the floor below. Having established the pet's presence as a central, cumbersome, and indeed *loud* fixture of the Quadri household, the director then undercuts the significance of its presence as Anna enters the picture and, as the saying goes, "steals the show." Bertolucci's bravado is also apparent in the subtly reflexive air of the scene. Anna's appearance as a femme fatale in the making is "rehearsed," for our benefit, just before Marcello sees her walk toward the door. We first see her, before he does, in a medium shot of her standing in a dark corner, holding her breath rather like a theater actor about to walk on stage (Figure 6.15). An element of the theatrical pervades the use of music

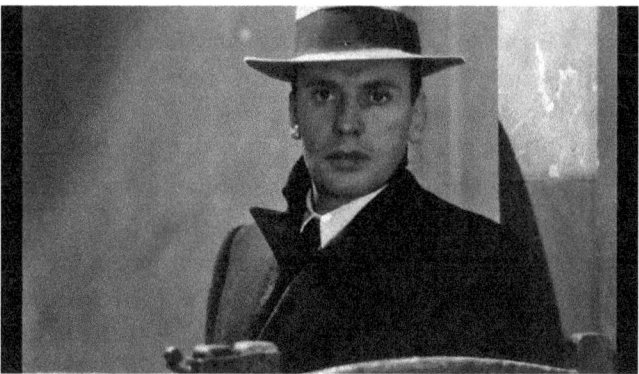

Figure 6.14 The Conformist.

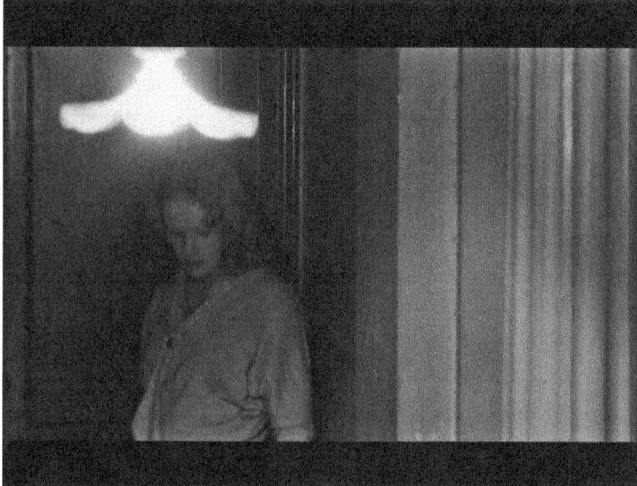

Figure 6.15 The Conformist.

as well. Delerue's doleful, stinger-like cue sounds like a deliberate throwback to an older phase of the history of film scoring (a habit the composer will indulge freely in upon writing the brilliant score for Truffaut's last film, *Confidentially Yours* [1983]). Such a brief intervention in the soundtrack is more characteristic of a classical score and would have been utterly out of fashion when the film was released. The conspicuously short cue is in keeping with Bertolucci's re-creation of the late 1930s via citations of film techniques from that period (a strategy common in the films of the nouvelle vague and, before them, central to the style of Welles's *The Magnificent Ambersons* [1942]).

The short music cue reprises the theme first heard during the newlyweds' arrival to Paris. The play on memory is significant: recognizing the motif foregrounds its presence. Synchronized to a shot of Marcello's intent gaze, the sighing, accordion-tinged motif telegraphs the impact Anna has on him, and possibly hints at her own awareness of the emotional traffic she has just caused. At the same time, the music also momentarily clouds our awareness of the fracas created by her huge dog as it barks menacingly at Giulia. It does so in two, mutually reinforcing ways. On the one hand, the score comes to occupy a sizeable portion of the mix. In view of the limited capacity of our attention, this attenuates the physical force of the competing sounds. In concert with the frontal shot of Marcello, moreover, Delerue's music cues us to weigh an alternative focus of attention—the sight of love at first sight—and thus a readjustment of our frame of reference. It is a case of what psychologists call "structural interference" as much as limited capacity, as the noise of the barking dog does not belong to the new configuration, and thus falls outside the attention's metaphorical spotlight despite being there.

Among the defining—and most enticing—aspects of the love-at-first-sight motif is its miraculous, almost talismanic suddenness. This is largely a myth, of course, and fictions have done much to keep it alive. *The Conformist* underscores this twice. By the time Marcello sees Anna, as I have already noted, we have already seen her once readying herself for a proper entrance, as if winking at us in acknowledgment of our expectation of a love story proper. This is significant since till then the film is sorely lacking in romantic interest. Marcello has married Giulia just to gain for himself the appearance of normalcy—hence the title. Years later, during the war and with a child in tow, Giulia comes across to him as more than just an instrument in his path toward normalcy. Then, Marcello finally sees her depth as a person, and it devastates him. It is *love at delayed* or *last sight* and naturally does not receive the same treatment as his sudden, irrepressible infatuation for Anna. Such a love is in some respects the obverse: a love borne out of habit, day-to-day acquaintance, the sharing of chores, hard work, and, in wartime, sacrifices and the entertaining of the possibility of death. Love at first sight, to the contrary, is shot through with a sense of recognition and owes much of its power to the feeling that one has always known the love object without ever being acquainted with her. Marcello acknowledges as much when tells an incredulous Anna, somewhat incredulous himself, that he already "met" her in the form of a prostitute in Ventimiglia, on the Italian-French border. This is how fate "cues him up"—and the film prepares us, twice over—for his fatal encounter with her.

Selective Attention as Memory

So secure is the place of the imagery associated with love at first sight in the history of cinema that a long stream of parodies pepper the history of the medium (albeit not all of them as subtle as Bertolucci's pastiche). By the time Scorsese's *Raging Bull* (1980) was released, the toolkit associated with it—close-ups, variable framing, strings—could not be used naively (without, that is, evoking an earlier phase of the history of filmmaking). Parodies had existed for a long time, of course, and subtle variants or derivations, such as a gentle underscore or special alteration of the balance in the mix, would continue to be used without a trace of irony in countless films (they do to this day). But within the microcosm of *Raging Bull*, so self-consciously faithful to the spirit of La Motta's chronicle but determined to forge an innovative language that did justice to the unique life trajectory of its protagonist, an unspoken rule would dictate that Scorsese and his team forge a subtle and daring staging of Jake's first meeting with Vickie. Their meeting is in line with the adventurousness and technical virtuosity that had been the signature of the so-called New Hollywood throughout the 1970s (and which owed a great deal to the personal approach to narrative filmmaking in the European and Japanese cinemas of the 1950s and 1960s). So while the scores of *The Thief of Bagdad* or *Vertigo*, for all their merits, have jelled into a highly stylized memento of a certain moment in the history of studio filmmaking, that of *Raging Bull* rings novel and idiosyncratic enough to resonate with more recent and even contemporary practices both in and outside Hollywood.

The aesthetics of opera informs the film as a whole without us hearing a single instance of the operatic voice. The "aria without words" of the credits, set to the music of the Intermezzo from Mascagni's *Cavalleria Rusticana*, establishes the credentials of Jake La Motta as a tragic, operatic character. The public sphere coexists uncomfortably with the private as images of the boxer, surrounded by thousands and photographed by dozens for tens of thousands more, and yet fundamentally alone in the ring, make palpable a sense of almost metaphysical loneliness. As in Verdi's *Rigoletto*, this deeply affecting overture is followed by a jarring anticlimax. A straight cut takes us to a far less glamorous setting: a changing room where an old, emaciated Jake is rehearsing the lines of a gig he's engaged for to pay the bills. The stylistic range and emotional scope of the film is thus revealed at once.

Operatic grandeur returns in the form of a ballroom sequence set in Webster Hall, a venerable New York dance hall. There, again as in opera, a drama unfolds against the background of festive—and indifferent—music. Jake is taken there by his brother Joey to consolidate his ascent by becoming friendly with influential members of the community feeding—and feeding off of—the lucrative business of boxing. There, he catches sight of Vickie. His exclusive focus on her throughout the episode is a quiet act of recklessness. He not only fails to accomplish what his brother had suggested he do—that is, mingle with and ingratiate friends and foes—but also casts his eyes in the direction of a woman who is close to an influential, and potentially dangerous, figure in the community ("Salvy" Batts).

Like Scottie in *Vertigo*, Jake is "cued up" for the encounter with Vickie. He is therefore in an ideal situation to be struck with the full force of love at first sight. Just before the party, he and his wife have a violent argument. Moreover, he has heard about Vickie from Joey himself. This much is subtly but unequivocally suggested by the way the two brothers talk about her as they sit down to order their drink. While the dialogue remains virtually unchanged, the realization on screen of the setting differs somewhat from the script.[34] In the latter, because of Vickie's young age—she is a minor when Jake meets her—the event is deemed a "neighborhood dance," and the guests young, boys separated from girls. In the

---

[34] Paul Schrader and Martin Madik, *Raging Bull: Shooting Script* (Alexandra, VA: Alexander Street Press, 2003), 21.

film the atmosphere is a decidedly more "grown-up" one, with alcohol clearly in sight, and people of different sexes mingling freely. The way the scene was shot most likely reflects awareness of the status the hall had in the early 1940s, and the plausibility of someone of Jake's age and status going there with his brother. So instead of Jake intruding on an event for adolescents, we have a precocious adolescent illegally sneaking into a soiree patronized by a much older crowd instead. More changes still further nuanced the realization of the screenplay's original conception during postproduction. Hardly a word is spent on sound and music in the script. In the film, by contrast, the sound design is sophisticated in the extreme. Along with Jake's glances in the direction of Vickie, it is sound that carries the action, conveying the depth and seriousness of the impact she has on him.

The sequence begins with the image of a poster announcing a "Summer Dance" sponsored by St. Clare's Church at Chester Palace. The lingering sound of Jake's wife's screaming at her husband, the subject of the previous sequence, makes for an ironic counterpoint. Her profanities are synchronized to a full view of the notice, which reads "Holy Name Society and/Mother Seton Guild/of St. Clare's Church/Annual Summer Dance, etc." As her voice fades out, there is a closer view of the poster, at which point the sound of the reed section of a jazz band segues till, a moment later, we see Joey walk into the venue, which is already packed with people chatting, drinking, and dancing. The two brothers have walked in as the party is in full swing already. Jake stands behind, shyly, as Joey almost drags him against his will to join a table of "guys" from which he "can at least see her." The hall is a veritable resonating chamber, the mix consisting of ambient noise—the patrons' chatter, footsteps, chairs moving, barmen making and serving drinks, all reverberated to boot—and the music. "Webster Hall" is an example of composed source music by Harth-Robertson, who also curated the entire soundtrack of the film. Scored for a piano trio and a small reed section, the piece is a classic instance of pastiche inspired, indeed dictated by, the exigencies of the setting. One may wonder whether it captures the time in which the sequence is set (that is, 1943). It resembles in both substance and form a jazz instrumental such as one might hear at a somewhat later time in the history of jazz, a time, that is, in which jazz began to divorce itself from dancing proper. While the AABA, thirty-two-bar song form is typical of the swing era and provides ample cues for the dancers seen in the background of some of the shots, the harmony changes and formal demarcations are sometimes clouded by the virtuosic work at the piano, particularly the right hand's clusters, grapples of chords, and quick, zig-zagging figurations with which Garth Hudson, who co-composed the track, creates momentum.

However one may wish to place it chronologically, the track is in every other respect a well-behaved instance of source music. Acoustically nuanced so as to betray a source in a specific point in space and at a certain distance from the focus of the action, it is pertinent to the setting and, in a concession to the perspective of the protagonists, unobtrusive. All components of the mix, including the indistinct yet ever-present roar of the crowd, are in fact subtly but constantly adjusted to privilege dialogue intelligibility. It is when Jake begins to scan the room and search with his gaze for Vickie that the soundtrack departs from tradition. Following a medium close-up of Jake looking off, a medium-long shot of the table at which she is sitting is the first hint (Figures 6.16 and 6.17). The

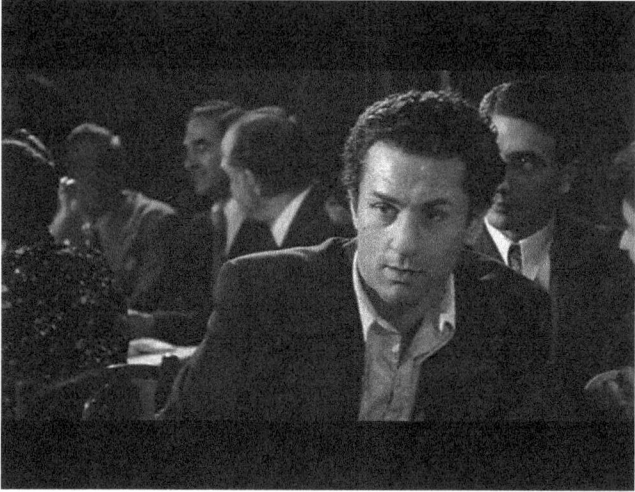

Figure 6.16 Raging Bull.

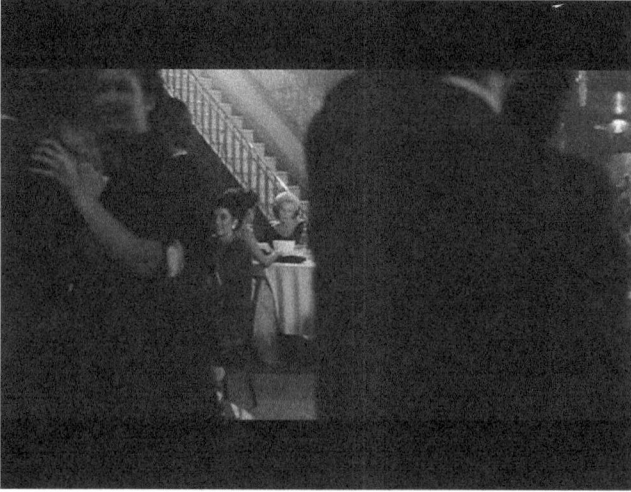

Figure 6.17 Raging Bull.

camera is moving, as if skating on ice, from right to left in the attempt to gain on Jake's behalf an optimal viewpoint. People are walking across the frame, restricting access to his line of sight, yet it is precisely as involuntarily framed by their moving torsos and legs that Vickie emerges as the true target of the gaze. The dyadic structure—image of him looking, followed by what he's looking at—repeats three times over, the point-of-view shots gaining more ground each time as we, in turn, are afforded a closer and closer view of Vickie. The camera keeps on gliding laterally, too, as if voyeuristically relishing her image from changing angles. This cannot be a literal point of view, yet it is a realistic depiction of Jake's attempts to cast a probing and already loving gaze from as many angles as possible.

In the soundtrack, the music takes center stage, pushing out all other sounds each time we are given his point of view. It's a selective presentation of selective attention—selective, that is, in what it chooses to pick out and when. Jake seemingly singles out only one stream of the auditory scene—the piano part, in particular—and latches on to it as the sole reminder of where he is and with whom, all the while focusing relentlessly on Vickie. He is temporarily treating ambient sound and music as two separate, and hence separable, streams: two distinct perceptual objects. This is convenient since the party music might be heard as doubling, an example of composed score drowning out ambient sound—as in the classic instances of the trope. However, the convention is here defamiliarized as the piano part is neither melodic nor particularly memorable, suggesting rather that its occasional resurfacing at the foreground of the mix merely follows from the arbitrary, almost capricious work of Jake's erratic attention to the sounds around him: the sonic equivalent of a blur. Adopting a principle of minimal intervention, Scorsese prefers to represent a state of anesthesia without adding any extra element into the mix, all the while exploiting the "accidental" homology between one of the two streams (the band music) and a composed score. The material homology enables—or, at least, encourages—a transfer of function, turning the snippets of piano music into the soundtrack to Jake's petit roman. By the simple device of staging the sequence in a dance hall filled with music, the subjectively inflected representation is made to serve two defining stylistic imperatives of the film: gritty realism punctuated by quasi-surreal foregrounding of seemingly arbitrary sounds and sights—such as the light and sound of the cameras before the boxing match, for instance—and the minimal use of scoring, reserved only for the montage sequences.

These stylistic choices also follow from the desire to represent the work of memory. The film is based on La Motta's memoir. The screenplay preserves this important aspect of La Motta's own memoir by intercutting between the present time of La Motta's career as an actor—the early to mid-1960s—and the peak of his career as a boxer, in the 1940s. The film changed that, and retained only two sequences of the older La Motta as bookends. Yet the change of structure did not erase the dimension of memory; rather, it made it more indirect, subtle, and poetic. The story contained between the two bookends is neither a conventional flashback nor an objective, third-person recounting of La Motta's life. In adopting something like the equivalent of free indirect discourse in literature, Scorsese and his collaborators tilted the narrative to reflect Jake's anxiety-ridden experience of his rise to stardom, his ineradicable jealousy for Vickie, and eventually his fall. Black-and-white cinematography, as well as the musical framing, moreover, envelops the film with an unmistakable veneer of nostalgia. Finally, the narration is peppered not only with point-of-view shots and fully fledged subjective sequences but also with seemingly objective and yet unaccountably distorted, muted, or enhanced sounds and sights. They are the cipher of Jake's memories, fragments of lived life that have impressed themselves on his mind and are called up at key junctures of his story (winning the title, meeting with Vickie, losing an important fight, and so forth). Like attention, memory is selective. The slow-motion flashing of the vintage camera bulbs, the gunshot-like sounds they make as they go off, and the acciaccaturas at the piano in Webster Hall are all cases in point. The sixteen weeks spent designing and perfecting the sound mix in postproduction brings testimony to the significance of these and myriad other sounds, and the selective nature of recall more generally.[35] In the Webster Hall sequence, it isn't just the tinkering with sound that suggests the work of memory; it is also the emphasis on Vickie's date, neighborhood boss "Salvy," seen approaching her in a frankly proprietary manner and in emphatic slow motion. Whether seen as conveying Jake's subjective perception, above and beyond his optical perspective, or as a tip from an omniscient narrator foreshadowing his almost maniacal jealousy, the slow-motion images suggest yet another interpretation, namely, that the image of Salvy menacingly approaching Vickie is a re-elaboration of that encounter, made by Jake at a later time upon looking back at the episode.

There is, of course, no need to press the point that this sequence is a flashback; the point, rather, is that a key element of the subtle poetry of the film lies in the ambiguity between subjective and objective narration and how this ambiguity, in turn, is folded within another, that between present- and past-tense narration. As Jake follows Vickie and her coterie out, almost like a stalker, there

---

[35] On the sound for this film, see the interview in Mary Pat Kelly, *Martin Scorsese: A Journey* (London: Secker and Warburg, 1992), 148, and David Thompson and Ian Christie, eds., *Scorsese on Scorsese* (London: Faber and Faber, 1990), 63.

is an insisted sequence of point-of-view shots from his position in space. What is more important, the epilogue is drastically compressed to include only those moments in which she is visible during the riot near the club exit. His last sight of her combines anesthesia and hyperacousia: a different music track, coming from the radio inside Salvy's car, takes over the soundtrack entirely, if only for a few fleeting seconds (Figures 6.18 and 6.19). Jake would seem to have the power to pick out a stream of sound even at great distance; at this time, the screaming

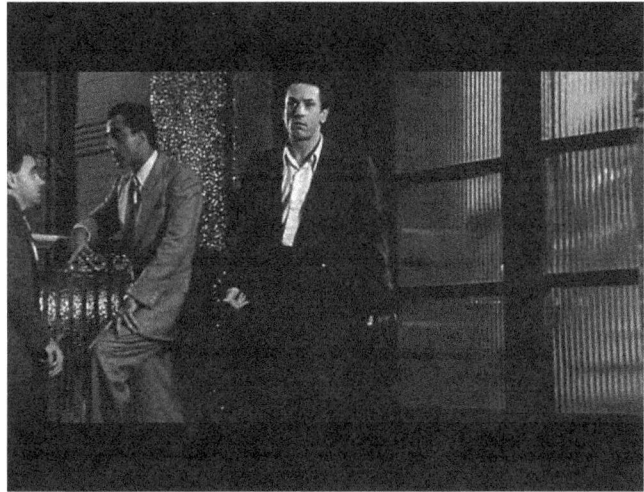

Figure 6.18 Raging Bull.

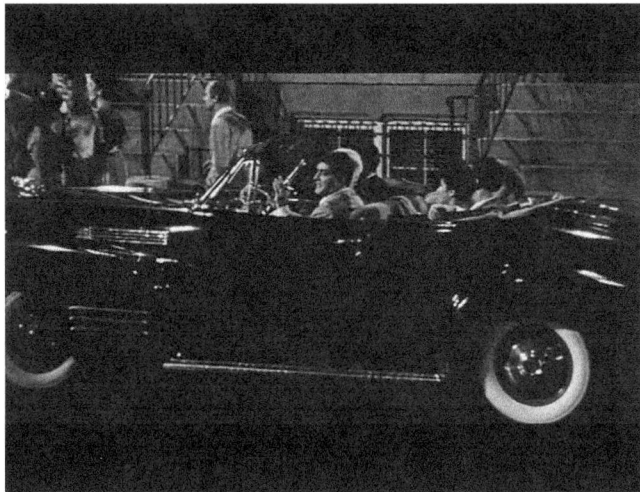

Figure 6.19 Raging Bull.

of the patrons by the entrance and the traffic noise are all but silent. This, I would argue, is how he remembers the event. It is in this sonically insulated space that the car exits the frame to the left carrying with it its precious cargo, till the unceremonious reappearance of sound briefly returns Jake—and us—to the prosaic world of the dance hall, its full coterie of sounds in full display again, untouched by the discriminating filter of Jake's interest.

Conclusion

Situating the Spectator

There is freedom only in a situation, and there is a situation only through freedom.
—Jean Paul Sartre, *Being and Nothingness*

A chief premise of this book has been what Michael Fried calls, with reference to painting, the primacy of the "single dramatic imperative."[1] I take the fulfillment of this imperative in the form of a single, intelligible, and compelling dramatic situation—a conversation between two characters, say, a visit to a bereaved relative, or a final showdown between rival gangs—to be the ultimate goal of the filmmaker's work in the construction of a scene. Fiction cinema is of course much more—occasionally, less—than a sequence of clearly demarcated episodes expressive of a singular predicament and centered around a clear-cut situation.[2] My focus on the dramatic dimension of cinema as the lynchpin to a theory of "situated listening" is a heuristic. In particular, I wish to reinstate the commonality between works of fiction and reality as hinging on recognizable situations. The impact of films, after all, depends in no small measure on their referring to circumstances we know and care deeply about outside the movie-watching experience per se.[3] It is at this juncture that, in my opinion, cinema becomes a productive vantage point in which and from which to revisit questions about the musical experience.

My emphasis on dramatic situations serves a more specific goal as well in that it gives weight to the argument that the spectator's attention, insofar as it is directed toward a situation or predicament, cannot be measured empirically.

---

[1] Michael Fried, *The Moment of Caravaggio* (Princeton, NJ: Princeton University Press, 2010), 2.

[2] On cinema as event or "novelty spectacle," for instance, see Tom Gunning, "The Cinema of Attraction," *Wide Angle* 8, no. 3–4 (1986): 63–70.

[3] For an illuminating discussion of the status of fictional worlds in literary theory and philosophy, see Thomas G. Pavel, *Fictional Worlds* (Cambridge, MA: Harvard University Press, 1989).

Let us leave aside for a moment the intractable question of how to observe auditory attention. We shall consider instead tracking eye movements, now made possible by a new generation of video-based eye trackers.[4] There is no doubting the exceptionally precise reconstruction of eye movements afforded by this technique, and the new picture it offers of the relationship between saccades and moments of fixation. But this information only provides a physiological measure. I may be looking at you while thinking about the pain in my left arm, for instance (attention being in this case self-directed or, at the very least, split between two tasks). Even assuming the attention is wholly committed to a film, complications arise. It is indisputable that we constantly process the various sounds and images a film presents us with. This level of engagement can be diagrammed the way eye-tracking studies are or verbalized via the sentence "Now I am watching the actor's eyes" or "What a loud noise from off screen." There is another level of engagement, however, at which these sights and hearings are but the path of access to a situation that can only be inferred, grasped, or imagined rather than sensed in any literal sense, and nevertheless be a target for the attention in its own right ("Now Alvie is wondering what to say to Louise"). This, in turn, may also precipitate an emotional response that could momentarily distract us from the putative object of the attention (the dramatic situation, now functioning as an emotion-producing machine). And so forth. Given this, to try and describe the spectator's attention empirically would be a formidable, indeed chimerical, task, for it would involve tracking not just the behavior of the relevant sensory organs but a complex, multidimensional cycle, one that yields potentially infinite realizations on account of the different kinds of inferences and responses to a given state of affairs likely to emerge from as many individuals.

Even when demarcated by a clear beginning and end, a dramatic situation is a construction, the aggregate result of seeing, hearing, thinking, and feeling

---

[4] Recent applications of eye-tracking measurements to the perception of moving images include Paul Marchant, David Raybould, Tony Renshaw, and Richard Stevens, "Are You Seeing What I'm Seeing? An Eye-Tracking Evaluation of Dynamic Scenes," *Digital Creativity* 20, no. 3 (2009): 153–63; and Tim J. Smith, "Watching You Watch Movies: Using Eye-Tracking to Inform Film Theory," in *Psychocinematics: Exploring Cognition at the Movies*, ed. A. P. Sinamura (New York: Oxford University Press, 2013), 165–91. Miguel Mera and Simone Stumpf, "Eye-Tracking Film Music," *Music and the Moving Image* 7, no. 3 (2014): 3–23, is to my knowledge the first attempt to study the impact of film music on the gazing of the film spectator. I should add that much of this scholarship rests on the assumption, to me simplistic, that duration and frequency of fixations are indices of looking at something in the sense of *attending* to it. For two experiments questioning this tenet, see Mika Koivisto, Jukka Hyönä, and Antti Revonsuo, "The Effects of Eye Movements, Spatial Attention, and Stimulus Features on Inattentional Blindness," *Vision Research* 44, no. 27 (2004): 3211–21; and Daniel Memmert, "The Effect of Eye Movements, Age, and Expertise on Inattentional Blindness," *Consciousness and Cognition* 15, no. 3 (2006): 620–27.

one's way along the chain of events that constitute a film narrative.[5] This creates scope for different, even contradictory accounts. You see an endearing address where I may see a thinly disguised threat. Not every situation is inherently ambiguous, of course. If I raise the possibility of a disagreement as to what is happening in a particular scene, this is to indicate how much more is at stake in the encounter with a dramatic situation than the uncontroversial determination of a state of affairs, let alone the mere registering of visual and auditory stimuli. The determination of what is happening, to the contrary, is already a form of *interpretation*.[6] In this book I have mapped the conditions of the deployment of the auditory attention along what, after Noël Carroll, we may call the "lines of least resistance" entailed by a given dramatic situation.[7] Such an effort is in one sense more modest than a full-blown empirical study in that it foregoes any attempt to describe what happens to real, flesh-and-blood spectators. In particular, it excludes those whose understanding and appreciation of film may not conform to the norms that film studios, as well as the scholars who study their work, assume on their behalf.[8] Yet theorizing the spectator is, in the last analysis, unavoidable.[9] The resulting theoretical construct, I hasten to add, does not represent the "ideal" in the sense of the best or more desirable; rather, it is meant to provide a workable model against which to consider empirical, particularized spectators.

My focus on dramatic situations, finally, entails that I understand film music to serve goals consistent with those pursued by dramatists, painters, and even novelists as they themselves enrolled or evoked the presence of music in their various efforts at world making. They include, but are not limited to, the

---

[5] For a now-classic example of a constructivist model of the spectator's experience, see David Bordwell, *Narration in the Fiction Film* (Madison: University of Wisconsin Press, 1985).

[6] George Wilson, "Interpretation," in *The Routledge Companion to Film and Philosophy*, ed. Paisley Livingston and Carl Plantinga (London and New York: Routledge, 2008), 162–72. Wilson's point is to some extent anticipated in the writings of the so-called Constance School of reception aesthetics. See, for instance, Wolfgang Iser, *The Act of Reading: A Theory of Aesthetic Response* (Baltimore: John Hopkins University Press, 1980). For his part, Bordwell seems to accord the inference of what happens, what he calls after the Russian formalists *fabula* construction, a role akin to inventorization (rather than interpretation, as I do here). He prefers "interpretation" to mean a hermeneutic reading: Bordwell, *Narration in the Fiction Film*, 48.

[7] Noël Carroll, "Film, Attention, and Communication: a Naturalistic Account," in *Engaging the Moving Image*, ed. Noël Carroll (New Haven, CT: Yale University Press, 2008), 10–58.

[8] Think of subjects affected by autism spectrum conditions, for instance. Their response to a film can be quite involved. Among the possible "deviations" from the norm is hypersensory acuity and difficulties with sensory integration. The subject is vast and remains woefully understudied.

[9] For a defense of the need to model the spectator in reception studies, see Carl Plantinga, *Moving Viewers: American Film and the Spectator's Experience* (Berkeley: University of California Press, 2009), and *Rhetoric and Representation in Non-Fiction Film* (Grand Rapids, MI: Chapbook Press, 2010).

construction of a plausible setting, creation of characters, and representation of their attitudes and states of mind. As is well known, both practitioners and theorists of the cinema have been reluctant to think of film in terms of drama. This is due to the latter's association with the theater and persistent anxiety that the cinema be defined apart from it.[10] This state of affairs goes back as far as the early debates on cinema's specificity and relative artistic merits vis-à-vis other art forms.[11] Possibly because of the polemics against theater and theatricality that animates his work, Fried must ironically refrain from explicitly articulating his own view of painting as a species of dramatic representation. I feel no such inhibitions here, as I understand the pursuit of the dramatic imperative and the construction of a situation to be dimensions of representation that cut across different art forms in different media—be they paintings, novels, plays, radio dramas, or sit-coms. While I acknowledge that practitioners of different arts may be pursuing the same or similar goals, I am naturally also aware that their efforts result in strikingly distinctive constructs, as they emerge from the strengths and limitations of the medium at hand. Too often, however, medium specificity has been taken to refer to that which is unique to, or uniquely possible through, a given medium. This bias was further accentuated by the principle, as pervasive as it was unspoken, that what is unique to a medium must also be the defining aspect of the corresponding art form and thus the one most in need of discussion.[12] And yet, it may well be that what is specific to the cinema as opposed to, say, the theater emerges in more vivid terms precisely when considering its investment in drama. This applies to both the extrinsic qualities of a film and the phenomenological qualities of the spectator's experience of it.

[10] A primer on the relationship between film and the theater would have to at least include Jean Epstein, *Cinéma* (Paris: Éditions de la sirène, 1921); Erwin Panofsky, "Style and Medium in the Motion Pictures," in *Three Essays on Style*, ed. Irving Lavin (Cambridge, MA: MIT Press, 1997); Allardyce Nicoll, *Film and Theatre* (New York: Thomas Y. Crowell, 1936); Rudolf Arnheim, *Film as Art* (Berkeley: University of California Press, 1957); André Bazin, "Theater and Cinema," in *What Is Cinema?*, vol. 1, trans. Hugh Gray (Berkeley: University of California Press, 2005), 76–124; and Susan Sontag, "Theatre and Film," in *Styles of Radical Will* (New York: Picador, 2002), 99–122.

[11] One thinks of the much-discussed notion of "pure cinema" in France in the 1920s, for instance. The relationship with the theater has not always been so fraught. The sense of presence associated with the theater, to give an example, became a selling point in the marketing of widescreen technologies in the 1950s. See John Belton, *Widescreen Cinema* (Cambridge, MA: Harvard University Press, 1992), 191–96.

[12] For a critique of the specificity thesis as it impinges on all art forms and the critical traditions that pertain to them, see Noël Carroll, "The Specificity of Media in the Arts," in *Theorizing the Moving Image* (Cambridge: Cambridge University Press, 1996), 25–26. Carroll rejects the idea that film is a specific medium or cultural form, preferring instead to refer to the "moving image," a rubric under which he subsumes film as only one of a number of related, overlapping art forms: Carroll, "Defining the Moving Image," in *Theorizing the Moving Image*, 49–74.

Beyond the Multimedia Model

Like opera and other theatrical and televisual genres, the fiction cinema mixes modes of representation—whether they are epic, dramatic, presentational, or spectacular in nature—to an extent that it is sometimes not just pedantic but simply impossible to define with any precision whether one prevails over the other.[13] One is dealing in differences of degrees, not kinds, and privileging one mode of analysis over the other is a matter of emphasis and terminological preferences. In film music studies, for example, narrative has been the preferred term of reference, and not without good reason.[14] Thinking of film in terms of narrative is of course compatible with the kind of closely observed analysis of dramatic situations I practice here. My focus, however, inevitably entails a shift in emphasis away from some of the traditional givens of film narratology, such as the question of narrative agency, for example, or the reformulation of subjectivity in terms of "focalization." For reasons that have, I hope, become clear in the course of the analyses, I also refrain from embracing the notion of film as multimedia. An analytical model predicated on media, and their different statuses and modes of functioning, may be viable when considering the music video, advertising, or, come to think of it, the lied. Upon considering the use of music as part of dramatic action, however, we should be cautious in breaking down the whole into discrete components, as if one could freely refer to "the music" as against a monolithically defined "image" under which to subsume, incongruously, framing, composition, lighting, and even acting.

Talk of music as one of two—or more—media, and of cinema as a form of multimedia, is the legacy of two distinct yet intimately tied developments in modernist criticism. The first is a bias for the medium at the expense of the imaginary content of an artwork. In certain quarters, this was precipitated by the critique of representation as "regressive," "bourgeois," if not an outright "lie," and the spectator focusing on narrative as "gullible."[15] It also

---

[13] A classic discussion of this subject is André Bazin, "Ladri di biciclette/Bicycle Thief," in *What Is Cinema?*, vol. 2, trans. H. Gray (Berkeley: University of California Press, 2005), 47–60. For a study of the various modes of presentation in opera, see Carl Dahlhaus, "Zeitstrukturen in der Oper," *Die Musikforschung* 34, no. 1 (1979): 2–11; Carolyn Abbate, *Unsung Voices: Opera and Musical Narrative in the Nineteenth Century* (Princeton, NJ: Princeton University Press, 1991), and Karol Berger, "Diegesis and Mimesis: The Poetic Modes and the Matter of Artistic Presentation," *Journal of Musicology* 12, no. 4 (1994): 407–33.

[14] Claudia Gorbman, *Unheard Melodies: Narrative Film Music* (London: BFI Publishing, 1987); Guido Heldt, *Music and Levels of Narration in Film: Steps across the Border* (Bristol: Intellect, 2013).

[15] Historically, cross sections of the moviegoing audience subject to patronizing attitudes were often treated as stand-ins for such a "naïve" spectator. In a telling anecdote, for instance, producer Darryl Zanuck tells of his wife that she was "usually never conscious of anything of a technical nature and concentrates only on the story or the actors," cited in Belton, *Widescreen Cinema*, 203.

followed from the pressing need to come to terms with the advent of nonrepresentational art. The second development is the continuation of a tradition
of endorsing, indeed encouraging, the separation and self-sufficiency of different art forms (lamentably on display in the segregated nature of the arts in
colleges and universities). Hanns Eisler's statement about "the insurmountable heterogeneity" of music and pictures is typical in this respect in that it
betrays a view of the cinema as a compound of already-constituted media
rather than constituent elements of an entity of a different order.[16] Rudolf
Arnheim's well-known rejection of the "talkie," too, springs precisely from
the unwillingness to consider the script, dialogue, score, and images of a film
as raw materials combinable in a new, integrated, composite art form. His
view of them as manifestations of already-constituted, independent media—
literature, theater, music, and the motion picture, respectively—led him to
deem the sound film an "impure" art form, one that, by the same token, over-
loads a spectator's attention.[17] More recently, Michel Chion has stressed the
spurious nature of the separation between sounds and images in analytical
discourse.[18] He has also repeatedly argued that the terms "soundtrack" and
"image track" are at best approximations of complex, nuanced constructions,
brimming with multiple relationships among components that are irreducible to either one or the other. Yet Chion's thinking is still very much an-
chored in the modernist rhetoric that stresses the component media or, to
be precise, their sensorial points of access—vision, audition—at the expense
of the representations that they serve as conduits. While he concedes that
images and sounds fuse into something like a complex gestalt, Chion falls
short of acknowledging that as an imaginary construct, a dramatic situation
may not be pruned into the notion of "audio-vision." This is because images

[16] See Hans Eisler, *Composing for the Films* (London: Dobson, 1947). Eisler's influence can be
felt today in, among others, Nicholas Cook's sophisticated theory of "musical multimedia": Cook,
Analysing Musical Multimedia (Oxford: Clarendon Press, 1998).

[17] See Rudolf Arnheim, "A New Laocoön: Artistic Composites and the Talking Film," in *Film
as Art* (London: Faber and Faber, 1958), 199–230 (first appeared in the Italian magazine *Bianco
e Nero* in 1938). In fairness to Arnheim, his argument is more subtle and rigorously worked out
than many contemporary theorists' rejection or, worse, indifference to it would seem to suggest. His pages about the integration of visual and auditory components in the theater, for instance, remain particularly cogent: Arnheim, "A New Laocoön," 165–67. A recent reappraisal
of Arnheim's work is Ian Verstegen, "A Formalist Reborn," *Film-Philosophy* 3, no. 46 (1999), accessed June 30, 2012, http://www.film-philosophy.com/index.php/f-p/article/view/528/441.
For a recent, persuasive critique of Arnheim's specificity thesis, see Noël Carroll, "The Specificity
Thesis," in *Philosophical Problems of Classical Film Theory* (Princeton, NJ: Princeton University
Press, 1988), 80–90.

[18] Michel Chion, *Audio-Vision*, trans. Claudia Gorbman (New York: Columbia University
Press, 1994).

and sounds are paths of access to objects, persons, events, and situations—it is to the latter that, in the model of spectatorship adopted here, the attention is primarily directed.

The separateness of the different components of a film, and their reconstitution into a "specious" whole, was of course a major theme in much film theory that emerged in the 1970s and 1980s. As an important corollary, constructing, as opposed to recording, reality was seen as a form of mystification. This was a time in which exposing the workings of the "cinematic apparatus" and the way in which it "positioned" the spectator was high on the agenda of much writing and theorizing about the cinema. So, for instance, Rick Altman redefined sound cinema as "ventriloquism," and the operations subtending the editing of sound and music as an elaborate ploy to disavow the fundamental separateness of sounds from their actual sources.[19] Such work espoused a somewhat crude version of empiricism whereby the material premises of a phenomenon constitute its sole, or at any rate most significant, "reality."[20] In the process, the capacity for imaginative, sustained engagement with fictional characters and dramatic situations was reduced to almost epiphenomenal status, when not denigrated altogether. Cognitive and phenomenological approaches have since shown the limitations of "subject positioning," "apparatus critique," and cognate theories, redefining spectatorship in terms of a productive engagement with film as narrative and providing a nuanced reading of the moment-to-moment experience of that engagement.[21]

[19] See Rick Altman, "Moving Lips: Cinema as Ventriloquism," *Yale French Studies* 60, Cinema/Sound (1980): 67–79, and also my discussion of the "naturalization" of sound technology in chapter 5.

[20] The separation between the actual and putative source of a sound is in any case a much older phenomenon than cinema. One need only think of puppetry, including puppet operas and shadow play. In the words of philosopher Jonathan Rée, "acting as a whole could be thought of as a generalized ventriloquism, or a form of puppetry without the puppets; and according to the assiduous theatregoer Søren Kierkegaard this kind of vocal play may even be a fundamental phase in the art of existence itself": Rée, "Dumbstruck: A Cultural History of Ventriloquism," *London Review of Books* 23, no. 9 (2001): 14.

[21] See Bordwell, *Narration in the Fiction Film*; and Vivian C. Sobchak, *The Address of the Eye: A Phenomenology of Film Experience* (Princeton, NJ: Princeton University Press, 1992). It is under the pressure of these, more persuasive, models of the spectator, not the disappearance of the "absorbed spectator" tout court, that the "subject positioning" film theory of the 1970s and 1980s became, in Miriam Hansen's words, "history": Hansen, "Early Cinema, Late Cinema: Permutations of the Public Sphere," *Screen* 34, no. 3 (1993): 197. Put another way, it is not that new scholarship on the cinema of attractions or the television functioned like real-time gauges of the "massive changes that have assailed the institution of cinema over the past two decades": Hansen, "Early Cinema, Late Cinema," 198. It is rather the case that this scholarly work revealed dimensions of spectatorship that had, in varying ratios, always coexisted with the old absorptive model. The spectator ensnared by illusion so dear to "subject positioning" theorists had in any case always been a parody of the real thing.

Filming the Spectator

The characters as situated listeners that form the main subject of this book are both a rich reservoir of behavioral types and instances of "objectified spectators": representations of spectatorship that are not only intersubjectively available but also appealingly reflexive.[22] They return to us a picture—now plausible, now troubling, now humorous—of ourselves in a similar situation. The situatedness of a character's listening experience can be measured in terms of his or her predicament, as it emerges from a given dramatic situation. That of the flesh-and-blood spectator sitting through a film, too, follows from his or her predicament—only, what is it? The subject is as vast as it is treacherous. In stressing the availability, internal coherence, and intelligibility of the dramatic imperative, and taking it axiomatic that it is the target of the spectator's attention, I am aware that I privilege one mode of film spectatorship, and the absorptive and optimally attentive disposition it implies. Clearly there are films or episodes thereof that, by their very nature, encourage neither an absorptive disposition nor an interest in character psychology nor, finally, the thorough parsing of motives that defines the engagement with narrative cinema. What is more, there are as many uses of a narrative film as there are viewers, and consideration of this well-known aspect of film spectatorship has opened up an area of research as exciting as any in film scholarship.[23] To examine the whole range of possible situations in which a person can watch a film would involve placing the moviegoing experience within yet another, and broader, frame of reference (the practice of the every day, for instance, against which to weigh the significance of such experience).[24] But, as per the gestalt principle that forms the main spine of my argument, lest we are prepared to chase an ever-receding subject, forever eluding our grasp, a narrower frame of reference was put in place, one that inevitably obscured the emergence of particularized spectators.[25] While the move may come at a cost, it

---

[22] Darrell W. Davis, *Saving Face: Spectator and Spectacle in Japanese Theatre and Film* (Hong Kong: David C. Lam Institute for East-West Studies, 2004), 3.

[23] Linda Williams, ed., *Viewing Positions: Ways of Seeing Film* (New Brunswick, NJ: Rutgers University Press, 1994).

[24] On what he calls "the cinematic heterotopia," the "range of possibilities for dismantling and reconfiguring the once inviolable objects offered by narrative cinema," see Victor Burgin, "Introduction: The Noise of the Marketplace," in *The Remembered Film* (London: Reaktion Books, 2004), 7–8.

[25] On the notions of the "marked," "unmarked," or normative body, as they pertain to questions about spectatorship, see Sobchak, *The Address of the Eye*, 145. See also my observations about attentional deficit at note 8. For the perceptual and hence epistemological shift precipitated by a change in framing, see the classic discussions in Thomas Kuhn, *The Structure of Scientific Revolutions* (Chicago: University of Chicago Press, 1962), and Erving Goffmann, *Frame Analysis: An Essay on the Organization of Experience* (New York: Harper and Row, 1974).

also brings certain advantages with it. Assuming the perspective of an unmarked, absorbed spectator does not merely allow me to embrace the scope and diversity of the various kinds of responses to music dramatized in various films; such a perspective is also the *condition* for the emergence, as against a background, of a "figure"—what I call situated listening—in the first place. The appreciation of the specifics of a character's predicament, be they the result of his or her personal history, cultural background, gender, or any other characteristics or life-defining events the film may wish to foreground, are contingent on our *performance as spectators*. In particular, they depend on our assuming, to the extent that is possible or at least sufficient, the perspective of the film unfolding before us.[26]

A case in point is Francesco Casetti's reading of Egoyan's *Artaud Double Bill* (2007), which he interprets as symptomatic of contemporary spectatorship.[27] In the film, the female leads, Anna and Nicole, are shown going to the movie theater and exhibiting forms of engagement with cinema that are not merely consistent but also follow from the availability of new technologies of communication (e.g., mobile phones). Taking stock of this, Casetti goes on to claim that Anna and Nicole are paragons of a new paradigm of the film spectator who no longer "receives" but rather "monitors" a movie, casting an equivocal "glance" onto it.[28] Casetti, in other words, extrapolates a general theory of how the contemporary spectator behaves from a study of stand-ins in the form of fictional characters. But what this approach misses is that in taking stock of what to him is an "epochal" shift, Casetti, as a self-appointed meta-spectator, must himself view *Artaud Double Bill* according to the old, and allegedly obsolete, paradigm of absorption—the one associated to Anna and Nicole's counterexample, the Nana of Godard's *Vivre sa vie* (1962). This is not only self-contradictory but also ultimately unsurprising, for only thus can knowledge about what the characters have in store for us, if at all, be gauged. While in traditional film theory and criticism, spectatorship often functioned as transcendent legitimization of claims about immanent, and eminently observable, textual structures, in some contemporary

---

[26] The point of view of the spectator and that of the film can never be isomorphic, identical. As Sobchak writes, albeit with respect to vision only: "I do not have a *point* of view. As a lived-body engaged in intentional acts of perception in an intended world, I have a *place* of viewing, a *situation*. My vision is informed by and filled with my other modes of access to the world, including the tactile contact of my posterior with the theater seat. In so far as the *visual space I see before me* is not completely isomorphic with the *bodily space from which I see*, there will be a pressure from, an echo of, the machine that mediates my perception. Again, however, . . . the machine's presence of 'echo' in the perceptual experience is secondary and latent. It is the world and its image as a terminus that is primary and active": Sobchak, *The Address of the Eye*, 178.

[27] Francesco Casetti, "Back to the Motherland: The Film Theatre in the Postmedia Age," *Screen* 52, no. 1 (2011): 1–12.

[28] Ibid., 3.

film theory the obverse is obtained: the film-text legitimizes transcendent claims about the spectator. Of course, character development, textual structures, and the conditions of film viewing do tell us a great deal about the people they are made for, but they should be treated as models, predictions, or marketing appeals, not infallible gauges of actual audience behavior. Extrapolating a theory of spectatorship from a film is a risky affair, too, for there are as many theoretical models as films about spectatorship.

The shifting relationship between the political uses of the performing arts, the design of venues, and the aesthetic attention is subtly yet memorably captured in all its complexity in the Taiwanese film masterpiece, Hou's *The Puppetmaster* (1993). An account of the life of Taiwan's most celebrated puppeteer, the film presents a view of the puppets, theater, and cinema as "folk" arts lying on a historical, social, and aesthetic continuum against the background of the Japanese colonization of the island (1895–1945). The insistence on the seasonality of spectacles and the temporary nature of some of the venues that hosted them remind one of the original circumstances surrounding the creation of the Festspielhaus in Bayreuth (which was conceived as a temporary structure). In *The Puppetmaster*, however, the point is rather that the calendar cycles, makeshift theaters, and popular participation that underpin the performances allow for a wide range of attitudes. The attempt to capture this variety of attitudes, in turn, has inspired the creation of a bold and original film language. Hou places the camera not in front but in the midst of or behind the audience, looking on in the same direction as they do, and filling the frame with multiple points of interest. To achieve this, he employs multiple frames within the same shot, typically in a deep-focus composition, so as to allow the viewer the simultaneous apprehension of different activities and spaces, and to clarify that the audience is as much the focus of his camera as the puppet or theatrical performances themselves. While these shots last a long time, allowing us to probe them at length, they also end suddenly and without preparation.

In a telling episode, Li revisits an event that marked the moment when the Japanese occupiers began to shape the daily lives of the islanders (banning Taiwanese opera, performed outdoors, and limiting performances to "approved" opera performances indoors only). Characteristically, the episode reflects the puppeteer Li's own special perspective, one informed by the history of Taiwanese stagecraft. A Peking opera performance is under way at night. The first image is a medium-long shot of the fully lit stage as seen, slightly off-center, from the much darker seating area (Figure 7.1). Two actors are engaged in an acrobatic number to a synchronized, off-stage musical accompaniment. Because of the camera angle and position, the wooden ceiling above the actors is visible near the upper edge of the frame. The audience and a Japanese officer who ostensibly oversees the seating arrangements and makes sure the evening runs in an orderly fashion fill the lower and lateral edges in soft focus. While the officer

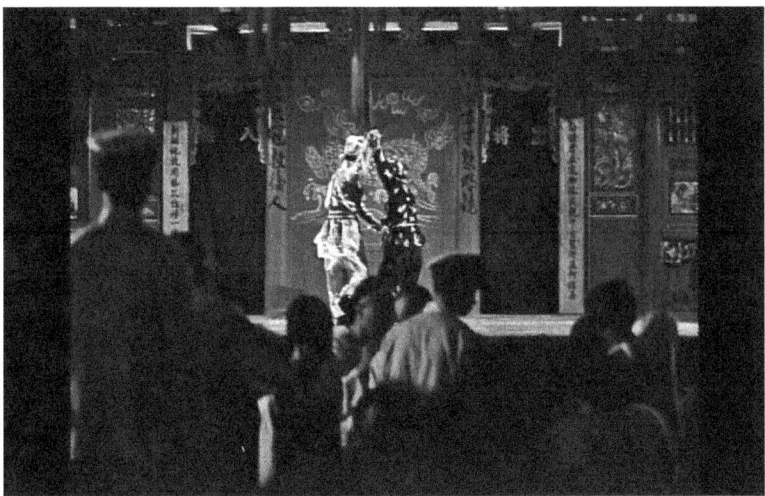

Figure 7.1 The Puppetmaster.

does occasionally obscure the sight of the stage, the seated audience forms a de-tectable yet indistinct presence well below it. The penumbra of the seating area makes their silhouettes barely recognizable, although they are all in focus. Over time, we begin to notice some of its members leave or newcomers take their seats. We also hear the hum of their chatting in the mix.

Having settled comfortably into this view of the performance, the camera suddenly steps farther back to offer an equally frontal but much longer view, along the same axis, of the stage. The latter consequently takes up now a far smaller portion of the frame.[29] As if the editing were dictated by the tempo of the onstage dance, the cut is neatly synchronized to the powerful strike of a cymbal. In reiterating our status as somewhat powerless subjects of a repre-sentation we cannot shape but only contemplate or walk away from, the new shot also grants the opportunity to explore a richer, more diverse field (Figure 7.2). Deep-focus composition, given the long duration of the shot, opens up a richly layered sight that draws our vision from the stage backward into the audi-ence, whether the audience members are seated or standing, coming or leaving, along the now-expanded middle plane of the shot. The darkness of the unlit areas encloses this newly expanded field of action in a distinctly painterly fash-ion, like a tertiary frame within the frame. The hanging paper lamps come to dominate the upper part of the composition, but it is the two standing Japanese officers, though presumably bored and thus in a sense absent, that now seem

---

[29] On cutting along the same camera axis in *The Puppetmaster*, see James Udden, *No Man an Island: The Cinema of Hou Hsiao-hsien* (Hong Kong: Hong Kong University Press, 2009), 121.

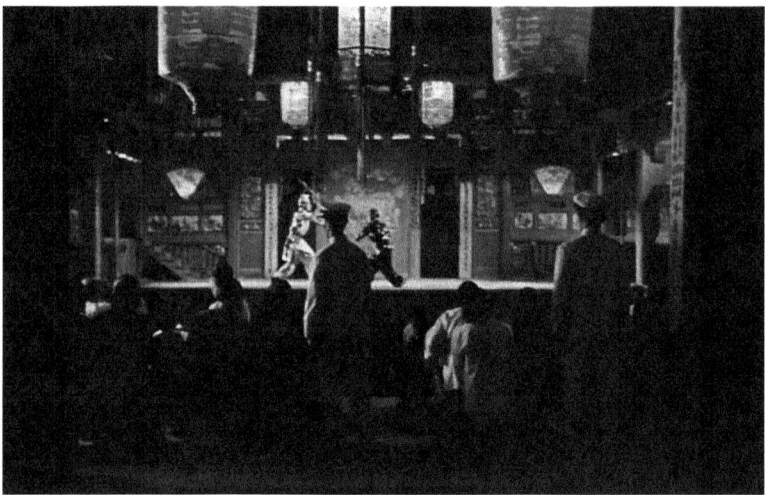

Figure 7.2 The Puppetmaster.

to anchor the scene. Moreover, the onstage action repeatedly claims our attention, if nothing else, on account of its position in the center of the frame and the actors' constant motion. Rather than deciding on our behalf by simply offering a closer view of it, the film now shows the performance obliquely, as something whose central status within the shot must be earned only to be lost again as our gaze is deflected now by the obstructing presence of the Japanese enforcers, now the sight of yet another member of the audience moving about or lighting a cigarette in the stalls. Like a prism breaking down a beam of light into a potentially infinite range of hues, this composite audience does not merely stand between the stage and us but effectively channels our attention toward or away from it, and indeed anything in between, along a similarly infinitesimal range of gradations.[30]

[30] There is a political dimension to the striking representation of spectatorship presented in this episode, one that is best elucidated by reference to the scene that precedes it (and functions as its premise). The performance is scheduled to take place after the Japanese have taken the step to force all the men to cut off their queue, in an apparent effort to visibly affirm their ownership of the island by shaping their new subjects' appearance (and disavow their ethnic Chinese background). The opera performance is sponsored as a form of appeasement of the population. No explicit link is made, in moving from one scene to the other, between the choice of camera setups, mise-en-scène, and the politically fraught circumstances in which the evening performance is put together. But it is hard not to acknowledge at least the suggestion that the diversity of responses on display at the opera is a veiled commentary on the equivocal role played by opera in a community whose self-determination has just been forfeited. The sequence, moreover, unceremoniously comes to an end in the middle of the performance. A straight cut takes us to the image of the Japanese burning the excess hair from all the male villagers' queues on a green slope.

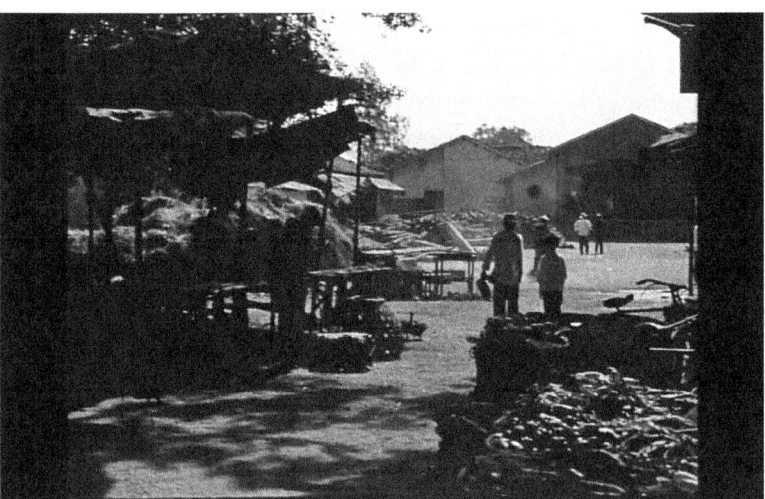

Figures 7.3 The Puppetmaster.

The Puppetmaster, as Nick Browne has observed, is "an autobiography in the third person."[31] Li's own narration features prominently at various junctures, often consisting quite simply of a frontal shot of him, in old age—that is, the present of the film production—talking to the camera. When a cut takes us to an image of where the episode referred to is taking place, his narration continues as voice-over. But the relationship between sound and image invariably takes some time for the spectator to resolve, prompting a self-reflexive play on our attention. I am thinking, in particular, of the use of what I would term an "advanced" master shot; this is an image of a locale that is cut in well before the appearance in the frame of a character, or Li's own explanatory words, clarifies its role in the narration. A paradigmatic example is the story of the onset, and quick worsening, of Li's mother's fatal illness (Figure 7.3). He begins to relate the incident, somewhat enigmatically, over a long shot of what appears to be a large, dusty village market in the scorching midday sun. Gradually, the narration touches on the fact that he was sent to the market with his foster father—Mr. Ko, otherwise known as "uncle"—to buy a duck so that a soup for his sick mother could be made. As he says this, our attention is captured by two moving figures in the middle plane of the frame whom we eventually recognize as, sure enough, Li and his father; only at this point do we finally begin to understand the image as an illustration of what is simultaneously being said.

---

[31] N. Browne, "Hou Hsiao Hsien's *The Puppetmaster*: The Poetics of Landscape," in *Island on the Edge: Taiwan New Cinema and After*, ed. Chris Berry and Feii Lu (Hong Kong: Hong Kong University Press, 2005), 81. For the special relationship between Hou and Li, see Udden, *No Man an Island*, 117.

Though it may seem peripheral, the image of the market is an image that is worth relating, and illustrating visually at that, because it touchingly captures the only instance of Li's direct involvement in the passing away of his mother (of which he was to be for the most part a distant witness).[32] Hou's fictional restaging not only doubles what is being heard but also entwines the visual and auditory channels. As Udden points out, the voice and the music cut across different episodes, erasing borderlines between past and future.[33] Because the image appears so much before its contents are touched upon in the voice-over, we may well wonder whether it is the image, rather like an involuntary memory, that has elicited Li's touching on his mother's death in the first place. His retelling of the episode is thus bound up with a powerful visual memory whose initial lack of appeal and clarity gives way to an appreciation of its lingering value in the mind of the now very old puppeteer. The somewhat whimsical temporal displacement between editing and voice-over enhances the poignancy of the scene. But it also makes us aware of our own deciphering operations as probing spectators, thereby encouraging a degree of self-observation (as when, upon observing a painting by Brueghel, for example, we catch ourselves casting about the canvas in search of what the title refers to).[34] This state of affairs is the striking counterpart of the scenes in which we are invited to observe the people sitting or standing before the stage where Li is performing (and thus engaged in spectatorial activities themselves). The initial concealment of the relationship between voice-over and the initially merely concomitant, yet eventually synchronized, image also signals the presence of another narrator (aside from Li, that is). Though we need not identify this narrator with the flesh-and-blood director himself, it is important that it be identified as a cinematic narrator all the same or at the very least a narrating agency whom we hold responsible for the particular, indeed idiosyncratic, combination of sounds and images that make up the film. One net result of causing a jolt as we parse the content of the film's long shots is to expose the manipulation of the relationship between the content and length of the takes, the timing of the editing, and that of the voice-over—that is, to make palpable the work of the cinema at the hands of a controlling intelligence.

Responding to the same reflexive impetus, albeit in a more explicit fashion, the film also shows the activities of puppeteers and opera actors from the backstage and side stage, so to speak, inviting us to see the spectacle as both illusion and a specialized type of work carried out by skilled professionals. To this the director adds the sight of the stage proceedings as seen under a third aspect, namely, as a

[32] Hou's explains the rationale to his elliptical manner in Peggy Chao, "History's Subtle Shadows: Hou Hsiao-hsien's *The Puppetmaster*," *Cinemaya*, 21 (1993): 4–11.

[33] Udden, *No Man an Island*, 125.

[34] I wish to thank Estela Ibáñez-García for this observation.

backdrop to various forms of socializing or the intermittent object of the dwellers' distracted gaze. Hou's lesson was not lost on fellow Taiwanese filmmaker Tsai Ming-liang, whose *Goodbye, Dragon Inn* (2003) is set in a famous Taipei movie theater about to close after a long and distinguished history. As a screening of King Hu's 1967 *Dragon Inn* is projected, Tsai sketches a few subplots featuring a member of the original cast of Hu's film teary with nostalgia, an old man with his grandson, and a Japanese tourist in search of a clandestine tryst. The farther away we are taken from the subject matter of the projected film, the more it resembles a television program playing in the background to other, wholly unrelated activities. The accidental sync points between a line of dialogue or theme of the score in Hu's film and the images of the goings-on in the nearly empty theater signal a trespassing of the fourth wall separating the filmic world from its putative audience. They are all phenomena enjoying equal status in a new frame (Tsai's own film).

Abbas Kiarostami's *Shirin* (2008) is even more radical, consisting entirely of frontal shots, with the camera turned 180 degrees away from the screen, of female spectators watching in rapt attention a film based on the traditional stories of Koshrow and Shirin (Figure 7.4). The audience members are striking not only for the homogeneity of their gender but also because they are all well-known Iranian actresses (with the sole exception of Juliette Binoche, who stands in as a *trait d'union* between her Iranian peers and the global audience). The film they are watching remains off screen for the entire time, its plot and locales inferable only through the soundtrack, a task that is none too easy given that the latter is deliberately not constructed like a radio drama (and is therefore insufficient for us as a gauge to follow the plot). With an incomplete film running as soundtrack only, the center of interest slowly yet inexorably shifts toward not so much the images of the actresses themselves as their responses to what they see and hear. These amount to no more than suggestions, however. As per the dominant etiquette, they do not articulate their thoughts in

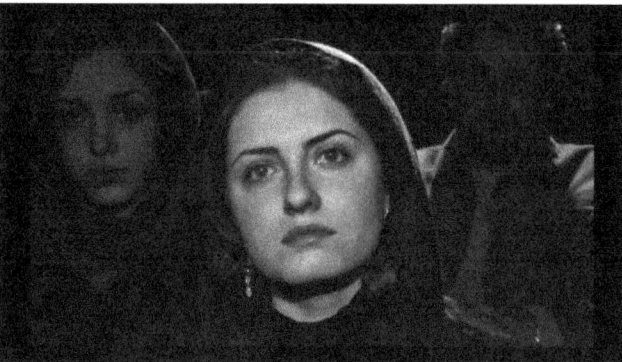

Figure 7.4 Shirin.

words and hardly betray any signs of emotion. Their condition of silent spectators slowly assumes the facets of an uncomfortable imposition, all the more so since the film running before them tells all-too-familiar stories of female self-sacrifice. Occasionally Kiarostami titillates the exercise of our selective attention by pulling us toward the soundtrack of the film playing off screen—on screen for the actresses/spectators—only to redirect it toward their faces again. These the camera studies lovingly, as if in search of a clue or even the merest hint of a drama that, albeit inspired by the film in the film, is separable from it. Yet, in the end, *Shirin* is the story of a failure. Capitulating, Kiarostami stages the absorbed spectator as an impossible subject for a film, a zero-sum game of subtractions, and acknowledges the status of whatever drama goes on inside his actresses/spectators as an activity whose specifics must forever remain private, occult, and thus unrepresentable. Dwelling on it plunges one into a hollow space. Absorption, we may deduce, is a good subject for a tableau, or a large-format photograph in the manner of a Thomas Struth, but not a time-based representation.

Cinema as Collective Intentionality

If musicology can be faulted for failing to question the implicit model of the attentive, contemplative listener for too long, film studies have done so almost to a fault. Narratives about the disappearance of the attentive film spectator have been around for some time. One such narrative came in response to the advent of television, and especially the "deviant" practice of watching films on the small screen, the televisual experience being more prone to distraction.[35] The introduction of new, portable, and frankly intrusive media platforms such as mobile phones, themselves nesting myriad social media within them, are now being put forward as evidence in favor of the "loss of the rituality of vision," or the revival of the old Benjaminian thesis that the "cinema is not an alternative to, but a continuation of, [our] daily world."[36] Surely films no longer sit at the center of social, artistic, and intellectual life as they did, for example, in the 1960s. But they were never the objects of undivided attention we (nostalgically) make them out to be.[37] A visit via a hypothetical time machine to a movie theater in Osaka ca. 1930, Rome ca. 1950, or Mumbai ca. 1970 would soon dispel any such idea (as would, for that matter, any summary

---

[35] Gerald Mast, *Film/Cinema/Movie: A Theory of Experience* (New York: Harper and Row, 1977).

[36] Casetti, "Back to the Motherland," 4.

[37] On this subject, see the masterful survey by Gian P. Brunetta, *Buio in sala: cent'anni di passione dello spettatore cinematografico* (Venezia: Marsilio, 1989).

review of the relevant written literature). Spectators cheered, reviled, or simply ignored the films being projected then as they do today. And governments and institutions bent them to their own agendas.[38] Conversely, the emergence of new technologies and the new media they give us access to does not necessarily come at the exclusion of others, which they allegedly supersede. It is not, of course, that they have not opened up new possibilities for distraction, the exercise of the attention across several different tasks in shorter spans, or the emergence of new creative forms (e.g., the mashup). Only in doing so they have not fundamentally altered, let alone neutralized, the capacity for sustained attention, and the need for a ritualized experience that nurtures it: "back to the Motherland," as Casetti himself acknowledges.[39] That is why countless films are still being written and produced with a probing viewer capable of long bursts of focused attention in mind. There is no indissoluble link that ties a medium to a mode of reception—witness novels written in the form of SMS messages or an Internet crawl, all of which demand not only the full attention of their "absorbed" readers but also the activation of that old chestnut, the "diegetic effect."[40] Such technologies as noise-cancelling headphones and mobile screens themselves, finally, both acknowledge the need for and explicitly encourage the practice of new forms of absorption, such as the creation of bubbles of contemplation during a noisy commute (itself a new, up-to-date version of the use of Walkmans in the 1980s).[41] To be sure, human agency is limited and technology has the proverbial "unintended consequences." But we must be careful not to write out the inertial force of established genres and practices upon considering new ones, nor do we want to end up unwittingly

---

[38] See, for example, Hideaki Fujiki, "Creating the Audience: Cinema as Popular Recreation and Social Education in Modern Japan," in *The Oxford Handbook of Japanese Cinema*, ed. Daisuke Miyao (New York: Oxford University Press, 2014), 79–100. See also Joseph L. Anderson and Donald Richie's dispassionate account of film presentation and spectatorship in Japan: "Theater and Audiences," in *The Japanese Film: Art and Industry* (expanded edition) (Princeton: Princeton University Press, 1982), 412-438.

[39] Casetti, "Back to the Motherland," 9.

[40] For a critique of "diegesis" as theorized in film and film music scholarship, see Anahid Kassabian, 'The End of Diegesis as We Know It," in *The Oxford Handbook of New Audiovisual Aesthetics*, ed. John Richardson, Claudia Gorbman, and Carol Vernallis (New York: Oxford University Press, 2013), 89–106. Kassabian states that the "strength of linear narrative itself is waning" under the pressure of interactive media such as the web and video games, and as film engages audiences "not through identification, but by a constant flow of sensory experience," 101. For a partial rejoinder to this argument, limited to Hollywood cinema, see in the same volume Jeff Smith, "The Sound of Intensified Continuity," 331–56.

[41] For an early and prescient exploration of what he calls "weak listening," see Shuhei Hosokawa, "L'ascolto debole," in *Estetiche del Walkman*, ed. Angela Ferraro and Gabriele Montagano (Napoli: Flavio Pagano Editore, 1990), 81–109. Hosokawa's term is a clear reference to Gianni Vattimo's philosophical program, "pensiero debole" (weak thought).

endorsing a simplistic form of technological determinism or, worse, the grand claims made by commercial entities who have a stake in the public's belief that their products have a transformative power.[42]

The absorbed spectator, one for whom the representation of human characters and actions is an attention-demanding, fulfilling, and occasionally exhausting experience, is alive and well. Such a spectator is not "positioned," let alone "constructed," by a film. He or she is not O'Doherty's "Eye," issuing forth from a body bleached out of a self.[43] Nor do the present conditions of the mediascape predetermine his or her experience entirely. Upon committing the attention to a fiction film, he or she takes part in a socially sanctioned game of make-believe.[44] Situatedness, like that of a participant to a ritual, is shared with others whom the representation summons as a collective before an ideally joint, albeit staggered and scattered, effort. The experience and subsequently the interpretation of films are in this respect a classic example of what philosophers refer to as collective intentionality: "the power of minds to be jointly directed at objects, matters of fact, states of affairs, goals, or values."[45] Joint directedness to shared artifacts or expressive gestures does not imply agreement, but it ensures that a meaningful debate about them is possible.

[42] Jonathan Sterne dubs this the "male birth model" of technological innovation. See Jonathan Sterne, *The Audible Past: Cultural Origins of Sound Reproduction* (Durham, NC: Duke University Press, 2003), 181. I should note in passing that Sterne is primarily concerned with the ways in which culture shapes the creation of the new technologies rather than the resilience of older forms of reception in the face of technological innovation.

[43] Thomas McEvilley, "Introduction," in *Inside the White Cube*, by B. O'Doherty (Santa Monica, CA: Lapis Press, 1986), 9.

[44] Kendall L. Walton, *Mimesis as Make-Believe: On the Foundations of the Representational Arts* (Cambridge, MA: Harvard University Press, 1990).

[45] David P. Schweikard and Hans B. Schmid, "Collective Intentionality," in *The Stanford Encyclopedia of Philosophy*, ed. Edward N. Zalta (Summer 2013), http://plato.stanford.edu/archives/sum2013/entries/collective-intentionality/.

Filmography

Blackmail, dir. by A. Hitchcock (1930)
A Night at the Opera, dir. by S. Wood (1935)
The Rules of the Game, dir. by J. Renoir (1939)
The Thief of Bagdad, dir. by M. Powell, L. Berger, and T. Whelan (1940)
The Magnificent Ambersons, dir. by O. Welles (1942)
Unfaithfully Yours, dir. by P. Sturges (1944)
One Wonderful Sunday, dir. by A. Kurosawa (1947)
Letter from an Unknown Woman, dir. by M. Ophuls (1948)
Ikiru, dir. by A. Kurosawa (1952)
Rear Window, dir. by A. Hitchcock (1954)
River of No Return, dir. by Otto Preminger (1954)
The Man Who Knew Too Much, dir. by A. Hitchcock (1955)
The Music Room, dir. by S. Ray (1958)
Paths of Glory, dir. by S. Kubrick (1958)
Vertigo, dir. by A. Hitchcock (1958)
L'avventura, dir. by M. Antonioni (1959)
North by Northwest, dir. by A. Hitchcock (1959)
La Notte, dir. by M. Antonioni (1961)
Vivre sa vie, dir. by J.-L. Godard (1962)
The Eclipse, dir. by M. Antonioni (1963)
High and Low, dir. by A. Kurosawa (1963)
The Leopard, dir. by L. Visconti (1963)
Antoine et Colette, dir. by F. Truffaut (1964)
Dr. Strangelove, dir. by S. Kubrick (1964)
Empire, dir. by A. Warhol (1964)
Zen for Film, dir. by N. J. Paik (1964)
Chelsea Girls, dir. by A. Warhol (1966)
2001: A Space Odyssey, dir. S. Kubrick (1968)
Romeo and Juliet, dir. by F. Zeffirelli (1968)
My Night at Maud's, dir. by E. Rohmer (1969)
The Conformist, dir. by B. Bertolucci (1970)
The Godfather I, dir. by F. F. Coppola (1972)
The Godfather II, dir. by F. F. Coppola (1974)
"Cheese Shop Sketch," by Monty Python (1974)
Barry Lyndon, dir. by S. Kubrick (1975)

Jaws, dir. by S. Spielberg (1975)
Annie Hall, dir. by W. Allen (1977)
Apocalypse Now, dir. by F. F. Coppola (1978)
Every Man for Himself aka *Slow Motion*, dir. by J.-L. Godard (1979)
Love on the Run, dir. by F. Truffaut (1979)
Manhattan, dir. by W. Allen (1979)
Raging Bull, dir. by M. Scorsese (1980)
A Woman Next Door, dir. by F. Truffaut (1981)
Rhapsody in August, dir. by A. Kurosawa (1991)
The Puppetmaster, dir. by H. H. Hsien (1993)
Schindler's List, dir. by S. Spielberg (1993)
The Shawshank Redemption, dir. by F. Darabont (1994)
Lost Highway, dir. by D. Lynch (1997)
In the Mood for Love, dir. by W. K. Wai (2001)
The Pianist, dir. by R. Polanski (2002)
Goodbye, Dragon Inn, dir. by T. M. Liang (2003)
"Montmartre," dir. by B Podalydès, in *Paris, je t'aime* (2006)
Artaud Double Bill, dir. by A. Egoyan (2007)
My Blueberry Nights, dir. by W. K. Wai (2007)
Shirin, dir. by A. Kiarostami (2008)

Bibliography

Abbate, Carolyn. "Music—Drastic or Gnostic?" *Critical Inquiry* 30, no. 3 (2004): 505–36.

———. *Unsung Voices: Opera and Musical Narrative in the Nineteenth Century.* Princeton, NJ: Princeton University Press, 1991.

Adorno, Theodor W. *In Search of Wagner.* London: Verso, 2005.

———. "The Radio Symphony: An Experiment in Theory." In *Radio Research, 1941*, edited by Paul F. Lazarsfeld and Frank Nicholas Stanton, 110–39. New York: Duell, Sloan and Pearce, 1941.

Alberti, Leon Battista. *On Painting.* New Haven, CT: Yale University Press, 1966.

Altman, Rick. "Cinema Sound at the Crossroads: A Century of Identity Crisis." In *Le Son En Perspective: Nouvelles Recherches*, edited by Dominique Nasta and Didier Huvelle, 13–46. Bruxelles: Peter Lang, 2004.

———. "Moving Lips: Cinema as Ventriloquism." *Yale French Studies: Cinema/Sound* 60, no. 2 (1980): 67–79.

———. "The Silence of the Silents." *Musical Quarterly* 80, no. 4 (Winter 1996): 648–718.

———. "Sound Space." In *Sound Theory/Sound Practice*, edited by Rick Altman, 46–64. New York: Routledge, 1992.

———. "Television/Sound." In *Studies in Entertainment: Critical Approaches to Mass Culture*, edited by Tania Modleski, 39–54. Bloomington: Indiana University, 1986.

———. *The American Film Musical.* Bloomington: Indiana University Press, 1987.

———. "The Technology of the Voice: Part I." *Iris* 3, no. 1 (1985): 3–20.

———. "The Technology of the Voice: Part II." *Iris* 4, no. 1 (1986): 107–18.

Anderson, Joseph L., and Donald Richie. *The Japanese Film: Art and Industry* (expanded edition). Princeton: Princeton University Press, 1982.

Arnheim, Rudolf. "A New Laocoön: Artistic Composites and the Talking Film." In *Film as Art*, 199–230 London: Faber and Faber, 1958.

———. *Film as Art.* London: Faber and Faber, 1958.

———. *The Power of the Center: A Study of Composition in the Visual Arts.* Berkeley: University of California Press, 1982.

Atkins, Irene K. *Source Music in Motion Pictures.* Rutherford, NJ: Fairleigh Dickinson University Press, 1983.

Auden, W. H. "Music in Shakespeare." In *The Dyer's Hand.* London: Faber, 2013.

Baltrušaitis, Jurgis. *Anamorphic Art.* New York: Harry N. Abrams, 1977.

Barr, Charles. "CinemaScope: Before and After." *Film Quarterly* 16, no. 4 (1963): 4–24.

———. *Vertigo.* London: BFI Publishing, 2002.

Barthes, Roland. *The Responsibility of Forms: Critical Essays on Music, Art, and Representation.* New York: Hill and Wang, 1985.

Batcho, James. "The Sonic Lifeworld: A Phenomenological Exploration of the Imaginative Potential of Animation Sound." *Journal of Sonic Studies* 6, no. 1, (January 2014). http://journal.sonicstudies.org/vol06/nr01/a05.

Bazin, André. "Ladri Di biciclette/Bicycle Thief." In *What Is Cinema?* Vol. 2, translated by Hugh Gray, 47–60. Berkeley: University of California Press, 2005.

———. "Theater and Cinema." In *What Is Cinema?* Vol. 1, translated by Hugh Gray, 76–124. Berkeley: University of California Press, 2005.

Beck, Jay, and Tony Grajeda. *Lowering the Boom: Critical Studies in Film Sound.* Urbana: University of Illinois Press, 2008.

Belton, John. *Alfred Hitchcock's Rear Window.* Cambridge: Cambridge University Press, 2000.

———. "Introduction: Spectacle and Narrative." In *Alfred Hitchcock's Rear Window*, 1–20. Cambridge: Cambridge University Press, 2000.

———. "The Phenomenology of Film Sound: Robert Bresson's *A Man Escaped.*" In *Lowering the Boom: Critical Studies in Film Sound*, edited by Jay Beck and Tony Grajeda, 23–35. Urbana: University of Illinois Press, 2008.

———. "The Space of Rear Window." In *Hitchcock's Rereleased Films: From Rope to Vertigo*, edited by Walter Raubicheck and Walter Srebnick, 76–94. Detroit: Wayne State University Press, 1991.

———. *Widescreen Cinema.* Cambridge, MA: Harvard University Press, 1992.

Benjamin, Walter. *The Work of Art in the Age of Its Technological Reproducibility, and Other Writings on Media*, edited by Michael W. Jennings, Brigid Doherty, and Thomas Y. Levin, and translated by E. F. N. Jephcott. Cambridge, MA: Belknap Press of Harvard University Press, 2008.

Berger, Karol. "Beethoven and the Aesthetic State." *Beethoven Forum* 7 (1999): 17–44.

———. "Diegesis and Mimesis: The Poetic Modes and the Matter of Artistic Presentation." *Journal of Musicology* 12, no. 4 (1994): 407–33.

Berry, Chris, and Feiyi Lu. *Island on the Edge: Taiwan New Cinema and After.* Hong Kong: Hong Kong University Press, 2005.

Besseler, Heinrich. *Das musikalische Hören der Neuzeit.* Berlin: Akademie Verlag, 1959.

———. "Grundfragen Des Musikalischen Hörens." *Jahrbuch Des Musikbiblothek Peters Für 1925* 32 (1926): 33–52.

Birdsall, Carolyn, and Anthony Enns. "Editorial: Rethinking Theories of Television Sound." *Journal of Sonic Studies* 3, no. 1 (October 2012). http://journal.sonicstudies.org/vol03/nr01/a01.

Biancorosso, Giorgio. "Sound." In *The Routledge Companion to Philosophy and Film*, edited by Paisley Livingston and Carl Plantinga, 260–67. New York: Routledge, 2008.

———. "The Harpist in the Closet: Film Music as Epistemological Joke." *Music and the Moving Image* 2, no. 3 (2009): 11–33.

———. "The Shark in the Music." *Music Analysis* 29, no. 1–3 (2010): 306–33.

———. "Where Does the Music Come From?: Studies in the Aesthetics of Film Music." PhD dissertation, Princeton University, 2002.

Blesser, Barry, and Linda-Ruth Salter. *Spaces Speak, Are You Listening? Experiencing Aural Architecture.* Cambridge, MA: MIT Press, 2007.

Borchmeyer, Dieter. *Richard Wagner: Theory and Theatre.* Oxford: Clarendon Press, 1991.

Bordwell, David. "Convention, Construction, and Vision." In *Post-Theory: Reconstructing Film Studies*, edited by David Bordwell and Noël Carroll, 87–107. Madison: University of Wisconsin Press, 1996.

———. "Intensified Continuity Visual Style in Contemporary American Film." *Film Quarterly* 55, no. 3 (2002): 16–28.

———. *Narration in the Fiction Film.* Madison: University of Wisconsin Press, 1985.

———. "Review of *To the Distant Observer*, by Nöel Burch," *Wide Angle* 3, no. 4 (1980): 70–73.

Bordwell, David, and Noël Carroll, eds. *Post-Theory Reconstructing Film Studies.* Madison: University of Wisconsin Press, 1996.

Bourdaghs, Michael K. *Sayonara Amerika, Sayonara Nippon: A Geopolitical Prehistory of J-Pop.* New York: Columbia University Press, 2012.

Branigan, Edward. *Point of View in the Cinema: A Theory of Narration and Subjectivity in Classical Film.* Berlin: Mouton, 1987.

Brooks, Peter. *The Melodramatic Imagination: Balzac, Henry James, Melodrama, and the Mode of Excess.* New Haven, CT: Yale University Press, 1976.

Brooks, William. "Pragmatics of Silence." *Silence, Music, Silent Music,* edited by Nicky Losseff and Jenny Doctor, 97–126. Aldershot, UK: Ashgate, 2007.

Brown, Carolyn. *Chance and Circumstance: Twenty Years with Cage and Cunningham.* Evanston: Northwestern University Press, 2009.

Browne, Nick. "Hou Hsiao-Hsien's Puppetmaster: The Poetics of Landscape." In *Island on the Edge: Taiwan New Cinema and After,* edited by Chris Berry and Feiyi Lu, 8: 79–88. Hong Kong: Hong Kong University Press, 2005.

———. "The Spectator-in-the-Text: The Rhetoric of *Stagecoach.*" *Film Quarterly* 29, no. 2 (1975–76): 26–38.

Brown, Royal S. "Herrmann, Hitchcock, and the Music of the Irrational." *Cinema Journal* 21, no. 2 (1982): 14–49.

Bruce, Graham Donald. *Bernard Herrmann: Film Music and Narrative.* Ann Arbor, MI: UMI Research Press, 1985.

Brunetta, Gian Piero. *Buio in sala: Cent'anni di passioni dello spettatore cinematografico.* Venezia: Marsilio, 1989.

Buckland, Warren. *Puzzle Films: Complex Storytelling in Contemporary Cinema.* Chichester, UK: Wiley-Blackwell, 2009.

Bull, Michael. "Remaking the Urban: The Audiovisual Aesthetics of Ipod Use." In *The Oxford Handbook of New Audiovisual Aesthetics,* 628–44. Oxford: Oxford University Press, 2013.

Burch, Noël. *To the Distant Observer: Form and Meaning in the Japanese Cinema.* Berkeley: University of California Press, 1979.

———. *In and Out of Synch: The Awakening of a Cine-Dreamer.* Aldershot, England: Scolar Press, 1991.

Burgin, Victor. "Situational Aesthetics." In *Art in Theory 1900–2000: An Anthology of Changing Ideas,* edited by Charles Harrison and Paul J. Wood. Oxford: Blackwell Publishing, 2002.

———. "Introduction: The Noise of the Marketplace." In *The Remembered Film,* 7–8. London: Reaktion, 2004.

———. "Situational Aesthetics." *Studio International/Ed. G. S. Whittet.,* 1969, 118–21.

Burnham, Scott G. *Beethoven Hero.* Princeton, NJ: Princeton University Press, 1995.

Byg, Barton. "Traces of a Life: Chronicle of Anna Magdalena Bach." In *Landscapes of Resistance: The German Films of Danièle Huillet and Jean-Marie Straub,* 51–70. Berkeley: University of California Press, 1995.

Calabretto, Roberto. *Antonioni e la musica.* Venezia: Marsilio, 2012.

———. "La sinfonia sopra una canzone d'amore: Per Il Gattopardo." *AAA TAC: Acoustical, Art and Artifacts: Technology, Aesthetics, Communication* 5 (2008): 5–125.

Campana, Alessandra. *Opera and Modern Spectatorship in Late Nineteenth-Century Italy.* Cambridge: Cambridge University Press, 2015.

Carroll, Noël. "Defining the Moving Image." In *Theorizing the Moving Image,* 49–74. Cambridge and New York: Cambridge University Press, 1996.

———. "Film, Attention, and Communication: A Naturalistic Account." In *Engaging the Moving Image,* edited by Noël Carroll, 10–58. New Haven, CT: Yale University Press, 2003.

———. "Notes on Movie Music." In *Theorizing the Moving Image,* 139–45. Cambridge and New York: Cambridge University Press, 1996.

———. "The Specificity of Media in the Arts." In *Theorizing the Moving Image,* 25–36. Cambridge and New York: Cambridge University Press, 1996.

———. "The Specificity Thesis." In *Philosophical Problems of Classical Film Theory,* 28: 80–90. Princeton, NJ: Princeton University Press, 1988.

Casetti F. "Back to the Motherland: The Film Theatre in the Postmedia Age." *Screen Screen* 52, no. 1 (2011): 1–12.

Cenciarelli, Carlo. "Dr Lecter's Taste for 'Goldberg,' or: The Horror of Bach in the Hannibal Franchise." *Journal of the Royal Musical Association* 137, no. 1 (2012): 107–34.

Chao, Peggy. "History's Subtle Shadows: Hou Hsiao-Hsien's *The Puppetmaster.*" *Cinemaya* 21 (1993): 4–11.

Chion, Michel. "Alfred Hitchcock's 'Rear Window': The Fourth Side." In *Alfred Hitchcock's Rear Window*, edited by John Belton, 110–17. Cambridge: Cambridge University Press, 2000.

———. *Audio-Vision: Sound on Screen*. New York: Columbia University Press, 1994.

———. *Film, a Sound Art*, translated by Claudia Gorbman. New York: Columbia University Press, 2009.

———. *Kubrick's Cinema Odyssey*. London: British Film Institute, 2001.

———. "What a Time It Was! An Essay on Antonioni's *L'eclisse*," translated by Alain Renaud and Don Siegel. *The Soundtrack* 3, no. 1 (2010): 5–9.

Chua, Daniel K. L. "Listening to the Self: *The Shawshank Redemption* and the Technology of Music." *19th-Century Music* 34, no. 3 (2011): 341–55.

Citron, Marcia J. "Operatic Style and Structure in Coppola's 'Godfather Trilogy.'" *Musical Quarterly* 87, no. 3 (2004): 423–67.

———. "Subjectivity in the Opera Films of Jean-Pierre Ponnelle." *Journal of Musicology* 22, no. 2 (2005): 203–40.

Clarke, David, and Eric F. Clarke. *Music and Consciousness: Philosophical, Psychological, and Cultural Perspectives*. Oxford: Oxford University Press, 2011.

Clarke, Eric. *Ways of Listening: An Ecological Approach to the Perception of Musical Meaning*. Oxford: Oxford University Press, 2005.

———. "Music Perception and Musical Consciousness." In *Music and Consciousness: Philosophical, Psychological and Cultural Perspectives*, edited by David Clarke and Eric Clarke, 193–214. Oxford: Clarendon Press, 2011.

Cohen, Anabel. "Congruence-Association Model of Music and Multimedia: Origin and Evolution." In *The Psychology of Music in Multimedia*, edited by Tan Siu-Lan, Anabel Cohen, and Roger A. Kendall, 17–47. New York: Oxford University Press, 2013.

Cone, Edward T. "Three Ways of Reading a Detective Story or a Brahm's Intermezzo." In *Music: A View from Delft*, edited by Edward T. Cone and Robert P. Morgan, 77–93. Chicago: Chicago University Press, 1989.

Cook, Nicholas. *Analysing Musical Multimedia*. Oxford: Clarendon Press, 1998.

———. *Beyond the Score: Music as Performance*. New York: Oxford University Press, 2013.

———. *Music, Imagination, and Culture*. Oxford: Oxford University Press, 1990.

Cooper, David. *Bernard Herrmann's Vertigo: A Film Score Handbook*. Westport, CT: Greenwood Press, 2001.

———. "Film Form and Musical Form in Bernard Herrmann's Score to *Vertigo.*" *Journal of Film Music* 1, no. 2/3 (2009): 239–48.

Crary, Jonathan. *Suspensions of Perception Attention, Spectacle, and Modern Culture*. Cambridge, MA: MIT Press, 1999.

———. *Techniques of the Observer: On Vision and Modernity in the Nineteenth Century*. Cambridge, MA: MIT Press, 1990.

Crimp, Douglas. *"Our Kind of Movie": The Films of Andy Warhol*. Cambridge, MA: MIT Press, 2012.

Crosby, Eric. "Widescreen Composition and Transnational Influence: Early Anamorphic Filmmaking in Japan." In *Widescreen Worldwide*, edited by John Belton, Sheldon Hall, and Steve Neale, 181–82. Herts: John Libbey Publishing, 2010.

Cronin, Theresa Anne. "Disciplining the Spectator Subjectivity, the Body and Contemporary Spectatorship." PhD dissertation, Goldsmiths, University of London, 2011.

Curtis, Scott. "The Making of Rear Window." In *Alfred Hitchcock's Rear Window*, edited by John Belton, 21–56. Cambridge: Cambridge University Press, 2000.

Dagrada, Elena. *Between the Eye and the World: The Emergence of the Point-of-View Shot.* Brussels: Peter Lang, 2015.

Dahlhaus, Carl. *Richard Wagner's Music Dramas.* Cambridge: Cambridge University Press, 1979.

———. "Zeitstrukturen in der Oper." *Musikforschung Die Musikforschung* 34, no. 1 (1981): 2–11.

Darwin, Charles. *The Expression of the Emotions in Man and Animals.* Oxford and New York: Oxford University Press, 1998.

Davis, Darrell William, and David C. Lam. *Saving Face: Spectator and Spectacle in Japanese Theatre and Film.* Hong Kong: David C. Lam Institute for East-West Studies, Hong Kong Baptist University, 2004.

Davison, Annette. *Hollywood Theory, Non-Hollywood Practice: Cinema Soundtracks in the 1980s and 1990s.* Aldershot: Ashgate, 2004.

Deleuze, Gilles, and Félix Guattari. *A Thousand Plateaus: Capitalism and Schizophrenia.* Minneapolis: University of Minnesota Press, 1987.

DeLillo, Don. *White Noise.* New York: Viking Press, 1985.

De Nora, Tia. "Musicalizing Consciousness: Aesthetics and Anaesthetics." In *Music Asylums: Wellbeing Through Music in Everyday Life.* London and New York: Routledge, 2014, 97–120.

Dermonourt, Bertrand. "Eric Rohmer, Le Son Au plus Vrai—L'Express. Interview by Bertrand Dermonourt." *L'Express*, January 13, 2010. http://www.lexpress.fr/culture/musique/eric-rohmer-le-son-au-plus-vrai_841713.html.

Deutelbaum, Marshall, and Leland A. Poague, eds. *A Hitchcock Reader.* Ames: Iowa State University Press, 1986.

Donnelly, Kevin J. *Occult Aesthetics: Synchronization in Sound Film.* New York: Oxford University Press, 2014.

Doty, Mark. *The Art of Description: World into Word.* Minneapolis: Graywolf Press, 2010.

Douchet, Jean. "Hitch and His Public." In *A Hitchcock Reader*, edited by Marshall Deutelbaum and Leland A Poague, translated by Verena Conley, 7–15. Ames: Iowa State University Press, 1986.

Douglas, Susan Jeanne. *Listening In: Radio and the American Imagination.* Minneapolis: University of Minnesota Press, 2004.

Doyle, Peter. *Echo and Reverb: Fabricating Space in Popular Music Recording, 1900–1960.* Middletown, CT: Wesleyan University Press, 2005.

Dretske, Fred. "Change Blindness." *Philosophical Studies: An International Journal for Philosophy in the Analytic Tradition* 120, no. 1–3 (2004): 1–18.

Dyer, Richard. *In the Space of a Song: The Uses of Song in Film.* New York: Routledge, 2012.

Eisler, Hanns. *Composing for the Films.* London: Dobson, 1947.

Ellis, John. *Visible Fictions: Cinema, Television, Video.* London and New York: Routledge, 1992.

Elsaesser, Thomas, and Malte Hagener. *Film Theory: An Introduction through the Senses.* New York: Routledge, 2010.

Epstein, Jean. *Cinéma.* Paris: Éditions de la Sirène, 1921.

Fawell, John Wesley. *Hitchcock's Rear Window: The Well-Made Film.* Carbondale: Southern Illinois University Press, 2001.

Feldman, Martha. *Opera and Sovereignty Transforming Myths in Eighteenth-Century Italy.* Chicago: University of Chicago Press, 2007.

Fox, Albertine. "Constructing Voices in Jean-Luc Godard's *Sauve Qui Peut (la vie)* (1979)." *Studies in French Cinema* 14, no. 1 (2014): 19–32.

Franz Waxman Papers, Special Collection Research Center, Syracuse University Libraries, Box OS 90.

Frege, Gottlob. "Über Sinn Und Bedeutung." *Wittgenstein Studien* 100 (1892): 25–50.

Fried, Michael. *Absorption and Theatricality: Painting and Beholder in the Age of Diderot.* Berkeley: University of California Press, 1980.

———. *The Moment of Caravaggio.* Princeton, NJ: Princeton University Press, 2010.

————. *Why Photography Matters as Art as Never Before.* New Haven, CT: Yale University Press, 2008.

Fujiki, Hideaki. "Creating the Audience: Cinema as Popular Recreation and Social Education in Modern Japan." In *The Oxford Handbook of Japanese Cinema*, edited by Daisuke Miyao, 79–100. New York: Oxford University Press, 2014.

Geary, Jason. *The Politics of Appropriation: German Romantic Music and the Ancient Greek Legacy.* New York: Oxford University Press, 2014.

Gell, Alfred. *Art and Agency: An Anthropological Theory.* Oxford: Clarendon Press, 1998.

————. "Vogel's Net: Traps as Artworks and Artworks as Traps." *Journal of Material Culture* 1, no. 1 (1996): 15–38.

Gilman, Lisa. "An American Soldier's iPod: Layers of Identity and Situated Listening in Iraq." *Music and Politics* 4, no. 2. http://quod.lib.umich.edu/m/mp/9460447.0004.201/--american-soldiers-ipod-layers-of-identity-and-situated?rgn=main;view=fulltext.

Goffman, Erving. *Frame Analysis: An Essay on the Organization of Experience.* New York: Harper and Row, 1974.

Goldmark, Daniel, Lawrence Kramer, and Richard D Leppert. *Beyond the Soundtrack Representing Music in Cinema.* Berkeley: University of California Press, 2007.

Gombrich, E. H. *Art and Illusion: A Study in the Psychology of Pictorial Representation.* New York: Pantheon Books, 1960.

————. *The Sense of Order: A Study in the Psychology of Decorative Art.* London: Phaidon Press, 1984.

Gorbman, Claudia. "Artless Singing." *Music, Sound, and the Moving Image* 5, no. 2 (2011): 157–71.

————. *Unheard Melodies: Narrative Film Music.* London: BFI Publishing, 1987.

Griffin, Alice. *Understanding Tennessee Williams.* Columbia, SC: University of South California Press, 1995.

Gunning, Tom. "The Cinema of Attraction." *Wide Angle* 3, no. 4 (1986): 1986.

Hamilton, Andy. "The Sounds of Music." In *Sounds and Perception*, edited by Matthew Nudds and Casey O'Callaghan, 146–82. Oxford: Oxford University Press, 2009.

Handel, Stephen. *Listening: An Introduction to the Perception of Auditory Events.* Cambridge, MA: MIT Press, 1989.

Hansen, Miriam. "Early Cinema, Late Cinema: Permutations of the Public Sphere." *Screen* 34, no. 3 (1993): 197–210.

Harvey, Adam. *The Soundtracks of Woody Allen: A Complete Guide to the Songs and Music in Every Film, 1969-2005.* Jefferson, NC: McFarland, 2007.

Heldt, Guido. *Music and Levels of Narration in Film: Steps across the Border.* Bristol, UK: Intellect, 2013.

Heidegger, Martin. "The Origin of the Work of Art." In *Basic Writings: From Being and Time (1927) to The Task of Thinking (1964)*, 143–87. New York: Harper and Row, 1977.

Hermann, Bernard. "Music in Films—A Rebuttal." In "Aesthetic Squabbles." *The Routledge Film Music Sourcebook*, edited by James Eugene Wierzbicki, Nathan Platte, and Colin Roust, 107–24. New York and London: Routledge, 2012.

Hess, Remi. *La valse: révolution du couple en Europe.* Paris: A. M. Métailié, 1989.

Hopkins, Robert. "What Do We See in Film?" *Journal of Aesthetics and Art Criticism* 66, no. 2 (2008): 149–59.

Hosokawa, Shuhei. "L'ascolto debole." In *Estetiche del Walkman*, edited by Angela Ferraro and Gabriele Montagano, 81–109. Napoli: Flavio Pagano Editore, 1990.

Hunt, Lester H. "The Paradox of the Unknown Lover: A Reading of Letter from an Unknown Woman." *Journal of Aesthetics and Art Criticism* 64, no. 1 (2006): 55–66.

Hunter, Mary. "Opera in Film: Sentiment and Wit, Feeling and Knowing: *The Shawshank Redemption* and *Prizzi's Honor*." In *Between Opera and Cinema*, edited by Jeongwon Joe and Rose Theresa, 93–119. New York: Routledge, 2002.

Huxley, Aldous. *The Art of Seeing.* London: Flamingo, 1994.

Iser, Wolfgang. *The Act of Reading: A Theory of Aesthetic Response.* Baltimore: Johns Hopkins University Press, 1980.

Jakobson, Roman. "Is the Film in Decline?" In *Language in Literature*, edited by Krystyna Pomorska and Stephen Rudy, 458–65. Cambridge, MA: Harvard University Press, 1987.

Johnson, James H. *Listening in Paris: A Cultural History*. Berkeley: University of California Press, 1994.

Jones, Kent. "My Night at Maud's: Chances Are . . ." *The Criterion Collection*. Accessed July 18, 2015. http://www.criterion.com/current/posts/436-my-night-at-maud-s-chances-are.

Joseph, Branden W. "'Factory Setting' [review of Douglas Crimp, 'Our Kind of Movie': The Films of Andy Warhol (Cambridge, MA: MIT Press, 2012)

and J. J. Murphy, The Black Hole of the Camera: The Films of Andy Warhol (Berkeley: University of California Press, 2012)]." *Artforum* 51, no. 2 (2012): 59–60.

Kahn, Douglas. *Noise, Water, Meat a History of Sound in the Arts*. Cambridge, MA: MIT Press, 1999.

Kahneman, Daniel. *Attention and Effort*. Englewood Cliffs, NJ: Prentice-Hall, 1973.

Kassabian, Anahid. *Hearing Film: Tracking Identifications in Contemporary Hollywood Film Music*. New York: Routledge, 2001.

———. *Ubiquitous Listening Affect, Attention, and Distributed Subjectivity*. Berkeley: University of California Press, 2013.

Kassabian, Anahid, Elena Boschi, and Marta Garcia Quinones, eds. *Ubiquitous Musics: The Everyday Sounds That We Don't Always Notice*. Burlington, VT: Ashgate, 2013.

Kelly, Mary Pat. *Martin Scorsese: A Journey*. London: Secker and Warburg, 1992.

Kerins, Mark. *Beyond Dolby (Stereo) Cinema in the Digital Sound Age*. Bloomington: Indiana University Press, 2011.

Kickasola, Joseph K. "Kie´slowski's Musique Concrète." In *Music, Sound, and Filmmakers: Sonic Style in Cinema*, edited by James Wierzbicki, 61–75. New York: Routledge, 2012.

Kivy, Peter. "Speech, Song, and the Transparency of Medium: A Note on Operatic Metaphysics." In *Musical Worlds: New Directions in the Philosophy of Music*, edited by Phil Alperson, 63–68. University Park: Pennsylvania State University Press, 1998.

Kline, T. Jefferson. "Pascal Victim: The Hidden Text in Rohmer's *Ma Nuit Chez Maud*." In *Screening the Text: Intertextuality in New Wave French Cinema*, edited by T. Jefferson Kline, 119–47. Baltimore: Johns Hopkins University Press, 1992.

Koch, Stephen. *Stargazer: Andy Warhol's World and His Films*. New York: Praeger, 1973.

Koestenbaum, Wayne. *Andy Warhol*. New York: Viking, 2001.

Koivisto, Mika, Jukka Hyönä, and Antti Revonsuo. "The Effects of Eye Movements, Spatial Attention, and Stimulus Features on Inattentional Blindness." *Vision Research* 44, no. 27 (2004): 3211–21.

Koss, Juliet. *Modernism After Wagner*. Minneapolis and London: University of Minnesota Press, 2010.

Kracauer, Siegfried, and Thomas Y Levin. "Cult of Distraction: On Berlin's Picture Palaces." *Newgermcrit New German Critique*, no. 40 (1987): 91–96.

Kramer, Lawrence. "Melodic Trains: Music in Polanski's *The Pianist*." In *Beyond the Soundtrack: Representing Music in Cinema*, edited by Daniel Goldmark, Lawrence Kramer, and Richard Leppert, 66–85. Berkeley: University of California Press, 2007.

Kripke, Saul A. *Naming and Necessity*. Cambridge, MA: Harvard University Press, 1980.

Krohn, Bill. *Hitchcock at Work*. London: Phaidon, 2000.

Kuhn, Thomas S. *The Structure of Scientific Revolutions*. Chicago: University of Chicago Press, 1962.

Kulezic-Wilson, Danijela. "Gus Van Sant Soundwalks and Audio-Visual *Musique concrète*." In *Music, Sound, and Filmmakers: Sonic Style in Cinema*, edited by James Wierzbicki, 76–88. New York: Routledge, 2012.

Kulvicki, John V. *On Images: Their Structure and Content*. Oxford: Clarendon, 2006.

Lacan, Jacques. *The Seminar of Jacques Lacan, Book XI: The Four Fundamental Concepts of Psychoanalysis*, edited by Jacques-Alain Miller, trans. Alan Sheridan. New York: Norton, 1998.

Lacey, Kate. *Listening Publics: The Politics and Experience of Listening in the Media Age*. Cambridge: Polity Press, 2013.

Laing, Heather. *The Gendered Score: Music in 1940s Melodrama and the Woman's Film*. Aldershot: Ashgate, 2007.

Lastra, James. *Sound Technology and the American Cinema Perception, Representation, Modernity*. New York: Columbia University Press, 2000.

Lazarsfeld, Paul Felix, and Frank Nicholas Stanton. *Radio Research, 1941*. New York: Duell, Sloan and Pearce, 1941.

Le Guin, Elisabeth. "One Bar in Eight: Debussy and the Death of Description." In *Beyond Structural Listening*, edited by Andrew Dell'Antonio, 233–51. Berkeley: University of California Press, 2004.

Leitch, Thomas M., and Leland A. Poague. *A Companion to Alfred Hitchcock*. Chichester, UK: Wiley-Blackwell, 2011.

Levin, David J. "A Picture-Perfect Man? Senta, Absorption, and Wagnerian Theatricality." *Opera Quarterly* 21, no. 3 (2005): 486–95.

Levinson, Jerrold. "Film Music and Narrative Agency." In *Post-Theory: Reconstructing Film Studies*, edited by David Bordwell and Noël Carroll, 248–82. Madison: University of Wisconsin Press, 1996.

———. *Music in the Moment*. Ithaca, NY: Cornell University Press, 1997.

London, Justin. "Leitmotifs and Musical Reference in the Classical Film Score." In *Music and Cinema*, edited by James Buhler, Caryl Flinn, and David Neumeyer, 85–96. Hanover: University Press of New England, 2000.

Magee, Gayle Sherwood. *Robert Altman's Soundtracks: Film, Music and Sound from M*A*S*H to a Prairie Home Companion*. Oxford: Oxford University Press, 2014.

Marchant, Paul, David Raybould, Tony Renshaw, and Richard Stevens. "Are You Seeing What I'm Seeing? An Eye-Tracking Evaluation of Dynamic Scenes." *Digital Creativity* 20, no. 3 (2009): 153–63.

Mast, Gerald. *Film/Cinema/Movie: A Theory of Experience*. New York: Harper and Row, 1977.

McEvilley, Thomas. "Introduction." In *Inside the White Cube: The Ideology of the Gallery Space*, edited by Brian O'Doherty, 7–12. Santa Monica, CA: Lapis Press, 1986.

McGowan, Todd. "Looking for the Gaze: Lacanian Film Theory and Its Vicissitudes." *Cinema Journal* 42, no. 3 (2003): 27–47.

McGurk, H., and J. MacDonald. "Hearing Lips and Seeing Voices." *Nature* 264, no. 5588 (1976): 23–30.

McQuiston, Kate. *We'll Meet Again: Musical Design in the Films of Stanley Kubrick*. New York: Oxford University Press, 2013.

Memmert, Daniel. "The Effects of Eye Movements, Age, and Expertise on Inattentional Blindness." *Consciousness and Cognition* 15, no. 3 (September 2006): 620–27.

Mendelsund, Peter. *What We See When We Read: A Phenomenology*. New York: Vintage Books, 2014.

Mera, Miguel, and Simone Stumpf. "Eye-Tracking Film Music." *Music and the Moving Image* 7, no. 3 (2014): 3–23.

Miller, David A. "Hitchcock's Hidden Pictures." *Critical Inquiry* 37, no. 1 (2010): 106–30.

Millington, Barry. "Bayreuth Idealism: The Catastrophe." In *Wagner*, 114–23. Oxford and New York: Oxford University Press, 1999.

Morgan, Daniel. *Late Godard and the Possibilities of Cinema*. Berkeley: University of California Press, 2013.

Münsterberg, Hugo. "The Photoplay: A Psychological Study." In *Hugo Münsterberg on Film: The Photoplay: A Psychological Study and Other Writings*, edited by A. Langdale. New York: Routledge, 2002.

Mulvey, Laura. "Visual Pleasure and Narrative Cinema." In *The Audience Studies Reader*, edited by Will Broker and Deborah Jermyn, 133–42. New York and London: Routledge, 2002.

Murphy, J. J. *The Black Hole of the Camera: The Films of Andy Warhol*. Berkeley: University of California Press, 2012.

Nagel, Thomas. *The View from Nowhere*. New York: Oxford University Press, 1986.

———. "What Is It Like to Be a Bat." *Philosophical Review* 83, no, 4 (1974): 435–50.

Neumeyer, David, and Nathan Platte. *Franz Waxman's Rebecca: A Film Score Guide*. Lanham, MD: Scarecrow Press, 2012.

Newark, Cormac. "Not Listening in Paris: Critical and Fictional Lapses of Attention at the Opera." In *Words and Notes in the Long Nineteenth Century*, edited by Phyllis Weliver and Katharine Ellis, 35–54. Woodbridge: Boydell and Brewer, 2013.

Nicoll, Allardyce. *Film and Theatre*. New York: Thomas Y. Crowell Co., 1936.

Nietzsche, Friedrich Wilhelm. "Richard Wagner in Bayreuth." In *Untimely Meditations*, 195–254. Cambridge: Cambridge University Press, 1997.

O'Doherty, Brian. *Inside the White Cube: The Ideology of the Gallery Space*. Berkeley: University of California Press, 1999.

Ondaatje, Michael. *The Conversations: Walter Murch and the Art of Editing Film*. New York: Knopf, 2002.

Orr, John. *Hitchcock and Twentieth-Century Cinema*. London: Wallflower, 2005.

Panofsky, Erwin. "Style and Medium in the Motion Pictures." In *Three Essays on Style*, edited by Irving Lavin, 91–126. Cambridge: MIT Press, 1997.

Parker, Roger. "'As a Stranger Give It Welcome': Musical Meanings in 1830s London." In *Representation in Western Music*, 33–46. Cambridge: Cambridge University Press, 2013.

Pasolini, Pier Paolo. "Comments on Free Indirect Discourse." In *Heretical Empiricism*, translated by Ben Lawton and Louise K. Barnett, 79–101. Washington, DC: New Academia Publishing, 2005.

———. "The Cinema of Poetry." In *Heretical Empiricism*, translated by Ben Lawton and Louise K. Barnett, 167–86. Washington, DC: New Academia Publishing, 2005.

Pavel, Thomas G. *Fictional Worlds*. Cambridge, MA: Harvard University Press, 1986.

Perkins, V. F. *La Règle Du Jeu*. Basingstoke: Palgrave MacMillan, on behalf of the British Film Institute, 2012.

Perloff, Marjorie. "Constructed Anarchy." *Lana Turner: A Journal of Poetry and Opinion* 3. Accessed October 3, 2013. http://www.lanaturnerjournal.com/archives/constructed-anarchy.

Plantinga, Carl. *Moving Viewers American Film and the Spectator's Experience*. Berkeley: University of California Press, 2009.

———. *Rhetoric and Representation in Nonfiction Film*. Grand Rapids, MI: Chapbook Press, 2010.

Polanyi, Michael. "Sense-Giving and Sense-Reading." In *Knowing and Being: Essays by Michael Polanyi*, edited by Marjorie Grene, 181–207. Chicago: Chicago University Press, 1967.

———. *The Study of Man*. Chicago: University of Chicago Press, 1959.

Polzonetti, Pierpaolo. *Italian Opera in the Age of the American Revolution*. Cambridge: Cambridge University Press, 2011.

Pomerance, Murray. *Alfred Hitchcock's America*. Cambridge: Polity, 2013.

———. "Finding Release: 'Storm Clouds' and The Man Who Knew Too Much." In *Music and Cinema*, edited by James Buhler, Caryl Flinn, and David Neumeyer, 207–46. Middletown, CT: Wesleyan University Press, 2000.

Pontara, Tobias. "Bach at the Space Station: Hermeneutic Pliability and Multiplying Gaps in Andrei Tarkovsky's *Solaris*." *Music, Sound, and the Moving Image* 8, no. 1 (2014): 1–23.

Puzo, Mario. *The Godfather*. New York: G.P. Putnam's Son, 1969.

Raubichek, Walter, and Walter Srebnick, eds. *Hitchcock's Rereleased Films: From Rope to Vertigo*. Detroit, MI: Wayne State University, 1991.

Reader, Keith. *La Règle Du Jeu: French Film Guide*. London: I. B. Tauris, 2010.

Rée, Jonathan. "Review of *Dumbstruck: A Cultural History of Ventriloquism*, by Steven Connor." *London Review of Books* 23, no. 9 (2001): 14.

Rewald, Sabine. *Rooms with a View: The Open Window in the 19th Century*. New York: Metropolitan Museum of Art, 2011.

Ries, Frank W. D. *The Dance Theatre of Jean Cocteau*. Ann Arbor, MI: UMI Research Press, 1986.

Rosar, William H. "Film Studies in Musicology: Disciplinarity vs. Interdisciplinarity." *Journal of Film Music* 2, no. 2–4 (2010): 99–125.

Rosenbaum, Jonathan. "*L'eclisse*: A Vigilance of Desire." *The Criterion Collection*. Accessed October 13, 2015. http://www.criterion.com/current/posts/359-l-eclisse-a-vigilance-of-desire.

Rosen, Charles, et al. *The Romantic Generation*. Cambridge, MA: Harvard University Press, 1995.

Sabaneev, L., and S. W. Pring. "Remarks on the Leit-Motif." *Music and Letters* 13, no. 2 (1932): 200–206.

Sala, Emilio. *L'opera senza canto: il mélo romantico e l'invenzione della colonna sonora*. Venezia: Marsilio, 1995.

Salt, Barry. *Film Style and Technology: History and Analysis*. London: Starword, 1992.

Schrader, Paul, and Mardik Martin. *Raging Bull (1980) Shooting Script*. Alexandria, VA: Alexander Street Press, 2003.

Sartre, Jean-Paul. "For a Theatre of Situations." In *Modern Theories of Drama: A Selection of Writings on Drama and Theatre 1850-1990*, edited by George W. Brandt, 42–44. Oxford: Oxford University Press, 1998.

Scarecrow Film Score Guides. Lanham, MD: Scarecrow Press, 19.

Schopenhauer, Arthur. *Parerga and Paralipomena: Short Philosophical Essays*. Vol. 1. Oxford: Clarendon Press, 1974.

Schroeder, David P. *Hitchcock's Ear: Music and the Director's Art*. New York: Continuum, 2012.

Schweikard, David P., and Hans Bernhard Schmid. "Author and Citation Information for 'Collective Intentionality.'" In *The Stanford Encyclopedia of Philosophy*, Summer 2013. http://plato.stanford.edu/cgi-bin/encyclopedia/archinfo.cgi?entry=collective-intentionality.

Sciannameo, Franco. *Nino Rota's The Godfather Trilogy: A Film Score Guide*. Lanham, MD: Scarecrow Press, 2010.

Scorsese, Martin, David Thompson, and Ian Christie. *Scorsese on Scorsese*. London and Boston: Faber and Faber, 1990.

Scott, A.O. "A Brief History of Kissing in Movies." *New York Times*, December 13–4, 17 and 19.

Sergi, Gianluca. *The Dolby Era: Film Sound in Contemporary Hollywood*. Manchester: Manchester University Press, 2004.

Sesonske, Alexander. *Jean Renoir, the French Films, 1924-1939*. Cambridge, MA: Harvard University Press, 1980.

Sharff, Stefan. *The Art of Looking in Hitchcock's Rear Window*. New York: Limelight Editions, 1997.

Shelley, James. "The Concept of the Aesthetic," edited by Edward N. Zalta. In *The Standford Encyclopedia of Philosophy*, Fall 2013. http://plato.stanford.edu/archives/fall2013/entries/aesthetic-concept/.

Simons, Daniel J., and Christopher F. Chabris. "Gorillas in Our Midst: Sustained Inattentional Blindness for Dynamic Events." *Perception* 28, no. 9 (1999): 1059–74.

Sitney, P. Adams. *The Cinema of Poetry*. New York: Oxford University Press, 2015.

Small, Christopher. *Musicking: The Meanings of Performing and Listening*. Hanover, NH: University Press of New England, 1998.

Smith, Jeff. "Bridging the Gap: Reconsidering the Border between Diegetic and Nondiegetic Music." *Music and the Moving Image* 2, no. 1 (2009): 1–25.

———. *The Sounds of Commerce: Marketing Popular Film Music*. New York: Columbia University Press, 1998.

Smith, Murray. "Altered States: Character and Emotional Response in the Cinema." *Cinema Journal* 33, no. 4 (1994): 34–56.

———. "Consciousness." In *The Routledge Companion to Philosophy and Film*, edited by Paisley Livingston and Carl Plantinga, 39–51. New York: Routledge, 2008.

Smith, Tim J. "Watching You Watch Movies: Using Eye Tracking to Inform Film Theory." In *Psychocinematics: Exploring Cognition at the Movies*, edited by A. P. Sinamura, 165–91. New York: Oxford University Press, 2013.

Sobchack, Vivian Carol. *Carnal Thoughts Embodiment and Moving Image Culture*. Berkeley: University of California Press, 2004.

———. *The Address of the Eye: A Phenomenology of Film Experience*. Princeton, NJ: Princeton University Press, 1992.

Sontag, Susan. "Theatre and Film." In *Styles of Radical Will*, 99–122. New York: Picador, 2002.

Spoto, Donald. *The Dark Side of Genius: The Life of Alfred Hitchcock*. Boston: Little, Brown, 1983.

Steege, Benjamin. *Helmholtz and the Modern Listener*. Cambridge: Cambridge University Press, 2012.

Steinberg, Michael P. *Listening to Reason Culture, Subjectivity, and Nineteenth-Century Music*. Princeton, NJ: Princeton University Press, 2004.

Sterne, Jonathan. "Sounds Like the Mall of America: Programmed Music and the Architectonics of Commercial Space." *Ethnomusicology* 41, no. 1 (1997): 22–50.

———. *The Audible Past: Cultural Origins of Sound Reproduction*. Durham, NC: Duke University Press, 2003.

Stilwell, Robynn J. "The Fantastical Gap between Diegetic and Nondiegetic." In *Beyond the Soundtrack: Representing Music in Cinema*, edited by Daniel Goldmark, Lawrence Kramer, and Richard Leppert, 184–202. Berkeley: University of California Press, 2007.

Stimilli, Davide. *The Face of Immortality: Physiognomy and Criticism*. Albany: State University of New York Press, 2005.

Sullivan, Jack. *Hitchcock's Music*. New Haven, CT: Yale University Press, 2006.

Taruskin, Richard. *The Oxford History of Western Music*. Vol. 3. New York and Oxford: Oxford University Press, 2010.

Théberge, Paul. "Almost Silent: The Interplay of Sound and Silence in Contemporary Cinema and Television." In *Lowering the Boom: Critical Studies in Film Sound*, edited by Jay Beck and Tony Grajeda, 51–67. Urbana: University of Illinois Press, 2008.

Thompson, Emily Ann. *The Soundscape of Modernity: Architectural Acoustics and the Culture of Listening in America, 1900-1933*. Cambridge, MA: MIT Press, 2002.

Thompson, Kristin. *Breaking the Glass Armor: Neoformalist Film Analysis*. Princeton, NJ: Princeton University Press, 1988.

Thompson, Kristin, and David Bordwell. "Categorical Coherence: A Closer Look at Character Subjectivity." *Observations on Film Art*, October 24, 2008. http://www.davidbordwell.net/blog/2008/10/24/categorical-coherence-a-closer-look-at-character-subjectivity/.

Tovey, Donald Francis. *Essays in Musical Analysis*. Vol. 6: *Miscellaneous Notes, Glossary and Index*. Oxford: Oxford University Press, 1939.

Truffaut, François, and Helen G Scott. *Hitchcock*. New York: Simon and Schuster, 1984.

Turvey, Malcolm. *Doubting Vision: Film and the Revelationist Tradition*. New York: Oxford University Press, 2008.

———. *The Filming of Modern Life: European Avant-Garde Film of the 1920s*. Cambridge, MA: MIT Press, 2011.

Udden, James. *No Man an Island: The Cinema of Hou Hsiao-hsien*. Hong Kong and London: Hong Kong University Press, 2009.

Ulrici, Hermann. *Gott Und Der Mensch*. Leipzig: T. O. Weigel, 1874.

Uroskie, Andrew V. *Between the Black Box and the White Cube: Expanded Cinema and Postwar Art*. Chicago: University of Chicago Press, 2014.

Verstegen, Ian. "A Formalist Reborn." *Film-Philosophy* 3, no. 46 (1999). http://www.film-philosophy.com/vol3-1999/n46verstegen.

Waeber, Jacqueline. *En musique dans le texte le mélodrame de Rousseau à Schoenberg*. Paris: Van Dieren, 2006.

Walker, Elsie M. *Understanding Sound Tracks through Film Theory*. Oxford: Oxford University Press, 2015.

Walton, Kendall L. *Mimesis as Make-Believe: On the Foundations of the Representational Arts*. Cambridge, MA: Harvard University Press, 1990.

Weiner, Marc A. *Richard Wagner and the Anti-Semitic Imagination*. Lincoln: University of Nebraska Press, 1995.

Weis, Elisabeth. *The Silent Scream: Alfred Hitchcock's Sound Track*. Rutherford, NJ: Fairleigh Dickinson University Press, 1982.

———. "The Sound of One Wing Flapping." *Filmsound.org*. Accessed February 2, 2015. http://filmsound.org/articles/Hitchcock.htm.

Welles, Orson, Peter Bogdanovich, and Jonathan Rosenbaum. *This Is Orson Welles*. New York: HarperCollins, 1992.

White, Armond. "Eternal Vigilance in Rear Window." In *Hitchcock's Rear Window*, edited by John Belton, 118–40. Cambridge: Cambridge University Press, 2000.

White, Susan. "A Surface Collaboration: Hitchcock and Performance." In *A Companion to Alfred Hitchcock*, edited by Thomas Leitch and Leland Poague, 181–98. Chichester, UK: Wiley-Blackwell, 2011.

Wierzbicki, James. "Grand Illusion: The 'Storm Cloud' Music in Hitchcock's *The Man Who Knew Too Much*." *Journal of Film Music* 1, no. 2/3 (2009): 217–38.

Wilder, Ken. "Michael Fried and Beholding Video Art." *Proceedings of the European Society for Aesthetics* 3 (2011): 294–315.

Williams, Alan. "Godard's Use of Sound." *Camera Obscura* 8 (1982): 194–209.

Williams, Linda. *Hard Core: Power, Pleasure, and the "Frenzy of the Visible."* London and Sydney: Pandora Press, 1990.

———, ed. *Viewing Positions: Ways of Seeing Film*. New Brunswick, NJ: Rutgers University Press, 1995.

Wilson, E. Courtenay. "Interactions between the Auditory and Vibrotactile Senses: A Study of Perceptual Effects." Master's thesis, Massachusetts Institute of Technology, 2010.

Wilson, George. "Interpretation." In *The Routledge Companion to Philosophy and Film*, edited by Paisley Livingston and Carl Plantinga, 162–72. New York: Routledge, 2008.

Winters, Ben. "Musical Wallpaper? Towards an Appreciation of Non-Narrating Music in Film." *Music, Sound, and the Moving Image* 6, no. 1 (2012): 39–54.

———. *Music, Performance, and the Realities of Film: Shared Concert Experiences in Screen Fiction*. New York: Routledge, 2013.

———. "The Non-Diegetic Fallacy: Film, Music, and Narrative Space." *Music and Letters* 91, no. 2 (2010): 224–44.

Wood, Michael. "Distraction Theory: How to Read While Thinking of Something Else." *Michigan Quarterly Review (United States)* 48, no. 4 (2009): 577–88.

Wood, Robin. *Hitchcock's Films Revisited*. New York: Columbia University Press, 1989.

Wright, Robb. "Score vs. Song: Art, Commerce, and the H Factor in Film and Television Music." In *Popular Music and Film*, edited by Ian Inglis, 8–21. London: Wallflower Press, 2003.

Yoshimoto, Mitsuhiro. *Kurosawa: Film Studies and Japanese Cinema*. Durham, NC: Duke University Press, 2000.

Žižek, Slavoj. *Looking Awry: An Introduction to Jacques Lacan through Popular Culture*. Cambridge, MA: MIT Press, 1991.

———. "The Talking Heads." In *Organs without Bodies: On Deleuze and Consequences*. New York and London: Routledge, 2012.

Zoppelli, Luca. *L'opera come racconto: modi narrativi nel teatro musicale dell'Ottocento*. Venezia: Marsilio, 1994.

Index